VALUING A COMPANY

PRACTICES AND PROCEDURES

GEORGE D. McCARTHY, C.P.A.
RETIRED PARTNER, PRICE WATERHOUSE & CO.

ROBERT E. HEALY, C.P.A.
PARTNER, PRICE WATERHOUSE & CO.

A RONALD PRESS PUBLICATION

JOHN WILEY & SONS

New York • Chichester • Brisbane • Toronto

ISBN 0 471 06542-0

Library of Congress Catalog Card Number: 74–166300

PRINTED IN THE UNITED STATES OF AMERICA

10

Preface

This work endeavors to cover all of the significant aspects of valuing corporate and non-corporate businesses. Its purpose is to present meaningful data on many types of transactions, and guidelines for arriving at a valuation of a company, whether large or small.

A unique feature of the book, providing a wealth of useful information in compact form, is a series of comprehensive tables presenting critical data for companies in various industries involved in acquisitions and merger transactions; public offerings; valuations for federal estate, gift, and income tax purposes; and tender offers. Pertinent statistics and financial data for a selected number of conglomerates are also provided in time-saving tabular format. These extensive tables are the result of a vast amount of research in various financial publications mentioned throughout the book. In addition, thousands of proxy statements, annual reports, stock listing applications, and decisions on litigated tax and other cases were comprehensively reviewed, as well as the voluminous files of Price Waterhouse & Co.

In addition to these major studies, other valuations covered include those required for a "stepped up" basis in a taxable acquisition of a company, valuations of small professional and personal service organizations, valuations in regulated industries, and those determined pursuant to state laws for appraisal rights of stockholders dissenting to a merger or sale of the major assets of a company.

The book contains many footnote annotations and other source references for those desiring to further explore particular topics. Though legal aspects of various valuation situations are discussed, advice of legal counsel is recommended when specific problems arise that require reference to laws, regulations, and court decisions.

iii

The book brings to bear the authors' many years of experience in assisting clients in various kinds of valuation situations and in handling the practical problems arising out of business combinations as dealt with in the earlier book by George McCarthy, *Acquisitions and Mergers*. Inasmuch as several years were required to complete the various studies represented here, it was not practicable to have all of them cover the same period of years. An endeavor was made, however, to have each study cover representative periods so that the results derived would be meaningful.

While the titling of Parts and Chapters reflects principal coverage of major topics, certain basic valuation factors and tax considerations arise in various sections of the book. Where this occurs, ample cross-references have been provided.

No work of this magnitude could have been completed without the generous help of the authors' associates. While the responsibility for the opinions and conclusions in this book is exclusively the authors', they gratefully acknowledge the help of a number of their associates, particularly that of Ernest G. Weiss. Others who were of assistance include John C. Frye, Philip V. Gerdine, Gayford L. Hinton, Edward J. Humann, Eleanor M. Kelley, John R. Mehrtens, Edward A. Money, Joseph J. Rigney, Jr., and George C. Watt.

GEORGE D. McCARTHY
ROBERT E. HEALY

New York, New York
August, 1971

Contents

Part II   Tax Valuations

Part III   Business Combinations

Appendixes

PART I

SECURITIES MARKETS AND INITIAL OFFERINGS

1

Basic Problems and Economic Considerations

CONCEPTS OF VALUE

"Value" Has Many Meanings

"Value" is a word of many meanings when applied in an accounting, economic, legal, or engineering sense. In an attempt to define more precisely the meaning of value, some of the following terms are used: actual, appraised, assessed, book, break-up, carrying, real, reproductive, depreciated, face, fair, fair market, going concern, insurable, intangible, intrinsic, liquidating, market, residual, sound, and true.

As Bonbright concluded in his two-volume work on the valuation of property, "As long as common law and statute law persist in using the term 'value' as a legal jack-of-all-trades, judges are forced, willy-nilly, to reject the precedent of economists and to follow instead the precedent of Humpty Dumpty (from *Through the Looking Glass*): 'When I use a word it means what I choose it to mean—neither more nor less.'" [1]

Willing Seller–Willing Buyer Concept. The Board of Tax Appeals in its decision in the *James Couzens* case expounded the following

[1] BONBRIGHT, VALUATION OF PROPERTY (1937).

3

concept of fair market value, which has been widely quoted and précised in the federal estate and gift tax regulations:

It has been said that value is a price at which a willing seller and a willing buyer would agree to trade if they both were aware of the facts. . . . Recognizing all the facts in existence or in contemplation . . . as shown by the evidence, and from them attempting reasonably to predict those to come, being neither unduly skeptical nor unduly optimistic, we sought to determine what an intelligent and reasonable seller and an intelligent and reasonable buyer would in their fairly mercenary interests have been most likely to agree upon as a price for the property in question.[2]

However, in valuing the stocks of closely held corporations for federal tax purposes, instead of the mythical willing seller and willing buyer, we have as traditional adversaries the taxpayer or his heirs or donees and the Internal Revenue Service. As shown by the many litigated cases and the far more numerous compromise settlements effected short of judicial decisions, each adversary considers the other anything but willing and reasonable.

Determining Values Not an Exact Science. The valuation of a company or a business is not an exact science; considering the same relevant facts, experts may differ widely in their appraisals of value. This is understandable because of the many factors generally involved in reaching a decision on overall valuation. The weight given these factors is a matter of judgment, which is influenced not only by the experience of the valuer, but by the motives and objectives of the buyer or seller.

Judicial Opinions Offer Limited Guidance. Judicial opinions, although they may indicate factors considered in arriving at valuations, do not mention the weight given to each such factor in their overall determinations. Thus, the Tax Court, although it appeared arbitrary in expressing the following philosophy in the *Schwabacher* case, was realistic in its appraisal of the problems involved in satisfying all parties concerned in a valuation case. "There is plenty of difference of opinion as to the value of this stock based upon the present record. We have no deep-seated conviction as to what the value of the stock may have been but a finding of value is necessary and has been made to the best of our ability. It would serve no useful purpose and might convince no one if

2 James Couzens, 11 B.T.A. 1040 (1928).

we were to explain in detail just how our conclusions have been reached." [3]

Purpose of Valuation Important

Before discussing the factors influencing the valuation of a company or business, one must first know the purpose of the valuation. For example, a close corporation, or a substantial block of its capital stock, may be valued for purposes of determining federal estate or gift tax. Usually such a valuation will be on the low side, when compared with valuations for other purposes. This is necessarily so because no bona fide arm's-length transaction takes place when such assets are transferred to a person who is the object of the bounty of the donor or testator. In the absence of such conclusive evidence, the courts have generally held that the computed value of stock or an interest in a closely held business enterprise should be discounted for lack of marketability.

On the ascending scale will be valuations for purposes of an initial public offering of capital stock. Such valuations, although generally higher than those for federal tax purposes, will, with notable exceptions, still be reasonably conservative because of the lack of an established market at the time of the offering.

On the top of the scale are valuations for purposes of acquisition or merger, which in recent years have been generously high, whether a deal is negotiated with or without the cooperation of management of the company proposed to be acquired. In order to induce the stockholders of the selling company to go along with a deal, a premium over the established market price invariably must be offered.

ECONOMIC INFLUENCES AND GENERAL VALUATION FACTORS

Regardless of the purpose of a valuation, the same general factors are relevant, i.e., the status and trend of the economy, the current view of a particular industry's prospects, securities market conditions, and government fiscal policies.

[3] James H. Schwabacher, 5 T.C.M. 971 (1946).

Long-Term Economic Influences

Unquestionably, general economic factors play a role in the valuation of businesses. Some of these factors have a current effect on the economy and others a more predictable and long-term result.

Government Fiscal Policies. Government fiscal policies and spending requirements have, in recent years, had more effect on the economy than any combination of other factors. For example, the following selected statistics on gross national product, which consists primarily of expenditures for personal consumption and private investment, and government (federal, state, and local) purchases of goods and services, show the increasing role played by government in sustaining the economy: [4]

	Billions of Dollars			
	1940	1946	1968	* 1970
In current dollars:				
Personal consumption	$70.8	$143.4	$535.8	$616.8
Gross private domestic investment	13.1	30.6	126.5	135.8
Net exports	1.7	7.5	2.5	3.6
Government purchases	14.0	27.0	200.2	220.5
	$99.6	$208.5	$865.0	$976.7

* Preliminary.

Defense Expenditures. During World War II national defense expenditures reached a peak in 1944 of $87.4 billion in terms of current dollars. However, after the cessation of hostilities, gross national product in terms of current dollars dropped only from $210.1 billion in 1944 to $208.5 billion in 1946, despite a decrease in national defense expenditures of $72.7 billion.[5] In other words, personal consumption expenditures, private domestic investments, and exports were able to fill the vacuum created by curtailment of government expenditures. Such a situation would probably not prevail today, if there should be a drastic reduction in defense expenditures, which amounted to $76.6 billion in 1970, because

[4] U. S. Dept. of Commerce, Office of Business Economics.
[5] *Ibid.*

we are currently spending record amounts for consumer goods and social programs.

Population Growth and Social Programs. Other long-term economic factors are the ever growing population with its increased demand for goods and services, and the additional disposable income in the hands of retirees and others through social security and private and insured pension plans.

The population of the United States increased from 132,600,000 in 1940 to 206,000,000 in 1970, and the labor force from 55,600,000 to 86,200,000.[6] The population increase created new markets and demands, and the labor force, with its spiraling wage increases, provided the wherewithal to finance them.

Payments Under Public and Private Pension Plans. Estimated payments from federal funds under social security and related government welfare programs, including aid to education, amounted to $143,000,000,000 for the fiscal year ended June 30, 1970, and represented almost 15% of the nation's output for goods and services; such payments for fiscal 1940 were $8,800,000,000.[7] Private and insured pension, annuity, health, and related payments under employee benefit plans amounted to $18,500,000,000 for the year 1968. Such payments were relatively nominal in 1940.[8]

These payments are not additional income created, but represent, for the most part, a shift in income obtained from tax collections. A substantial portion of such payments goes to retirees and has created a market for homes and mobile housing in equable climates. The tremendous population increases in California and Florida since World War II are in no small part due to the influx of retirees and their families.

Growth of the Leisure Market. The home entertainment market for television receivers, radios, recording equipment, records, books, magazines, musical instruments, hobby and craft material, and games has expanded considerably in recent years. Expenditures for vacation travel, food, and lodging are reaching new

[6] *Ibid.*

[7] Skolnik and Dales, *Social Welfare Expenditures, 1968, 1969,* Soc. SEC. BULL., December 1970.

[8] Kolodrubetz, *Employee-Benefit Plans, 1950–68,* Soc. SEC. BULL., April 1970.

heights annually, as are outlays for sports equipment. It is estimated that the leisure market, in all its aspects, accounted for expenditures exceeding $150,000,000,000 during 1970.

Current Economic Influences

Governmental Tax Policies. Economic factors having a current rather than a long-term effect include federal tax and governmental money policies. For example, the investment credit against federal income taxes and the liberalization of depreciation guidelines placed additional disposable income in the hands of business in the estimated amount of $15,500,000,000 for the years 1962 to 1965 inclusive.[9] Also, the reduction in federal tax rates on individuals and corporations for the years 1964 to 1966 provided an estimated additional $38,800,000,000 (primarily to individuals) of disposable income.[10] Conversely, the speed-up of corporate payments of estimated tax reduced corporate disposable income an estimated $4,500,000,000 for the years 1964 to 1966.[11]

Federal Reserve Control of Credit. The Federal Reserve Board, which operates through twelve regional banks, exercises awesome powers over the credit available in the nation and in international finance. All national banks must be members of the system, and state-chartered banks may elect to be members. The Federal Reserve establishes (a) the discount rate at which member banks borrow from it, (b) the percentage of reserves required to be set aside against net demand and time deposits of such members, (c) the maximum interest rates which may be paid on time and savings deposits and negotiable certificates of deposit, and (d) stock market margin requirements. It also makes open market transactions for fixed income government securities.

The best source of funds for banks is deposits, but when the ceilings fixed by the Federal Reserve for allowable interest rates are low, funds are withdrawn by corporate treasurers and others and flow to competing types of short-term investments such as commercial paper and Treasury bills and notes. Savings deposits and certificates of deposit drawing interest at relatively low rates

---

[9] U. S. Treasury Dept., Office of Tax Analysis.
[10] *Ibid.*
[11] *Ibid.*

are no longer attractive when high-grade utility and industrial bonds may be purchased at yields as high as 8 to 9% per annum.

Thus, banks resort to the Federal Reserve for short-term borrowings at the current discount rate. This rate was successively increased from 4% on December 5, 1965, to 6% on April 4, 1969.[12] The Federal Reserve also increased its reserve requirements against net deposits on April 17, 1969, from 16½ to 17%, on amounts up to $5,000,000 for city banks, and 17½% on amounts above that figure. Reserve requirements for country banks were increased from 12 to 12½% on amounts up to $5,000,000 and to 13% on amounts above that figure. The reserve requirements for all classes of banks were 3% on savings deposits and on other time deposits under $5,000,000, and 6% on time deposits over $5,000,-000.[13] These reserve requirements raised the effective cost of utilizable bank borrowings. However, commencing in November 1970, the discount rate was successively lowered from 6 to 4¾% on February 12, 1971, and the reserve requirements on time deposits lowered to 5%.

The prime interest rate of banks, available only to the top credit rated borrowers, was 4½% at December 1, 1965. This rate was successively raised, as a result of the restraining policies on bank credit, to an unprecedented 8½% on June 9, 1969, 1¾% of which increase occurred after December 1968. This governmental policy of credit restraint had as its objective the control of inflation. The prime interest rate of banks started to decelerate in March 1970, as a result of the slackening in demand for loans, and following the drop in the discount rate, was successively reduced during 1970 and again in March 1971, to 5¼%.

Banks have traditionally purchased the bulk of new municipal bond issues. During the 1966 credit crunch they sold substantial amounts of such holdings to obtain funds for higher-yield lending purposes. Although this improved their earnings, it affected their liquidity, and the Federal Reserve sent them a letter warning against a continuation of this practice. In 1969, because of the scarcity of loan and investment funds, they virtually ceased purchasing municipal bonds. This caused the interest rates on these

[12] FED. RES. BULL., August 1969, p. A–9.
[13] Ibid., p. A–10.

to soar; a 7% yield on such tax exempts was not uncommon during 1969 and 1970. Because of such high rates, and statutory restrictive ceilings on rates, many municipalities postponed marketing securities and correspondingly their capital expenditure programs.

Banks had less money available for other than prime borrowers, and banks, insurance companies, and mortgage companies were loath to accept mortgage loans on individual homes because of state usury laws which restricted them to rates of 8–8½% per annum in some cases. Also, the Federal Housing Authority and other lenders adopted more stringent down-payment requirements for mortgage borrowers. This situation adversely affected the amount of new housing starts and the construction and building materials industries during 1969 and 1970.

The cost of commercial and industrial construction soared not only because of high union wage scales but also due to the interest rates on construction loans, running in the area of 12 to 14% per annum. After paying the high prices for construction caused by these factors, commercial and industrial borrowers were paying rates as high as 10% per annum for mortgage money, often with a kicker for the lender in the form of options or warrants to purchase capital stock of the borrowing company at attractive prices.

The effect of the Federal Reserve's control of credit was graphically illustrated when its discount rate and the prime interest rate of banks eased off during the latter part of 1970 and early in 1971. The stock market surged, and yields on corporate bonds went from the 8½ to 9% range to 7¼ to 7½%. The most dramatic change, however, took place in the municipal bond market and short-term Treasury bills. Moody's Municipal Bond Yield averages for long-term issues went from slightly over 7% on composite and approximately 7% for Aaa rated bonds in June 1970, to approximately 5¼% for composite and less than 5% on Aaa rated bonds early in February 1971. Short-term Treasury bills during this period went from a yield of about 7½% to less than 4%.

Wage–Price Spiral. Regardless of the Federal Reserve's efforts to curb too rapid an expansion of credit and the money supply, inflation cannot be reasonably controlled without some form of restraints, self-imposed or otherwise, on wage and price increases. As long as wage increases are not accompanied by increased productivity, so that unit costs remain reasonably in line, relative price increases must inevitably follow. With substantial wage increases during 1970, in the construction, automotive, transit, airlines, printing, and metals industries, among others, prices have been increasing at an obviously inflationary rate. Despite fare increases, the public transportation industries have been falling further behind in attempting to keep abreast of rising operating costs. Another facet of settling the substantial wage demands of major industries is a forced cutback in employment. In the face of a sluggish economy during 1970, for example, industry had no alternative but to cut back on labor costs, so that while a number of persons benefited from wage increases, many others were laid off from their jobs. At the close of the year 1970, 6.2% of the civilian labor force was unemployed, the highest rate since 1961. The rate was 3.5% at the close of 1969.[14]

Effect of a Slump in a Major Industry. General Motors preliminarily reported sales of $18,800 million and net income of $609 million for 1970, compared with $24,300 million and $1,711 million for the preceding year. Chrysler preliminarily reported sales of $7,000 million and a loss of $7.6 million for 1970 compared with sales of $7,100 million and net income of $99 million for the preceding year.

General Motors also reported that the UAW strike against the company for ten weeks ended November 12, 1970, accounted for $135 million of its decrease in net profits, and it was further estimated that the workers lost $637 million in payroll as a result of the strike.

The decrease in new car sales from 10,147,000 in 1969 to approximately 8,240,000 in 1970 [15] adversely affected steel, rubber, glass, and other suppliers to the industry, as well as rail and motor carriers.

Approximately 20% of steel output goes into automobile production, and there are many thousands of suppliers of other materials and components to the automotive industry. Thus, a reduction of business in one major industry can affect the general economy.

[14] U. S. Dept. of Commerce, Office of Business Economics.
[15] WARDS AUTOMOTIVE MANUAL, 1970.

Effects of the Stock Market on the Economy. The main thrust of this chapter has been to show factors that affect the economy and therefore the stock market and the valuation of companies. A reverse action may also take place when the stock market affects the economy. Excessive speculation, with its inevitable aftermath of a stock market slump, had a far-reaching adverse effect on the economy, as indicated in Chapter 2. During 1969 and the first half of 1970, both public and institutional stock market investors lost many billions of dollars. A number of stock exchange firms, including some larger ones, suffered such severe losses that they had to be liquidated, were forced into shotgun mergers with others, or had to go outside of the investment fraternity for needed capital. Hundreds of branch offices of these and other stock exchange firms were closed, and thousands of employees lost their jobs.

The psychological aspects of this major market break and the losses sustained by the public had a definitely adverse effect on consumer spending, particularly for luxury goods and services.

SPECIFIC VALUATION FACTORS

More specific factors considered in the valuation of a company or business are (a) potential earnings, (b) dividend paying capacity, (c) net assets, and (d) market prices of capital stock or of publicly traded stocks of similar companies in the industry.

For an operating company whose worth is largely dependent on its continuance as a going concern, potential earnings are generally the most important valuation factor. On the other hand, for a company with substantial holdings of disposable assets, such as securities or real estate, overall valuation would usually be related to the fair market value of such underlying assets.

In addition to obvious tangible valuation factors, there are many others, some favorable and some adverse, that merit consideration in valuing a company for a specific purpose. These will be discussed in later chapters.

Influence of Stock Market Prices

The market price of the capital stock of a company involved in a valuation problem, or of the stocks of public companies in the same industry, is always a potent factor in arriving at overall valuation. However, such prices should not be the only criteria of value. The importance, as well as the limitations, of stock market indexes and quoted prices of stocks of public companies will be discussed in the next chapter.

Validity of Some "Guideline" Factors

Over the years some guidelines have been considered in valuing a business, such as one year's gross revenues for an accounting business, an insurance agency, or other service-type enterprise. Also, the courts from time to time have expressly or overtly regarded "book value" as an appropriate measure of the valuation of a business. The validity of these and other criteria, such as the use of mathematical formulas, will be discussed in later chapters where appropriate.

Valuations That Defy Logical Explanation

There was a considerable amount of speculation going on in the stock market during the late 1960's, primarily in unlisted securities of companies in modern technological fields. This speculative fever affected new issues in so-called exotic industries to the point where companies that had no operations floated initial offerings at prices many times their computed net worth per share, including proceeds of the offering; others were priced at 50 or more times their latest year's earnings. Furthermore, many such stocks sold at substantial premiums within a week or less after the initial offerings.

The investing public has a short memory and apparently forgot the fate of innumerable issues marketed in the uranium and electronics fields, and recently of companies having the magic word "computer" as part of their corporate names. The only obvious explanation for such a Russian roulette type of purchase is the hope of finding a bigger fool who is willing to pay a still higher price for the excessively valued security. With no scientific explanation for such valuations, we defer to those who underwrite and maintain a market in such securities for their fertile imagination in the field of valuations.

ROLE OF INDEPENDENT PROFESSIONALS

Valuation Experts

Valuing a company or business, or an interest therein, usually requires the expertise of independent professionals. Depending upon the purpose of a valuation, such experts should be carefully selected for their knowledge of the rules, regulations, precedents, and current conditions applying to the particular type of evaluation.

The accounting and reporting requirements prescribed by the American Institute of Certified Public Accountants, the Securities and Exchange Commission, and the stock exchanges for an initial public offering, tender offer, or an acquisition or merger are designed to provide information that is germane in arriving at appropriate valuations by experts involved. The Internal Revenue Code, regulations, and significant rulings affect valuations for estate, gift, and income tax purposes, as well as those for public offerings and acquisitions and mergers. The impact of such federal taxes, and in some cases state taxes, may significantly influence the method of effecting a transaction for any of the purposes cited.

The opinion of a valuation expert should not be based on the knowledge which he professes but the knowledge he actually possesses. In judging the competence of an expert, consideration should be given to his apparent grasp of the essential facts in the case, his ability and experience in interpreting the facts, and his competence in arriving at a valuation that is meaningful and consistent with such facts. The several classes of experts involved in valuations are discussed briefly below.

In Public Offerings. In initial public offerings, the investment bankers who underwrite the issue are the valuation experts. In such a role they have an apparent conflict of interest, being valuers as well as purchasers of the issue. This is the only case in the three major areas of valuations—i.e., for initial public offerings, for federal estate, gift, and income tax purposes, and for business combinations—where there is, in effect, a unilateral determination of value. However, as illustrated by the study of 200 initial common stock offerings in Chapter 4, most investment bankers appear to arrive at reasonably objective valuations by and large.

In Federal Tax Evaluations. Valuations for federal estate, gift, and income tax purposes will generally require experts who are familiar with the intricacies of the Internal Revenue Code, regulations, rulings, and court decisions pertaining to such valuations. In submitting such valuations, the taxpayer or his representatives have an adversary in the Internal Revenue Service. In preparing or endeavoring to sustain such valuations legal counsel is customarily required, in addition to valuation experts. Such experts may include accountants, appraisal engineers, investment analysts, economists, or other specialists.

In Acquisitions and Mergers. Valuations for purposes of acquisitions and mergers, whether with or without the consent of the management of the company proposed to be acquired, often have their origin in the opinion of management of the would-be acquirer. This may be based on a quick appraisal of what financial benefits would be derived from the business combination.

In other cases a proposed acquisition may be brought to the attention of a would-be acquirer by an investment banking firm or a business broker. In many cases the valuation proposed for the selling company is based on its management's views without any sound basis for such valuation. Conversely, a company may be romanced to sell out at an equally unsound valuation proposed by the would-be acquirer. The fact that a go-between has brought a prospective acquirer and a seller together gives no assurance of his objectivity and expertise regarding the propriety of a proposed valuation. In appropriate cases, each party at interest may employ such experts as investment bankers, accountants, financial consultants, or management engineers to represent them in arriving at suitable valuations.

Need for Professional Guidance

It is of the utmost importance that the appraiser of a business enterprise and the parties involved in negotiations have a detailed knowledge of what is being valued. This will invariably require professional accounting studies of pertinent data, and will often involve other experts such as engineers, marketing analysts, investment bankers, and legal counsel.

Published Financial Statements. While companies listed on national securities exchanges and those otherwise reporting to the Securities and Exchange Commission under the various securities acts are subject to the accounting and financial disclosure requirements of the latter, such companies comprise a small percentage of the total business enterprises in the country.

A substantial number of companies, not subject to such requirements, have regular examinations of their financial statements by certified public accountants or licensed public accountants. However, they do not, in all cases, have examinations performed in accordance with generally accepted auditing standards nor do they always follow generally accepted accounting principles. Accordingly, a careful reading of an auditor's report is necessary to determine if statements submitted present fairly the financial position and results of operations of an enterprise in conformity with such standards and principles.

Furthermore, regulated industries such as airlines, banks, insurance companies, public utilities, and railroads employ certain accounting practices which differ from those followed by business enterprises in general. These practices are discussed in Chapter 15.

Last but not least, within the framework of generally accepted accounting principles there is some latitude permitted in the preparation of financial statements. Thus, company accounting practices may range from the conservative to the barely permissible, provided consistency in such practices is maintained *or changes therein disclosed.*

Importance of Current Knowledge

Many laws, rules, regulations, administrative practices, and court decisions, variously pertaining to the Securities Acts, major stock exchange releases, federal and state taxes, and antitrust laws are analyzed and discussed in this book. These data were current at the time the manuscript was submitted for publication. However, the reader should check, where such information is significant, to determine what changes, if any, have been effected subsequently.

2

Influence of
Securities Markets

Securities market prices admittedly play a dominant role in valuing public companies whose stocks are actively traded. They also are of importance in valuing public companies whose stocks are not actively traded, and stocks of closely held corporations, by means of comparative industry data. It would be well, therefore, to review the manner in which securities markets operate, the controls exercised over trading and prices, and some of the limitations of quoted prices and stock price indexes. Among key matters dealt with in this chapter are performance factors of actively traded common stocks, pricing policies for public offerings and "block transactions" involving such stocks, and speculation in so-called "hot issues."

To begin with, securities markets are influenced by the law of supply and demand, the same as commodity markets. When a company is in need of financing, depending upon current economic conditions and the purpose for which the funds are to be used, its management may decide on a short- or long-term bank or insurance company loan, a mortgage loan, the issuance of bonds, or equity financing in the form of common or preferred stock issues.

COMPARATIVE MARKET DATA ON
STOCKS AND BONDS

Since the close of World War II, stocks have been increasing in popularity with individual investors, pension funds, and nonprofit organizations. The market value of common and preferred stocks listed on the New York Stock Exchange increased from $68,595 million at the close of 1946 to $692,337 million in 1968. Because of a prolonged bear market during 1969 and the first half of 1970, these values had decreased to $636,380 million at the close of 1970. Average prices of stocks at these several year-ends would have no significance because of new listings, eliminations, stock splits, and stock dividends.

As a contrast, the market value of all bonds listed on the New York Stock Exchange at the close of 1946 was $140,793 million at an average price of $102.64 of face value. This compares with a market value of such listings at the close of 1968 of $120,407 million at an average price of $86.62, and $112,600 million at the close of 1970 at an average price of $83.59. While it is true that 50% of the bond values at the close of 1970 applied to U. S. Government, New York City, and other miscellaneous issues, the corporate issues comprising the remaining 50% of the total valuation were at an average price of $80.72.

Industry Summary of Stocks and Bonds

A summary, by industry, of listed stocks and bonds on the New York Stock Exchange at December 31, 1968 and 1970, appears in Tables 2–1 and 2–2.[1]

Many Bonds Not Traded on Exchanges. It should not be inferred from the industry summary that the volume of bond issues has remained static. Most federal, state, and municipal bonds, and many utility and industrial issues, are and always have been traded in the over-the-counter market and purchased in large blocks primarily by banks, insurance companies, and other institutional investors. State and municipal bonds have been gaining favor with individual investors in the higher income brackets be-

[1] New York Stock Exchange.

TABLE 2-1   Listed Stocks—By Industry
(Shares and Market Value in Millions)

| | All Stocks—Common and Preferred | | | | | |
| | 1968 | | | 1970 | | |
	No. Issues	No. Shares	Market Value	No. Issues	No. Shares	Market Value
Industrials:						
Aircraft	32	242	$ 11,674	32	248	$ 5,161
Amusement	19	118	5,776	20	139	3,771
Automotive	58	617	37,406	56	672	35,309
Building	65	207	9,798	66	311	8,772
Chemicals (including						
glass)	106	1,006	63,456	99	1,115	55,318
Drugs, cosmetics	46	504	31,067	47	712	40,687
Electronics, electrical.	125	939	83,211	132	1,175	75,355
Foods, commodities..	105	701	30,944	106	805	30,866
Furniture, office						
equipment	18	103	11,894	17	188	11,199
Leather, shoes	18	51	2,508	14	64	2,072
Machinery, metals	208	951	44,582	205	1,162	36,510
Mining	59	448	19,999	63	548	16,587
Paper, publishing	66	387	19,366	67	554	19,395
Petroleum, natural						
gas	72	1,516	102,401	72	1,787	81,622
Retail trade	101	723	31,972	109	898	36,129
Rubber	18	125	6,517	17	179	5,579
Steel	43	286	11,311	43	310	7,322
Textiles	55	168	6,706	57	208	5,635
Tobacco	16	103	4,545	15	123	5,916
Other	37	118	6,521	68	307	9,626
Total industrials	1,267	9,312	$541,654	1,305	11,508	$492,829
Transportation	109	552	23,918	101	608	15,899
Utilities	272	2,643	98,229	294	2,864	93,699
Finance, real estate	119	689	28,537	140	1,084	33,053
Grand total	1,767	13,196	$692,337	1,840	16,065	$636,380

Note: Some columns do not total because of rounding out.

cause they are exempt from federal income tax. Also, in recent years, there has been a surge of offerings of bonds of public utility companies on a high-yield basis and convertible debentures of industrial companies, either directly to the public for cash, or through acquisition and merger exchange offerings. Many such securities were purchased or received by individual investors.

TABLE 2-2   Listed Bonds—By Major Groups
(Par Value and Market Value in Millions)

	1968			1970		
	No. Issues	Par Value	Market Value	No. Issues	Par Value	Market Value
Total U. S. companies....	1,142	$ 47,778	$ 39,297	1,480	$ 69,500	$ 56,100
Foreign companies.........	42	609	500	32	800	700
U. S. government and New York City............	34	85,727	76,546	30	59,200	51,400
International banks........	32	2,475	2,087	35	3,000	2,600
Foreign governments......	205	2,311	1,978	152	2,200	1,900
Total	1,455	$138,901	$120,407	1,729	$134,700	$112,600

Note: Some columns do not total because of rounding out.

Number of Public Stockholders

The New York Stock Exchange has held six stockholder census surveys at periodic intervals since 1952. These surveys have shown a most substantial increase in the number of individual shareowners in public corporations, from 6,500,000 in 1952 to 30,850,000 in more than 10,000 public corporations in 1970. What is particularly startling is that 53.3% of this increase took place since the 1965 census when there were 20,120,000 shareowners.[2]

Disposable personal income, i.e., personal income less tax and non-tax payments to governments, increased during this period from $238,300 million in 1952 to $685,000 million (preliminary figure) for 1970.[3]

Institutional Investors

Institutional investors have also contributed to the increased demand for stock investments. The following tabulation shows a comparison of estimated holdings of New York Stock Exchange listed stocks by institutions at the close of 1949, 1968, and 1970:

[2] New York Stock Exchange, "Census Shareowners 1970."
[3] U. S. Dept. of Commerce, Office of Business Economics.

	Billions of Dollars		
	1949	1968	1970
Insurance companies	$2.8	$ 22.1	$ 23.1
Investment companies	3.0	49.4	43.8
Non-insured pension plans	0.5	55.4	59.7
Foundations, endowments, and other non-profit organizations	3.2	30.9	30.2
Other	0.2	5.0	5.1
Total	$9.7	$162.8	$161.9

These estimated holdings accounted for a formidable 25.4% of the market value of stocks listed on the Exchange at December 31, 1970.[4] The holdings by these financial institutions of stocks traded on other securities exchanges and on the over-the-counter market would increase this total by some billions of dollars. Furthermore, institutional investors have increased their trading activity; in 1969 they accounted for more than half of the dollar volume of shares publicly traded on the New York Stock Exchange. In other words, their trading activity was at a rate of more than three times that of the remaining public sector of stockholders.

The impact on securities market prices of institutional investors has been a matter of such concern to the Securities and Exchange Commission that Congress authorized it, in 1968, to undertake a study of this situation and other aspects of institutional investing. A substantial appropriation has been allocated for this project, which was carried out by a study group composed of economists, lawyers, financial analysts, statisticians, and others. Also, in 1969, the Commission appointed an advisory committee of persons prominent in the financial world, "for the purpose of advising and consulting with the Commission on a regular basis on matters coming within the purview of such study."

Bonds Versus Stocks in Inflationary Economy

What are the reasons for the dramatic increase in the number of public stockholders in recent years? Undoubtedly, public con-

[4] New York Stock Exchange.

fidence in the continued growth of the economy is one of the obvious reasons, but another and more fundamental one is that common stocks are a hedge against inflation. From 1946 to 1970 the purchasing power of the dollar, as measured by the consumer price index, dropped 51%, or at the rate of 2% per annum. The rate of decrease in purchasing power was about 4% in 1970. In other words, it took $1.38 in 1970 to buy what cost $0.68 in 1946.[5] Accordingly, one would have required a very high rate of interest on a fixed principal investment to offset the deflation in real value of such a security. Furthermore, the unit values of earlier issues of bonds decreased as interest rates on current offerings continued to increase. This is in sharp contrast with the considerable increment in the Standard & Poor's composite 500 stock price index from 15.30 to 92.15, or approximately 500% at the close of the above twenty-four-year period.

Principal Financial Assets of Individuals in Stocks

As shown in the following tabulation, 46% of financial assets of individuals (includes households, unincorporated businesses, trust funds, and non-profit institutions) was in common and preferred stocks at the close of 1968, and 40% at the close of 1970: [6]

	Billions of Dollars	
	1968	1970
Common and preferred stocks	$ 873	$ 748
Time deposits and savings	357	407
Insurance and pension reserves, private and government employee funds	323	361
Currency and demand deposits	111	122
U. S. Government, state, and municipal bonds	130	134
Corporate and foreign bonds	20	40
Miscellaneous financial assets	63	71
Total	$1,877	$1,883

The relative reduction in the value of stocks in 1970 was due to the market slump commencing in 1969 and lasting through the first half of 1970. Such adverse stock market conditions also

[5] U. S. Dept. of Commerce, Office of Business Economics.
[6] Board of Governors of the Federal Reserve System.

caused some shift by individual investors to bond purchases and the retention of greater amounts of cash.

Number of Stock Issues Traded

At the close of 1968, there were more than 1,500,000 active income-reporting companies in the country.[7] At that date there were approximately 3,500 stock issues admitted to trading on national securities exchanges, eliminating duplications where traded on more than one exchange.[8] At the same time there were more than 50,000 over-the-counter stocks, the vast majority of which were inactively traded.[9]

Most Active Common Stocks Traded. It is interesting to note that, of the 1,190 common stocks listed on the New York Stock Exchange, the 50 most active stocks accounted for a turnover of 388,312,500 round-lot shares, or 25% of the 1,556,300,000 total share volume in 1965.[10] At the other end of the spectrum were 72 listed common stocks having a turnover of less than 100,000 shares each, and an aggregate volume of only 4,008,000 shares or ¼ of 1% of the total for that year.[11] Thus, listing does not always insure an active market.

The 50 most active common stocks in 1970, of 1,350 listed, accounted for approximately 22.4% of all reported volume.[12]

Turnover Ratio of Stocks Traded. During 1970 industrial companies accounted for 76% of reported share volume on the New York Stock Exchange. The turnover rate of all stocks was 19% for 1970, compared with 16% for 1965. For 1970, the miscellaneous categories, such as vending, leasing, and other service groups, led with a 53% ratio, and the amusement industry was second with a 37% ratio; utility stocks were easily last in turnover with a 10% rate.[13]

The American Stock Exchange had 910 common and preferred stock issues listed at December 31, 1965, and 1,249 at December

---

[7] Internal Revenue Service, latest data available in 1970.
[8] Securities and Exchange Commission.
[9] National Association of Securities Dealers, Inc.
[10] New York Stock Exchange, "1965 Fact Book."
[11] Study made by authors.
[12] New York Stock Exchange.
[13] *Ibid.*

31, 1970. However, because of the lower average price of shares on this Exchange, speculative interest increased its turnover of shares traded from 30.9% in 1965 to 65.5% in 1968. However, there was a marked decline in turnover rate of stocks traded on the Amex in 1970.[14]

SECURITIES EXCHANGES

Securities and Exchange Commission

The Securities and Exchange Commission, an independent regulatory body having executive and quasi-judicial powers, has overall authority regarding trading in securities on organized exchanges, as well as over-the-counter markets. This authority was vested in the Commission under the Securities Exchange Act of 1934.

Among objectives of the Act are (a) to provide disclosure of financial and other information about publicly held companies to enable public investors to evaluate the securities of these companies on an informed and realistic basis, (b) to insure fair and honest markets in securities transactions, (c) to regulate transactions of brokers and dealers with their customers, (d) to supervise insider trading, i.e., securities transactions by officers, directors, and principal stockholders, and (e) to prevent excessive speculation and sudden and unreasonable market fluctuations resulting from the manipulation and control of security prices.[15]

National Securities Exchanges

There were 13 registered national securities exchanges at December 31, 1970. The total volume of stocks traded on such exchanges during the year then ended amounted to 4,535 million shares, of which the New York Stock Exchange accounted for 71%, the American Stock Exchange 19%, and all other exchanges 10%.[16]

A security may be traded on more than one national exchange,

---

[14] American Stock Exchange.
[15] Securities and Exchange Commission.
[16] *Ibid.*

or on an exchange and in the over-the-counter market. Also, New York Stock Exchange members engage in what is described as "off-board" trading in listed common stocks. Such transactions are mainly for the purpose of personal investment and arbitrage.

The New York exchanges are well organized for self-regulation of securities markets and have rules governing issuers as well as broker–dealer members. Both exchanges have minimum eligibility requirements for the number of shares of stock of a company to be listed and the number of round-lot shareholders to be included in such listing in order to insure an active market in the stock.

Listing Requirements of the Exchanges

The New York and American stock exchanges have been upgrading their listing requirements over the years, but do not apply them retroactively to companies whose securities are already listed. For example, the exchanges had minimum requirements for initial and for continued listing, as outlined below.

New York Stock Exchange.[17]

To be listed on the New York Stock Exchange, a company is expected to meet certain qualifications and to be willing to keep the investing public informed on the progress of its affairs. The company must be a going concern, or be the successor to a going concern. In determining eligibility for listing, particular attention is given to such qualifications as: 1) the degree of national interest in the company; 2) its relative position and stability in the industry; and 3) whether it is engaged in an expanding industry, with prospects of at least maintaining its relative position.

Initial Listing

While each case is decided on its own merits, the Exchange generally requires the following as a minimum. [These requirements were approved in principle by NYSE Board of Governors on April 18, 1968.]

1. Demonstrated earning power under competitive conditions of $2.5 million before Federal income taxes for the most recent year and $2 million pre-tax for each of the preceding two years.
2. Net tangible assets of $14 million, but greater emphasis will be placed on the aggregate market value of the common stock.
3. A total of $14 million in market value of publicly held common stock.

[17] New York Stock Exchange, "1970 Fact Book."

4. A total of 800,000 common shares publicly held out of 1,000,000 shares outstanding.

5. Round-lot shareholders numbering 1,800 out of a total of 2,000 shareholders.

Continued Listing

The appropriateness of continued listing of a security on the Exchange cannot be measured mathematically, and the Exchange may at any time suspend or delist a security where the Board considers that continued dealings in the security are not advisable, even though a security meets or fails to meet any specified criteria. For example, the Exchange would normally give consideration to suspending or removing from the list a common stock of a company when there are:

1. Less than 900 round-lot holders, with less than 1,000 shareholders of record.
2. 400,000 shares or less in public hands.
3. $4,000,000 or less aggregate market value of publicly held shares.
4. $7,000,000 or less in aggregate market value of all outstanding common stock or net tangible assets applicable thereto, combined with an earnings record of less than an average of $600,000 after taxes for the past three years.

Listing Agreement

The listing agreement between the company and the Exchange is designed to provide timely disclosure to the public of earnings statements, dividend notices, and other information which may affect security values or influence investment decisions. The Exchange requires actively operating companies to agree to solicit proxies for all meetings of stockholders.

Voting Rights

As a matter of general policy, the Exchange has for many years refused to list non-voting common stocks, and all listed common stocks have the right to vote.

American Stock Exchange.[18]

Initial Listing

The minimum requirements for listing on the American Stock Exchange at November 21, 1967, were as follows:

Shares Publicly Held [a] 300,000
Market Value of Publicly Held Shares [b] $2,000,000

[a] Exclusive of the holdings of officers and directors and other concentrated or family holdings.

[b] Price per share: A minimum of $5 for a reasonable period of time prior to the filing of a listing application.

[18] American Stock Exchange, 1970.

Number of Stockholders 900
Round-Lot Stockholders 600
Net Income Last Fiscal Year (pre-tax) $500,000
Net Income Last Fiscal Year (after all charges) $300,000
Net Tangible Assets $3,000,000

Continued Listing

Delisting guidelines, established in 1962 and revised in 1965 and again in 1968, make a company eligible for removal if (a) it has net tangible assets of less than $1,000,000 and sustained net losses in its two most recent fiscal years or (b) it has net tangible assets of less than $3,000,000 and sustained net losses in three of its four most recent fiscal years. Other requirements for continued listing include:

Shares Publicly Held 150,000
Market Value of Shares Publicly Held $750,000
Number of Stockholders 450
Number of Round-Lot Holders 300

Trading Specialists on Exchanges

The New York Stock Exchange operates as a continuous auction market through members who act primarily (in 75.8% of transactions in 1970 [19]) as agents for buyers and sellers. In order to insure an orderly market, the Exchange has appointed specialists for all its listed stocks. These specialists operate under partnership or other joint arrangements and specialize, on an average, in eleven different stocks. They work at particular trading posts on the floor of the Exchange where the stocks in which they specialize are traded. The American, Midwest, and Pacific Coast Exchanges operate under a similar system of specialists. Specialists may act as brokers or as dealers in a transaction. As broker, the specialist executes other brokers' orders on commission; as dealer, he acts for his own account, profit, and risk.

In addition to matching current purchases and sales of stocks, the specialist has two primary functions. He accepts orders, for subsequent disposition, from other members of the Exchange when the current market prices of his specialist stocks are away from the prices of the orders. His other primary function is to maintain, insofar as practicable, fair and orderly markets on the Exchange in the stocks that he services. This is done by buying or selling for his own account, to a reasonable degree, when there

[19] New York Stock Exchange.

is a temporary disparity between supply and demand. Of the 24.2% of round-lot purchases and sales during 1970 by New York Stock Exchange members for their own accounts, 61% were by specialists in performing their function of maintaining orderly markets, 32% were off-the-floor transactions, and 7% were by odd-lot dealers and registered traders.[20]

OVER-THE-COUNTER MARKET

The term "over the counter" encompasses all transactions in securities not consummated on an organized exchange. Such transactions, to a large extent, are carried out through a network of brokers and dealers who are members of the National Association of Security Dealers (NASD). Over-the-counter securities are traded in a negotiated rather than an auction market, in contrast to securities traded on an exchange.

The over-the-counter market substantially increased its share of total sales of corporate stocks in post-World War II years. For the year 1961 it is estimated that over-the-counter sales of stocks amounted to approximately $39 billion (excluding mutual funds), compared with $64 billion of stock sales on all national exchanges. However, a study reported on in 1966 indicated that over-the-counter sales declined in the several years following 1961,[21] while the dollar volume of common stock sales on the national exchanges continued to increase during this period. There were no figures available regarding over-the-counter sales for later years through 1970, although the number of issues traded had greatly increased in recent years.

Over-the-Counter Published Quotations

Over-the-counter market quotations are supplied by brokers or dealers to the National Association of Securities Dealers. Until February 1971, these "quotations" consisted of opinions of major dealers in tabulated issues as to what they would expect to give or take for a specific stock in a transaction with another dealer.

---

[20] *Ibid.*

[21] Booz, Allen & Hamilton, Inc., for NASD, "Over the Counter Market Study," August 22, 1966, p. 29.

The quotations on such stocks were based on information as of noon of the day before publication. There was no figure of such stocks identifiable as the price at which an actual trade took place, nor could a customer be assured he could obtain shares at a specified price over that of the dealer.

Daily quotations on more than 1,700 securities nationally traded were furnished on this basis to over 300 newspapers, and quotations on an additional 600 or so less active securities were furnished weekly. These quotations were subject to a markup, markdown, or commission in transactions with the public. Quotations were also furnished on some thousands of other issues to local newspapers.[22]

Commencing in 1971, through the National Association of Securities Dealers Automated Quotations System (NASDAQ), a registered representative or dealer will be able to obtain immediate quotations compiled on some 2,500 stocks through transmission devices such as those in use for securities listed on national exchanges. The dealer or representative, in answer to his query, will be furnished with the bid or asked prices of all dealers interested in buying or selling a particular stock. The system also enables the NASD to publish daily price ranges and volume of shares traded. It is expected to continue to add over-the-counter issues through NASDAQ, with an ultimate goal of many thousands of daily transactions.

STOCK MARKET INDEXES

There are various stock market indexes, the oldest and best known of which are the Dow Jones averages of 30 industrials, 20 transportation companies, and 15 utilities, and Standard & Poor's "500" averages of 425 industrials, 20 rails, and 55 utilities. All stocks included in these indexes are listed on the New York Stock Exchange.

Dow Jones

Although the Dow Jones industrial stock price index has been adjusted over the years to reflect stock splits and stock dividends,

---

[22] Merrill Lynch, Pierce, Fenner & Smith, Inc., "Over the Counter Securities, a National Market," November 1965.

as well as substitutions of the stocks used in it, some experts believe that it does not contain a sufficient number of issues to give a sound statistical result of price movements. For example, this index showed an increase from 874.13 to 969.26 during the year 1965. However, 9 of the 30 stocks included in the index decreased in market price per share during the year, and another 5 showed only slight improvement. In other words, approximately 50% of the stocks included in the industrial averages accounted for the improvement in the Dow Jones index during 1965.

Standard & Poor's

The Standard & Poor's stock price indexes are more representative of stock price movements than the Dow Jones. The 500 stocks covered in the S & P averages represent about 90% of the market value of all common stocks listed on the New York Stock Exchange.

Exchanges' Own Indexes

In 1966 the American Stock Exchange launched its own index; shortly thereafter the New York Stock Exchange followed suit. The Amex Index was constructed retroactively to the last quarter of 1962, while the NYSE Index set December 31, 1965, as its base. Both indexes include all the common stocks listed on the respective exchanges, weighted by the number of shares listed for each issue.

Statistics on Composite Indexes

The statistics shown on page 31 are furnished on Standard & Poor's composite stock price index and the New York Stock Exchange common stock index for the eleven years ended December 31, 1970. The tabulation straddles the periods covered by the various studies reported on in later chapters of this book. It will be noted that the relative percentage changes in the two indexes, from year to year, closely parallel each other.

During the period covered in the tabulation, there were three major stock market slumps. The first, commencing in May 1962, followed a period of "hot issue" initial offerings that began in the

	S & P's Composite Stock Price Index			NYSE Common Stock Index		
Year	High	Low	Close	High	Low	Close
1960	60.39	52.30	58.11	31.99	28.38	30.94
1961	72.64	57.57	71.55	38.60	31.17	38.39
1962	71.13	52.32	63.10	38.02	28.20	33.81
1963	75.02	62.69	75.02	39.92	34.41	39.92
1964	86.28	75.43	84.75	46.49	40.47	45.65
1965	92.63	81.60	92.43	50.00	43.64	50.00
1966	94.06	73.20	80.33	51.06	39.37	43.72
1967	97.59	80.38	96.47	54.16	43.74	53.83
1968	108.37	87.72	103.86	61.27	48.70	58.90
1969	106.16	89.48	92.06	59.32	49.31	51.53
1970	93.46	69.29	92.15	52.36	37.69	50.23

1950's. An SEC study showed that many of the companies whose stock was marketed during this period had failed. The second market slump, in 1966, and the third, starting around the beginning of 1969 and continuing to gain momentum during that year and the first half of 1970, may be attributable in large part to the tight money situation prevailing during those periods. Although stock market action is reputed to be a precursor of economic changes, general business indicators such as gross national product, disposable personal income, industrial production, and corporate profits continued to increase during the market stress periods of 1962 and 1966. However, industrial production and corporate profits trended lower during the latter part of 1969 and in 1970.

Limitations of Composite Indexes

In the burgeoning market of 1967, when its common stock index for the year advanced 23%, the New York Stock Exchange stock price profile showed that 1,038 of its issues had advanced, 162 had declined, and 6 had remained unchanged. Furthermore, the ratio of the number of stocks showing a decline in market value, to the total listed, was generally much higher in other years than it was in 1967, during periods of composite price advances. A holder of stocks in the declining group would probably not consider that a substantial increase in a composite index appropriately indicated a trend.

SOME QUESTIONABLE FACTORS INFLUENCING STOCK PRICES

Public Relations Activities

Public relations activities, at their best, act as a supplement to a company's annual report to stockholders by giving timely disclosure of important corporate developments. At their worst, they may be used to promote an unwarranted increase in the market price of a stock. The Securities and Exchange Commission in its special study of securities markets had this to say on the subject:

Although many companies and their financial public relations publicists who specialize in communicating between issuers on the one hand and the financial press, the investment community and stockholders on the other, conduct their activities with restraint and propriety, nevertheless a segment of this industry has been involved in the dissemination of inaccurate and misleading information. . . .

. . . Given a generally bullish market or existing public interest in a particular company or industry, a well-planned publicity campaign can have an immediate and dramatic effect on the price of a security. Examples were found in which a single carefully "placed" article had the effect, within a few days, of trebling the price of a stock with a thin floating supply. The business editor of a national publication for several years made a practice of purchasing the stock of small companies which the publication was about to write up, and selling his holdings shortly after the article appeared, usually at a considerable profit.

. . . Publicity may also be distributed for the personal gain of company officials or the personal advantage of public relations men who acquire securities of their clients either as part of their fee or otherwise. The Special Study found instances of persons in these categories selling substantial amounts of stock shortly after the public announcement of favorable corporate developments.

The publicity material reviewed by the Special Study had a broad range of accuracy—from straightforward reporting to material that appeared to be deliberately misleading. Most of the inaccurate publicity, however, appeared to have some basis in fact but erred in being overoptimistic. One issuer, over a period of several months, repeatedly announced plans to expand its business—plans which never came to fruition, if indeed they were ever seriously contemplated. Other companies announced earnings projections which were without basis and were not fulfilled, descriptions of new products which were still in the experimental stage, and announcements of mergers or acquisitions which were only vague possibilities. Related to the premature disclosure of corporate "news" were the problems of withholding information that should have been published and the generation or encouragement of optimistic rumors, thus giving "insiders" an unfair advantage over members of the public.[23]

Stabilizing Function in Public Offerings

In addition to the stabilizing function performed by exchange specialists for stocks they service, another type of stabilizing operation is permitted under the Securities Exchange Act of 1934. This involves open market purchases of securities during the period of distribution of a public offering, to prevent or retard a decline in the market price of such securities. The fact that stabilizing transactions are to be conducted during a distribution period must be disclosed in an offering prospectus and in reports filed with the Securities and Exchange Commission, showing purchases and sales of such securities by persons conducting the distribution.

Market Manipulation of Stocks

Manipulation and speculation are not to be confused with stabilizing operations. Over the years the Securities and Exchange Commission and the major stock exchanges have had to take disciplinary action on a number of occasions where various forms of market manipulation were indicated. In some cases trading in the manipulated stock was suspended for a period, and in others orders were issued requiring the offending persons to desist from the prohibited manipulative activities. Some manipulative practices reported on by the SEC and the Attorney General of the State of New York are commented on later in this chapter.

Speculation in Stocks

Speculation in the stock market is more difficult to control than manipulation. The presidents of the New York and American stock exchanges were so concerned about this problem that on April 23, 1966, both issued statements announcing measures being taken to discourage uninformed speculation by investors. The restrictive requirements applied primarily to "day traders," i.e., per-

[23] "Report of Special Study of Securities Markets of the Securities and Exchange Commission," Part 3, 1963.

sons whose accounts showed a pattern of buying and selling stocks before they had paid for them. The New York Stock Exchange, even prior to this period, required higher margin payments on certain stocks that showed volatile performance patterns.

Speculators and the "Hot Issues" Market

The prices of securities in which there is a relatively thin market may be subject to wide fluctuations. An example of runaway prices took place during the period of the "hot issue" market, commencing in 1959 and terminating with the sharp decline in securities market prices late in May 1962. Most of these "hot issues" were traded over-the-counter.

The Securities and Exchange Commission in its Special Study of Securities Markets noted the surge of initial offerings of stocks during this period. The following portion of the SEC report succinctly describes what transpired: [24]

This activity in new issues took place in a climate of general optimism and speculative interest. The public eagerly sought stocks of companies in certain "glamour" industries, especially the electronics industry, in the expectation that they would quickly rise to a substantial premium—an expectation that was often fulfilled. Within a few days or even hours after the initial distribution, these so-called "hot issues" would be traded at premiums of as much as 300 percent above the original offering price. In many cases, the price of a "hot" issue later fell to a fraction of its original offering price.

Apparently, many investors were not particularly concerned about the lack of basic underlying values of many stocks as long as prices continued to advance.

The newly elected president of the American Stock Exchange issued a warning on the speculative nature of prices of many of the stocks listed on the Exchange in July 1967. In the wake of this warning the *Investor's Reader* published a list of some 250 stocks on the New York and American stock exchanges that showed gains of from 100% to 1200% over their 1967 lows, and stated, "This very fact drives home the highly speculative nature of many (but far from all) of the stocks which have shot up so fast." This article further stated, "The list could have been ex-

24 *Ibid.*, Part 1.

panded by another 100 names (mostly Amex) had it not excluded stocks which now sell below $10, even after doubling, tripling and in at least a couple of cases quintupling." [25]

Trading in stocks continued at an accelerated pace during 1968. In the wake of a warning to its members and member organizations that speculation was approaching dangerous levels, the American Stock Exchange, early in February 1969, imposed a temporary ban on member transactions for their own account in 103 volatile issues listed on that exchange.

Study of New Issues Market by New York State

A study was made by the office of the Attorney General of the State of New York of the "hot new issues" market of securities sold during the 1968--1969 business period. The report on the study had some scathing things to say about corporate and customer "insiders" and underwriters handling the issuance and aftermarket of such securities.[26] Excerpts from this report are furnished as Appendix A to this book.

Of 103 issues reviewed in the study the public investors purchasing at the offering price found the book equity of their shares reduced on an average of 65% upon purchase. Earnings per share of 16% of the companies reviewed were non-existent (presumably they had not commenced operations) and another 29% showed losses.

A number of persons who bought these issues were interviewed and it developed that the majority who purchased them did so with the intention of making quick resales at premiums. Approximately 73% of the group who bought such securities at the original purchase price did resell them quite soon thereafter. Underwriters used various devices to run up the prices of such securities shortly after their issuance, but persons purchasing them at their high price levels were not so fortunate. A random sampling of these new issues indicated that the majority of them had declined more than 40% below the original issue prices from the end of January 1969 through August 27, 1969.

[25] Merrill Lynch, Pierce, Fenner & Smith, Inc., *Investor's Reader*, August 23, 1967.

[26] Report to the Hon. Louis J. Lefkowitz, Attorney General, State of New York, dated October 1969.

The study concluded that many of the companies studied were merely manufactured by underwriters for stock profits rather than bona fide new enterprises seeking capital in the securities market.

Despite SEC warnings to be wary of new stock issues of questionable value, the hope of quick profits continued to motivate a large segment of the investing public during 1969. There were 1,836 corporate primary common stock offerings marketed in 1969 with gross proceeds of $7.7 billion, compared with 1,130 issues valued at $3.9 billion the previous year. Of the total offerings in 1969 there were 1,270 issues by corporations registering common stock for the first time, compared with 650 issues during 1968.[27] These ran the gamut of food franchising, nursing homes, science, computer, and leasing companies. Apparently businesses were still able to raise venture capital, despite adverse stock market conditions, and underwriters seemed to have little difficulty in finding buyers of such shares.

Spin-offs and Shell Corporations

The Securities and Exchange Commission has expressed concern with methods employed by a growing number of companies and perons to effect distributions to the public of unregistered securities generally of questionable value. The following excerpts from an SEC release in July 1969 are of interest in this regard: [28]

Frequently, the pattern involves the issuance by a company, with little, if any, business activity, of its shares to a publicly-owned company in exchange for what may or may not be nominal consideration. The publicly-owned company subsequently spins off the shares to its shareholders with the result that active trading in the shares begins with no information on the issuer being available to the investing public. Despite this lack of information, moreover, the shares frequently trade in an active market at increasingly higher prices.

Another pattern has come to the Commission's attention in which certain promoters have acquired corporations which have ceased active operations, or which have little or no assets ("shell corporations"), and which have a substantial number of shares outstanding, generally in the hands of the public. Thereafter the promoters have engaged in activities to quickly increase the market value of their shareholdings. For example, in some cases promoters have initiated a program of acquisitions, transferring assets of

---

[27] Securities and Exchange Commission.
[28] Releases Nos. 4982 and 8638 of the 1933 and 1934 Acts.

dubious value to the "shell corporations" in exchange for substantial amounts of newly issued shares. This activity is frequently accompanied by publicity containing exaggerated or misleading statements and designed to stimulate interest of public investors in the company's shares in violation of the anti-fraud provisions of the Securities Exchange Act of 1934. Thereafter the market prices of these securities have risen sharply under circumstances which bear no relationship to the underlying financial condition and business activities of the company. In some of these cases the promoters or other corporate insiders, to take advantage of the market activity and the price rise which they have generated, have sold their shares at the inflated prices to the public in violation of the registration and anti-fraud provisions of the Federal securities laws. Similar activities have also been noted in a number of cases involving shares which a publicly held company has spun off to its shareholders.

STANDARD PRICING FACTORS

Performance Criteria for Actively Traded Common Stocks

Fundamentally, an investor in listed and other actively traded common stocks considers his return on investment to be dividend income plus market appreciation. Both of these are to a large extent dependent upon earnings. In determining return on investment, a year is too short a period in which to judge results. Probably a seven- to ten-year historical period would be a fairer measure of such return. Also, results will be influenced by conditions at the start and finish of an historical period. If the market is depressed at the start of the period but hits a high note at the finish, results will look better than if the reverse is true.

Over a period, depending upon yields on high-grade bonds, and tax-exempt municipals, an investor in common stocks, which are higher-risk securities, theoretically should be looking for a return on investment (dividend income plus market appreciation) in the area of 10% per annum or better on high-grade stocks.

Formula Approach—Deficiencies

Some investment analysts seek to test market values of specific stocks by discounting the value of estimated future earnings and dividends for a period of up to ten years. In the case of so-called growth stocks, where dividends are relatively small or non-existent, the estimated earnings growth alone is used for the computation. In addition a price–earnings multiple is used, which may be relatively constant for a company with little growth prospects, and progressively higher each year for one with favorable prospects.

Unfortunately, the main factor in the computation, earnings growth, is seldom predictable within a reasonable degree of variance. A perusal of the New York Stock Exchange's periodic publication of "Stocks on the Big Board" shows increases in compounded annual rates of earnings for the most recent five years for hundreds of companies listed on the Exchange. The vast majority of these show relatively sporadic earnings patterns rather than pronounced earnings trends. The many mergers and acquisitions during recent years have also increased the difficulty of forecasting earnings for long periods.

An assumed steady increase in price–earnings ratios in such projected computations for growth stocks is also debatable. As evidenced in recent years, many growth stocks have shown wide fluctuations in market prices and price–earnings ratios. During the ten-year period ended December 31, 1969, composite price–earnings ratios of Standard & Poor's 425 industrial stocks varied from a high of 22.93 to a low of 14.08.

From the standpoint of return on investment in common stocks, the investor fared far better during the decade from 1949 to 1959 than in that running to 1969. The New York Stock Exchange common stock index was 9.91 at the close of 1949, 32.15 at the close of 1959, and 51.53 at December 31, 1969. In other words the index increased 224%, or at a compounded annual growth rate of 12.5% during the earlier decade, and 60% for a compounded annual growth rate of only 4.8% during the decade ended December 31, 1969.

Median dividend yields on New York Stock Exchange common stocks paying dividends (about 90% of the total listed) averaged approximately 5.7% during the decade ended in 1959, compared with an average of slightly better than 3% for that ended December 31, 1969.

Pricing Additional Public Offerings
and Block Transactions

The requirements for registration under the Securities Act of 1933 are discussed in Chapter 3, and aspects of pricing initial public offerings in Chapter 4.

When a company whose shares are already publicly traded in an established market makes a public offering of additional shares, or an offering is made by selling stockholders of the company, fixing the offering price per share is a relatively simple matter. The price is generally fixed at the closing price the day before the issue is offered, or in some cases slightly below that price.

The prospectus covering the offering, under the section "Price Range of Common Stock," generally shows the high and low sales prices, if listed on an exchange, or bid prices in the over-the-counter market. Prices are given by quarters for the two latest years, and by years for four or five earlier years. The last reported sale or bid price at the close of the day preceding the offering is also noted. Thus, the prospective investor has an opportunity to determine whether there has been a significant advance in the price of the stock, during a period preceding the offering, that does not appear to be justified by the financial data in the prospectus.

If there is no established trading market in the securities to be offered (limited or sporadic quotations are not deemed to constitute such a market) the prospectus has to so indicate, and any quotations given should be suitably qualified. In such instances, the offering price per share usually is determined on a basis similar to an initial public offering.

Large block transactions, usually involving institutional investors, where a seller would disrupt the market by breaking down the shares into many smaller blocks, are disposed of in various ways, often at a price several points below the market. These may be sold to another institutional investor, outside the regular market, or as a secondary distribution to customers of brokers, or by accumulating orders on the floor of the exchange at prices between the current bid and asked quotations, or by a special bid offering open to all members of the exchange and their customers, but not as part of the auction market.

PROPER VALUES FOR LISTED STOCKS

Who is right in valuing listed common stocks? The brokers, dealers, and their customers, who create the auction market for stocks, or the management of companies who make tender offers to stockholders of other companies, often as an initial step in acquiring or merging with such companies? During recent years, a number of cash tender offers for common stocks, involving listed companies, were made to stockholders.

Premiums on Tender Offers

Of the companies offering to acquire the common stocks of others, many tenders were made at premiums ranging as high as 50% above the market prices at which such stocks were selling prior to the offers. (Pertinent information regarding selected tender requests is discussed in Chapter 11.)

In some of these cases the management of companies whose stock was sought vigorously opposed such tender actions, and in a few they were successful. However, in many instances the offers were made with the approval of such managements. Usually, the tender offers were for the purpose of immediate or ultimate merger with the companies whose stock was sought. In some few cases, it appeared that those making tender offers did so with investment objectives, because they perceived values in the stock beyond those reflected in current market prices.

Propriety of Market Prices

To sum up, a fair market generally exists only with respect to stocks that are actively traded, although even some of these stocks are so volatile that the propriety of their market prices at any instant is questionable. Public relations programs and public fervor, or in some cases gambling fever, may affect the price of a stock far more than current and forecasted financial statistics.

Although the Securities and Exchange Commission, the national securities exchanges, and the National Association of Securities Dealers are maintaining surveillance over trading of securities under their jurisdictions, they cannot stop public speculation, and generally learn of manipulation after the fact. Moreover, the vast majority of stocks of "publicly owned" companies do not enjoy an active market, and are subject to substantial price fluctuations on a relatively low trading volume.

Even where an active market exists, there frequently is a difference of opinion between traders and investors, on the one hand, and persons making tender offers for blocks of stock, or merger minded acquirers, on the other, as to the real value of a company.

Market Prices as a Valuation Factor

In considering market prices as a factor in buying, selling, or merging with a company, or in valuations for estate, gift, or income tax purposes, it is desirable, therefore, to review the market action of a stock for a reasonable period to ascertain that no extraneous factors have unduly influenced its current price. With respect to common stocks of companies whose trading volume is low or virtually non-existent, market prices should seldom be regarded as a significant valuation factor.

3

SEC Requirements—Initial Offerings

SECURITIES LAWS

Any discussion of public offerings of securities should start with an explanation of certain federal statutes known as the "Securities Laws." Principal among these are the Securities Act of 1933 and the Securities Exchange Act of 1934. As a result of these laws considerable information is available on the majority of initial public offerings of common stock, and on many such stocks in the "after-market."

Securities Act of 1933

The basic objectives of the Securities Act of 1933 are to provide investors with financial and other information of material importance concerning securities offered for sale to the public in interstate commerce or by use of the mail, and to prohibit misrepresentation, deceit, and other fraudulent practices in the offer and sale of securities.

Securities Exchange Act of 1934

Under the Securities Exchange Act of 1934, the Securities and Exchange Commission was created as an independent regulatory agency having executive and quasi-judicial powers for the purpose of administering the securities laws. The 1934 Act is primarily a regulatory statute involved with trading in securities, both on the organized exchanges and over the counter. It is not concerned with the public offering of securities, except that the majority of companies making public offerings are thenceforth subject to the financial and other reporting requirements under the 1934 Act.

Exemptions Under 1933 Act

With few exceptions, a company contemplating a public offering will be subject to the provisions of the 1933 Act.

Among these exceptions are certain exemptions from the registration requirements that fall into two general categories, "exempted securities" and "exempted transactions." The Securities Act of 1933 is remedial in nature and exemptions from the Act have been narrowly construed by the courts. The burden of proving the availability of an exemption rests with the person asserting it, and a section of the Act dealing with fraud applies regardless of whether a security is exempted. Accordingly, the advice of competent legal counsel should be sought before proceeding with any unregistered offering of securities. With these words of caution the ensuing comments relate to exemptions.

> *Exempted Securities*—Section 3(a) of the 1933 Act exempts from registration securities issued by: banks, common carriers, the federal and state governments and their instrumentalities, religious, charitable and educational, and other non-profit organizations. It also exempts short-term notes, drafts, bills of exchange, insurance policies, and certificates issued by a receiver or trustee in bankruptcy.
>
> *Exempted Transactions*—These include:
> 1. Certain securities issued in recapitalizations
> 2. Securities that are the subject of an intrastate offering
> 3. Securities offered under the provisions of Regulation A of the 1933 Act
> 4. Transactions by any person other than an issuer, underwriter, or dealer
> 5. Transactions by an issuer not involving any public offering
> 6. Brokers' transactions [1]

It is not the purpose of this chapter to discuss SEC rules and regulations, except as they may affect public offerings of common

[1] Securities Act of 1933, §§ 3(a) and 4.

stock issues. However, several types of exempted transactions are worthy of comment.

The *intrastate exemption* from registration under the Act is provided for any security that is part of an issue sold only to *persons resident within a single state or territory*, where the issuer of such security is a *person resident and doing business within such state or territory*.[2] Every security that is a part of the issue must ultimately come to rest within the state and in the hands of resident investors when the distribution is completed. Thus the risk of relying on the intrastate exemption is great, for it is virtually impossible to control the distribution of securities after they leave the issuer's hands, particularly if a substantial number of shares are offered.

The exemption available under Regulation A generally applies to offerings of securities not in excess of $500,000 by issuers and not in excess of $100,00 by certain persons other than the issuers.[3] The utilization of this exemption depends upon compliance with the terms and conditions prescribed by the Securities and Exchange Commission. These include, among other things, the filing and effecting of a notification and copies of the offering circular with a regional office of the Commission, disclosing specified items of information.[4]

A transaction by an issuer, not involving a public offering, is commonly referred to as a "private sale" exemption.[5] Neither the statute nor the rules and regulations define the terms "private sale" or "public offering." The question of whether a transaction involves a public offering is essentially one of fact, after consideration of all attendant circumstances. As in the case of other transaction exemptions, a person claiming the "private sale" exemption must sustain the burden of proof of its availability.

The SEC has indicated that the following factors must be considered in determining the availability of this exemption: (a) the number of offerees and their relationship to each other and to the

---

[2] *Ibid.*, § 3(a).
[3] *Ibid.*, § 3(b) and Rule 254 thereunder.
[4] Form 1–A.
[5] Securities Act of 1933, § 4(2).

issuer, (b) the number of units offered, (c) the amount of the offering, and (d) the manner of offering.[6]

Where the number of persons offered a security does not exceed 25, generally the Commission will not investigate the exemption claim. It should be noted, however, that this numerical test refers to offerees and not to ultimate purchasers. Also, if a purchaser intends to further distribute securities, the ultimate number of offerees must be considered in determining whether a public offering has taken place.

The question of whether there has been a public offering generally depends upon the need to protect the particular class of offerees. Consequently, if an offering is made only to key executies, investment funds, banks, trusts, or similarly sophisticated investors whose need for protection is substantially less than that of the investing public, the likelihood that a "public offering" will be deemed to have been made is lessened. Also, if the smallest investment unit is a large sum, the offerees are less likely to be persons who need the protection of the Act. Other factors warranting consideration, in determining whether an offering is public, are whether the offer was negotiated directly by the issuer or through an underwriter, and whether any securities of the issuer are being actively traded.

Further amplification is offered in the following words from SEC Release No. 33–4445:

> Public advertising of the offerings would, of course, be incompatible with the claim of a private offering.
>
> . . . An important factor to be considered is whether the securities offered have come to rest in the hands of the initial informed group or whether the purchasers are merely conduits for a wider distribution. Persons who act in this capacity, whether or not engaged in the securities business, are deemed to be underwriters within the meaning of Section 2(ii) of the Act. If the purchasers do in fact acquire the securities with a view to public distribution, the *seller* (issuer) assumes the risk of possible violation of the registration requirements of the Act and consequent civil liabilities.

Exemptions Under Rule 133. In addition to the "private sale" there is another type of transaction by an issuer considered not to involve a public offering and therefore exempt from the registra-

---

[6] Securities Act Release No. 4552, November 6, 1962.

tion requirements. The SEC has held that no offer or sale is involved when a plan of consolidation or merger is submitted to a vote of security holders and the affirmative vote of the required majority binds the minority holders. The theory behind this interpretation is that the transaction occurs as a corporate rather than an individual act.

To provide protection to companies relying on this administrative policy, the SEC adopted Rule 133 under the 1933 Act.[7] The rule describes the conditions under which a "no sale" transaction must be consummated and specifically provides for registration of securities previously issued in a Rule 133 transaction, if offered for sale by any person defined as an "underwriter" in the rule. It should be noted that the exemption provided by the rule relates only to the registration requirements of Section 5 of the Act and does not provide any protection from the antifraud, civil, and criminal liability provisions of the Act. Rule 133 is discussed further in Chapter 10.

FORMS FOR SECURITIES REGISTRATION

Registration requires the filing of a statement in the form and content prescribed by the Securities and Exchange Commission.

The various forms for registration may be classified under the following broad categories: (a) for commercial and industrial companies,[8] (b) for companies in the promotional, exploratory, or developmental state,[9] (c) for management investment companies and investment trusts,[10] and (d) for offerings relating to foreign issues,[11] and others.[12] In addition, certain issues that are exempt from registration under Regulation A of the 1933 Act, because of the size of the offering, still require the filing of data with the SEC.[13]

An underwriter and the Securities and Exchange Commission have the same disclosure objective in an offering of securities:

---

[7] Securities Act of 1933, § 5(a).
[8] Forms S–1, S–7, and S–9.
[9] Forms S–2 and S–3.
[10] Forms S–4, S–5, and S–6.
[11] Form S–12.
[12] Forms S–8, S–10, S–11, S–14, and S–16.
[13] Forms 1–A, etc.

to see that the prospective investor is properly informed. Form S–1 is the basic form for registration under the Securities Act of 1933. When no other form is prescribed, it is used in filings by commercial and industrial companies other than those in the promotional, exploratory, or developmental stage. The form is prepared in two parts. Part I consists of information that is included in the prospectus, and Part II contains all other information and is captioned "Information Not Required in the Prospectus." Generally a copy of the printed prospectus to be distributed for the purpose of selling the stock becomes Part I of the Registration Statement.

Guides for Preparation of Registration Statements

The Securities and Exchange Commission, in 1968, issued a release entitled, "Guides for Preparation and Filing of Registration Statements" under the Securities Act of 1933.[14] The cover of the release bears the following legend:

These guides are not rules of the Commission nor are they published as bearing the Commission's official approval. They represent policies and practices followed by the Commission's Division of Corporation Finance in the administration of the registration requirements of the Act, but do not purport to furnish complete criteria for the preparation of registration statements.

Also, a preface to the "Guides" mentions that notwithstanding their provisions, Rule 408 applies, regarding additional information to be furnished in a registration statement. This rule reads as follows:

In addition to the information expressly required to be included in a registration statement, there shall be added such further material information, if any, as may be necessary to make the required statements, in the light of the circumstances under which they are made, not misleading.

The following general provisions in the "Guides" are worthy of mention.

Pre-Filing Conferences with Registrants

The Commission has a long established policy of holding its staff available for conferences with prospective registrants or their representatives in

[14] Securities Act Release 4936, December 9, 1968.

advance of filing a registration statement. These conferences may be held for the purpose of discussing generally the problems confronting a registrant in effecting registration or to resolve specific problems of an unusual nature which are sometimes presented by involved or complicated financial transactions.

Occasionally a registrant will request a pre-filing review of a registration statement, but such a review has been refused since it would delay the examination of material which has already been filed and would favor certain issuers at the expense of others. Registrants or their representatives also occasionally request the staff to draft a paragraph or other statement which will comply with some requirement or request for disclosure. The staff cannot undertake to prepare material for filing but limits itself to stating the kind of disclosure required, leaving actual drafting to the registrant and its representatives.

Voluminous and Verbose Prospectuses

Prospectuses are sometimes difficult to read and to understand. Registrants have been encouraged to reduce the size of the prospectus by careful organization of the material, appropriate arrangement and subordination of information, use of tables and the avoidance of prolix or technical expression and unnecessary detail. . . .

Material on the cover page of the prospectus should be as brief as possible with an appropriate cross reference to more complete information elsewhere in the prospectus, particularly where the underwriters receive multiple benefits that cannot be completely described on the cover page.

Registration of Options, Warrants or Rights, and Other Securities Issued or Sold to Underwriters

Transferable options, warrants or rights and the stock to be issued upon the exercise thereof which are issued to underwriters in connection with a registered public offering are to be considered a part of such offering. Similarly, stock, or securities convertible into another security, sold to underwriters in connection with a registered public offering are to be considered a part of such offering. Accordingly, such options, warrants or rights and the stock which is subject thereto or such other security which is to be sold to underwriters must be registered along with the securities to be offered to the public, notwithstanding that it is represented that such options, warrants, rights, stock or other security have been acquired for investment and not with a view to the distribution thereof.

THE REGISTRATION STATEMENT—FORM S–1

There are 21 items of information required to be covered in Part I of the registration statement (the printed prospectus), and 10 items in Part II.

Form S–1 is not a "form" in the sense that one fills in information in blank spaces. It is rather a set of instructions regarding information to be supplied by the securities issuer in the registration statement. Accordingly, the information furnished in the prospectus often combines answers to some of the required items. Brief explanations of certain items of interest, typically furnished in a prospectus for an offering of capital stock, are set forth below.

Distribution Spread and Expenses of Issuance and Distribution

On the cover page are shown the underwriting discounts and commissions, per share and in the aggregate, that are received by the underwriter from the proceeds of the issue. The estimated expenses of the offering, such as legal and accounting fees, printing costs, filing fees, etc., are set forth in the aggregate in a note to the net proceeds column.

Underwriting compensation includes, in addition to cash discounts or commissions, options, warrants, or rights to purchase shares (including those sold or given to underwriters within 12 months before the filing), expense allowances, continuing fees for services, and first refusal on future financing.

Disclosure as to Listing on Exchange

This disclosure is usually on the cover page also. Unless there is reasonable assurance that the securities to be offered will be acceptable to a securities exchange for listing, the prospectus may be misleading if it conveys the impression that the registrant may apply for listing of the securities on an exchange or that the underwriters may request the registrant to apply for such listing.

Indication of Initial Offering

Typical language under this item would be:

At the date of this prospectus there is no quoted market value for the common stock of the Corporation, which has been closely held. The public offering price has been determined by negotiation between the Corporation (and/or selling stockholders, in applicable cases) and the underwriters.

These shares are offered by the several underwriters subject to prior sale and when, as, and if delivered to and accepted by the underwriters, and subject to approval of certain legal counsel for the underwriters.

Finders' Fees

Appropriate disclosure is required on the cover page of any finders' fees or similar payments. The finder and the nature of his relationship with the company and others involved in the offering should be disclosed. If a finder is deemed to be an underwriter by reason of the receipt of securities, he should be identified as such in the prospectus.

Speculative or High-Risk Offerings and Related Matters

Where a security offering is considered speculative, or involves more than the usual element of risk, the principal factors that contribute to this situation are required to be summarized immediately following the cover page. Such factors include but are not limited to the absence of an operating history or of profitable operations in recent periods, a poor financial position, or merely the nature of the business in which the company is engaged or proposes to be engaged.

Also, where there is a substantial disparity between the public offering price and the cash cost to officers, directors, promoters, and others for shares acquired or to be acquired by them, the following information is required: (a) the net tangible book value per share before and after the distribution; (b) the amount of increase in such net tangible book value per share attributable to the cash payments made by purchasers of the shares being offered; and (c) the amount of immediate dilution from the public offering price which will be absorbed by such purchasers.

Stabilizing Operations

If stabilizing operations are to be conducted during a period following the effective offering date, the following legend is required, in boldface type, on the cover or the inside cover page:

In connection with this offering the underwriters may overallot or effect transactions which stabilize or maintain the market price of the common stock of the corporation at a level above that which might otherwise prevail in the open market. Such stabilizing, if commenced, may be discontinued at any time.

Disclosure of Operations by Product Lines

Pursuant to amendments in July 1969, companies engaged in more than one line of business are required to disclose for each of the last five fiscal years after December 31, 1966, the approximate amount or percentage of total sales and operating revenues and contribution to income before income taxes and extraordinary items attributable to each line of business which contributed, during either of the last two fiscal years, a certain proportion to the total of sales and revenues or income before income taxes and extraordinary items. For companies with total sales and revenues over $50 million, the proportion is 10%; for smaller companies it is 15%. Where the percentage tests as applied to both sales and earnings contribution result in more than ten lines of business, the disclosure may be limited to the ten most important lines. For disclosure purposes, contributions to sales or earnings contemplate losses as well as gains.[15] The amendments continue the existing disclosure requirements on breakdown of total volume of sales and revenues by principal products or classes of similar products or services, except that the percentage test has been reduced from 15% to 10% in the case of companies having total sales and revenues in excess of $50 million during either of their last two fiscal years.

Principal and Selling Stockholders

A table is required setting forth the names, type of ownership, number of shares, and approximate percentage of each class of stock of the company for each person who owned of record, or was known to own beneficially more than 10% of the outstanding stock of the company. Any pertinent transactions or agreements between any such principal stockholder, or any officer or director, and the company are required to be described.

If a secondary offering is involved, the number of shares being sold by each stockholder must be shown, as well as the number to be held after the offering. A statement is required by the Commission from such selling stockholders, setting forth the reason or

[15] Releases Nos. 4988 and 8650 under the 1933 and 1934 Acts, July 14, 1969.

reasons for selling their securities, and verifying that they are familiar with the registration statement. If any material adverse information, not disclosed in the registration statement, is known by such persons, they are required to reveal it or to make a negative representation if they know of none.

Capital Stock Being Registered

A description of the common stock being registered should be set forth, including (a) dividend rights, (b) voting rights, with a statement to the effect that the shares do not have cumulative voting rights, if such is the case, and that holders of more than 50% of the shares may elect all of the directors, if they choose, and (c) liquidation and redemption rights. A statement should be made as to the assessable status of the shares, and whether the holders of the stock have pre-emptive or other subscription or conversion rights. Also, a description of any other securities, including preferred stock or debt securities, the terms of which may affect the rights of the holders of the common stock, is set forth under this section.

Experts

The independent public accountants, whose opinion is furnished on the financial statements and schedules included in the prospectus and registration statement, are named herein together with a statement to the effect that these financial data have been included in reliance upon their report and the authority of the accountants as experts in auditing and accounting. Any other experts such as engineers and appraisers are also named in this section and reference made to their reports.

Sales at Special Prices

Any securities that have been sold during the preceding six months, or are to be sold by the company or selling stockholders at a price varying from that at which the securities are being offered to the general public, pursuant to the registration statement, must be disclosed along with the consideration therefor. These include sales pursuant to stock options, purchase warrants, employees' stock purchase plans, etc.

Recent Sales of Unregistered Securities

Pertinent information is required with respect to any securities not registered under the 1933 Act, whether reacquired or new issues, which have been sold or issued during the preceding three years in exchange for cash, property, services, or other securities, etc. These include debt as well as equity securities, and typically cover securities issued in connection with an acquisition or merger of another company, private placements, bonds, long-term notes, and interim notes issued under a long-term revolving credit agreement.

Supplemental Information
(Not Part of Registration Statement)

If, within the past twelve months, any engineering, management, or similar report or memorandum relating to broad aspects of the business or operations or products of the registrant, or in connection with the proposed offering, has been prepared for or by the registrant, the principal security holder (owning more than 10% of any class of securities), or the principal underwriter, this report or memorandum should be furnished as "supplemental information," prior to a pre-filing conference, if any, or at the time of filing the registration statement, or as soon as practicable thereafter.

PREPARATION OF STATEMENT A JOINT UNDERTAKING

During the course of the preparation of the registration statement, the issuer, its legal counsel and independent accountants, and the principal underwriter and its legal counsel generally work closely together. Although the prospectus will contain considerable information, it must be reasonably concise and understandable to the prospective investor.

An underwriter and his legal counsel generally will make extensive inquiries of the issuer and his experts regarding data to be covered in the prospectus as well as other relevant matters. These investigations will entail visits to the principal offices of the company and its major plants, discussion of products and plans for future products, meetings with principal officers and executives to ascertain the caliber of the management and plans for management succession, and discussions with legal counsel and independent accountants of the company on matters with which they are familiar. Also, an underwriter will often ascertain from the company's principal commercial banks, and some of its customers, how they regard the company management and its products.

FINANCIAL DATA IN PROSPECTUS

Ordinarily, the most important data contained in a prospectus prepared under the 1933 Act are the summary of earnings, statements of source and application of funds, balance sheet, notes to financial statements, and other financial information. These have a significant bearing on investment decisions to be made by offerees of securities. The form and content of the financial statements are governed by Regulation S–X of the Securities and Exchange Commission.[16] This regulation sets forth the data that must be shown for proper disclosure of financial position and results of operations and the rules governing the certification of these data by independent accountants.

Summary of Earnings and/or Income Statement

The summary of earnings, shown in the forepart of the prospectus, covers the last five fiscal years of a company's operations, except where its life and that of its immediate predecessors is shorter. In addition, the summary covers any period between the latest fiscal year and the date of the latest balance sheet furnished, and the corresponding interim period of the preceding fiscal year.

As permitted, the income statement of a company is usually substituted in its entirety for the summary of earnings, thus obviating the necessity of repeating these data in the financial statements section of the prospectus. The income statement must be certified for the last three fiscal years, and for any interim period between the close of the latest of these years and the date of any

---

[16] Regulation S–X, "Form and Content of Financial Statements."

later certified balance sheet furnished. Retroactive adjustments should be reflected in the income statement. Although comparability as between years is of the utmost importance in constructing the income statement, care should be taken to avoid "normalizing" income to the extent that the data thus reflected do not give a true picture of historical operations of a company.

Explanation of items of material significance in appraising the results shown is required in the statement, or in notes thereto, or by reference to information set forth elsewhere in the prospectus. The footnotes to the income statement should be limited to information essential to an understanding of the statement. Compuations of per-share earnings and dividends are required for each year or portion thereof included in the statements.

Certified statements summarizing the sources from which funds or working capital were obtained and their disposition for the last three fiscal years are required for registration statements filed after December 31, 1970.[17]

In addition to the above-described financial data contained in the prospectus, there are various supporting schedules included in Part II of the registration statement. These are required to be certified whenever the balance sheet or statements of income to which they relate are certified. The schedules are described in Regulation S–X, numbers from I to XVII, although it would be rare to find a case where all would be applicable in an initial public offering.

Balance Sheets and Other Statements

The latest balance sheet in Form S–1 must be as of a date within 90 days of the filing date. If the issuer has filed reports pursuant to Section 13 or 15(d) of the Securities and Exchange Act of 1934, and meets other specified conditions, the latest balance sheet may be as of a date within six months prior to filing. However, only companies already registered with the Securities and Exchange Commission could meet the latter conditions.

If the latest (interim) balance sheet is not certified, a certified balance sheet as of the latest fiscal year-end is required, unless

[17] *Ibid.*

such fiscal year has ended within 90 days prior to the date of filing. In the latter case the certified balance sheet may be as of the end of the preceding fiscal year. Nevertheless, underwriters or legal counsel will often request that the latest financial statements included in the registration statements be certified, particularly in an initial public offering.

Also, when numerous or involved financial transactions have been effected, or unusual conditions affect the determination of earnings, certified interim financial statements may be required by the Securities and Exchange Commission as a condition to acceleration of the processing of the registration statement, under Section 8(a) of the 1933 Act. New registrants with no established record of earnings, and old registrants showing a weak financial condition, should be prepared to furnish more current financial statements to the Commission than would ordinarily be required.

Other Financial Data

Other financial data, some of which are customarily included in annual reports, are required in a prospectus prepared under the 1933 Act. These include (a) a company's rates and its policies regarding depreciation and accounting for sales and retirement of fixed assets, (b) a description of stock option and pension plans, (c) data on non-consolidated subsidiaries, in certain instances, (d) amounts for rents and royalties, (e) charges for maintenance and repairs, depreciation, depletion and obsolescence of physical properties, and for the amortization of intangible assets, and (f) details or various types of taxes, such as payroll, franchise, and property taxes. This information may be submitted in schedule form or in the financial statements or the notes thereto.

ACCOUNTING RULES AND REGULATIONS

Regulation S–X

Regulation S–X is intended for use only as a guide to the preparation of financial statements. There has been a tendency on the part of some registrants to look upon its provisions as a tax-return type of form in which amounts applicable to each item, regardless of size, are required to be set forth in the financial statements. Such an approach has resulted in statements that contain such a volume of information that material items are lost in a maze of insignificant detail. Thus, two rules contained in this regulation are important: first, that financial statements may be set forth in such form and employ such generally accepted terminology as will best indicate their significance and character in the light of applicable S–X provisions, and second, that the amounts that are not material need not be separately set forth in the manner prescribed. The Commission's definition of "material" information relates to those matters that an average prudent investor ought reasonably to be informed of before purchasing the security registered.

The various statutes administered by the Commission give it broad rule-making powers regarding the preparation and presentation of financial statements contained in SEC filings. Among other things, the Commission may prescribe the methods to be followed in the preparation of accounts; appraisal or valuation of assets and liabilities; and the determination of recurring and non-recurring items, income, and expense.

Accounting Series Releases

In addition to Regulation S–X, the Securities and Exchange Commission publishes rules and regulations relating to major accounting questions or administrative policies regarding financial statements. These are called Accounting Series Releases and are of considerable importance in preparing financial statements. The first such release was issued in 1937, and since that time there have been 118 issued through December 31, 1970.

Accounting Series Release Number 4, issued by the Commission in 1938, is probably the most significant of all its accounting rules. The essence of the release is that if statements filed with the Commission are based on unsupportable accounting principles, disclosure of this information in the accountants' opinion or in notes to financial statements will not correct them. Furthermore, if a company files financial statements that reflect accounting principles that have been formally disapproved by the Commission, such financial statements will be presumed to be misleading.

Accordingly, a company filing financial statements with the Commission is charged not only with knowledge of the rules and regulations of the Commission but also with its accounting opinions and administrative procedures, whether in the form of accounting series releases, or in official decisions and releases under the various securities acts. If the accounting treatment for a given transaction is not clearly indicated, either because principles have not been well established or because there are differences of opinion regarding the weight to be given the known facts, it may be desirable to discuss such problems with the Commission's staff in advance of filing a registration statement.

Certification of Financial Statements

The financial statements (including the statements of source and application of funds) contained in the prospectus forming part of a registration statement filed with the Securities and Exchange Commission must be certified by certified public accountants or licensed public accountants who are in good standing and entitled to practice under the laws of their place of residence or principal office. Rules regarding the qualifications, independence, representations, and opinions expressed by accountants with respect to financial statements are contained in Regulation S–X.[18]

MISCELLANEOUS ASPECTS OF SECURITIES REGISTRATION

Offering Circular Under Regulation A

Item 11 in Schedule I, under a Regulation A offering (described on page 44), sets forth the financial information required to be included in an offering circular prepared for distribution to offerees.[19] This information is not nearly as detailed as that required in a prospectus included as part of a registration statement under the 1933 Act. Also, although Item 11 calls for appropriate financial statements of the issuer and its predecessors, such statements need not be certified. The Commission stipulates that these statements be prepared in accordance with generally ac-

---

[18] *Ibid.*, Art. 2.
[19] Item 11, Schedule I, Regulation A (reproduced as Appendix B).

cepted accounting principles and practices. However, without the certification requirement, there can be no assurance that statements prepared and included in an offering circular, under Regulation A, are in accordance with such principles and practices.

Timely Filing of Registration Statements

All registration statements under the 1933 Act must be filed with the Commission sufficiently prior to the proposed public offering to permit review by the staff of the Commission. Upon receipt of a registration statement, the staff of the Commission examines it to determine whether it complies with the standards of accurate and fair disclosure established by the Act and usually notifies the registrant by an informal letter of comment of any material respects in which the statement fails to conform to such requirements. The registrant is then afforded an opportunity to file an amendment to the registration statement to clear up any deficiencies cited.

Failure by the staff of the Commission to cite a deficiency may not always be indicative of its agreement with the material filed, but could result from a lack of information. The examination staff is not in the position of the company or its experts; it does not have available the details known to them. The absence of deficiencies does not condone the inclusion in the prospectus of information subsequently found to be misleading when the true facts come to light. Furthermore, to rebut specifically any inference that its review constitutes approval of the contents of a prospectus, the Commission requires the following legend to appear in capital letters on the cover of every prospectus or offering circular:

THESE SECURITIES HAVE NOT BEEN APPROVED OR DISAPPROVED BY THE SECURITIES AND EXCHANGE COMMISSION NOR HAS THE COMMISSION PASSED UPON THE ACCURACY OR ADEQUACY OF THIS PROSPECTUS. ANY REPRESENTATION TO THE CONTRARY IS A CRIMINAL OFFENSE.

Preliminary Prospectus

After a registration statement has been filed initially, pending the time when it becomes effective, offers to sell the securities may be made orally or by means of the preliminary prospectus. This is known as the "red herring" prospectus because of the notice which appears in red across its cover and the following legend, in red, at the left side of the cover:

Preliminary Prospectus dated _____

A registration statement relating to these securities has been filed with the Securities and Exchange Commission, but has not yet become effective. Information contained herein is subject to completion or amendment. These securities may not be sold nor may offers to buy be accepted prior to the time the registration statement becomes effective. This prospectus shall not constitute an offer to sell or the solicitation of an offer to buy nor shall there be any sale of these securities in any State in which such offer, solicitation or sale would be unlawful prior to registration or qualification under the securities laws of any such State.

Each time an amendment to the registration statement is filed affecting Part I (the prospectus), the updated preliminary prospectus must be distributed if the changes made are significant.

Due Diligence Meetings

Section 11 of the Securities Act of 1933 relates to civil liabilities of persons involved in a registration statement. Involved persons include those signing the statement, directors of the company, "experts" (accountants, appraisers, and engineers), and underwriters. Notwithstanding the civil liabilities provisions, no person other than the issuer shall be liable, if he had, *after reasonable investigation,* reasonable ground to believe, and did in fact believe, that at the time the registration became effective the statements therein were true and there was no omission to state a material fact required to be stated therein or necessary to make the statements therein not misleading. The burden of proving reasonable belief would, of course, rest with individuals asserting such a defense.

As a part of this *reasonable investigation* it has become the practice to hold a "due diligence meeting," or meetings at several locations in the case of a large public offering. These meetings are usually held after the registration statement has been filed and, hopefully, after the first letter of comment on the filing has been received from the Securities and Exchange Commission.

The participating underwriters attend these meetings, at which they have an opportunity to meet and ask questions of the company's officers, counsel, and independent accountants. Their questions may aim to clarify material included in the prospectus, or to go beyond such material. Company officials should be guided by counsel as to how far they can go in their answers, particularly as to representations of future earnings prospects.

In addition to the due diligence meetings, the underwriters require letters from the various experts involved in the registration statement. The letter from the independent accountants of the company, known as a "comfort letter," is discussed briefly below.

Underwriting Agreement

Although drafting of the "underwriting agreement" between the underwriters and the issuer of the securities is commenced by their respective counsel at a relatively early stage, this document is generally not executed until the morning of the day the registration is expected to become effective. This is because the underwriter will not definitively agree on the price at which the securities are to be offered until he determines (a) current stock market conditions and (b) the general outlook for the sale of the securities, including sales to dealers in the selling group.

The preliminary or red herring prospectuses that have been distributed prior to this time do not show the price at which the securities are to be offered. Although the managing underwriter undoubtedly has indicated an approximate price to the issuer, the actual price is revealed in a "pricing amendment" filed with the Securities and Exchange Commission immediately before the registration statement becomes effective.

Comfort Letters from Independent Accountants

Customarily there is included in an underwriting agreement a provision requiring a letter from the independent accountants regarding (a) the audited financial statements and supporting schedules in the registration statement and prospectus, (b) any unaudited financial statements included therein, and (c) comments pertaining to events subsequent to the date of the audited financial statements. Furthermore, as a result of recent litigation and court decisions, underwriters often request accountants to give comfort on additional accounting data contained in the prospectus under various captions. The letter issued is commonly referred to as a "comfort letter" and may be addressed either to the company or jointly to the company and underwriters.

Processing Time for Registration Statement

The 1933 Act provides that a registration statement shall become effective on the twentieth day after it has been filed, or 20 days after the filing of any amendment thereto, although acceleration may be requested.[20] Since most registration statements require one or more amendments, it usually takes considerably longer than a 20-day period after an original filing. As a matter of fact, for the fiscal year ended June 30, 1970, it required 70 days to complete the registration process for the "median" registration statement.

Follow-up Reports on Initial Offerings

Issuers filing a registration statement for the first time that is effective after May 19, 1971, are required to furnish follow-up reports to the Commission on Form SR (securities sold and proceeds applied), three months after the effective date of the registration statement and thereafter at six-month intervals during the period of the offering and until the proceeds thereof have been applied (SEC Release No. 33–5141).

Blue Sky Laws

State statutes governing the regulation of the offering for sale of securities are generally referred to as "blue sky laws." This term of reference was explained by a United States Supreme Court opinion, in which it was stated: "The name that is given to the law indicates the evil at which it is aimed, that is, to use the language of a cited case, 'speculative schemes which have no more basis than so many feet of blue sky.'" [21]

20 Securities Act of 1933, § 8(a).
21 Hall v. Geiger-Jones Co., 242 U.S. 539 (1916).

Blue sky laws vary among the states, from those designed primarily to provide penalties for the fraudulent sale of securities to those that are quite comprehensive in regulating their sale. The states that have comprehensive laws governing the issuance of securities are in the majority. The administrators of the securities laws in many such states have adopted a uniform application form for qualification of securities and certain other uniform policies.

Depending upon the proposed plans for distribution of an issue, legal counsel will investigate the up-to-date requirements of the various states involved and process the necessary applications. Although this may be done by counsel for the company or counsel for the underwriter, generally it is handled by the latter. However, the company will usually pay all or an agreed maximum amount of such cost.

Although it may be clear in some states that a security, or the issuer, must be qualified in order to offer securities for sale, in others it is necessary to request a ruling as to the necessity for so doing. Generally, a ruling will be forthcoming on the basis of a preliminary prospectus under an SEC registration filing or preliminary offering circular for a Regulation A issue.

When qualifying in a state, it is necessary to forward to authorities thereof the initial prospectus (or circular), plus each amendment thereto, filed with the Securities and Exchange Commission. When final approval has been obtained from the latter for release of the offering, it is necessary to obtain clearance, generally by telegram, from the Securities Commissioners of each state where applications and prospectuses were required, before proceeding with the offering in such jurisdictions.

Correlation of SEC and Listing Requirements

At times companies having initial public offerings will apply for listing of such securities with a national securities exchange upon completion of the offering or some months thereafter. The listing requirements of the New York and American stock exchanges with regard to the general and industry status of a company, its earning power, net tangible assets, number of shares outstanding, value of shares publicly held, and "round-lot" shareholders are set forth in Chapter 2.

Before a security is traded on a national securities exchange, it must be registered for trading under the Securities Exchange Act of 1934.[22] The only exceptions to this are for "exempt"[23] securities (as defined in the Act), securities that have unlisted trading privileges, and certain securities traded temporarily on a "when-issued" basis.[24] Registration is accomplished by filing a listing application with the applicable stock exchange and concurrently filing an application for registration of securities (Form 10) with the Securities and Exchange Commission.

As permitted by Rule 12b–35 of the Securities Exchange Act of 1934, an issuer may use a 1933 Act registration statement (Form S–1) that has been effective for not more than one year and incorporate it as part of the application under the 1934 Act. Any data required in the application that are not contained in the Form S–1 registration statement would then be added as a supplement thereto. Registration will become effective and the securities listed either 30 days after the stock exchange has notified the Commission that the application has been approved "or within such shorter period of time as the Commission may determine."[25] In practice, the Commission has granted acceleration in most cases, in accordance with its policy to "cooperate with registrants and with the exchanges by acting upon requests for acceleration as promptly as possible."[26]

Listing Applications. The New York Stock Exchange has two kinds of listing applications (as does the American Stock Exchange): one for original listing and another for subsequent listings. These are designed to meet the following basic objectives:

1. Original listing application
   a. To provide the stock exchange with the necessary information for determining the suitability of the securities for trading on the exchange

---

[22] Securities Exchange Act of 1934, § 12(a).
[23] *Ibid.*, § 3(a)(12).
[24] *Ibid.*, Rule 12a–5.
[25] *Ibid.*, § 12(d).
[26] *Ibid.*, Release No. 34–3085.

　　b. To provide the investing public with the necessary information for making an intelligent decision on the investment merits of the security

2. Subsequent listing application
　　a. To provide the stock exchange with full information regarding the purpose for which the securities are to be issued and the consideration to be received therefor
　　b. To bring up to date certain significant information to the extent this has not been done in preceding applications

Companies making application for the listing of their securities on either the New York or American Stock Exchange, as a regular part of the listing procedure, enter into a listing agreement with the exchange through which they commit themselves to a code of performance, regarding the matters dealt with by the agreement. As the public interest in corporate affairs has become more clearly defined, the listing agreement has expanded in scope.

The *New York Stock Exchange Company Manual* defines the basic objectives that the listing agreement attempts to achieve, as follows:

1. Timely disclosure, to the public and to the Exchange, of information which may affect security values or influence investment decisions, and in which stockholders, the public and the Exchange have a warrantable interest;
2. Frequent, regular and timely publication of financial reports prepared in accordance with accepted accounting practice, and in adequate but not burdensome detail;
3. Providing the Exchange with timely information to enable it to perform, efficiently and expeditiously, its function of maintaining an orderly market for the company's securities and to enable it to maintain its necessary records;
4. Preclusion of certain practices not generally considered sound;
5. Allowing the Exchange opportunity to make representations as to certain matters before they become accomplished facts.[27]

Thus, it is clear that the overriding objective of the listing agreement is the timely disclosure of information. The American Stock Exchange also has similar basic objectives.

Subsequent listing applications required as the result of acquisitions and mergers are discussed in Chapter 10.

---

[27] *New York Stock Exchange Company Manual*, pp. A28 and 29, July 18, 1968.

4

Tax, Procedural, and Pricing Considerations

TAX FACTORS TO CONSIDER

A large number of initial offerings involve the stock of principals of a corporation. Federal income tax, the rate of which will vary depending on the holding period, is assessed on the difference between the owner's basis and the net proceeds received from the public offering. In addition, many other matters having tax implications require consideration.

A closely held company operates in a manner that best suits its principals from the standpoint of guarding its privacy and minimizing taxes. Going public requires full and complete disclosure of current and past operations which heretofore have been known by relatively few people in the organization. Some of the problems generally arising from past practices require consideration in going public because they may result in additional federal income tax assessments. Such items include unreasonable compensation of principals, improper accumulation of surplus, Section 306 stock exposure, transactions between the company and principal stockholders and their families, multiple corporate organizations, disposal of excess assets, and inventory valuations.

In the usual case, a company will have filed its federal income tax returns in good faith, although resolving doubtful issues in its favor.   Any substantial risk of a material tax deficiency requires disclosure in an SEC registration statement and prospectus. It therefore requires careful planning prior to filing a registration statement to minimize or eliminate exposure to material tax deficiencies. It would be ideal to have several years in which to implement such planning before going public. However, this step must often be accomplished in a much shorter period because of the need for additional financing or to take advantage of favorable market conditions.

Unreasonable Compensation

Often management shareholders, particularly when other family members have substantial ownership interests in a company, will have generous compensation arrangements for themselves. These arrangements must be reviewed in the light of the public offering, and if there is a material decrease in compensation this could result in a disallowance to the company of excessive compensation for open years and be treated as a dividend to the management shareholders.

Improper Accumulation of Surplus

Under Section 531 and several subsequent sections of the Internal Revenue Code, an accumulated earnings tax is imposed on corporations improperly accumulating surplus to avoid income tax on the shareholders.[1]   The fact that the earnings and profits of a corporation are permitted to accumulate beyond the reasonable needs of the business shall be determinative of the purpose to avoid income tax.   A closely held corporation may need to retain more of its earnings for expansion and for financing peak working capital requirements than a large public corporation, because of its greater difficulty in obtaining needed financing at attractive rates.   However, if substantial amounts of accumulated earnings are retained by a closely.held corporation, a punitive tax under the aforementioned sections of the Internal Revenue Code may be imposed.

---

[1] I.R.C. §§ 531–537.

The term "reasonable needs of the business" includes: [2]

1. The "reasonably anticipated needs of the business." For purposes of determining the improper accumulation of earnings a minimum statutory credit of $100,000 is allowed, exclusive of amounts required as below.
2. The "section 303 redemption needs of the business." The term "section 303 redemption needs" means the amount needed to make a redemption of stock included in the gross estate of a deceased stockholder in the year of death or subsequent thereto, limited to the amount required to pay various death duties, funeral costs, and administration expenses.
3. The "excess business holdings redemption needs of the business." The term "excess business holdings redemption needs" means the amount needed or anticipated to be needed to redeem stock from a private foundation when its holdings of such stock in a functionally unrelated corporation exceed certain limitations. This applies to stock held by a foundation on May 26, 1969, or acquired from a trust which was irrevocable on that date, or under a will executed on or before that date.

Multiple Corporate Organizations

At times a business enterprise will operate under a multiple corporate arrangement to facilitate operations in different states, or to limit liability with respect to a particular activity or product line, or for some other reason. The fact that multiple surtax exemptions were availed of has brought many organizations under scrutiny by the Internal Revenue Service. Under certain circumstances the multiple surtax exemptions, as well as the $100,000 accumulated earnings credits referred to in the preceding section, have been denied.

In any case, for years beginning after December 31, 1969, corporations that are members of a controlled group (parent–subsidiary, brother–sister, combined, and certain insurance companies) will be limited to one surtax exemption, one $100,000 minimum accumulated earnings credit, and one $25,000 small business deduction (available for life insurance companies), plus a diminishing amount of such benefits available to each other member of the group, to be phased out over a transitional period

[2] *Ibid.*, § 537.

for 1970 through 1974.   After the transitional period only a single surtax exemption, accumulated earnings credit, and small business deduction will be available for the entire group.[3]   Also, the group may take into account only $10,000 for first-year depreciation allowances.

A special rule permits a more than three-year retroactive termination of a multiple surtax election by an affiliated group electing to file a consolidated return for the taxable year which includes December 31, 1970.   The termination will apply to the prior December 31, which is included in the taxable year of any member of the group from which there is a net operating loss carryover to the 1970 consolidated return year.

It may be desirable before going public to simplify a complex structure of controlled corporations by means of a non-taxable reorganization.   This subject is discussed in some detail in Chapter 8.

Section 306 Stock

At times, in close corporations, preferred stock will be issued as a dividend to holders of common stock.   At the time of the distribution no income or acquisition rights accrue to the recipient of such stock.   However, if the stockholder sells or otherwise disposes of such stock, the amount realized therefrom may be treated as ordinary income to the recipient to the extent that accumulated earnings and profits were ratably available at the time of the distribution of the stock.   If Section 306 stock is redeemed by the corporation, the same situation applies.   However, if the stock is exchanged for common stock in the same corporation, the taint of 306 stock is removed and the usual capital gains rules apply upon disposition of the common stock.[4]

Transactions Between Corporation and Principal Stockholders

In a closely held corporation, transactions between the corporation and principal stockholders and their families are not uncom-

---

[3] *Ibid.*, §§ 1561–1564.
[4] *Ibid.*, § 306.

mon. These transactions may include loans; leases of the corporate premises or of plant or equipment from major stockholders or their relatives, or from corporations controlled by them; and purchases and sales of products or services between the corporation and brother–sister corporations, i.e., those which are commonly owned.

Loans. The existence of substantial loans by stockholders to a corporation, particularly if they are of long standing, may indicate a thin equity capitalization. If there is a high ratio of debt to equity capital, the corporation's interest expense deductions could be disallowed for open years, and the principal repayments treated as dividend income to the shareholders.

The problem of determining when corporate indebtedness shall be considered as equity capitalization has become more acute in recent years, as a result of which a new Section 385 has been added to the Internal Revenue Code. This section authorizes the Secretary of the Treasury or his delegate to prescribe such regulations as may be necessary or appropriate to determine whether an interest in a corporation is to be treated as stock or indebtedness. Among the factors to be taken into account in these guidelines are the following:

1. Whether there is a written unconditional promise to pay on demand or on a specified date a sum certain in money in return for an adequate consideration in money or money's worth, and to pay a fixed rate of interest.
2. Whether there is subordination to or preference over any indebtedness of the corporation.
3. The ratio of debt to equity of the corporation.
4. Whether there is convertibility into stock of the corporation.
5. The relationship between holdings of stock in the corporation and holdings of the interest in question.

A determination made under this section will be applicable for all purposes of the Internal Revenue Code rather than being limited to corporate acquisition indebtedness situations (discussed in Chapter 8), and the deductibility of interest under the latter provisions will not necessarily preclude application of the new projected regulations. The determination of whether an obligation constitutes debt or equity (under this section of the Code) may affect all open tax years.[5]

If the stockholders have the requisite 80% control of a corporation, they could exchange the debt for additional shares of stock under the non-taxable provisions of Section 351 of the Internal Revenue Code.[6] Although this would not solve the problem of possible interest expense disallowance prior to such an exchange, or of principal repayments previously made being treated as dividend income to the stockholders, it would eliminate any future problems in this regard.

Loans from the corporation to stockholders pose other problems. The Internal Revenue Service may contend that such loans, particularly if they are of long standing, in fact represent dividends to the stockholders. Repayment by the stockholders will generally establish the fact that the loans were bona fide.

Leased Property. Frequently a closely held corporation will lease premises or equipment from principal stockholders or their families under excessive rental arrangements. Prior to going public the property may be transferred or sold to the corporation, or long-term arm's-length lease arrangements may be entered into with such persons, possibly with an option to purchase. The more desirable procedure is to transfer or sell the property to the corporation, because any substantially different lease arrangements are more likely to result in partial disallowance by IRS of rental deductions in open years and dividend treatment for stockholders on these disallowances.

Transactions with "Brother–Sister" Corporations. The definition of a brother–sister controlled group heretofore has been two or more corporations in which at least 80% of the voting stock or total value of shares is owned by one person who is an individual, estate, or trust. This definition has been enlarged so that for years ending on or after December 31, 1970, the following definition prevails for the purpose of subjecting corporations of this type to certain limitations that apply to multiple corporations.[7]

[5] *Ibid.*, § 385.
[6] *Ibid.*, § 351.
[7] *Ibid.*, § 1563(a)(2).

Brother–Sister Controlled Group—Two or more corporations if 5 or fewer persons who are individuals, estates, or trusts own (within the meaning of subsection 1563(d)(2)) stock possessing—

(A) at least 80 percent of the total combined voting power of all classes of stock entitled to vote or at least 80 percent of the total value of shares of all classes of the stock of each corporation, and

(B) more than 50 percent of the total combined voting power of all classes of stock entitled to vote or more than 50 percent of the total value of shares of all classes of stock of each corporation, taking into account the stock ownership of each such person only to the extent such stock ownership is identical with respect to each such corporation.

At times a corporation may purchase and sell products and services from or to business enterprises owned by related taxpayers (brother–sister corporations). These arrangements must be reviewed, before going public, to determine that they are at arm's length. Any changes in procedures and policy will raise a question of the good faith of such arrangements, particularly if operations through the several enterprises resulted in a lower effective tax rate for the combined entities.

Under Section 482 of the Internal Revenue Code, the government is empowered to reallocate income among related enterprises to prevent the evasion of taxes or to clearly reflect their incomes, whether or not they qualify under the rules as parent–subsidiary or brother–sister corporations for tax purposes.[8] It may be desirable to discontinue such transactions, if they are not too substantial, or conversely to have a non-taxable reorganization which would combine the enterprises, if transactions among them are significant.

Excess Assets

Inasmuch as earnings, potential earnings, and dividend-paying capacity are the primary factors in pricing an initial offering, it is generally desirable to dispose of excess assets prior to going public. These may include real estate and properties having no present or apparent future use for company operations; unrelated security investments; large insurance policies on the lives of officers, etc. Often the principals of the corporation will purchase some of these or receive them as a "dividend in kind"; alternatively, they

[8] *Ibid.,* § 482.

may be sold to outsiders and the proceeds distributed as cash dividends before going public. Although the disposal of excess assets may raise the question of accumulated earnings being beyond the reasonable needs of the business (under Section 531 and subsequent sections), the stockholders will have an opportunity to rebut the contention. Even if unsuccessful, they may still be better off financially if the tax under these sections is asserted against the corporation.

Inventories

In many cases closely held corporations follow accounting practices, whether generally acceptable or not, which are designed to minimize current income tax payments. One of the most common areas of subjective accounting pertains to the valuation of inventories. Where the valuation of inventories is substantial and significant in the determination of income, past practices may have to be revised and income figures reconstructed for purposes of the registration statement and prospectus. Management's view of obsolete and unsalable merchandise may have been extremely conservative, overhead may have been excluded in pricing work in process and finished goods in inventories, or a general reserve may have been applied against the aggregate inventory valuations.

If a change in the tax reporting practices regarding inventories is desirable, the adjustment might be reflected in the return for the current year or spread back over prior years by filing amended returns. If the adjustment could be considered the result of a change in accounting method, pursuant to Section 481, it might be advantageous to have the Internal Revenue Service initiate the change. Where overhead is to be included in inventories for the first time, a ten-year spread of the adjustment may be available under Revenue Procedure 70–27.

Gift Tax Planning

Gifts of shares of a closely held corporation may be valued at less than the price of the initial offering if there is no market for the shares at that time or because of the size of the block being valued. It is generally desirable to make such gifts prior to formalizing arrangements with an underwriter. In several recent cases, the courts approved valuations below those of the initial public offering prices of stock in valuing gifts.[9]

PREPARING FOR PUBLIC OFFERING

As discussed elsewhere, when a company is being valued for federal tax purposes or for a proposed acquisition or merger, consideration is usually given to values attributable to (a) non-operating assets; (b) prospective earnings that would accrue through a different and supposedly less conservative method of accounting; or (c) an earnings potential not yet realized or indicated in its historical earnings trend. On the other hand, in an initial public offering, or any public offering for that matter, the financial and other data reflected in the prospectus must tell the issuer's entire story. Accordingly, it is often necessary for a company whose stock is closely held to get its house in order for such an offering.

Capital Structure and Other Considerations

In addition to the tax aspects of going public, matters that may require consultation with legal counsel and others for possible remedial action include the following:

1. Refinancing of undesirable types of borrowing, such as those requiring the pledging of accounts receivable or inventories, or chattel mortgages against equipment.
2. Recapitalization where the authorized number of shares would be insufficient for a contemplated offering. In conjunction with amending the company's certificate of incorporation for an increase in the amount of authorized shares, consideration may be given to the advantages of changing its state of incorporation.
3. Elimination of restrictive provisions on capital stock such as preemptive rights, stockholders' repurchase agreements, voting trusts, and limitations on the payment of dividends because of loan agreements or bond indenture provisions.
4. The establishment or revision of stock option, pension, or other fringe benefit plans for executive and key personnel, to compete with other public companies.

[9] Estate of Heinhold v. Comm'r, 363 F.2d 329 (7th Cir. 1966); and Morris M. Messing, 48 T.C. 502 (1967).

5. Reconstruction of financial statements in conformity with generally accepted accounting principles, so that an appropriate opinion on the financial statements may be obtained from an independent accountant, as required by the Securities Act of 1933.

Guidance of Competent Professionals

Anyone contemplating an initial public offering or, for that matter, any subsequent public offering of common stock should consult with his attorney and his independent accountants, and with an underwriter. In Chapter 2, the role of brokers and dealers in the purchase and sale of securities was discussed. A large number of brokers and dealers also function as underwriters. Underwriters are also known as investment bankers, as distinguished from commercial bankers.

It is most desirable that legal counsel and independent public accountants engaged to assist in the preparation of statements and documents for public offerings be experienced and competent in that field. The Securities Act of 1933 is complex and provides for civil liabilities for the issuer, its directors and certain officers and controlling stockholders, underwriters, and any experts involved, where there have been materially false or inadequate representations.[10] The Act also provides for criminal penalties under certain conditions which could lead to a maximum fine of $5,000, or imprisonment up to five years, or both, for any person convicted under applicable sections of the Act.[11] Accordingly, the need for engaging competent professionals and underwriters cannot be overemphasized.

Timing of Offering

Timing is another important matter to be considered in a contemplated initial public offering. If the principal stockholders of a company are not under any immediate compulsion to sell some of their own or company stock, it is sometimes advisable to delay such action. Conditions that would indicate the desirability of postponing an initial public offering include a period of generally sharp decline in stock market prices or in prices of stocks of

10 Securities Act of 1933, §§ 11–16.
11 Ibid., §§ 17–24.

the companies within the prospective issuer's particular industry. Also, if the company's earnings through the period to be included in the prospectus are not satisfactory, but might be substantially improved during the following year, postponement of the offering might be prudent.

Underwriting

Public offerings of securities are sometimes handled by a single underwriter, if an issue offered is small. For the most part, however, several underwriters participate in a public offering. Where a group of underwriters is involved, the issuer customarily carries out his discussions and negotiations with the managing underwriter.

Underwriting Agreements. There are three basic methods of underwriting, i.e., fixed commitment, best efforts, and all or none. Under the fixed commitment method, the underwriter or underwriters agree to purchase stock from the issuer at a fixed price, thereby relieving the issuer of responsibility for the success of the offering.

Under the best efforts method, the underwriter merely acts as a distributing agent in offering the stock to the public, and has no obligation to purchase any unsold stock. This type of offering is undertaken where a stock is considered speculative and an issuer is unable to induce an underwriter to make a firm commitment to purchase the stock.

The all or none basis is a variation of a best efforts commitment, whereby the issuer and underwriter agree that if an entire issue or specified portion thereof is not sold the agreement shall be terminated. There is usually a time limit for distribution under this type of agreement and funds received from subscribers are placed in escrow. If the terms of agreement under an all or none basis commitment are not met, it automatically terminates and the monies received from subscribers to the common stock are refunded in full.

Underwriters' Investigations. As previously mentioned, an underwriter will conduct certain investigations and make sufficient inquiries to be assured that he should sponsor an initial common stock offering. He will be primarily concerned with:

1. The earnings record over a period of years. A steady improvement in sales and earnings, particularly during the usual five-year period covered in the summary of earnings, is a plus factor. Conversely, a static or sporadic pattern of sales and earnings, or a steady increase in sales without a reasonable improvement in earnings, would be regarded adversely.

2. If any company stock is being offered (many initial offerings are entirely by selling stockholders), it is important that the proceeds be beneficially utilized. Even where the entire offering is by selling stockholders, the investment banker will generally prepare a cash flow and forecast to see that the company will not run into financial difficulties in the foreseeable future.[12]

3. The company's position in its industry and the apparent future of the industry. A company that is at least maintaining and possibly improving its position in an industry will be well regarded. Also, a company that has 10% of the market in its industry will be considered a better risk than one with only 1%.

4. The company's ability to pay dividends on the stock being offered, so that affirmative action in this regard may be indicated in the prospectus.

5. The adequacy of the number of shares being offered to create a reasonable after-market in the stock. In many cases, substantial amounts of stock, in an initial offering, are proposed to be reserved for officers, employees, directors, suppliers, and customers of the company.

6. The proportion of stock offered by the principal stockholders relative to their holdings. If it is substantial, this may indicate a lack of confidence in the future of the company.

---

[12] "Accounting Research Study No. 2," published by the American Institute of Certified Public Accountants in 1961, defines "cash flow" as follows:

" 'Cash flow' in financial analysis means net income, after adding back expense items which currently do not use funds such as depreciation. It may also involve deducting revenue items which do not currently provide funds, such as the current amortization of deferred income. It corresponds to the 'funds derived from operations' in a statement of source and application of funds.

"The concept of 'cash flow' can be used effectively as one of the major factors in judging the ability to meet debt retirement requirements, to maintain regular dividends, to finance replacement and expansion costs, etc.

"In no sense, however, can the amount of 'cash flow' be considered to be a substitute for or an improvement upon the net income, properly determined, as an indication of the results of operations or the change in financial position."

7. The all-important aspects of the strengths, abilities, and progressiveness of the management, management successors, and technical executives and personnel.

PRICING THE INITIAL PUBLIC OFFERING

General Conservatism

The foregoing discussion is germane to arriving at a price for an initial public offering of common stock. With an investment banker, a public offering is not a one-time affair. He and the participating underwriting and selling groups are in the business of marketing securities. Although some underwritten public offerings will prove to have been overpriced, or perhaps should not have been marketed at all, in the majority of cases investment bankers do an excellent job in protecting the customers to whom they sell securities.

Does this result in general conservatism in pricing initial public offerings of common stock? Possibly; but for the most part such conservatism in pricing is not necessarily inimical to the interests of selling stockholders or to an issuing company. It may be of some concern to the management or principal stockholders of a company, if the price of a stock increases substantially shortly after being offered, but it would be far worse if the price were to decline substantially in the after-market. This not only has an adverse affect on all of the issue outstanding, besides the shares offered, but renders it difficult to undertake future public offerings of the stock on an advantageous basis.

Most Initial Offerings Less Than Majority of Shares. In most cases, initial public offerings will not represent the major portion of common stock to be outstanding after the offering. Accordingly, any increase in price in the after-market enhances the value of all shares, in addition to those included in the offering. Some principals of companies, on the advice of underwriters, undertake to market, on a two-step basis, common stock that they ultimately wish to be publicly owned. The initial offering may consist of, say, 20% of the total to be outstanding, and additional amounts will be offered one or several years later, at a higher price, as the result of public acceptance and seasoning of the stock.

Methods of Valuing Companies

There are basically two methods of valuing companies for purposes of an initial public offering. Those with substantial disposable assets, such as securities or real estate, have an overall valuation generally related to the fair market value of such assets, with consideration given to problems of liquidation and federal taxes involved. The offerings of such companies generally do not entail too many valuation problems for the underwriter.

The vast majority of initial public offerings involve operating companies whose worth is largely dependent on continuance as a going concern. Potential earnings are the primary factor in the valuation of such companies.

How Are Initial Public Offerings Priced?

At what price should a common stock of such an operating company be valued for purposes of an initial public offering? The answer is startlingly simple. It is purely a matter of judgment, exercised by the underwriter and his associates in the deal. Theirs is a merchandising problem. At what price will the public buy the stock, so that after the period of market-stabilizing operations the underwriters will not be the unwilling owners of substantial amounts of the offered stock? Like merchandisers in other lines they do not wish to have their capital unproductively tied up.

Guidelines in Pricing. Certainly, guidelines are used in the exercise of judgment by the underwriters in pricing an initial public offering of common stock. Potential earnings have been mentioned as the primary factor in such valuations. Inasmuch as these are largely conjectural, some known factors are used in lieu thereof—that is, the latest year's earnings of the company, the trend of earnings in recent years, general stock market conditions, market prices of stocks of other companies in the industry, and the company's performance compared with its competitors.

With some exceptions, all these factors are distilled into an offering price based on a price–earnings ratio, approximately so many times the latest year's earnings. If, however, the latest year's earnings indicate a misleading trend, a pro forma figure may be used for such a computation. As a rough measure, an initial offering may be priced at, say, 5% to 10% below the median price–earnings ratio of actively traded stocks of companies in the same industry. The differential will generally be greater if the company is in a high price–earnings multiple industry. However, there have been periods, such as that prevailing during 1969, when, because of a dull market in listed stocks, speculative demand resulted in high offering prices for some new issues that had little relation to their intrinsic values.

Significance of Latest Interim Earnings. Interim earnings figures generally are required in prospectuses for the period subsequent to the latest fiscal year, with figures for the comparable period of the preceding year. Besides indicating the earnings trend, such figures are important to the underwriter and the investing public in giving assurance that the latest full year's earnings have not been improved at the expense of subsequent earnings. Also, a substantial improvement shown in subsequent interim earnings, particularly if they cover a period of six months or more, may warrant a better offering price for the stock.

Quality of Earnings. The quality of earnings is of the utmost importance in valuing a company for an initial public offering, as well as for other purposes, and does not always receive the consideration it deserves. Earnings resulting from normal operations of a company are of the highest quality; "earnings" generated by means of accounting changes or one-shot transactions generally are not. Such items distort earnings trends and other information intended to facilitate comparisons with results of prior years, and at times affect future earnings adversely.

All or most of these practices, if properly disclosed, have had approval of the accounting profession, although consideration is being given to requiring disclosure of the comparative significance of certain accounting changes in relation to previously reported and current net income. A list of some of these practices follows:

1. Reducing depreciation provisions, either by a reduction in rates or by changing from an accelerated to a straight-line method.

2. Changing from an amortization to a flow-through method of handling the investment tax credit.

3. Changing from LIFO to a current cost or market basis for valuing inventories.

4. Changing from a write-off basis for research and development expenses to a basis of amortizing such costs over a period of years.

5. Reflecting in a single year, rather than over a period, a reduction in or an elimination of the provision for pensions, resulting from changing actuarial assumptions as to future earnings under the plan.

6. Taking as income full amounts of land development sales or certain types of franchise sales, the proceeds of which are collectible over a period of years.

7. Deferring the cost of overruns on completed contracts in the expectation of receiving renewal contracts.

8. Reflecting in conglomerate companies the net realized capital gains on securities sold by insurance company subsidiaries, and ignoring unrealized depreciation during the year on their portfolio securities still on hand.

Profits resulting from the disposal of plants, from subsidiaries that have been operating successfully, and from investments (except for companies engaged in buying and selling securities), although they benefit the year in which transactions take place, adversely affect the future to the extent they have benefited earnings up to the time of disposal. Also, earnings generated through the redemption of company debt and by means of cost reduction programs are generally of a one-shot nature.

Differences in accounting practices of companies in the same industry also should be recognized in valuing their capital stocks. Although, over a period, companies deferring and amortizing certain major costs produce earnings results which are comparable with those of companies using the write-off method, their resultant deferred "assets" may have little or no intrinsic value. Also, some of these companies from time to time have to face up to a major write-off of deferral accumulations, with disastrous results to the market values of their capital stocks.

Current Popularity of Industry Important. Fundamentally, if a company is in a cyclical industry, or is largely dependent upon government business, or is in an industry that has reached a relatively static position, the stock will probably be valued at a relatively low price–earnings ratio. Conversely, if a company is in a fast-growing industry, at times including aerospace, hospital supplies, chemicals, drugs, cosmetics and toiletries, and printing and publishing, the stock will probably be marketed at a relatively high price–earnings ratio. As shown in Table 4–2 (pages 86–99), discussed later in this chapter, stocks of companies in such industries were offered at relatively high price–earnings ratios; those of companies engaged in the manufacture of apparel, household products, and steel, and those in the retail trade, were at low multiples. These observations are made on the assumption that a company's common stock meets the normal criteria for a successful public offering. Incidentally, the investing popularity of industries and individual stocks varies from time to time; those that are "in" this year may be "out" the next.

Price–Earnings Ratios of Primary Importance. Evidence of the significance of price–earnings ratios of stocks is found in the periodic disclosure of such information in many financial publications on listed and over-the-counter stocks actively traded. The *Monthly Stock Digest*,[13] which has a very large circulation, shows summary information on thousands of stocks that are actively traded. In addition to other information, this service significantly shows price–earnings ratios of stock based on the current market price, and the latest available or estimated twelve months earnings. It also shows the yield on such stocks, i.e., the annual rate of dividend related to the current market price.

Standard & Poor's method of rating the quality of common stocks is based primarily on a weighting formula which combines earnings and dividends.[14] The New York Stock Exchange, in periodic studies, shows similar statistics, in addition to other data, on most of its listed stocks.[15]

If these data are of primary importance in appraising the market price of actively traded common stocks they must be

---

[13] Data Digests, Inc., "Monthly Stock Digest."
[14] Standard & Poor's Corp., "Stock Guide" (published monthly).
[15] New York Stock Exchange, "Stocks on the Big Board."

equally significant in valuing stocks for purposes of initial public offerings.

STUDY OF INITIAL PUBLIC OFFERINGS

Table 4–1 (page 84) provides selected price–earnings ratios by industries, as background data for the studies of individual offerings described below.

Arrangement of Study

Pertinent data on 200 selected initial public offerings of common stock during the period from July 1, 1962, to December 31, 1966, are compiled in Table 4–2 (pages 86–99). This period begins after the "hot issue" market that terminated late in May 1962, and does not include offerings during that earlier time. It was chosen as a representative period because it includes approximately four and one-half years of steadily rising market prices, the sharp decline in 1966, and the slight recovery taking place later in that year. Market values of stocks are carried through to April 28, 1967, a substantial recovery period, to obtain a more reasonable appraisal of the after-market action of stocks offered late in 1966.

Offerings Grouped by Industry. The offerings have been homogeneously grouped by industry for ready comparison of the financial data and statistics summarized in Table 4–2. However, some companies may not fit the offering price pattern of others classified in their industry because of involvement in other major activities. One company that stands out particularly in this respect is Jefferson Corporation which is in the ready-mixed concrete business. Its stock was offered late in 1965 at 131 times the latest fiscal year's earnings, principally on the basis of a substantial investment in a life insurance company.

Composite Price–Earnings Ratios of Selected Industries. Table 4–1 shows price–earnings ratios for Standard & Poor's 425 industrial stocks and for selected industry classifications included therein. These correspond reasonably with some of the larger groupings of companies in Table 4–2. Ratios of seasoned companies, which are furnished for comparison with those in the

TABLE 4–1 Selected Price–Earnings Ratios of Stocks*
(June 30, 1962, to April 30, 1967)

	June 30, 1962	Dec. 31, 1962	June 30, 1963	Dec. 31, 1963	June 30, 1964	Dec. 31, 1964	June 30, 1965	Dec. 31, 1965	June 30, 1966	Dec. 31, 1966	June 30, 1967
425 industrial stocks—composite	14.13	17.64	17.93	18.78	17.04	17.49	18.99	17.90	15.66	14.75	17.32
Selected industry classifications:											
Apparel–textile manufacturers	12.9	12.8	12.7	14.3	14.7	13.5	13.8	16.2	14.4	12.8	15.1
Chemical products (excluding duPont; see notes 1 and 2)	16.5	18.9	19.3	21.4	21.0	20.0	18.3	19.1	15.0	12.8	15.7
Drugs	20.6	22.9	23.8	24.6	24.0	25.5	24.3	27.9	24.4	24.0	28.6
Electronics	21.8	24.1	28.6	27.1	21.1	21.6	20.2	27.8	30.0	27.0	31.2
Food products	18.7	20.8	21.7	22.8	22.6	21.0	20.2	20.1	16.2	15.2	15.9
Household furnishings	13.5	11.5	13.7	14.4	13.9	12.1	11.8	12.5	10.7	8.7	14.1
Machinery	12.9	14.6	16.1	15.3	16.0	14.9	13.5	14.9	12.2	10.3	14.6
Office and business equipment (excluding IBM; see note 2)	25.0	26.6	43.2	46.5	44.0	33.4	36.5	46.4	49.5	36.9	49.2
Printing and publishing (excluding Curtis Publishing; see note 3)	15.9	18.7	22.4	19.5	23.7	18.3	20.0	26.5	22.2	20.7	25.9
Retail trade—composite	17.8	18.9	20.9	21.0	23.3	23.1	23.3	21.1	17.7	14.7	18.4
Retail trade—food chains	15.4	15.3	17.2	16.1	18.2	18.2	17.4	15.7	12.8	11.2	12.5

*Furnished by Standard & Poor's.
Notes:
1. Computer and Allied Services are included in this category.
2. duPont and IBM have been excluded because their figures are so relatively substantial that they would unduly influence the industry composite figures.
3. Curtis Publishing has been excluded because its losses were so substantial during the period that they would greatly distort the industry composite price–earnings ratios.

initial offerings study, are shown at six-month intervals commencing June 30, 1962, to June 30, 1967. The ratios in Table 4–1 indicate some of the favored industries during the period, some whose performance varied from the averages, and some that were consistently below average.

Offerings Included

For the most part, the offerings selected for analysis, out of the many hundreds reviewed, were of issues aggregating $1,000,000 and over. A relatively few smaller issues have been included in order to show the relationship of underwriters' discounts and other expenses of the offerings to their gross proceeds. Offerings were selected on a random basis during the period covered by the study, with primary emphasis on obtaining a reasonable cross section of industries, and a sufficient number of issues marketed in each year (or part thereof for 1962). Also, the availability of the considerable amount of information required for each issue necessarily had some bearing on the selection or rejection of an offering for inclusion in the study.

No Regulation A offerings (those not exceeding $300,000 at the time of the study) have been included because most of these are underwritten on a best efforts basis or not underwritten at all. Accordingly, data such as those summarized in Table 4–2 could not be reasonably obtained on such offerings. Furthermore, the substantial underwriting houses generally do not handle Regulation A offerings, because so many of them are speculative in nature, and the commissions and expenses of underwriting are too great relative to the gross proceeds.

Findings

Characteristics of Offerings. The median price–earnings ratios at which stocks in Table 4–2 were offered during the period were: 12 for the six months ended December 31, 1962; and 13, 13, 16, and 13 for the respective years ended December 31, 1963, 1964, 1965, and 1966. These median price–earnings ratios were consistently lower than the Standard & Poor's 425 industrial stock averages but do show the influence, on such offerings, of general stock market prices, particularly in the six months ended Decem-

TABLE 4-2 Statistics on Selected
(July 1, 1962, to

		Number of Shares		Price to Public	
Industry Classification and Company	Offering Date	Offered	Outstanding After Offering	Per Share	Aggregate
Oil and Gas Field Resources					
1 Permeator	12/14/62	250,000			$ 1,250,000
		50,000 emp.	1,135,000	$ 5.00	250,000
2 Southeastern Drilling...	5/11/65	315,000	1,790,000	15.00	4,725,000
Manufacturing					
Apparel					
3 Leslie Fay	9/11/62	200,000	600,000	9.875	1,975,000
4 Red Kap Inc.	6/ 4/63	230,000		20.00	4,600,000
		10,000 emp.	500,000	18.60	186,000
5 Evans Inc.	7/17/63	180,000	540,000	12.00	2,160,000
6 Lilli Ann	3/23/64	150,000	299,000	22.50	3,375,000
7 Susan Thomas	5/27/65	375,000	1,065,000	21.50	8,062,500
8 Eagle Clothes	9/13/65	375,000	1,500,350	12.50	4,687,500
9 Charles Pindyck	10/ 7/65	165,000	430,000	7.50	1,237,500
10 Fairfield Noble	10/27/65	300,000	1,150,000	5.00	1,500,000
11 The Villager	11/16/65	600,000	2,000,000	16.50	9,900,000
12 Koret of California	5/ 2/66	497,200	2,023,971	24.75	12,305,700
13 Bali Co.	5/25/66	251,750	1,325,000	13.75	3,461,562
Cement, Concrete, etc.					
14 Puerto Rican Cement..	3/25/63	600,000	2,000,000	19.50	11,700,000
15 Jefferson Corp.	11/ 9/65	115,000	583,000	17.00	1,955,000
Chemical Products					
16 Cabot Corporation	4/24/63	296,560	2,573,837	41.50	12,307,240
17 Phillip A. Hunt...........	2/25/64	225,000	800,000	6.50	1,462,500
18 Fisher Scientific	3/23/65	175,000	1,630,900	30.00	5,250,000
19 Big Three Gas	4/ 6/65	373,122	1,764,052	32.00	11,939,904
20 National Chemsearch ..	9/28/65	289,832		26.50	7,680,548
		20,000 emp.	1,408,314	25.10	502,000
21 Mercury Chemical	12/20/65	80,000	240,000	7.50	600,000
22 Fine Organics	5/12/66	275,000 min.	830,000	5.00	1,375,000
23 Buckbee Mears	9/27/66	530,730 min.	1,901,980	23.00	12,206,790
24 Elcor Chemical	12/ 6/66	300,000	1,153,931	10.00	3,000,000
Drugs and Hospital Supplies					
25 A. H. Robins	3/26/63	425,000	3,897,460	29.00	10,150,000
26 C. R. Bard	7/ 9/63	204,095	863,287	16.50	3,367,567
27 Marion Laboratories ...	8/19/65	187,470	669,400	21.00	3,936,870
28 Barnes-Hind Pharm. ...	9/28/65	270,300	700,000	18.25	4,932,975
29 Massengill	11/ 4/65	100,000	1,000,000	20.00	2,000,000
30 Mem Company	4/28/66	300,000	1,180,800	23.50	7,050,000

emp. = shares offered to employees.
min. = minimum number of shares.

Initial Public Offerings of Common Stock
December 31, 1966)

Underwriters' Discounts and Commissions	Estimated Expenses	Earnings per Share for Fiscal Years Prior to Offering			P/E Ratio— Fiscal Year Prior to Offering	Approximate Market Price		
		Latest	First Prior	Second Prior		Highest Since Offering	April 28, 1967	
$ 93,750	$ 85,000	New company				$25\frac{1}{4}$	$14\frac{1}{4}$	1
378,000	85,000	$1.96	$2.43	$2.21	8	$49\frac{3}{4}$	$48\frac{1}{2}$	2
177,750	57,000	1.09	.50	.33	9	$29\frac{1}{4}$	$20\frac{7}{8}$*	3
322,000	65,000	1.92	1.40	1.21	10	$25\frac{1}{2}$	Merged	4
194,400	35,250	1.01	.93	.85	12	17	17	5
294,000	43,000	2.03	1.27	.88	11	$33\frac{3}{8}$	16 *	6
525,000	85,188	1.26	.90	.50	17	$27\frac{3}{4}$	$12\frac{1}{4}$	7
326,250	78,000	1.14	.61	.36	11	$14\frac{1}{4}$	$10\frac{7}{8}$	8
111,375	57,000	1.32	.49	.57	6	$7\frac{1}{2}$	$3\frac{7}{8}$	9
120,000	67,500	.62	.25	.15	8	$13\frac{1}{2}$	9	10
675,000	118,570	.88	.65	.41	19	$49\frac{5}{8}$	$44\frac{1}{2}$*	11
820,380	150,000	1.50	.31	.18	16	34	$20\frac{3}{4}$	12
259,302	71,400	1.05	.81	.54	13	$18\frac{5}{8}$	$18\frac{5}{8}$	13
810,000	135,000	1.96	1.54	1.27	10	$24\frac{3}{4}$	$20\frac{5}{8}$	14
175,950	72,000	.13	.12	.23	131	17	$11\frac{1}{4}$	15
667,260	145,000	2.66	2.88	3.50	16	$54\frac{1}{2}$	$54\frac{1}{2}$	16
123,750	40,600	.43	.29	.22	15	$58\frac{1}{4}$	$58\frac{1}{4}$*	17
262,500	50,000	1.70	1.00	1.05	18	$47\frac{1}{4}$	45	18
708,932	64,500	1.41	.98	.78	23	$74\frac{3}{8}$	$67\frac{3}{4}$*	19
405,765	75,000	1.33	1.04	.81	20	$57\frac{1}{2}$	$57\frac{1}{2}$	20
75,000	29,500	.41	.22	.21	18	$9\frac{1}{4}$	$8\frac{1}{2}$	21
115,500	60,400	.38	.21	.09	13	$7\frac{1}{4}$	$7\frac{1}{4}$	22
769,559	141,200	.84	.40	.21	27	49	$40\frac{3}{4}$	23
255,000	80,000	.73	.38	.16	14	22	$21\frac{1}{4}$	24
507,500	10,950	1.16	.80	.70	25	$85\frac{1}{2}$	$85\frac{1}{8}$*	25
234,709	130,000	.92	.71	.70	18	$97\frac{1}{2}$	$97\frac{1}{2}$*	26
281,205	51,200	1.12	.21	.10	18	80	$77\frac{1}{2}$*	27
337,875	89,000	.82	.33	.27	22	$35\frac{3}{4}$	$28\frac{3}{4}$	28
130,000	65,520	1.00	.76	.89	20	25	16	29
525,000	91,000	2.30	1.33	.32	10	26	16	30

*Approximate market prices at April 28, 1967, and "highest since offering" have been adjusted upward for stock splits and stock dividends of 10% or more, for comparison with initial offering prices.

TABLE 4–2 (cont.) Statistics on Selected

(July 1, 1962, to

Industry Classification and Company	Offering Date	Number of Shares		Price to Public	
		Offered	Outstanding After Offering	Per Share	Aggregate
Manufacturing (cont.)					
Electronics and Components					
31 Computer Control	2/13/63	200,000	1,010,006	$ 8.00	$ 1,600,000
32 Continental Device	4/ 2/63	275,000	1,382,500	5.50	1,512,750
33 Tektronix	9/11/63	540,000	8,072,700	19.75	10,655,000
34 Scientific Data Syst. ...	6/ 3/64	382,375	2,104,800	25.00	9,559,375
35 E. F. Johnson	9/15/64	240,000	1,081,040	15.50	3,720,000
		10,000 emp.		14.35	43,500
36 Tracor	10/20/64	110,000	448,701	19.50	2,145,000
37 Essex Wire	1/19/65	1,090,288	4,000,000	25.50	27,802,344
38 Memorex	3/ 3/65	220,926	977,106	25.00	5,523,150
39 Philbrick (George A.) ..	1/27/65	350,000 min.	985,000	16.50	5,775,000
40 Kearney National	8/11/65	200,000	1,100,000	10.00	2,000,000
41 Dickson Electronics	4/26/65	120,000	454,220	11.50	1,380,000
42 Ameco Inc.	10/ 5/65	400,000	1,200,000	19.00	7,600,000
43 General Electro Dyn. ..	10/ 7/65	285,000 min.	443,179	7.00	1,995,000
44 Space Craft Inc.	12/ 9/65	100,000	391,368	12.50	1,187,500
45 K. M. Electronics	3/16/66	450,000	1,649,500	2.00	900,000
46 Technitrol Inc.	4/19/66	170,000	635,000	16.00	2,720,000
47 Optical Scanning	5/ 5/66	200,000	419,000	20.00	4,000,000
48 Methode Electronics ...	6/17/66	200,000	842,760	12.75	2,550,000
49 Space Ordnance Syst...	8/ 3/66	75,640	392,800	7.00	529,480
50 Space Corp.	11/30/66	130,000	325,329	9.75	1,267,500
Food Products					
51 Hawthorn–Melody	9/ 9/63	497,500	1,000,000	22.50	11,193,750
52 International Milling ...	1/23/64	450,000	2,351,083	27.75	12,487,500
53 Spencer Packing	6/10/65	336,000	840,000	12.00	4,032,000
54 Marhoefer Packing	6/22/65	192,000	467,047	10.00	1,920,000
55 Assoc. Coca-Cola Bot..	5/ 3/66	300,000	1,392,630	20.75	6,225,000
56 Sun City Dairy	6/23/66	125,000	262,500	8.25	1,031,250
57 Havatampa Cigar	6/29/66	160,000	2,815,029	9.00	1,440,000
		40,000 emp.		8.46	338,400
Footwear					
58 Consolidated Nat. Shoe	3/ 2/65	240,000	500,000	16.00	3,840,000
59 Penobscot Shoe Co.	9/ 9/65	270,525	1,108,050	12.25	3,313,931
Household Products					
60 Fieldcrest Mills	10/ 9/62	300,000	2,270,000	14.00	4,200,000
61 Lenox Incorporated	4/23/63	172,500	466,100	16.25	2,803,125
62 Rival Manufacturing ...	4/ 7/64	260,000	410,000	14.00	3,640,000
63 Overhead Door	4/28/64	600,000	1,414,208	10.00	6,000,000
64 Magic Chef	5/ 5/64	272,000	1,052,262	16.50	4,488,000
65 Shelby Williams	5/26/65	160,000	350,000	10.75	1,720,000

emp. = shares offered to employees.
min. = minimum number of shares.

Initial Public Offerings of Common Stock
December 31, 1966)

Underwriters' Discounts and Commissions	Estimated Expenses	Earnings per Share for Fiscal Years Prior to Offering			P/E Ratio— Fiscal Year Prior to Offering	Approximate Market Price		
		Latest	First Prior	Second Prior		Highest Since Offering	April 28, 1967	
$ 125,000	$ 67,000	$ .32	$ .06	$ –	25	$ $25\frac{3}{4}$	Merged	31
123,750	75,000	.33	.22	.10	17	$24\frac{1}{4}$	$ $19\frac{1}{8}$	32
540,000	106,000	.72	.58	.62	27	$44\frac{1}{4}$	$40\frac{3}{4}$	33
573,562	60,000	.69	(.27)	–	36	$117\frac{1}{4}$	$110\frac{5}{8}$	34
276,000	37,500	.75	.96	.68	21	$26\frac{5}{8}$	$24\frac{3}{4}$	35
193,050	57,000	.67	.41	.25	29	52	52	36
1,362,860	148,463	2.06	1.87	1.18	12	$71\frac{3}{4}$	$65\frac{1}{2}$*	37
353,482	40,000	1.08	.27	(.85)	23	116	116	38
462,000	39,000	.89	.65	.46	18	$21\frac{3}{4}$	Merged	39
180,000	76,000	1.08	.44	.22	9	$42\frac{1}{8}$	$42\frac{1}{8}$	40
114,000	65,000	1.05	.96	.79	11	41	$27\frac{1}{2}$	41
600,000	143,160	1.04	.19	.15	18	$38\frac{3}{8}$	$9\frac{7}{8}$	42
159,600	82,763	.83	1.61	.89	8	$23\frac{3}{4}$	19	43
95,000	17,500	.82	.47	.38	15	$12\frac{3}{4}$	$10\frac{1}{2}$	44
54,000	21,000	Losses since inception			–	$4\frac{1}{2}$	$4\frac{3}{8}$	45
229,500	71,000	1.06	.68	.18	15	$34\frac{1}{2}$	$34\frac{1}{4}$*	46
400,000	50,000	Losses since inception			–	93	$78\frac{3}{4}$	47
190,000	63,250	.49	.32	.27	25	$15\frac{1}{4}$	$13\frac{3}{4}$	48
52,948	38,080	1.01	(.52)	(1.12)	5	$16\frac{3}{8}$	$16\frac{3}{8}$	49
126,750	48,000	1.02	.49	.89	9	$9\frac{3}{4}$	$8\frac{3}{4}$	50
771,125	53,553	1.70	1.53	1.01	13	$35\frac{3}{4}$	$19\frac{1}{8}$	51
630,000	105,700	2.13	1.58	2.36	13	$28\frac{1}{8}$	$22\frac{1}{4}$	52
362,880	50,000	.62	.24	.40	19	$34\frac{5}{8}$	$20\frac{1}{4}$	53
192,000	54,000	1.35	.39	.70	8	10	$8\frac{7}{8}$	54
390,000	57,600	1.67	1.36	.95	12	$20\frac{3}{4}$	$17\frac{1}{2}$	55
92,500	37,226	.95	.50	.38	9	$8\frac{1}{2}$	8	56
86,400	54,600	.81	.87	.70	11	9	$6\frac{1}{8}$	57
336,000	83,000	1.48	1.17	1.54	11	16	$10\frac{1}{8}$	58
265,114	65,000	.89	.59	.46	14	$12\frac{1}{2}$	$11\frac{7}{8}$	59
270,000	100,000	1.13	.70	1.25	12	$37\frac{5}{8}$	$25\frac{1}{2}$	60
207,000	61,000	1.49	.99	1.00	11	$49\frac{1}{8}$	38*	61
291,200	50,000	2.00	–	–	7	$46\frac{1}{2}$	37	62
540,000	53,290	1.00	.73	.41	10	$14\frac{1}{4}$	$12\frac{5}{8}$	63
340,000	103,000	1.50	.71	.18	11	$25\frac{1}{2}$	23*	64
152,000	48,000	1.09	.76	.54	10	$16\frac{1}{2}$	$16\frac{1}{8}$	65

*Approximate market prices at April 28, 1967, and "highest since offering" have been adjusted upward for stock splits and stock dividends of 10% or more, for comparison with initial offering prices.

TABLE 4-2 (cont.)   Statistics on Selected
(July 1, 1962, to

			Number of Shares		Price to Public	
Industry Classification and Company	Offering Date	Offered	Outstanding After Offering	Per Share	Aggregate
Manufacturing (cont.)						
Household Products (cont.)						
66	Henredon Furniture ...	6/17/65	304,098	1,327,500	$ 16.75	$ 5,093,641
67	C. H. Masland & Sons..	9/21/65	250,000	1,036,680	13.50	3,375,000
68	Miller Industries	10/ 7/35	110,000	240,000	5.00	550,000
69	Springs Mills	10/27/66	675,000	8,607,843	17.00	11,475,000
70	Huffman Manu-facturing	11/15/66	250,000	858,744	12.50	3,125,000
Iron, Steel and Aluminum						
71	Wehr Corp.	4/14/64	186,000	750,000	12.00	2,232,000
72	James B. Clow	5/20/64	250,980	1,303,128	23.25	5,835,285
			10,000 emp.		21.97	219,700
73	Tyler Pipe & Foundry .	9/21/64	150,000	994,888	13.50	2,025,000
74	Diversified Metals	3/ 2/66	275,000	1,012,897	9.00	2,475,000
75	U. S. Reduction	3/17/66	320,000	794,468	15.25	4,880,000
76	Proler Steel	6/29/66	400,000	1,615,000	20.00	8,000,000
Machinery and Equipment						
77	Berns Air King	5/15/63	100,000	350,000	7.50	750,000
78	Landis Tool Co.	6/24/65	110,000	878,608	66.00	7,260,000
79	Cascade Corp.	7/12/65	200,000	728,680	11.00	2,200,000
80	Keuffel & Esser	9/14/65	250,000	1,280,000	26.00	6,500,000
			40,000 emp.		23.40	936,000
81	Process Plants	12/15/65	200,000	1,040,000	5.50	1,100,000
82	Kliklok Corp.	12/20/65	270,000	1,500,000	11.00	2,970,000
83	Raymond Corp.	4/ 5/66	240,000	818,205	15.00	3,600,000
84	Stapling Machines	4/19/66	230,000	898,784	15.25	3,507,500
85	Voss Engineering	5/ 5/66	100,000	450,000	10.00	1,000,000
86	Tridair Industries	6/16/66	110,000	497,520	16.00	1,760,000
87	Vermont American	7/21/66	200,000	1,104,285	13.50	2,700,000
88	Penn Engineering	12/ 6/66	260,000 min.	815,000	10.00	2,600,000
Office Furniture and Equipment						
89	Acme Visible Records .	7/ 2/63	150,000	622,069	16.00	2,400,000
90	Home-O-Nize Co.	4/20/66	20,000	258,407	35.00	700,000
Printing and Publishing						
91	Scripps-Howard	4/ 3/63	375,000	2,588,750	19.25	7,218,750
92	Dow Jones	5/28/63	103,500	1,562,200	112.00	11,592,000
			6,500 emp.		107.00	695,500
93	Safran Printing	6/11/63	225,720	553,476	16.25	3,667,950
94	Baltimore Bus. Forms .	11/15/65	150,000	591,600	8.00	1,200,000
95	De Luxe Check Print...	12/ 8/65	300,000	2,957,656	21.50	6,450,000
96	Richmond Newspapers	5/26/66	350,983	1,438,423	22.00	7,721,626

emp. = shares offered to employees.
min. = minimum number of shares.

Initial Public Offerings of Common Stock
December 31, 1966)

Underwriters' Discounts and Commissions	Estimated Expenses	Earnings per Share for Fiscal Years Prior to Offering			P/E Ratio—Fiscal Year Prior to Offering	Approximate Market Price		
		Latest	First Prior	Second Prior		Highest Since Offering	April 28, 1967	
$ 364,918	$ 48,000	$1.29	$ .83	$ .58	13	$ 25	$ 17	66
275,000	78,500	1.07	.56	.87	13	$15\frac{1}{2}$	$9\frac{1}{4}$	67
55,000	51,780	.66	.27	—	8	5	4	68
742,500	95,000	2.48	2.18	1.66	7	$19\frac{7}{8}$	$18\frac{3}{8}$	69
250,000	73,000	1.41	1.53	1.28	9	$17\frac{1}{2}$	$16\frac{1}{4}$	70
204,600	40,000	1.63	—	—	7	$22\frac{3}{4}$	$17\frac{1}{2}$*	71
321,254	76,025	2.10	1.78	1.83	11	$27\frac{1}{2}$	$27\frac{3}{8}$	72
172,500	42,000	1.22	1.14	1.36	11	$14\frac{1}{4}$	$12\frac{1}{4}$	73
198,000	61,070	.84	.40	.18	11	$61\frac{1}{2}$	$42\frac{7}{8}$	74
416,000	73,000	1.71	.63	.50	9	$18\frac{3}{8}$	15	75
540,000	112,500	1.60	1.63	.99	12	$21\frac{7}{8}$	$21\frac{3}{4}$	76
75,000	32,500	.91	.88	.86	8	14	10*	77
385,000	107,000	5.83	3.96	3.40	11	$84\frac{1}{2}$	80*	78
150,000	39,500	.87	.69	.53	13	$17\frac{1}{4}$	$13\frac{3}{4}$	79
375,000	110,950	1.25	.92	.92	21	$42\frac{1}{4}$	$41\frac{3}{8}$	80
110,000	60,000	.42	(.03)	.07	13	$12\frac{1}{4}$	$12\frac{1}{8}$	81
270,000	59,000	.61	.57	.49	18	12	$11\frac{1}{2}$	82
288,000	65,000	1.26	.94	.78	12	21	$19\frac{3}{4}$	83
287,500	74,500	1.40	.90	1.09	11	$22\frac{1}{2}$	$20\frac{1}{4}$	84
85,000	58,600	.97	.70	.26	10	$12\frac{5}{8}$	$12\frac{5}{8}$	85
121,000	54,700	.81	.63	.62	20	55	$54\frac{1}{2}$	86
200,000	62,300	1.06	.79	.67	13	$13\frac{3}{4}$	$13\frac{3}{4}$	87
234,000	56,565	.76	.51	.37	13	$25\frac{1}{8}$	$24\frac{5}{8}$	88
180,000	64,798	1.19	.75	—	14	$76\frac{1}{8}$	$76\frac{1}{8}$*	89
56,000	23,000	3.11	2.19	1.58	11	$37\frac{1}{2}$	$37\frac{1}{2}$	90
468,750	96,000	1.20	1.09	1.04	16	35	33	91
517,500	105,000	4.17	4.34	4.08	27	$292\frac{1}{2}$	$282\frac{3}{8}$*	92
293,436	62,500	1.18	.89	.78	14	26	$17\frac{1}{4}$	93
112,500	64,008	.51	—	.04	16	$8\frac{1}{4}$	$8\frac{1}{4}$	94
420,000	57,312	1.23	.95	.95	17	$28\frac{1}{4}$	$19\frac{5}{8}$	95
526,474	94,900	1.37	1.22	1.18	16	$22\frac{1}{2}$	$22\frac{1}{2}$	96

*Approximate market prices at April 28, 1967, and "highest since offering" have been adjusted upward for stock splits and stock dividends of 10% or more, for comparison with initial offering prices.

TABLE 4-2 (cont.) Statistics on Selected

(July 1, 1962, to

		Number of Shares		Price to Public	
Industry Classification and Company	Offering Date	Offered	Outstanding After Offering	Per Share	Aggregate
Manufacturing (cont.)					
Transportation Equipment					
97 General Automotive Parts	5/ 7/63	200,000	1,352,661	$ 12.50	$ 2,500,000
98 Keystone Railway Equip.	10/28/64	200,000	495,000	16.00	3,200,000
99 Lear Jet	11/30/64	500,000	2,000,000	10.00	5,000,000
100 Fleetwood Enterprises.	3/ 4/65	250,000	565,000	10.00	2,500,000
101 Tenna Corp.	11/10/65	160,000	590,911	12.25	1,960,000
102 R. J. Enstrom Corp. ...	1/31/66	100,000	254,715	12.00	1,200,000
Miscellaneous Products					
103 Mosler Safe	9/11/62	260,000	1,654,519	13.50	3,510,000
104 Pak–Well Paper	3/25/63	153,620	750,000	11.50	1,766,630
105 J. L. Clark Mfg.	2/26/64	155,600	800,000	15.00	2,334,000
		30,000 emp.		13.90	417,000
106 Cyclotron Corp.	11/16/65	100,000	150,000	10.00	1,000,000
107 Automatic Sprinkler ...	11/17/65	242,210	1,211,750	19.50	4,723,095
108 American Welding & Mfg.	3/24/66	365,400	900,000	20.00	7,308,000
Communications and Transportation					
Communications					
109 Subscription TV	10/30/63	1,700,000	3,028,972	12.00	20,400,000
110 Cox Broadcasting	4/21/64	665,231	2,650,000	16.25	10,810,004
		20,000 emp.		15.05	301,000
111 Communications Satel.	6/ 2/64	5,000,000	5,000,000	20.00	100,000,000
		5,000,000 †	5,000,000	20.00	100,000,000
112 Lin Broadcasting	3/24/66	200,000	523,093	8.50	1,700,000
Transportation					
Air					
113 Pac. Southwest Air...	2/13/63	313,000	509,000	19.00	5,947,000
114 Trans Internat. Air...	4/28/65	224,000	1,047,360	10.375	2,324,000
115 Airborne Freight	9/ 8/65	323,000	845,850	5.00	1,615,000
116 World Airways	4/18/66	975,000	5,000,000	25.00	24,375,000
Other					
117 Twenty Grand Marine	7/ 7/65	300,000	1,022,434	17.00	5,100,000
118 Chemical Leaman Tank	10/13/65	250,000	930,192	10.00	2,500,000
119 Wilson Freight	2/23/66	200,000	846,000	12.50	2,500,000

emp. = shares offered to employees.
† Shares subscribed to by authorized communications carriers.

Initial Public Offerings of Common Stock
December 31, 1966)

Underwriters' Discounts and Commissions	Estimated Expenses	Earnings per Share for Fiscal Years Prior to Offering			P/E Ratio— Fiscal Year Prior to Offering	Approximate Market Price		
		Latest	First Prior	Second Prior		Highest Since Offering	April 28, 1967	
$ 200,000	$ 40,000	$1.11	$1.05	$ .83	11	$ $15\frac{3}{4}$	$ $11\frac{1}{2}$	97
320,000	35,500	2.03	.99	.06	8	57	$37\frac{3}{4}$*	98
450,000	140,000	New company				$83\frac{1}{2}$	$25\frac{1}{8}$	99
200,000	56,250	.57	.57	.54	17	$11\frac{1}{4}$	$11\frac{1}{4}$	100
166,400	81,400	1.57	1.16	.72	8	$17\frac{3}{8}$	$11\frac{3}{4}$	101
120,000	50,000	Losses since inception			—	12	11	102
260,000	226,000	.93	.48	.24	15	43	$42\frac{3}{8}$*	103
138,258	75,615	1.01	.87	.86	11	$18\frac{3}{4}$	$18\frac{1}{4}$	104
171,160	36,000	1.29	1.13	.93	12	$22\frac{1}{2}$	$20\frac{1}{4}$	105
100,000	24,000	New company				$14\frac{1}{2}$	$8\frac{3}{8}$	106
399,646	100,400	1.01	—	—	19	$99\frac{3}{8}$	94*	107
584,640	55,500	2.51	1.11	.80	8	$45\frac{1}{4}$	$37\frac{7}{8}$	108
1,375,500	155,000	New company				15	$2\frac{1}{2}$	109
798,277	107,500	1.04	.97	.71	16	55	$52\frac{1}{4}$	110
4,000,000	650,000	New company				$71\frac{1}{2}$	$68\frac{3}{4}$	111
144,000	67,000	.56	.30	.20	15	$18\frac{3}{8}$	$18\frac{1}{2}$	112
500,800	64,750	2.84	.78	—	7	141	$135\frac{3}{4}$	113
185,920	70,000	1.05	1.18	.82	10	$110\frac{1}{4}$	$110\frac{1}{4}$	114
151,810	30,000	.29	.30	.20	17	$20\frac{3}{8}$	$16\frac{1}{4}$	115
1,462,500	133,625	1.39	.81	.28	18	64	$57\frac{7}{8}$	116
375,000	86,100	1.00	.74	.32	17	$22\frac{5}{8}$	$20\frac{3}{8}$	117
205,627	35,000	1.06	1.04	.96	9	$18\frac{3}{4}$	$13\frac{1}{4}$	118
200,000	50,000	1.39	1.01	.76	9	$12\frac{7}{8}$	$9\frac{1}{4}$	119

*Approximate market prices at April 28, 1967, and "highest since offering" have been adjusted upward for stock splits and stock dividends of 10% or more, for comparison with initial offering prices.

TABLE 4–2 (cont.)   Statistics on Selected

(July 1, 1962, to

	Industry Classification and Company	Offering Date	Number of Shares		Price to Public	
			Offered	Outstanding After Offering	Per Share	Aggregate
	Retail Trade					
	Drug Stores					
120	Revco D. S. Inc.	11/18/64	224,800	556,500	$ 18.75	$ 4,215,000
121	Eckerd Drugs	6/23/65	350,000	1,439,188	22.00	7,700,000
122	White Cross Stores	9/ 9/65	400,000	1,000,000	22.50	9,000,000
123	Skaggs Drug Center	11/10/65	355,347	1,896,232	18.25	6,485,083
124	Cole Drug Co.	7/ 6/66	175,000	468,400	13.50	2,362,500
	Food Stores					
125	Stater Bros.	2/18/65	250,000	1,339,920	18.00	4,500,000
126	Weis Markets	3/ 2/65	611,000	3,055,000	21.00	12,831,000
127	Star Supermarkets.......	6/15/65	350,000	602,320	14.00	4,900,000
128	Village Supermarkets ..	8/10/65	100,000	500,000	8.50	850,000
129	Foodarama Super- markets	9/14/65	160,000	1,000,000	12.75	2,040,000
130	Applebaum's Food Mkts.	10/13/65	240,000	800,000	13.50	3,240,000
131	Harvest Markets	4/28/66	210,000	556,000	12.00	2,520,000
	Other Retail and Discount Stores					
132	Miracle Mart	9/19/62	180,000	450,009	10.00	1,800,000
133	Zayre Corp.	9/26/62	350,000	1,681,500	12.00	4,200,000
134	Automatique	6/27/63	254,975	955,230	7.50	1,912,312
135	Mammoth Mart	12/ 1/64	200,000	500,000	10.00	2,000,000
136	Roos/Atkins	5/18/65	212,000	931,493	12.75	2,703,000
137	Hardlines Distr.	6/14/65	300,000	700,000	16.50	4,950,000
138	Cornelius Co.	7/29/65	207,000	749,000	18.00	3,726,000
139	Merco Enterprises	8/ 9/65	140,000	350,000	9.25	1,295,000
140	Morton's Shoe Stores ..	3/24/66	400,000	1,000,000	8.00	3,200,000
141	Barbara Lynn Stores ...	6/21/66	310,000	828,500	8.50	2,635,000
142	Jamesway Corp.	6/14/66	142,000	522,746	7.50	1,065,000
143	Gaylords National	6/29/66	255,000	628,304	11.50	2,932,500
144	Sperry & Hutchinson ..	4/27/66	950,000	10,603,372	33.00	31,350,000
			50,000 emp.		31.35	1,567,500
	Restaurants					
145	Denny's Restaurants ...	10/21/63	167,000	555,556	10.00	1,670,000
146	McDonalds Corp.	4/20/65	285,000	1,500,000	22.50	6,412,500
			15,000 emp.		21.00	315,000
147	Royal Castle System ...	9/14/65	360,000	1,187,700	19.00	6,650,000
148	Jack in the Box	11/23/65	270,000	1,020,000	12.50	3,375,000
149	Aristo Foods	2/ 9/66	100,000	267,500	10.00	1,000,000
150	Fred Harvey	5/18/66	159,500	484,800	17.75	2,831,125
			3,000 emp.		16.51	49,530

emp. = shares offered to employees.

Initial Public Offerings of Common Stock
December 31, 1966)

Underwriters' Discounts and Commissions	Estimated Expenses	Earnings per Share for Fiscal Years Prior to Offering			P/E Ratio— Fiscal Year Prior to Offering	Approximate Market Price		
		Latest	First Prior	Second Prior		Highest Since Offering	April 28, 1967	
$ 314,720	$ 51,600	$1.37	$1.27	($ .62)	14	$ 40	$ $36\frac{1}{2}$*	120
462,000	60,000	1.16	.71	.52	19	$25\frac{3}{8}$	$25\frac{3}{8}$	121
560,000	125,000	1.58	.69	.10	14	$40\frac{1}{2}$	$40\frac{1}{4}$	122
390,882	96,000	.89	.58	.57	20	$19\frac{3}{4}$	$19\frac{3}{4}$	123
210,000	53,000	1.03	.69	.30	13	14	11	124
330,000	52,000	1.26	.90	.73	14	$23\frac{3}{8}$	$14\frac{1}{2}$	125
824,850	90,133	1.21	.89	.84	17	$23\frac{7}{8}$	$19\frac{3}{4}$	126
367,500	98,000	1.14	.72	1.08	12	$15\frac{5}{8}$	$7\frac{5}{8}$	127
65,000	34,600	.75	.62	.41	11	$15\frac{1}{2}$	$7\frac{1}{8}$	128
152,000	60,258	.71	.42	.28	18	$24\frac{1}{4}$	$15\frac{1}{2}$	129
194,400	90,000	.95	.76	.24	14	$13\frac{3}{4}$	$11\frac{1}{2}$	130
210,000	85,504	.97	.33	.39	12	$11\frac{3}{4}$	$8\frac{3}{4}$	131
162,000	58,000	1.04	.58	.08	10	$10\frac{1}{4}$	$1\frac{1}{2}$	132
315,000	108,000	.75	.36	.29	16	$58\frac{1}{8}$	$51\frac{1}{4}$*	133
173,383	110,000	.39	—	—	19	$7\frac{1}{4}$	$4\frac{1}{2}$	134
170,000	40,000	.85	.44	.67	12	$23\frac{3}{8}$	$19\frac{5}{8}$*	135
212,000	95,358	1.05	.41	—	12	$14\frac{1}{4}$	Merged	136
390,000	81,000	1.73	1.10	.43	10	$16\frac{3}{4}$	Merged	137
283,590	40,500	1.69	1.16	.59	11	$47\frac{7}{8}$	$47\frac{7}{8}$	138
129,500	38,868	.88	.52	.70	11	$9\frac{3}{4}$	$9\frac{3}{4}$	139
240,000	59,500	.90	.51	.09	9	$8\frac{1}{8}$	$7\frac{1}{4}$	140
237,150	89,000	1.07	.58	.40	8	$12\frac{1}{8}$	$11\frac{1}{8}$	141
85,200	51,500	.99	.63	.41	8	$8\frac{1}{8}$	8	142
255,000	87,500	1.37	1.02	.39	8	$13\frac{3}{4}$	$13\frac{3}{4}$*	143
1,567,500	35,000	2.16	1.82	1.31	15	$33\frac{1}{4}$	26	144
150,300	80,000	1.18	.69	.36	9	$66\frac{3}{4}$	$62\frac{1}{2}$*	145
427,500	89,325	1.34	.70	.29	17	78	74*	146
420,000	42,000	.95	.69	.59	20	$19\frac{7}{8}$	$6\frac{7}{8}$	147
270,000	65,000	.61	.11	.13	20	$25\frac{3}{8}$	$25\frac{3}{8}$	148
80,000	31,500	1.60	1.41	1.39	6	13	$9\frac{1}{4}$	149
197,780	45,875	1.54	.98	.94	11	$23\frac{1}{4}$	$23\frac{1}{4}$	150

*Approximate market prices at April 28, 1967, and "highest since offering" have been adjusted upward for stock splits and stock dividends of 10% or more, for comparison with initial offering prices.

TABLE 4-2 (cont.)   Statistics on Selected
(July 1, 1962, to

	Industry Classification and Company	Offering Date	Number of Shares		Price to Public	
			Offered	Outstanding After Offering	Per Share	Aggregate
	Finance, Insurance, etc.					
	Financial Institutions					
151	American Savings & Loan	2/12/63	242,581	823,115	$ 8.00	$ 1,940,648
152	Florida Bankgrowth	2/14/63	250,000	350,000	12.625	3,156,250
153	Pacific Savings & Loan	3/13/63	171,002	937,440	15.75	2,693,282
154	Southeastern Mortgage	6/10/63	1,000,000	1,000,000	10.00	10,000,000
155	Travelers Express	6/24/63	267,740	694,944	13.50	3,614,490
156	Buttonwood Capital....	9/22/64	100,000	104,040	25.00	2,500,000
157	Capital Bankshares	4/14/65	243,333 min.	550,000	10.00	3,433,330
158	First Bancorporation ..	5/13/65	200,000	1,201,000	11.00	2,200,000
	Insurance Companies					
159	Superior Benefit Life ..	6/24/63	600,000	917,000	2.50	1,500,000
160	Sun Life	3/24/64	320,000	1,708,000	42.50	13,600,000
161	Louisiana & Sou. Life..	6/17/64	525,000	885,500	10.00	5,250,000
162	Windsor Life	12/ 9/64	625,000	625,000	5.00	3,125,000
163	American Presidents Life	12/14/64	2,000,000	2,000,000	5.00	10,000,000
164	First American Title ...	12/23/64	250,107	843,516	14.00	3,501,498
165	Volkswagen Insurance Co.	12/23/64	727,275	909,093	12.00	8,727,300
166	Minn. National Life	4/22/65	600,000	700,000	10.00	6,000,000
167	Time Insurance Co.	4/13/66	107,543	546,000	45.00	4,839,435
	Equipment Operators and Lessors					
168	Granite Equip. Leasing	6/20/66	240,000	725,604	5.00	1,200,000
169	Solon Automat. Serv...	7/28/66	104,000	852,500	5.50	572,000
	Services					
	Advertising Firms					
170	Foote, Cone & Belding	9/10/63	475,000	1,744,609	15.50	7,362,500
			25,000 emp.		14.45	361,250
171	Doyle, Dane, Bernbach	8/24/64	222,080	256,750	27.00	5,996,160
			25,000 emp.		25.38	634,500
172	John Blair	12/ 9/65	345,000	1,066,870	22.50	7,762,500
173	Ogilvy & Mather..........	4/26/66	349,883	1,086,601	22.00	7,697,426
	Audio-Visual Services					
174	Wilding Inc.	4/15/64	200,000	399,420	15.50	3,100,000
175	Inflight Motion Pict. ...	2/17/66	225,455	664,000	18.50	4,170,917
176	Maryland Telecom.	4/ 4/66	145,000	482,380	8.00	1,160,000
177	Superscope Inc.	5/20/66	290,000	1,200,000	10.00	2,900,000
178	Riker Video	6/22/66	135,000	465,000	7.50	1,012,500
179	Graphic Controls.........	8/ 4/66	290,000	790,148	13.00	3,770,000
180	Visual Electronics	10/20/66	170,000	1,030,000	10.00	1,700,000

emp. = shares offered to employees.
min. = minimum number of shares.

Initial Public Offerings of Common Stock
December 31, 1966)

Underwriters' Discounts and Commissions	Estimated Expenses	Earnings per Share for Fiscal Years Prior to Offering			P/E Ratio— Fiscal Year Prior to Offering	Approximate Market Price		
		Latest	First Prior	Second Prior		Highest Since Offering	April 28, 1967	
$ 164,955	$ 20,000	$ .90	$ .92	$ .84	9	$ 8	$ 5$\frac{1}{2}$	151
265,000	50,000	New company				12$\frac{5}{8}$	9$\frac{5}{8}$	152
192,377	38,500	1.86	1.22	.91	8	19$\frac{1}{4}$	13$\frac{1}{4}$	153
1,000,000	320,000	New company				12	6	154
294,514	77,500	1.01	.23	.09	13	17$\frac{3}{4}$	Merged	155
100,000	27,000	—	New company	—	—	25	Liquid.	156
291,833	95,000	.21	—	—	48	11	10$\frac{7}{8}$	157
180,000	39,000	.64	.59	.50	17	11	5$\frac{5}{8}$	158
135,000	15,000	New company				2$\frac{1}{2}$	$\frac{3}{4}$	159
816,000	117,000	1.15	1.18	.95	37	49$\frac{1}{4}$	25$\frac{3}{4}$	160
472,500	48,000	New company				18$\frac{3}{8}$	8$\frac{3}{4}$	161
312,500	28,000	New company				15$\frac{1}{2}$	8$\frac{3}{4}$	162
1,200,000	45,000	New company				7	2$\frac{1}{4}$	163
227,597	103,500	1.68	.96	.85	8	14$\frac{1}{4}$	7$\frac{3}{4}$	164
727,275	65,000	Losses since inception			—	11$\frac{7}{8}$	9$\frac{1}{4}$	165
120,000	46,200	New company				10	8$\frac{1}{2}$	166
365,646	42,896	2.85	.58	.82	16	45	35	167
120,000	50,000	.21	.13	.06	25	29$\frac{3}{8}$	29$\frac{3}{8}$	168
57,200	24,000	.33	.19	.12	17	5$\frac{1}{2}$	4	169
498,750	148,000	.81	.79	.68	19	24$\frac{3}{4}$	23$\frac{3}{4}$*	170
359,770	70,000	.81	.42	.23	33	75$\frac{1}{4}$	68$\frac{3}{4}$*	171
465,750	66,134	1.51	1.30	1.34	15	26$\frac{1}{4}$	23$\frac{1}{8}$	172
472,342	154,425	1.31	.97	.47	17	23	17$\frac{3}{4}$	173
232,000	50,000	1.29	.72	.12	12	15$\frac{3}{4}$	15$\frac{1}{2}$	174
311,128	86,240	.78	.29	(.17)	24	26$\frac{1}{4}$	16$\frac{5}{8}$	175
92,800	22,800	.43	.38	.24	19	18$\frac{1}{2}$	16$\frac{1}{2}$	176
232,000	54,000	.62	.43	.34	16	18$\frac{3}{4}$	17$\frac{3}{4}$	177
101,250	58,000	.50	.28	—	15	37$\frac{1}{2}$	36$\frac{1}{2}$	178
304,500	63,844	.99	.91	.73	13	27$\frac{3}{4}$	27$\frac{5}{8}$	179
153,000	63,000	.56	.06	.02	18	24$\frac{3}{4}$	22$\frac{3}{4}$	180

*Approximate market prices at April 28, 1967, and "highest since offering" have been adjusted upward for stock splits and stock dividends of 10% or more, for comparison with initial offering prices.

TABLE 4–2 (cont.)   Statistics on Selected
(July 1, 1962, to

	Industry Classification and Company	Offering Date	Number of Shares		Price to Public	
			Offered	Outstanding After Offering	Per Share	Aggregate
	Services (cont.)					
	Computer and Allied Services					
181	Computer Sciences	9/19/63	200,000	815,000	$ 12.50	$ 2,500,000
182	University Computing .	9/ 9/65	250,000 min.	805,000	4.50	1,125,000
183	Applied Data Research	9/21/65	120,000	471,520	5.50	660,000
184	Redcor	10/26/65	157,170	279,150	11.50	1,807,455
185	Tabulating Business	11/ 9/65	100,000	400,000	6.50	650,000
186	Technology Inc.	11/22/65	95,000	311,000	12.00	1,140,000
187	Dynamic Research	12/ 8/65	150,000	311,274	12.50	1,875,000
188	Data Process. Financial	12/ 8/65	300,000	1,245,000	11.00	3,300,000
189	Digitek Corp.	1/20/66	80,000	399,000	6.00	480,000
190	Systems Engineering ...	3/16/66	120,000	927,749	7.00	840,000
191	Electronic Memories ...	3/29/66	137,500	757,120	13.00	1,787,500
192	Infotronics Corp.	4/ 5/66	80,000	491,018	7.50	600,000
193	Randolph Computer ...	4/13/66	100,000	527,500	20.00	2,000,000
194	Informatics Inc.	5/10/66	70,000	566,000	7.50	525,000
195	G. C. Computer	8/17/66	500,000	3,700,000	20.00	10,000,000
196	Computax Services	9/26/66	60,000 min.	1,370,001	19.50	1,170,000
	Miscellaneous Services					
197	Murphy Pacific Marine	1/25/66	360,000 min.	649,940	10.00	3,600,000
198	Sales Follow-up Corp.	3/ 3/66	100,000	393,000	8.75	875,000
199	Wackenhut Corp.	4/26/66	247,300	921,000	12.50	2,918,750
200	Medicenters of America	7/21/66	150,000	467,000	10.00	1,500,000

min. = minimum number of shares.

ber 1962, following the market collapse in May of that year, and in the bull market during the year 1965.

The following median price–earnings ratios, for industries having the larger number of companies included in the study, support the view that industry popularity, or the lack thereof, influences offering prices: computer and allied services 21, chemical products 18, electronics and components 18, machinery and

Initial Public Offerings of Common Stock

December 31, 1966)

Underwriters' Discounts and Commissions	Estimated Expenses	Earnings per Share for Fiscal Years Prior to Offering: Latest	Earnings per Share for Fiscal Years Prior to Offering: First Prior	Earnings per Share for Fiscal Years Prior to Offering: Second Prior	P/E Ratio—Fiscal Year Prior to Offering	Approximate Market Price: Highest Since Offering	Approximate Market Price: April 28, 1967	
$ 212,000	$ 43,125	$ .61	$ .20	$ .09	20	$114	$\$110\frac{5}{8}$*	181
101,250	35,000	.19	—	—	24	63	63	182
66,000	40,000	.30	(.35)	(.19)	18	$10\frac{7}{8}$	$6\frac{3}{8}$	183
149,311	38,600	1.07	.79	.11	10	21	$7\frac{1}{2}$	184
65,000	42,500	.37	.35	.15	18	$10\frac{1}{4}$	8	185
95,000	23,000	.76	.40	.19	16	$27\frac{1}{4}$	$24\frac{1}{4}$	186
165,000	45,000	.59	.57	.43	21	$12\frac{3}{4}$	$5\frac{1}{4}$	187
300,000	66,810	.18	.04	.02	61	$63\frac{5}{8}$	$57\frac{1}{2}$	188
38,400	14,000	.15	.07	.03	40	13	$7\frac{1}{2}$	189
72,000	72,000	.67	.36	.26	10	$26\frac{1}{4}$	25	190
116,875	38,500	.66	.46	.23	20	26	22	191
44,800	29,000	.30	.26	(.04)	25	18	$17\frac{1}{4}$	192
150,000	38,000		New company			$57\frac{1}{2}$	$55\frac{1}{4}$	193
42,000	53,555	.37	.19	.15	30	$22\frac{1}{2}$	$23\frac{1}{4}$	194
667,000	69,000	.61	.27	.09	33	41	33	195
105,000	70,000		New company			28	$17\frac{1}{4}$	196
306,000	75,000		New company			$15\frac{5}{8}$	$14\frac{3}{4}$	197
75,000	29,000	.60	.11	.08	15	$14\frac{1}{4}$	$8\frac{5}{8}$	198
210,150	53,500	.86	.43	.36	15	$12\frac{1}{2}$	$9\frac{1}{4}$	199
127,500	38,000		New company			45	$40\frac{1}{2}$	200

*Approximate market prices at April 28, 1967, and "highest since offering" have been adjusted upward for stock splits and stock dividends of 10% or more, for comparison with initial offering prices.

equipment 13, food products 12, apparel 11, other retail and discount stores 11, and household products 10.

The number of shares of common stock offered, relative to the total to be outstanding after the public offerings, ranged from approximately 6% to a high of 100% in some newly formed companies. Most initial offerings were in the range of 20% to 40% of the total shares to be outstanding. Where a company had more than one class of common stock outstanding or to be outstanding, these were combined in Table 4–2.

Only 8 of the 200 offerings were on a "best efforts" basis. The remainder were covered by generally conventional underwriting arrangements. As shown in the table, most of the offerings involved a substantial number of shares. In two smaller issues, the offeree was warned that, in view of the limited number of shares being offered, there was no assurance that an established market would develop upon completion of the offerings.

Where a security offering was considered speculative, the Securities and Exchange Commission required that this be indicated in the offering prospectus. Some 20 prospectuses designated that the securities were offered as a speculation or involved more than the usual element of risk.

Company Offerings and Offerings by Stockholders. Of the total offerings, 57 were by selling stockholders alone, 87 included company and selling stockholders' stock, and in only 56 cases (of which 17 were new companies) was company stock alone offered. These statistics are not surprising because principal stockholders in a closely held company invariably reach a position where they not only wish to establish a market for their stock for gift, trust, and estate tax purposes, but also desire the protection generally afforded by diversification of investments.

Shares Reserved for "Insiders." In almost half of the offerings, some shares were reserved, usually for a limited time, for purchase by officers, directors, and employees, and, in a number of instances, by business associates. In some cases such shares could be purchased net of the underwriter's commission, and in others no such concession was granted. In approximately 10% of the offerings, underwriters were granted purchase warrants or options, or otherwise were recipients of special concessions for the purchase of the issuers' stock, in addition to cash underwriting discounts or commissions. This is not a common arrangement, inasmuch as the majority of such concessions were made to one underwriting house.

"After-Market" Action of Offerings. With few exceptions, issues subsequently reached a higher price than that at which they were initially offered. However, in some cases this may have been due to stabilizing operations by the underwriters.

The following tabulation shows how the 200 issues fared in the "after-market," by comparing adjusted offering prices to approximate market prices at April 28, 1967:

		Year of Offering			
	Total	1966	1965	1964	1963	1962 (six months)
Market—April 28, 1967:						
Above offering price	128	43	44	18	18	5
Below offering price	64	21	25	8	9	1
Same as offering price........	1			1		
Merged or acquired, etc.	7		3	1	3	
	200	64	72	28	30	6

Approximate market prices at April 28, 1967, and "highest since offering" prices shown in Table 4–2, have been adjusted upward for stock splits and stock dividends of 10% or more, for comparison with initial offering prices. On actively traded stocks such prices were computed from Standard & Poor's "Stock Guide." Prices used on less active stocks were obtained generally by reference to copies of "The National Monthly Stock Summary." [16] Since only bid prices are used in compiling ranges in the latter publication, it is possible that transactions have taken place at higher prices than those quoted.

Of the 64 companies whose stocks, at April 28, 1967, were selling below the adjusted offering prices, such market action, in a number of cases, appeared due to poorer earnings (estimated) for the latest twelve-month period to April 28, 1967. In others, such as chain food stores, insurance companies, and financial institutions, lower market prices generally prevailed because of the investing public's unfavorable view of the prospects of such industries at that time.

Earnings Figures Shown in Prospectuses. Historical earnings figures shown in prospectuses were used in Table 4–2, except in

[16] National Quotation Bureau, "The National Monthly Stock Summary."

instances where it appeared that "pro forma earnings" had more significance in computing price–earnings ratios.

It was difficult to determine where substantially improved interim earnings, subsequent to the latest fiscal year, resulted in a better offering price. Approximately 15% of the companies included in the study appeared to be candidates for such treatment. However, in the absence of definitive information in this regard, their price–earnings ratios have been computed in the table based on the latest year's earnings.

Offering Price Determined by Negotiation. In most cases, the public offering price was indicated to have been determined by negotiation between the company and/or selling stockholders, and the underwriters. However, in at least eleven offerings the price was said to have been "arbitrarily" determined by negotiation. Two of these went further and mentioned that such arbitrary prices were not based on earnings and assets. In one offering, the price was based "particularly on the six months interim earnings" subsequent to the latest fiscal year with a comment to the effect that there was no assurance that this rate of earnings could be maintained.

Significance of Dividend Payments. Sixty-six of the companies included in the study paid dividends prior to their public offerings. However, 58 companies that had not previously paid dividends announced initial cash dividends on the stock offered in their prospectuses, an illustration of the general importance of dividend payments to the investing public. Of the remaining 76 companies, 17 were new and 33 were in industries currently considered fast growing—electronics, computer, and audio visual services. Those that had no immediate prospects or intention of declaring dividends on the stock offered so indicated with a statement to the effect that earnings would be used for expanding working capital requirements.

Incidentally, 1,127 out of 1,267 common stocks listed on the New York Stock Exchange paid cash dividends during 1966 with a median yield of 4.1%, and 1,116 out of 1,255 listed common stocks in 1967 yielded 3.2%, based on their year-end market prices. For the ten years ended December 31, 1967, such yields varied from a high of 6.1% in 1957 to a low of 3.2% in 1965 and 1967, with a simple arithmetical average for the period of approximately 4%. In absolute figures, estimated aggregate cash dividend payments on the New York Stock Exchange common stocks increased from $8,807,000,000 in 1957 to $16,866,000,000 in 1967.[17]

Use of Several Classes of Common Stock.   Where the payment of dividends on all common shares to be outstanding might have caused a financial hardship, some companies created several classes of common stock, generally only one of which would be initially entitled to dividends. In the usual case, the other classes of stock were convertible into the dividend-paying stock, in installments over a period. Among such companies were 30 that had two classes of stock, and two with three classes. In one case, where there was a single class of common stock outstanding, the principal stockholder waived dividends for a period of years. However, federal income tax complications can arise through the use of this method of limiting dividend payments, as opposed to the safer course of creating several classes of common stock.

Lack of Significance of "Book Value."   Book value, or net equity per share, appeared to have no significance, and was not indicated in prospectuses generally, except for relatively unseasoned companies, where the immediate dilution per share of book value to offerees was substantial because of the spread between the offering price and the book value per share prior to the offering. In such cases the increment in book value per share accruing to existing stockholders as a result of the offering was also indicated.

Forbes periodically lists companies traded on the New York Stock Exchange that are selling below "book value" per share. In its September 1, 1968, issue were listed 86 such companies that sold in the previous month at discounts from "book value." Conversely, many stocks that were selling at high price–earnings multiples concurrently were quoted at five or even more times "book value."

In mid-1970, because of the depressed state of the stock market, *Forbes* found that stocks of one-third of the 1,800 public com-

---

[17] New York Stock Exchange, "1968 Fact Book."

panies reviewed were selling below book value per share. In order to get on their list for 1970 a stock had to sell around 40% or more below book value. Seventy-one companies listed on the New York Stock Exchange made this list, including some very well known ones.[18]

Table 4–3 shows a comparison of the offering prices to net assets per share, after the offering, of the 52 stocks of four industries included in Table 4–2. These industries—chemical products, electronics and components, food products, and computer and allied services—provide a reasonable field for such a comparison. The results of this study indicate the evident lack of significance of "book value" as a valuation factor.

Communications Satellite Offering. The largest public offering included in the study, and probably the most interesting, was that of Communications Satellite Corporation, which offered 10,000,-000 shares of common stock at $20 a share for aggregate gross proceeds of $200,000,000. This corporation, although not an agency of the United States Government, was authorized under the Communications Satellite Act of 1962, but the stock or the profitability of its operations was in no manner guaranteed by the government. Its stated purpose was to establish and operate a global commercial communications satellite system to be placed in orbit around the earth.

One half of the 10,000,000 shares of stock were reserved and sold to a number of communications common carriers, including American Telephone and Telegraph Company and International Telephone and Telegraph Corporation, and the remaining 5,000,-000 shares were sold to the general public.

Although this offering has not been considered in the study as speculative, three pages of the prospectus were devoted to a discussion of "The Venture and Its Risks." This issue is an example of the public's eager acceptance of a glamour stock. It was offered in June 1964 at $20 per share, shot up to $71½ during the year, declined to a low of $36¾ during 1965 and closed at $68¾ on April 28, 1967. This despite the fact that commercially profitable operations had barely been achieved in 1968.

[18] "Loaded Laggards," *Forbes*, September 1, 1968, and July 15, 1970.

TABLE 4-3 Comparison of Offering Price to Net Assets per Share After Offering

	Offering Price	Net Assets per Share*	
		Amount	Per Cent of Offering
Chemical Products:			
Cabot Corporation	$41.50	$43.00	104%
Phillip A. Hunt	6.50	1.37	21
Fisher Scientific	30.00	14.20	47
Big Three Gas	32.00	11.05	35
National Chemsearch	26.50	4.82	18
Mercury Chemical	7.50	3.52	47
Fine Organics	5.00	1.89	38
Buckbee Mears	23.00	4.04	18
Elcor Chemical	10.00	4.65	47
Computer and Allied Services:			
Computer Sciences	$12.50	$ 3.28	26%
University Computing	4.50	1.77	39
Applied Data Research	5.50	1.55	28
Redcor	11.50	4.90	43
Tabulating Business	6.50	1.89	29
Technology Inc.	12.00	5.32	44
Dynamics Research	12.50	4.45	36
Data Process. Financial	11.00	2.72	25
Digitek Corp.	6.00	1.47	25
Systems Engineering	7.00	1.83	26
Electronic Memories	13.00	3.89	30
Infotronics Corp.	7.50	2.02	27
Randolph Computer	20.00	11.21	56
Informatics Inc.	7.50	1.67	22
G. C. Computer	20.00	5.41	27
Computax Services	19.50	.28	1

	Offering Price	Net Assets per Share*	
		Amount	Per Cent of Offering
Electronics and Components:			
Computer Control	$ 8.00	$ 1.96	25%
Continental Device	5.50	1.50	27
Tektronix	19.75	4.00	20
Scientific Data Syst.	25.00	3.34	13
E. F. Johnson	15.50	5.29	34
Tracor	19.50	6.53	33
Essex Wire	25.50	19.30	76
Memorex	25.00	2.60	10
Philbrick (George A.)	16.50	2.66	16
Kearney National	10.00	4.19	42
Dickson Electronics	11.50	5.25	46
Ameco Inc.	19.00	4.66	25
General Electro Dyn.	7.00	4.34	62
Space Craft Inc.	12.50	4.34	35
K. M. Electronics	2.00	.63	32
Technitrol Inc.	16.00	3.85	24
Optical Scanning	20.00	9.48	47
Methode Electronics	12.75	3.96	31
Space Ordnance Syst.	7.00	1.42	20
Space Corp.	9.75	6.97	72
Food Products:			
Hawthorn–Melody	$22.50	$11.50	51%
International Milling	27.75	23.16	83
Spencer Packing	12.00	2.58	22
Marhoefer Packing	10.00	13.23	132
Assoc. Coca-Cola Bot.	20.75	14.80	71
Sun City Dairy	8.25	4.25	52
Havatampa Cigar	9.00	9.67	107

*Net Assets = common stockholders' equity before offering, plus proceeds to company from offering, less underwriting commissions and expenses payable by company, divided by the number of shares outstanding after the offering.

105

Lear Jet Offering. Lear Jet Corporation, another glamour stock offered late in 1964 at $10 a share, registered a high of $83½ and a low of $8¼ in the following year, and closed at $25⅛ on April 28, 1967.

Range of Underwriters' Discounts and Commissions. Underwriters' discounts and commissions ranged from a low of 2% of the gross proceeds of the offering (Communications Satellite) to 12% on proceeds of $10,000,000 from a speculative offering on a best efforts basis (American Presidents Life). The most frequent range was from 6½% to 8½% with many larger issues averaging less than the low of this range.

Other Expenses of Offerings. Estimated expenses of offerings other than underwriting costs ranged from less than 1% up to 10% of the gross proceeds of offerings. It is impracticable to establish a yardstick for legal and accounting fees and, in some cases, printing costs incidental to a public offering. One company may have minimal expenses of this nature because its legal work is current, it has had annual examinations of its financial statements by independent public accountants who have rendered their opinions, and its latest annual financial statements are current enough for a registration statement, under the 1933 Act.

Another may require extensive legal work because of having failed to seek proper advice in this regard in the past, or because there is a need for a corporate or business reorganization in order to go public. Also, accountants' fees will be substantially higher if a company has not had appropriate annual examinations by independent public accountants. Printing costs will vary depending upon the degree of care used in presenting material to the printer, the number of different proofs desired, the time allotted for the printing, and the number and nature of amendments requested, by the SEC, to the registration statement initially filed.

Where stock is being offered jointly by companies and selling stockholders, practices vary greatly in regard to expense allocations to the two groups. In some cases, the companies pay all of the expenses, or all but an allocable share of the cost of such items as filing fees, cost of stock certificates, etc. In others, expenses are allocated substantially in accordance with the ratio of shares offered by each group.

PART II

TAX VALUATIONS

5

Analysis of Rules and Regulations

CLOSELY HELD CORPORATIONS, PARTNERSHIPS, AND PROPRIETORSHIPS

The valuation of capital stocks of closely held corporations or of sole proprietorships or partnerships, for estate or gift taxes, generally presents the most perplexing problems in the field of valuations. In a public offering of common stock, or in an acquisition or merger, the de facto consummation of such transactions results in the establishment of market prices, under the "willing buyer–willing seller" concept. Although various pertinent revenue rulings use the term "fair market value" in referring to determinations of value of capital stock of closely held corporations, such valuations necessarily are hypothetical, because of the general absence of arm's-length transfers of ownership.

The Internal Revenue Code, regulations, and rulings relating to estate and gift taxes and the determination of basis for federal capital gains tax are voluminous and complex. Anyone having problems in these tax areas should not attempt to proceed without competent legal advice.

Because of the problems that arise in valuations for federal estate and gift tax purposes, special rules have been established for valuing various kinds of property or interests in property.

These cover valuations of real estate, stocks and bonds, including "those corporations the shares of which are owned by a relatively limited number of stockholders," interests in non-corporate businesses, secured and unsecured notes, cash, household and personal effects, life estates, remainder and reversionary interests, and miscellaneous other property.[1]

However, before examining these rules it will be useful to review briefly the nature of federal estate and gift taxes. The procedures available to taxpayers in valuation cases will be found at the end of this chapter.

ESTATE AND GIFT TAXES

The federal estate tax is an excise tax levied upon the transfer of a deceased person's taxable estate and is determined by applying specific tax rates thereto.[2] The taxable estate is arrived at by valuing all property or property interests of the decedent, and subtracting specified deductible items and exemptions.[3] The representative of an estate has an election to value property as of the date of the decedent's death, or, as alternatives, the date or dates of distribution within a six-month period, or six months after the date of death for remaining assets. Estate tax returns shall be filed within nine months of the decedent's death. Extensions of time for the payment of such tax may be granted for a period not exceeding twelve months, *except where the payment would result in undue hardship to the estate,* when the time for payment may be extended for a reasonable period not exceeding ten years from the normally prescribed date.[4]

The federal gift tax is an excise tax levied upon transfers of property made without adequate and full consideration.[5] The tax, although levied annually, is cumulative in effect, so that the most recent gifts are added to those previously made, after deducting applicable lifetime and annual exemptions, in determining the rate bracket. Gift tax rates are at three-fourths of those of

[1] Treas. Reg. § 20.203.1.
[2] I.R.C., § 2001.
[3] *Ibid.*, § 2051.
[4] *Ibid.*, §§ 2032, 6161.
[5] *Ibid.*, § 2512.

estate taxes, and value of gifts is determined as of the effective date of the transfer. Effective for periods after December 31, 1970, gift tax returns (with certain specified exemptions) shall be filed for each calendar quarter on or before the fifteenth day of the second month following the close of such calendar quarter.[6]

Up to a certain point, particularly in an estate of substantial value, the making of gifts during a lifetime will result in a reduction of combined gift and estate taxes. Property transferred by gift is removed from the estate, at the top tax bracket, into the lowest gift tax bracket at the commencement of a giving program. However, any property acquired by gift subsequent to December 31, 1920, has the same basis to the donee as it would in the hands of the donor, or the last preceding owner by whom it was not acquired by gift, increased by the amount of gift tax paid, with certain limitations. However, if the fair market value at the date of gift is less than the basis so derived, such fair market value will become the basis for determining loss only.[7]

There has been some consideration in Congress about revising the estate and gift tax laws, within the next few years, to impose a capital gains tax on appreciated estate assets; having the initial estate tax bracket begin with the decedent's final gift tax bracket; exempting transfers of property between husband and wife; increasing lifetime exemptions; and reducing tax rates at lower levels.

Estate Tax Code Section

Section 2031(b) of the Code, covering valuation for estate tax purposes of unlisted securities, provides for consideration of listed stocks of comparable companies:

> **Valuation of unlisted stock and securities.**—In the case of stock and securities of a corporation the value of which, by reason of their not being listed on an exchange and by reason of the absence of sales thereof, cannot be determined with reference to bid and asked prices or with reference to sales prices, the value thereof shall be determined by taking into consideration, in addition to all other factors, the value of stock or securities of corporations engaged in the same or a similar line of business which are listed on an exchange.

[6] *Ibid.,* §§ 2502, 2504, 2521.
[7] *Ibid.,* § 1015.

Estate Tax Regulations

The estate tax regulations of the Code, dealing with the valuation of stocks of closely held corporations and with business interests in partnerships and sole proprietorships, follow:

Reg. 20.2031–2–

(f) *Where selling prices or bid and asked prices are unavailable.* If the provisions of paragraphs (b), (c), and (d) of this section are inapplicable because actual sale prices and bona fide bid and asked prices are lacking, then the fair market value is to be determined by taking the following factors into consideration:

(1) In the case of corporate or other bonds, the soundness of the security, the interest yield, the date of maturity, and other relevant factors; and

(2) In the case of shares of stock, the company's net worth, prospective earning power and dividend-paying capacity, and other relevant factors.

Some of the "other relevant factors" referred to in subparagraphs (1) and (2) of this paragraph are: the good will of the business; the economic outlook in the particular industry; the company's position in the industry and its management; the degree of control of the business represented by the block of stock to be valued; and the values of securities of corporations engaged in the same or similar lines of business which are listed on a stock exchange. However, the weight to be accorded such comparisons or any other evidentiary factors considered in the determination of a value depends upon the facts of each case. Complete financial and other data upon which the valuation is based should be submitted with the return, including copies of reports of any examinations of the company made by accountants, engineers, or any technical experts as of or near the applicable valuation date.

Reg. 20.2031–3–**Valuation of interests in businesses.** The fair market value of any interest of a decedent in a business, whether a partnership or a proprietorship, is a net amount which a willing purchaser, whether an individual or a corporation, would pay for the interest to a willing seller, neither being under any compulsion to buy or to sell and both having reasonable knowledge of relevant facts. The net value is determined on the basis of all relevant factors including—

(a) A fair appraisal as of the applicable valuation date of all the assets of the business, tangible and intangible, including good will;

(b) The demonstrated earning capacity of the business; and

(c) The other factors set forth in paragraphs (f) and (h) of § 20.2031–2 relating to the valuation of corporate stock, to the extent applicable.

Special attention should be given to determining an adequate value of the good will of the business in all cases in which the decedent has not agreed, for an adequate and full consideration in money or money's worth, that his interest passes at his death to, for example, his surviving partner or partners.

Complete financial and other data upon which the valuation is based should be submitted with the return, including copies of reports in examinations of the business made by accountants, engineers, or any technical experts as of or near the applicable valuation date.

Gift Tax Regulations

The gift tax regulations [25.2512.2(f) and 25.2512.3] regarding the valuation of stocks of closely held corporations and business interests in partnerships and sole proprietorships are similar to those for estate tax valuations.

IRS RULINGS ON VALUATIONS

The Internal Revenue Service rulings for determining the valuation of closely held businesses are primarily guidelines of some of the more important factors to be considered. Rarely will the facts and circumstances in two valuation cases be so similar that they would lead to identical conclusions. A brief review of revenue rulings that have influenced valuations for federal tax purposes follows.

Early Rulings

Valuing Prohibition Law Business Losses. The Committee on Appeals and Review Memoranda issued in 1920 Appeals and Review Memorandum (ARM) 34 for the purpose of providing suggested formulas for determining the amount of intangible asset value lost as of March 1, 1913 (the effective date of the first federal income tax law) by breweries, distilleries, and related businesses, particularly those put out of business by the passage of the Eighteenth Amendment (Volstead Act). This ruling proposed three different methods for determining loss of goodwill or trademarks upon disposition of the abandonment of such assets, products, or businesses.

The third of these methods, suggested as having the widest application, consisted of a two-part formula, i.e., to allow 10% return on average tangible assets over a period of no less than five years prior to March 1, 1913, and to consider the earnings in excess of this return attributable to intangibles and capitalized at a 20% rate.

The ruling did not stop at this point, however, but went on as follows:

> The foregoing is intended to apply particularly to businesses put out of existence by the prohibition law, but will be equally applicable so far as the third formula is concerned, to other businesses of a more or less hazardous nature. In the case, however, of valuation of goodwill of a business which consists of the manufacture or sale of standard articles of everyday necessity not subject to violent fluctuations and where the hazard is not so great, the Committee is of the opinion that the figure for determination of the return on tangible assets might be reduced from 10 to 8 or 9 per cent and that the percentage for capitalization of the return upon intangibles might be reduced from 20 to 15 per cent. . . .

ARM 68, also issued in 1920, merely clarified ARM 34 to the effect that the return of 10% mentioned in the latter ruling was to be applied to the *net* tangible assets.

It is unfortunate that the Committee mentioned the tangible–intangible asset formula approach as having application to businesses other than those then affected by the Volstead Act. Through the years since its issuance, the ARM 34 formula approach has been widely used and referred to in valuing closely held corporate and non-corporate businesses. In many of those cases, other factors such as the market price of actively traded stocks in similar lines of business, or indicated earnings trends, may have been far more significant in arriving at fair market values.

Later Rulings—Closely Held and Limited Market Corporations

The next important ruling affecting the valuation for estate and gift taxes of stock in closely held corporations was Revenue Ruling 54–77 issued in 1954. This ruling recognized and discussed the many factors to be considered in the determination of "fair market value," based on experiences of the Internal Revenue Service and numerous court decisions in litigated cases. The ruling was superseded in 1959 by Revenue Ruling 59–60 which reflected certain revisions and refinements in the 1954 ruling.

Valuation Under Revenue Ruling 59–60.   Revenue Ruling 59–60 (reproduced as Appendix D) refers to the applicable section of the 1954 Internal Revenue Code and the Estate and Gift Tax Regulations that govern the valuation of stock of closely held corporations, or those where market quotations are unavailable or are so scarce that they do not reflect fair market value.

Reference is made in Revenue Ruling 59–60 to the sections of the regulations which

. . . define fair market value, in effect, as the price at which the property would change hands between a willing buyer and a willing seller when the former is not under any compulsion to buy and the latter is not under any compulsion to sell, both parties having reasonable knowledge of relevant facts. Court decisions frequently state in addition that the hypothetical buyer and seller are assumed to be able, as well as willing, to trade and to be well informed about the property and concerning the market for such property.

In Section 3 of the ruling, paragraphs .01 and .03 form part of a preamble, "Approach to Valuation," to the factors to be considered. These paragraphs follow, with appropriate comments:

.01   A determination of fair market value, being a question of fact, will depend upon the circumstances in each case. No formula can be devised that will be generally applicable to the multitude of different valuation issues arising in estate and gift tax cases. Often, an appraiser will find wide differences of opinion as to the fair market value of a particular stock. In resolving such differences, he should maintain a reasonable attitude in recognition of the fact that valuation is not an exact science. A sound valuation will be based upon all the relevant facts, but the elements of common sense, informed judgment and reasonableness must enter into the process of weighing those facts and determining their aggregate significance.

This is further supported by a statement in Section 6 that "no standard tables of capitalization rates applicable to closely held corporations can be formulated," and another in Section 7 that "no useful purpose is served by taking an average of several factors (for example, book value, capitalized earnings and capitalized dividends) and basing the valuation on the result."

.03   Valuation of securities is, in essence, a prophecy as to the future and must be based on facts available at the required date of appraisal. As a generalization, the prices of stocks which are traded in volume in a free and active market by informed persons best reflect the consensus of the investing public as to what the future holds for the corporations and industries represented. When a stock is closely held, is traded infrequently, or is traded in an erratic market, some other measure of value must be used. In many instances, the next best measure may be found in the prices at which the stocks of companies engaged in the same or a similar line of business are selling in a free and open market.

This paragraph gives recognition to the valuation of a company based on market prices of publicly owned companies. Valuation experts generally consider such comparisons to be the primary factor in valuing stock of a closely held corporation, other than an investment or real estate holding company.

Section 4 of Revenue Ruling 59–60 lists the factors to be considered in valuations, as follows:

.01   It is advisable to emphasize that in the valuation of the stock of closely held corporations or the stock of corporations where market quotations are either lacking or too scarce to be recognized, all available financial data, as well as all relevant factors affecting the fair market value, should be considered. The following factors, although not all-inclusive are fundamental and require careful analysis in each case:

(a) The nature of the business and the history of the enterprise from the inception.
(b) The economic outlook in general and the condition and outlook of the specific industry in particular.
(c) The book value of the stock and the financial condition of the business.
(d) The earning capacity of the company.
(e) The dividend-paying capacity.
(f) Whether or not the enterprise has good will or other intangible value.
(g) Sales of the stock and the size of the block of stock to be valued.
(h) The market price of stocks of corporations engaged in the same or a similar line of business having their stocks actively traded in a full and open market, either on an exchange or over-the-counter.

A review of these factors with appropriate comments and relevant case citations follows.

Nature and History of the Enterprise.   Consideration of this factor should highlight operating and financial information, product or services changes, and growth or the lack thereof over a long historical period. The importance of recent significant changes in the character of the business, and the discounting of past events unlikely to recur is emphasized.

Economic Outlook.   The importance of the condition of the general economy and particular industry prospects has been discussed earlier in this book. The discussion of this factor in the ruling emphasizes the need to know how a company is progressing vis-à-vis its competitors, and an industry's ability to compete with other industries that furnish similar or substitute products or services. Under this factor is also discussed the effect of the loss of the manager of a so-called one-man business, the absence of management succession, and the possible ameliorating effects of key man life insurance to offset such adversities. (Management loss and succession, being a specific company problem, probably should have been discussed in the ruling under "History of the Enterprise.")

Book Value and Financial Condition. It is recommended that balance sheets be obtained for several years and for a recent interim period, together with necessary supplemental schedules for review. From these data the appraiser may determine the capital structure, net worth, and financial ratios customarily regarded as significant in determining the soundness of a business enterprise.

Recognition is given to the fact that investments in securities, real estate, and other non-operating assets should be separately considered:

> In computing the book value per share of stock, assets of the investment type should be revalued on the basis of their market prices and the book value adjusted accordingly.

Unquestionably, non-operating assets should be revalued at their current market prices, but the figure thus obtained, less any potential capital gains tax liability, should be added to the value determined for the operating assets and business, and not to the book value of assets other than those of the investment type. In the usual case of a going concern, other than one with disposable assets, its fair value would best be ascertained by a capitalization of earnings, or a price–earnings ratio computation, based on a study of market prices of stocks of companies in the industry.

Furthermore, combining the words "book" and "value" is anomalous. In a going industrial company, it would be sheer chance if its fair market value and the net book equity (book value) applicable to its common stock were the same. Bonbright commented as follows on the term "book value."

In all respects the relationship between the commercial value of a business and the so-called physical values of its assets is highly indirect and uncertain. Almost never does it justify an assumption that the "values" (that is, the depreciated costs) of the latter even roughly measure the value of the former.[8]

The United States Court of Appeals in *Ketler v. Commissioner*[9] rejected book value as a primary valuation factor stating, "It is quite evident that the book value of a stock is a very unreliable basis upon which to determine the fair market value." The Court referred to the 1934 case of *Anson Evans*,[10] to the effect that "Book value frequently bears no relationship to actual cash or fair market value."

Despite the early and widespread recognition of the inadequacy of "book value" as a primary valuation factor, there have been litigated cases[11] in relatively recent years where either the Internal Revenue Service or the taxpayer contended that the fair market value of stock approximated its "book value." It is interesting to note that the courts in all such cases rejected the contention that book value approximated the fair market value of capital stock.

As mentioned in Chapter 4, some common stocks listed on the New York Stock Exchange may be selling at five or more times their underlying net book equity, at any one time, while others are selling at prices substantially below their per-share equity figures. Such market prices generally reflect the investing public's view of the earnings potential or lack thereof of the particular stocks, without regard to net book values.

Earning Capacity. It is recommended that detailed profit and loss statements be obtained and reviewed for a representative period, preferably five or more years, immediately prior to the required date of appraisal. Recognizing that potential future income is a major factor in valuing stocks of closely held corpora-

---

[8] BONBRIGHT, VALUATION OF PROPERTY 265 (1937).

[9] Ketler v. Comm'r, 196 F.2d 822 (1952).

[10] Anson Evans, 29 B.T.A. 710 (1934).

[11] Among these were Colonial Trust Co. v. Kraemer, 63 F. Supp. 866 (D. Conn. 1945); Bartram, Exec. v. Graham, Admx., 157 F. Supp. 757 (D. Conn. 1957); Estate of Dorothy Cookson, 24 T.C.M. 1776 (1965); Estate of Samuel E. Montgomery, 12 T.C.M. 1380 (1953); Estate of Mary K. Miller, 18 T.C.M. 1127 (1959).

tions, Revenue Ruling 59–60 suggests a review of prior earnings as an approach to predicting the future. Officers' salaries and contributions made are singled out for a review as to reasonableness. Also, non-recurring items of income and expense and the possible abandonment of loss lines of business with benefit to the company are considered as affecting potential earnings.

Resort to arbitrary five- or ten-year averages of earnings to project future trends is decried, and recognition is given to the fact that the most recent year's earnings may be more significant for this purpose in appropriate cases.

Prospective earnings is acknowledged by valuation experts to be the most important factor in valuing operating companies whose worth is generally dependent upon continuation as a going concern. As indicated in the preceding chapter, investment bankers in valuing an industrial common stock for an initial public offering will generally compute its value at a price–earnings ratio based on the latest year's earnings. "Book value" is of significance only to the extent that the net assets of the company are sufficient to support a continuance of such earnings.

Among the cases [12] in which earnings was determined to be the most important factor in valuing the capital stock of a corporation are the following:

1. *Daniels v. United States:* "However, of these [asset values, etc.] factors, earnings reflect most of the other factors listed and are therefore often the most reliable guide to the value of the stock. The value of corporate shares is determined more by what income they will bring than by any other single consideration." [62–2 U. S. TAX CAS. 12,113 (D. Ore. 1961)] (This case is reviewed in Chapter 7.)

2. *Bader, Exec. v. United States:* "I am certain the investor is inclined to give earnings power and dividend prospects much more weight in appraising the worth of any security. What the buyer is acquiring are the profits and dividends which the business will provide in the future." [172 F. Supp. 833 (S.D. Ill. 1959)]

---

[12] Additional cases are: Central Trust Co. v. United States, 305 F.2d 393 (Ct. Cl. 1962); O'Malley v. Ames, 197 F.2d 256 (8th Cir. 1952); Estate of J. L. Snyder, 285 F.2d 857 (4th Cir. 1961); Inga Bardahl, 24 T.C.M. 841 (1965); Estate of Elizabeth A. Wilson, 10 T.C.M. 750 (1951); Drayton Cochran, 7 T.C.M. 325 (1948). (Three of these cases are reviewed in Chapter 7.)

3. *Borg v. International Silver Co.:* "The value of shares in a commercial or manufacturing company depends chiefly on what they will earn, on which balance sheets throw little light." [11 F.2d 147 (2nd Cir. 1925)]

4. *Estate of James P. Hooper:* "In our opinion, the factor which we would consider as the most important would be what the stock would earn." [41 B.T.A. 114 (1940)]

Dividend-paying Capacity. A comment under this section of Revenue Ruling 59–60 states that dividends (paid) are a less reliable criterion of market value than other applicable factors. This is so in a closely held corporation because of the ability of an individual or group to control dividend payments to meet the needs of the stockholders or to substitute salaries or other emoluments therefor. However, if dividends are a factor in valuing a company, the appraiser should determine the indicated capacity for such payments rather than the historical record.

Section 4(e) of the Ruling also contains the following statement: "Recognition must be given to the necessity of retaining a reasonable portion of profits in a company to meet competition." This appears to be an acknowledgment that a closely held corporation needs to retain a larger portion of its earnings for working capital and internal expansion than a publicly held company, which has readier access to credit and at more reasonable terms.

Dividends, although important, are not always a major factor in stock valuations, particularly in the case of the newer growth industries. If there is indication that a company's future earnings will be steadily improved by the retention of, say, 70% or more of its current earnings, the demand for its stock will generally reflect better than average market performance.

However, in the case of cyclical or mature industries, or for companies whose earnings are relatively static or show only a modest improvement, prospective dividend payments are a more significant factor in valuations. The importance of dividends was graphically illustrated when United States Steel Corporation (in a cyclical industry) coupled an announcement of a decrease in earnings for the nine months ending September 30, 1966, with an increase in the annual rate of dividend from $2.00 to $2.40. The market price of the company's common stock rose 2½ points on the announcement, and registered a percentage gain that was as good as or better than several other steel companies that reported improved earnings.

Goodwill or Other Intangible Value. The discussion under this section of the ruling, prior to 1965, is as follows:

In the final analysis, goodwill is based upon earning capacity. The presence of goodwill and its value, therefore, rests upon the excess of net earnings over and above a fair return on the net tangible assets. While the element of goodwill may be based primarily on earnings, such factors as the prestige and renown of the business, the ownership of a trade or brand name, and a record of successful operations over a prolonged period in a particular locality, also may furnish support for the inclusion of intangible value. [In some instances it may not be possible to make a separate appraisal of the tangible and intangible assets of the business. The enterprise has a value as an entity.] Whatever intangible value there is, which is supportable by the facts, may be measured by the amount by which the appraised value of the tangible assets exceeds the net book value of such assets.][13]

The first two sentences adequately summarize the real measure of goodwill in an industrial or commercial enterprise, i.e., premium earnings. Trademarks, trade names, copyrights, formulas, patents, know-how, product acceptance, and strategic market position all serve to create the goodwill of a company, provided they produce premium earnings. In an actively traded common stock, premium earnings and the prospects of their continuation at a high level will generally result in a market price reflecting a better than average price–earnings ratio.

Revenue Ruling 65–193, issued in 1965, modified Revenue Ruling 59–60 to the extent of deleting the material indicated above. The following explanation was given for the deletion:

The instances where it is not possible to make a separate appraisal of the tangible and intangible assets of a business are rare and each case varies from the other. No rule can be devised which will be generally applicable to such cases.

This appears to be an illogical reason for deleting a statement that "an enterprise *may* have a value as an entity." As a practical

---

[13] The bracketed sentences were deleted by Rev. Rul. 65–193, 1965–2 CUM. BULL. 370.

matter, an industrial or commercial enterprise operating at a profit should be valued *only as an entity, in most instances*. The gist of this explanation is to contradict other statements in Revenue Ruling 59-60 that indicate, and properly so, that price-earnings ratios derived through comparisons of market prices of companies in similar industries, or by a capitalization of a company's own earnings, are a primary method of valuation. On one hand, the Internal Revenue Service indicates the limited use of the two-step tangible-intangible method of valuation set forth in ARM 34, and on the other it seeks to extend its use through the explanation in Revenue Ruling 65-193.

Presumably, this comment relates to industrial and commercial enterprises operating at a profit, because goodwill, generally, would not be a factor in the valuation of companies holding real estate, securities, or other disposable assets, or companies operating at a loss.

It is unlikely that anyone could arrive at a *fair market valuation* of a going enterprise, with the few exceptions mentioned, by resorting to a so-called sound or reproductive valuation of individual assets, and measuring goodwill by the amount by which such an appraisal exceeded the net book value of the enterprise.

Opinions in a long line of litigated cases have discredited the use of appraisals of tangible assets as a means of determining the fair market value of the stock of a company. As was held by the Tax Court in *Philadelphia Steel & Iron Corp.*: [14] "Suffice it to say the courts will not be bound by adherence to the rule of reproduction cost less accrued depreciation." In *National Packing Corp.*, [15] the court emphasized the impropriety of "theoretical values" determined by means of appraisals, and concluded that "market value is a definite thing, and it may have no particular

[14] Philadelphia Steel & Iron Corp., 23 T.C.M. 558 (1964), aff'd 344 F.2d 964 (3rd Cir. 1965).
[15] National Packing Corp., 24 B.T.A. 952 (1931).

relation to replacement cost and is in no wise determined by it." [16]

A more detailed discussion of methods of valuing and accounting for goodwill is set forth in Chapter 8.

Size of Block To Be Valued. It is mentioned that forced or distressed sales, or isolated sales in small amounts do not ordinarily reflect fair market value of stock of a closely held corporation. The view is expressed that a block of stock representing controlling interest may justify a higher value per share than a minority interest, which is more difficult to sell. Also, because of the absence of prevailing market prices the blockage theory of discounting the "fair market value" is not considered appropriate in valuing stock of closely held corporations.

Market prices of stock present objective evidence of value, and, in the absence of any showing to the contrary, reflect the consensus of the investing public. As discussed in a previous chapter, there are not too many stocks listed on national exchanges or traded over the counter for which the volume of trade is substantial relative to total outstanding shares.

Despite the apparent endeavor to deprecate the use of the blockage theory of discounting the "fair market value" of stock, it seems appropriate to value any large block of stock, except in unusual circumstances, at less than its fair market value because of the difficulty of disposing of it. In the ordinary course the holder would have to dribble out his shares over a period of time to prevent saturating the market and substantially depressing the price, or he would have to engage in a secondary public offering with the consequent fees and expenses involved, or sell the stock in a large block transaction at a price from one to possibly four points below the market.

A notable exception to discounting the fair market value of a relatively large block of stock would be where another company was seeking to acquire control of the company whose valuation

---

[16] Other cases in which there were similar findings include: Georgia Ry. & Power Co. v. Railroad Comm'r of Ga., 262 U.S. 625, 630 (1923); A. M. Byers Co., 10 B.T.A. 660, 665 (1930); American Steel Wool Mfg. Co., 14 B.T.A. 762, 765 (1928); Jerecki Mfg. Co., 12 B.T.A. 1165, 1178 (1928); Donaldson Iron Co., 9 B.T.A. 1081, 1086 (1928); Rockford Malleable Iron Works, 2 B.T.A. 817 (1925); Frost Mfg. Co., 13 B.T.A. 802 (1928).

was under tax review, or where a definitive offer had been received from an institutional buyer. In the absence of such evidence, and without confirmation that the would-be acquirer was willing to pay a higher value than that claimed by the taxpayer, the application of blockage discount should invariably be a matter for consideration.

There have been many litigated cases where the use of blockage discount from market value has been upheld. One of particular interest was that of *Helvering v. Maytag*,[17] wherein the U. S. Circuit Court of Appeals for the Eighth Circuit affirmed the decision of the U. S. Board of Tax Appeals applying blockage discount from the market value of a listed stock, where two blocks to be valued represented over twice the number of shares in the hands of the public, as follows:

> Where, as in this case, the taxpayer affirmatively shows that a block of listed stock to be valued is very great in comparison with the amounts of the stock which have been traded in on the exchange where it is listed, that the block of stock could not be sold on such market at its quoted prices within a reasonable time by skilled brokers following prudent practices for liquidation and that the true value of the block of stock is in fact different from the price quotations, then the taxpayer is entitled to have all other proper evidence of the value of the block of stock considered together with the market quotations. Thus, where only about 250,000 out of over 1,600,000 shares of listed stock were in the hands of the public and where several thousand shares were the most sold in a single day, the Board properly valued a block of 133,859 shares of stock in a decedent's estate and another block of 400,000 shares transferred by gift at amounts less than the stock market price.

Another interesting case, in which the court decided that the value of a stock traded over the counter was less than the quoted market price, was that of the *Estate of Marjorie Gilbert Brush*.[18]

Market Price of Stocks of Similar Corporations. Section 4(h) of the ruling makes reference to Section 2031(b) of the Internal Revenue Code of 1954 (see page 111), substantially carried over from the 1939 Code. But the ruling goes beyond Section 2031(b) in recognizing that the appraiser may have to resort to a comparison of actively traded over-the-counter stocks, in addition to,

---

[17] Helvering v. Maytag, 125 F.2d 55 (8th Cir. 1942), *cert. denied* 316 U. S. 689 (1942).

[18] Estate of Marjorie Gilbert Brush, 22 T.C.M. 900 (1963). This case is reviewed in Chapter 7.

or in lieu of, those traded on exchanges. It is stressed that comparisons should be made only with companies whose stocks are actively traded in a "free public market." As mentioned in Chapter 2, the annual dollar trading volume of over-the-counter industrial and commercial stocks is relatively substantial.

Section 4(h) of the ruling also contains a comment to the effect that a corporation having preferred stock, bonds, or debentures in addition to its common stock should not be considered to be directly comparable to one having only common stock outstanding. This is not a valid concept because an appraiser may readily determine the value attributable to common stock of a company, regardless of its capital structure.

Revenue Ruling 59–60: Miscellaneous Provisions. Section 5 of Revenue Ruling 59–60 discusses weight to be accorded the relevant valuation factors and mentions that earnings may be the most important criterion in valuing stocks of companies that sell products or services to the public, whereas the greatest weight may be accorded to the value of underlying assets of an investment or real estate holding company. Operating expenses and the cost of liquidation are to be considered in appraising the underlying assets of holding companies.

Although it is not mentioned specifically in this section of the ruling, federal income and other taxes that would be incurred in liquidating underlying assets at appraised values are among the "costs" that should be considered.

Section 6 deals with the subject of capitalization rates and reiterates that no standard tables can be formulated because wide variations will be found in selling prices of listed companies in the same industry. The important factors mentioned for consideration of capitalization rates are the nature of the business, the risk involved, and the stability or irregularity of earnings.

Section 7 rejects the mathematical averaging of several factors in accordance with a prescribed formula as unrealistic and tending to exclude active consideration of other pertinent factors.

Section 8 deals with agreements restricting the sale or transfer of closely held stocks, and states that where shares of stock acquired by a decedent are subject to repurchase by the issuing corporation, the option price is usually accepted as the fair market value for estate tax purposes. However, for gift tax purposes such option prices are not considered determinative of fair market value.

Where the option or buy and sell agreement is the result of voluntary action by the stockholders and is binding during the life as well as at the death of the stockholders, such agreement may or may not, depending upon the circumstances, fix the value for estate tax purposes. Where the stockholder is free to dispose of his shares during life and the option is to become effective only upon his death, the fair market value is not limited to the option price. It is not the intent of the law to have such agreements used as a device for the decedent to pass on his share interests to his heirs for less than adequate and full consideration.

Revenue Ruling 68–609

The next significant Revenue Ruling was 65–192 (1965–2 CUM. BULL. 259), which affirmed the applicability of the procedures outlined in Revenue Ruling 59–60 (now modified by Revenue Ruling 65–193) in valuing closely held stocks and business interests for income and other taxes, as well as for estate and gift tax purposes. It also discussed the limitations of the formula approach set forth in ARM 34 and ARM 68.

Revenue Ruling 68–609, issued in 1968, is the latest ruling and superseded ARM 34, ARM 68, and Revenue Ruling 65–192. The purpose of the ruling was to update and restate the formula approach in the determination of fair market value of intangible assets of a business. The gist of the ruling is that the formula approach may be used only if there is no better basis available for making the determination. The ruling gives suggested rates of return on investment and capitalization of earnings "in excess of a fair rate of return on net tangible assets." It further states that such rates are used as examples and are not appropriate in all cases. It also affirms the applicability of Revenue Ruling 59–60, as modified, in valuing closely held stocks and business interests.

The three final paragraphs of Revenue Ruling 68–609, which is reproduced in its entirety as Appendix F, sum up its applicability in valuations:

1. The "formula" approach should not be used if there is better evidence available from which the value of intangibles can be de-

termined. If the assets of a going business are sold upon the basis of a rate of capitalization that can be substantiated as being realistic, though it is not within the range of figures indicated here as the ones ordinarily to be adopted, the same rate of capitalization should be used in determining the value of intangibles.

2. Accordingly, the "formula" approach may be used for determining the fair market value of intangible assets of a business only if there is no better basis available.

3. See also Revenue Ruling 59–60 (1959–1 Cum. Bull. 237), modified by Revenue Ruling 65–193 (1965–2 Cum. Bull. 370), which sets forth the proper approach to use in the valuation of closely held corporate stocks for estate and gift tax purposes. The general approach, methods, and factors outlined in Revenue Ruling 59–60, as modified, are equally applicable to valuations of corporate stocks for income and other tax purposes as well as for estate and gift tax purposes. They apply also to problems involving the determination of the fair market value of business interests of any type, including partnerships and proprietorships, and of intangible assets for all tax purposes.

IRS PROCEDURES IN VALUATION CASES

The administrative procedures followed in valuation cases before the Internal Revenue Service start with the examination, by an agent of the audit branch of the Service, of the estate, gift, or income tax returns filed by the taxpayer or his representative. If agreement cannot be reached as to the valuation claimed with the examining revenue agent, the taxpayer will be issued a "30-day letter" and complete examination report, and is entitled to a District Conference, upon the filing of a protest within that period. The District Conference is conducted by a full-time conferee, independent of the agent and his supervisor.

If the taxpayer and conferee are unable to reach an agreement at the District Conference (or if the taxpayer decides to waive the District Conference possibly at the suggestion of the Internal Revenue Service), the taxpayer may request a hearing before the Service's Appellate Division. Here the taxpayer will have an opportunity to sign a waiver which permits the District Director to assess any deficiency against him or schedule for refund any overpayment agreed upon. If agreement is not reached with the Appellate Division, the taxpayer will receive a "90-day letter." This is a statutory notice of the proposed deficiency and contains a statement that if the taxpayer does not file a petition with the U. S. Tax Court within 90 days, the deficiency will be assessed against him.

Following receipt of the 90-day letter the taxpayer may elect to pay the proposed deficiency, sign the waiver of restriction on assessment, or challenge the Internal Revenue Service's determination in court.

Challenging a Determination in Court

If the taxpayer chooses to go to court, three federal tribunals are available: The Tax Court, the District Court, and the Court of Claims. It should be noted that the Tax Court may be used *only* in the case of a deficiency determination. An advantage of the Tax Court is that payment of the asserted tax is not required prior to the trial. However, the taxpayer may pay the proposed deficiency, if he wishes, in order to stop the running of interest during litigation.

However, the taxpayer is precluded from appealing his case to the Tax Court if he pays the proposed deficiency or signs the waiver *before* the mailing of the 90-day letter; in the latter case he must pay the deficiency, file a claim for refund with the Internal Revenue Service, and eventually sue for refund, if he deems it desirable, in either the District Court or Court of Claims. Possible advantages of the District Court are that a jury trial is available, which may be of some importance in borderline factual issues, and, in some areas of taxation, the taxpayer has fared better in the District Courts and Court of Claims than in the Tax Court.

If the taxpayer is not successful in maintaining his position either in the U. S. Tax Court or District Court, then he may appeal to the U. S. Court of Appeals, and, if unsuccessful at this level, he then may seek review by the U. S. Supreme Court. If the taxpayer is unsuccessful in the Court of Claims, he may seek review directly by the U. S. Supreme Court. Generally, the Supreme Court hears only a few tax cases each year. Needless to say, a taxpayer should get sound legal advice before deciding upon a particular course of action in arguing his claim for valuation.

6

Illustrative Examples

BASIC CONSIDERATIONS

This chapter is devoted to suggestions and examples of valuations for federal tax purposes, based on applicable sections of the Internal Revenue Code and Regulations and Revenue Rulings reviewed in Chapter 5. However, these examples are necessarily limited, as several volumes could be written on this aspect of valuations. Additional insight on the subject, particularly on special situations, may be gained by referring to court decisions in litigated cases reviewed in Chapter 7.

Ultimate Tax Effect

In submitting a valuation for estate tax purposes, the taxpayer's representatives should consider the ultimate tax effect of a claimed valuation for capital stock or a business interest. If the estate tax would be at a low rate because of deductions for various expenses and claims, the statutory exemption, and the marital deduction, it may be desirable to value such stock or interest at the highest reasonable range. This is particularly applicable where the beneficiaries of the estate are in a high income tax bracket and would pay the maximum capital gains tax (reaching a 35% rate in 1972), on disposing of the stock or interest.

Accounting Principles

At this point it is appropriate to discuss a matter that concerns the statements submitted for a determination of the financial condition, profit and loss, and earning capacity of a business, i.e., the principles of accounting under which such financial statements have been prepared.

The limitations of financial statements that have not been audited and reported on by independent public accountants were discussed in Chapter 3. Not only are there no authoritative requirements under the Internal Revenue Code, Regulations, or Rulings for independent audits of corporate taxpayers' financial statements, but, by law, any of several different methods of accounting may be used if consistently followed by the taxpayer.

It therefore is incumbent upon the appraiser to determine what principles of accounting have been followed in preparing financial statements for estate, gift, and other federal tax purposes. If such statements have not been prepared in conformity with generally accepted accounting principles, they should be revised, to the extent practicable, to reflect properly the financial condition, net income, and other pertinent data for the periods under review.

Revenue Rulings

Despite the few seeming defects or inconsistencies noted in Chapter 5, Revenue Ruling 59–60, as modified, and its companion Revenue Ruling 68–609 are a valuable contribution to the taxpayer and his representatives, and present a comprehensive guide for valuing closely held corporate stocks or business interests. They present the official views of the Internal Revenue Service, and it behooves anyone involved with a valuation problem to show that all relevant factors set forth in these rulings have been considered in presenting a case.

Case Citations

Discussions of a valuation case, for federal tax purposes, will be carried out with Internal Revenue Service personnel, whose training, whether legal or otherwise, is oriented around rules, regulations, and precedent. If litigated, the case will be tried by a judge (lawyer), who will be similarly guided. It is well, therefore, to cite rules, regulations, and adjudicated cases to support the presentation.

Discounts for Lack of Marketability

One of the most important factors in valuing closely held corporate stocks is the discount from computed value in arriving at fair market value. As mentioned, no arm's-length transaction takes place when a donor, or testator, passes on to his relatives or friends shares of stock or business interests. Therefore, in valuing such stock or interests, it is customary to deduct a discount from the theoretically computed value.

The size of the discount is a matter of judgment, based on all of the relevant facts; regardless of whether an interest represents a majority or minority holding of the outstanding stock in question, a discount is usually appropriate. In the case of a majority interest, this may be in consideration of how salable the stock would be, based on its earnings trend, cash flow available for dividends, depth of management, vulnerability to competition, etc., and is not confined to the estimated costs of a theoretical public offering. A greater discount usually would be appropriate for a minority interest. In addition to factors affecting the marketability of a majority interest, a minority stockholder generally has no say in the dividend policies of a corporation or a decision on whether to liquidate it, or any influence on operating decisions.

Accordingly, it will be noted in the examples in this chapter, and the case analyses in Chapter 7, that the various factors to be considered in discounting share values play an important role in valuation findings.

COMPANY WHOSE WORTH IS DEPENDENT ON CONTINUING AS A GOING CONCERN

In the following illustration, valuation was made for estate tax purposes of an interest in a trucking company.

John Jones, who died on June 20, 1967, left a 55% interest in Acme Trucking Company as the major item among his estate assets. The remaining 45% of the capital stock was owned by four other officer-directors of the company who constituted its active management. The entire estate was willed to Jones's widow, who had never taken an active part in the management of the company. Jones also left sufficient life insurance and other liquid assets to pay federal estate and state inheritance taxes.

The company operated a general trucking business in the eastern part of the United States and had a fiscal year ending June 30. Jones had been chairman of the board of the company at a salary of $50,000 per annum. Although he had not been devoting a great deal of his time to company affairs for several years before his death, it was felt that this compensation was reasonable for consulting services, because of his long background in the business. It was agreed by the other officer-director-stockholders that Jones's widow would succeed her deceased husband as chairman of the board of the company at a salary of $5,000 per annum, primarily for attending directors' meetings, which were held monthly.

Pertinent Financial Data

Pertinent financial statistics taken from audited financial statements of the company at June 30, 1967, are shown on pages 133 and 134. The company's earnings and the dividends per share paid on the common stock for the three years ended June 30, 1967, were as follows:

Year Ended June 30	Earnings	Dividends	Percentage of Payout of Earnings
1967	$2.64	$0.80	30%
1966	2.32	0.70	30
1965	1.98	0.55	28

Although the company's dividend payout was somewhat on the low side, there would be no problem in increasing the payout to 40% or more of earnings. This policy has already been agreed to by the stockholders in view of the savings on the salary formerly paid to Jones, and the fact that his widow depends upon such dividends as her principal source of income.

ACME TRUCKING COMPANY
BALANCE SHEET
June 30, 1967

Properties	$4,464,000	
Less: reserves for depreciation	1,839,000	
	2,625,000	
Intangibles	90,000	
Total properties and intangibles		$2,715,000

Current assets:

Cash	$ 504,000	
Short-term U. S. Government bonds	285,000	
Receivables	544,000	
Inventories	78,000	
Prepaid items	188,000	
Other current assets	87,000	
Total current assets		1,686,000
Total assets		$4,401,000

Liabilities and capital:

Common stock—140,000 shares no par value	$ 500,000	
Long-term debt	1,270,000	
Deferred federal income tax	220,000	
Earned surplus	1,230,000	
		$3,220,000

Current liabilities:

Current debt maturing	$ 420,000	
Accounts payable	284,000	
Liability for loss and damage	183,000	
Tax reserve	103,000	
Other current liabilities	191,000	
Total current liabilities		1,181,000
Total liabilities and capital		$4,401,000

Net current assets	$ 505,000
Per share	$3.61

Net tangible assets	$3,130,000
Per share	$22.36

ACME TRUCKING COMPANY
CONDENSED STATEMENT OF INCOME

Year Ending June 30, 1967

Operating revenues		$8,778,000
Operation and maintenance expenses	$7,115,000	
Operating taxes and licenses	591,000	7,706,000
Operating income		1,072,000
Other income		12,000
Total income		1,084,000
Depreciation	$ 294,000	
Interest expense	69,000	
Miscellaneous deductions	6,000	
Federal income tax	346,000	715,000
Net income		$ 369,000
Common shares outstanding		140,000
Earnings per share		$2.64

Significant Revenue Ruling Factors

Although all factors mentioned in Revenue Ruling 59–60, as well as any other relevant factors, should be given consideration in valuing a company, the appraiser must decide which of the factors are of particular significance in making his determination in a specific case.

In the case of Acme Trucking Company, it appears that the following factors, listed in the Ruling, are most significant:

1. Financial condition of the business
2. Earning capacity of the company
3. Dividend-paying capacity
4. Size of the block of stock to be valued
5. Market price of stocks of corporations engaged in the same or similar lines of business, whose stocks are actively traded in a free and open market, either on an exchange or over the counter.

Comparison With Other Companies

For the purpose of valuing the stock of Acme, the appraiser should compile significant financial data of other companies in the trucking industry. Standard & Poor's Stock Guide for September, 1967, lists 31 companies in the industry, of which 13 are not ranked (rated). It is explained that no ranking is possible for these companies "because of insufficient data, non-recurring factors, or some other reason."

To illustrate the principle of valuation by means of comparison of financial data, selected information is set forth below on the seven trucking companies listed in the New York Stock Exchange's "Stocks on the Big Board." Ordinarily, the appraiser should endeavor to obtain data on a larger number of companies, ascertaining, however, that their stocks are actively traded in a free market.

		Earnings per Share—Fiscal Years		
		1966	1965	1964
Associated Transport	December	$ 2.47	$ 2.60	$ 2.28
Consolidated Freightways	December	2.19	1.69	1.16
Interstate Motor Freight	December	3.20	2.87	2.50
Leaseway Transportation	December	1.50	1.75	0.87
McLean Trucking	* June	2.65	2.62	1.93
Overnite Transportation	December	2.06	2.24	2.15
Pacific Intermountain Exp.	December	1.73	1.41	1.30
Totals		$15.80	$15.18	$12.19
Average		$ 2.26	$ 2.17	$ 1.74

	Earnings for Twelve Months Ending Latest Reported Quarter in 1967	Market Price June 20, 1967	Price—Earnings Ratio Based on Latest Twelve Months' Earnings
Associated Transport	March	$ 2.30	16⅜	7
Consolidated Freightways	March	2.27	29⅞	13
Interstate Motor Freight	April	3.00	28	9
Leaseway Transportation	March	1.35	14¾	11
McLean Trucking	* June	2.65	22¼	8
Overnite Transportation	March	1.95	18	9
Pacific Intermountain Exp.	March	1.61	18⅜	11
Totals		$15.13	147⅝	68
Average		$ 2.16	21	9.7

* Year ended June 30, 1967.

	Dividends per Share— Fiscal Years		Latest Twelve Months		
	1966	1965	Indicated Rate	Percentage of Payout of Earnings	** Yield
Associated Transport	$0.85	$0.75	$1.00	43%	6.0%
Consolidated Freightways	0.75	0.45	0.80	35	2.7
Interstate Motor Freight	1.20	1.00	1.20	40	4.3
Leaseway Transportation	0.50	0.19	0.50	37	3.4
McLean Trucking	* 0.75	0.65	0.80	28	3.6
Overnite Transportation	0.80	0.725	0.80	41	4.4
Pacific Intermountain Exp.	0.90	0.80	1.05	65	5.7
Totals			$6.15	289%	30.1%
Average			$0.86	40%	4.1%

	Latest Fiscal Year End per Share		
		Net Tangible Assets	
	Net Current Assets	Amount	Percentage of Market Price
Associated Transport	$7.51	$13.38	82%
Consolidated Freightways	3.99	10.02	33
Interstate Motor Freight	2.31	20.45	73
Leaseway Transportation	0.14	7.25	49
McLean Trucking	2.41	11.95	54
Overnite Transportation	0.78	9.87	55
Pacific Intermountain Exp.	3.49	9.61	52

* Year ended June 30, 1967.
** Based on market price June 20, 1967.

Value per Share

Using the above data, a preliminary per-share valuation of Acme stock would be as follows:

Earnings year ending June 30, 1967	$ 2.64
Average price—earnings ratios of seven companies	9.7
Computed market price, before discount	$25.61

The following observations are in order:

1. The financial condition of the company is good, although net current assets of $3.61 per share appear to be low relative to net tangible assets.

2. Net tangible assets of $22.36 per share are 87% of the computed market price of $25.61 before discount.
3. The company should have no difficulty in raising its dividend pay-out to 40% of earnings. Such a payout would have amounted to $1.05 for the fiscal year ending June 30, 1967, which would have yielded 4.1% on the computed market price, before discount.

As set forth in Chapter 4, investment bankers would have approached the valuation of Acme on the above basis. This is truly an illustration of a willing-buyer–willing-seller concept, because the underwriters would be pricing the stock to sell, rather than making a theoretical computation.

Furthermore, considering that the experts were pricing the stock for an initial offering, they probably would shade the price–earnings ratio to nine times earnings or slightly under. Also, the net proceeds of the stock would be after underwriting discounts, commissions, and other expenses.

Accordingly, the appraiser would be justified in making the following computation of value of the 77,000 shares of Acme in Jones's estate:

Computed market price per share, before discount	$25.61
20% discount for lack of marketability	5.12
Computed price per share	$20.49
Shares to be valued	77,000
Total value for estate tax purposes	$1,577,730

If the shares in Jones's estate had been a minority instead of a majority interest, a larger discount for lack of marketability would have been appropriate.

Valuing Non-operating Assets

Assume that Acme Trucking Company had the following non-operating assets, in addition to those listed on its balance sheet on page 133:

	Per Books (Cost)	Market Value
2,000 shares of common stock of Star Transportation Co. (listed company)	50,000	111,000
Land	50,000	200,000

The stock of Star Transportation, a large transcontinental trucking company, represented only a fraction of a 1% interest. The
land investment represented ten acres of unimproved property
that had been acquired some years prior, in another area, for the
purpose of constructing the company's main depot, head office,
and other facilities. However, it was found that the loss that
would have been sustained on existing head office and main depot
facilities, plus the cost of constructing the new facilities, would
have severely taxed the company's finances. Accordingly, the
project was abandoned for the time being.

The common stock of Star Transportation would thus be valued:

Market value, June 20, 1967, based on quoted price of 55½		$111,000
Less:		
Brokerage commission and state tax on assumed sale ......$ 1,000		
* Federal capital gains tax (25% of $111,000—$51,000)...... 15,000		16,000
Adjusted market value		$ 95,000

The investment in land would be valued:

Market value of land (based on average of three appraisals by		
qualified real estate appraisers)		$200,000
Less:		
Brokerage commission of 10% $20,000		
Legal and other fees 4,000		
* Federal capital gains tax (30% of $200,000—$74,000)...... 37,800		61,800
Adjusted market value		$138,200

* Rates used in this and other examples are for illustrative purposes only.

A recomputation of the value of Acme Trucking Company
stock, including these additional non-operating assets follows:

Computed market price per share, after discount	$20.49
Add: Value per share of non-operating assets	
($95,000 + 138,200 ÷ 140,000)	1.66
Adjusted price per share	$22.15
Shares to be valued	77,000
Total value for estate tax purposes	$1,705,550

The recomputation could be refined by deducting assumed
dividends of $4,400 (4% yield) on Star Transportation stock, less

federal income taxes, from net income of $369,000 of Acme. However, the effect of such an adjustment on the computed market price of Acme would be insignificant.

Wide Variation in Price–Earnings Ratios of Comparative Stocks

In the Acme illustration, the price–earnings ratio of the lowest trucking industry stock differed only 2.9 from the average; the highest was 3.3 above average. Other more volatile industries may not produce such a uniform pattern.

Under such circumstances the appraiser could attempt to *select* certain actively quoted stocks in the industry for comparison of their financial data with those of the company to be valued. However, in doing this he might be accused of bias in his selection. A better technique would be to list all such companies in the industry, from a given source, and then eliminate high and low ratio stocks that deviate from the average.

The list of drug stocks on page 140, taken from the New York Stock Exchange's "Stocks on the Big Board," illustrates how adjusted averages can be computed. In the drug industry and other industries where listed stocks are currently selling at a high price–earnings ratio, the appraiser may be justified in deducting a large discount, say 35%, for lack of marketability, in valuing a closely held stock.

Apparent Lack of Significance of Book Values

In the tabulation on page 136, two of the seven trucking companies appear to be in a very tight working capital position and several have a low ratio of net tangible assets, relative to the average. This bears out the study shown on page 104 in Chapter 4, as to the general lack of significance of net book equity (book value) per share.

However, in the sale of the entire capital stock of a company that is in a tight position for liquid assets as the result of having paid out too much in dividends or otherwise overextending itself, the prospective purchaser would normally discount the purchase price by the amount of additional capital or borrowed money he

		Twelve Months' Earnings Ending Latest Reported Quarter in 1967	Market Price June 20, 1967	Price–Earnings Ratio Based on Latest Twelve Months' Earnings
Abbott Laboratories	March	$ 2.01	47¼	24
American Home Products	March	1.88	56¾	29
Baxter Laboratories	March	1.13	68¼	62
Bristol-Myers Co.	June	1.69	74⅜	45
Carter Wallace	March	1.31	14¼	11
Merck & Company	March	2.38	84½	34
Miles Laboratories	March	1.83	38½	21
Norwich Pharmacal	March	2.78	76½	27
Parke, Davis Co.	March	2.05	28⅛	14
Pfizer, Chas. & Co.	March	3.00	88½	29
Plough Inc.	March	2.98	78¾	27
Richardson-Merrell	March	4.16	82	19
Robins, A. H.	March	1.68	52¾	31
Rorer, William H.	March	2.25	47⅜	21
Schering Corp.	March	2.16	62¾	29
Searle, G. D. & Co.	March	1.63	52½	34
Smith, Kline French Lab.	March	2.80	56⅝	20
Sterling Drug Inc.	March	1.66	48⅝	28
Upjohn Company	March	2.35	59¼	26
Warner-Lambert Pharmaceutical	March	1.83	50⅛	28
Totals		$43.56	1,167½	559
Eliminate extreme high- and low-ratio stocks:				
Baxter Laboratories		$ 1.13	68¼	62
Bristol-Myers Co.		1.69	74⅜	45
Carter Wallace		1.31	14¼	11
Parke, Davis Co.		2.05	28⅛	14
		$ 6.18	185	132
Adjusted totals		$37.38	982½	427
Average		$ 2.34	61⅜	26

would have to furnish to support the current volume of business and earnings.

Other Considerations

If the principal stockholder of Acme had been the active head of the business at the time of his death and it had become necessary to engage an outsider to replace him, for substantial compensation with options and other benefits, the value of the decedent's stock would have been adversely affected.

Also, if mutual buy and sell agreements had existed between the stockholders and/or the corporation, in which a specific price formula had been agreed to, the stock would have been valued on that basis for estate tax purposes.

Such other factors as the general economic outlook, nationwide and in the specific industry, and goodwill or other intangible values would all be distilled into a price–earnings ratio of actively traded stocks in the particular industry.

COMPANY OPERATING AT A LOSS

Valuation for estate tax purposes of an interest in a company operating at a loss is illustrated as follows.

William Baker, who died on March 14, 1966, owned 2,000 shares, or 20%, of the total outstanding shares of capital stock of Merit Machine Tool Company, of which he was president. His will provided that his estate, which contained negotiable securities and insurance as well as the aforementioned stock, be divided equally between his sons, Robert and Joseph, after payment of all taxes due. There were approximately 100 other stockholders of Merit, no one of whom owned more than 5% of the outstanding stock of the company.

The company, which manufactured a variety of non-standardized metal-cutting machine tools, on order only, had suffered losses in two of the three years preceding Baker's death and there had been virtually no trading activity in the stock for some time. Baker's sons, who were co-executors under his will, decided to use the optional date of March 14, 1967, one year after date of death at that time, to value the stock of Merit, inasmuch as the company suffered a further loss from operations for the year 1966.

Also, the company was in default on its three-year term bank loan because its stockholders' equity account was less than the minimum requirement of $1,450,000. Accordingly, the loan had been placed on a demand basis.

Pertinent Financial Data

Pertinent statistics follow, as taken from audited financial statements of the company for the year 1966, as well as for previous years:

MERIT MACHINE TOOL COMPANY
BALANCE SHEET

December 31, 1966

Assets:
Current assets:
Cash ....$ 161,000
Accounts receivable 470,000

Inventories:
Raw materials, parts, and finished stock 720,000
Contracts in process 540,000
Prepaid expenses   41,000
Total current assets $1,932,000
Land ....$ 150,000
Buildings, machinery, and equipment, at cost, less
accumulated depreciation of $1,824,000 778,000

928,000

Total assets $2,860,000

Liabilities and capital:
Current liabilities:
Notes payable to banks $1,000,000
Accounts payable and accrued liabilities 510,000
Mortgage installments due within one year   40,000
Total current liabilities $1,550,000

Mortgage payable   200,000

Stockholders' equity:
Common stock, no par value, authorized and issued
10,000 shares ....$ 500,000
Retained earnings 610,000

1,110,000

Total liabilities and capital $2,860,000

Net tangible assets per share .... $ 111.00

MERIT MACHINE TOOL COMPANY
CONDENSED STATEMENT OF INCOME
Year Ended December 31, 1966

Sales, less discounts, returns, and allowances		$5,640,000
Costs and expenses:		
Cost of goods sold	$5,042,000	
Selling, general, and administrative expenses	476,000	
Depreciation	138,000	
Research and development	81,000	
Interest expense	79,000	
		5,816,000
(Loss) for the year		($ 176,000)
(Loss) per share		($ 17.60)

The company's earnings or (losses), and dividends per share, for the five years ended December 31, 1966, were as follows:

Year Ended December 31	Earnings or * (Losses)		Dividends Paid per Share
	Total	Per Share	
1966...........	($176,000)	($17.60)	—
1965...........	(129,000)	(12.90)	—
1964...........	(186,000)	(18.60)	—
1963...........	148,000	14.80	$10.00
1962...........	162,000	16.20	10.00

* Losses for 1964 and 1965 were after federal income tax credits from net operating loss carrybacks. No such credits were available for 1966.

Significant Revenue Ruling Factors

For the purpose of valuing the stock of Merit, it appears that the following factors, listed in Revenue Ruling 59–60, are most significant:

1. Nature of the business and history of the enterprise
2. Condition and outlook of the specific industry
3. Book value of the stock and financial condition of the business
4. Earning capacity of the company
5. Dividend-paying capacity
6. Size of block of stock to be valued

The company obviously was in a tight financial position, having more than 60% of its current assets in inventory. Its machinery and equipment were approximately two-thirds depreciated, despite the fact that its composite rate of depreciation was only 5%. Its total short- and long-term debt amounted to $1,240,000, compared with equity capital of $1,110,000. The default on the term loan with the bank speaks for itself.

Condition of Industry

The metal cutting machine tool industry had been depressed for the past 15 years, as illustrated by comparing the sporadic results of the industry with the growth of manufacturing–industrial production: [1]

Year	* Shipments of Domestic Metal-cutting Machine Tools	* Manufacturing–Industrial Production
1952	100%	100%
1953	108	109
1954	81	101
1955	60	114
1956	80	118
1957	75	118
1958	36	109
1959	36	124
1960	39	128
1961	34	129
1962	42	139
1963	49	147
1964	64	156
1965	83	170
1966	103	186

* 1952 = 100%

As further evidence of the condition and outlook of the industry at that time, the following statistics are cited regarding the seven large machine tool companies listed on the New York Stock Exchange in "Stocks on the Big Board":

[1] Computed from statistics furnished by U. S. Dept. of Commerce, Office of Business Economics.

	Per Share, for Year Ended December 31, 1966			Price–Earnings Ratio
	Net Assets	Market Price	Earnings	
Browne & Sharpe	$41.95	29½	$2.91	10
Bullard Co.	28.41	15⅞	2.61	6
Cincinnati Milling	28.16	33	4.11	8
Monarch Machine Tool	18.06	14½	2.19	6½
National Acme	34.11	38⅞	5.11	7½
* U.T.D. Corp.	17.42	20⅝	2.57	8
Warner & Swasey	27.74	27½	3.71	7½

* Year ended June 30, 1966.

The seven leading companies in the industry were thus selling on an average of 7.6 times earnings at December 31, 1966, compared with Standard & Poor's average of 14.8 for 425 industrial common stocks listed on the New York Stock Exchange. Furthermore, three of the seven companies were selling below net book assets per share at that date, and one was selling at approximate net asset value.

The earning and dividend-paying capacity of the company can be covered very briefly. After three successive years of losses and non-payment of dividends these factors should be considered from an adverse point of view.

Value per Share

Under the circumstances, the adjusted book value or, to be more precise, the estimated liquidating value of the company appeared to be the indicated approach for the valuation of the shares in question. An appraisal of the net assets of the company carried out by an appraisal engineering firm, relative to inventories, machinery, and equipment, and by real estate appraisers, relative to the land and buildings, was assembled by the company's accountants, who made estimates of the liquidation values of other assets, less liabilities. This appraisal showed an estimated liquidating value of the stock of $54 per share.

Any arm's-length value to be placed on the stock would be based on its speculative appeal, which did not appear to be too strong, considering the eventual liquidating value of the stock. However, the size of the blocks of stock, together constituting only

20% of the outstanding shares, would preclude any efforts toward liquidating the company, and would constitute a further negative factor in the valuation of the stock.

Under the circumstances, and considering the declining net book asset values as a result of losses, a prudent investor would require a substantial discount from the estimated current liquidating value of $54, as an inducement to purchase the shares. Accordingly, a discount of 33⅓%, or $18 per share, for a valuation of $36 per share would appear reasonable.

On this basis each block of 1,000 shares of Merit stock bequeathed to Baker's two sons would be valued at $36,000, for an aggregate of $72,000.

A FAMILY INVESTMENT COMPANY

An illustration of the valuation for gift tax purposes of an interest in a family investment company follows.

Richard Smith owned 300 shares of a total of 1,000 outstanding shares of the capital stock of Smithfield Corporation, whose assets consisted primarily of a diversified portfolio of common stocks listed on the New York Stock Exchange. His cousin William Field also owned 300 shares, and the remaining 400 shares were held by their wives and close family relatives. Smith and Field were the original stockholders of the company.

On December 31, 1966, Smith made a gift of 50 shares each of Smithfield stock to his daughter Mary and his son Richard, Jr. The company was a "personal holding company" for the year 1966, as it had been for many prior years. That is to say, at least 50% of the value of its outstanding capital stock was owned directly or indirectly by not more than five individuals, and more than 60% of its income was from dividends and interest, i.e., "personal holding company" income. Accordingly, any undistributed personal holding company income for any year would be subject to an additional tax of 70%.

Pertinent Financial Data

Pertinent statistics taken from audited financial statements of the company at December 31, 1966, appear on pages 147 and 148.

SMITHFIELD CORPORATION
BALANCE SHEET

At December 31, 1966

	Per Books (Cost)	Market Value
Assets:		
Investments:		
Common stocks	$2,865,000	$4,419,000
U. S. Treasury bills	302,000	304,000
	$3,167,000	$4,723,000 *
Other assets:		
Dividends receivable	$ 10,200	$ 10,200
Accrued interest	5,800	5,800
Other	3,500	3,500
	$ 19,500	$ 19,500
Total assets	$3,186,500	$4,742,500
Less: liabilities:		
Federal income tax	$ 30,100	$ 30,100
Dividends declared but not paid	15,000	15,000
Accounts payable	2,900	2,900
	$ 48,000	$ 48,000
Net assets	$3,138,500	$4,694,500
Represented by:		
Capital stock, 1,000 shares	$2,500,000	$2,500,000
Earned surplus:		
Beginning of year	$ 564,950	$ 564,950
Net income	243,550	243,550
Dividends paid or declared	(170,000)	(170,000)
End of year	** $ 638,500	$ 638,500
Unrealized appreciation on investments, less estimated federal capital gains tax	—	$1,556,000
	$3,138,500	$4,694,500

* Net of estimated federal capital gains tax.

** Earned surplus had been accumulated primarily from realized capital gains, less federal tax applicable thereto.

Significant Revenue Ruling Factors

For the purpose of valuing the stock of Smithfield, it appears that the following factors, listed in Revenue Ruling 59–60, are most significant:

    1. Book value of the stock ("In computing the book value per share of stock, assets of the investment type should be revalued on the

SMITHFIELD CORPORATION
STATEMENT OF INCOME

For the Year 1966

Income:

Cash dividends		$174,000	
Discount realized on U. S. Treasury bills		12,000	
Gain on sale of securities		110,000	$296,000
Expenses:			
Fee for investment advisory service	$	8,000	
Legal and auditing		5,200	
Other		1,000	14,200
			$281,800
Federal income tax			38,250
Net income			$243,550

Note: Federal income tax is computed after an 85% "dividend received deduction" on cash dividends, and at 30% of the gain on sale of securities. Capital gains are not considered to be personal holding company income and need not be distributed.

basis of their market prices and the book value adjusted accordingly.")

2. Earning capacity of the company
3. Dividend-paying capacity
4. Size of the block of stock to be valued

The adjusted "book value" of the stock of Smithfield has been computed in the foregoing financial statements by valuing the security portfolio at market quotations at December 31, 1966, less a reserve for federal capital gains tax which would have been payable upon the liquidation of such securities.

The company's earnings are approximately in line with average yields on dividend-paying stocks listed on the New York Stock Exchange. Smithfield is able to pay out, as dividends, its entire ordinary income, less federal taxes thereon, without creating any financial problem.

Each of the blocks of stock to be valued constituted only 5% of the total outstanding capital stock of Smithfield, and the recipients were therefore in no position to force liquidation of the company. Furthermore, if it were desired to liquidate Smithfield, some time and expense would be involved. Accordingly, any outsider approached to purchase one of these blocks of stock would undoubtedly want a discount from the so-called liquidation value per share.

Also, Mary and Richard, Jr., under the Internal Revenue Code and Regulations, had to assume their father's basis for the stock regardless of its value at the date of receipt by them. They therefore had a "built-in" capital gains tax on any gift tax valuation above $2,500 per share, the donor's basis, increased by the applicable gift tax.

Value per Share

Based on the above factors, a reasonable approach to valuing the stock of Smithfield would be as follows:

Preliminary value per share, adjusted "book value" ÷ 1,000 shares . . . . $	4,694.50
Less: 30% discount for lack of marketability, and assumed liquidating and other expenses	1,408.35
Adjusted value per share . . . . $	3,286.15
Number of shares	50
Total value of each block	$164,307.50

Thus, Richard Smith, Sr. would compute his gift tax on a total of $328,615 ($164,307.50 × 2) adjusted for any cumulative lifetime gifts and annual exemptions.

As support for the theory of discounting the per-share price of an investment holding company, from the value based on market quotations of its portfolio securities, the following statistics have been extracted from an Arthur Wiesenberger annual study [2] regarding the leading closed-end diversified investment companies:

As of December 31, 1966

Name of Company	Asset Value per Share	Market Price	Discount or (Premium)
Abacus Fund	$15.79	13	18%
Adams Express	28.59	26⅞	6
American International Corp.	16.31	14¼	13
Boston Personal Property Tr.	23.56	21¼	11
Carriers & General Corp.	32.04	26	19
Consolidated Investment Co.	12.13	10⅞	10
Dominick Fund	26.42	21¼	20

[2] Arthur Wiesenberger & Co., "Investment Companies—1967."

As of December 31, 1966

Name of Company	Asset Value per Share	Market Price	Discount or (Premium)
General American Investment Co. .	34.46	30½	11
General Public Service	6.50	5⅝	13
International Holdings	19.22	14⅜	25
Lehman Corp.	33.08	30⅛	9
Madison Fund	19.15	22⅝	(18)
Niagara Share	19.85	17⅜	12
Tri-Continental	30.69	23	25
U. S. & Foreign Securities	38.95	27½	29

The discount of 30% applied in valuing the gifts of Smithfield stock was in consideration of the company's size relative to the above giant investment companies and the fact that the gifts represented minority interests in the company.

A REAL ESTATE HOLDING COMPANY

The case method of illustrating valuation principles was used in this chapter for (a) an operating company whose worth is dependent on continuance as a going concern, (b) non-operating assets of such a company, (c) a company operating at a loss, and (d) a family investment company. Certain of the principles illustrated in these cases would be equally applicable to valuing an interest in a closely held or family owned real estate holding company. Accordingly, in lieu of using the case method of illustration, the considerations and principles involved in valuing such companies will be applied to the discussion of a real estate holding company.

Valuing an interest in a closely held or family owned real estate holding company requires a combination approach if its holdings consist of both income and non-income-producing properties.

Non-Income-producing Properties

Use of the method of valuing non-income-producing properties is discussed on page 137 under "Valuing Non-operating Assets."

If holdings of undeveloped land or non-operating properties are extensive, the appraiser would ordinarily be justified in discounting any valuations arrived at by means of appraisals, adjusted by brokerage commissions, fees, and capital gains taxes. This discount might justifiably range from 20% to 40%, depending upon the intent of the owners to develop or liquidate such holdings, and the time and expense involved in so doing.

Income-producing Properties

With regard to income-producing properties, such as apartments or industrial and commercial buildings, the net income and "cash flow" generated from such properties would be of primary importance. Thus, the quality and financial stability of the tenants and the length and terms of leases would need careful reviewing. In the case of industrial leases, it is quite common to have "net leases" whereby the tenant pays real estate taxes and certain other expenses. In office building rentals it is becoming the practice to have escalation clauses in leases to cover increased taxes, maintenance, and other costs. In this type of industrial and commercial rental, lease terms are generally for a number of years, say 5 to 25.

Apartment leases, however, may run for only 2 to 3 years, so that the landlord, in many cases, receives a fixed rental regardless of his expenses. Also, neighborhood obsolescence becomes a factor in attempting to project income for a number of years. This may come about through a change in zoning restrictions that would permit the encroachment of industrial or commercial properties, or through changing socioeconomic neighborhood patterns.

Theoretically the value of income-producing properties should be based on a capitalization of an income projection. Where long-term leases are involved, this may be done by determining the present worth of future net lease income, and the estimated residual value of the property at the expiration of the major leases. However, such a determination is more difficult when leases are of short duration and constantly "rolling over."

Customarily, an investment in a new apartment building will show no income return for a number of years. It may take one, two, or more years before the building is fully occupied, and generally depreciation will be claimed under one of the accelerated methods, so that the earlier years' income will bear substantially higher charges than later years. This results in a reduction or elimination of income tax in such years, and also a larger "cash flow" to meet mortgage interest and principal amortization payments. Accordingly, it will generally be necessary to reconstruct the statement of income on a pro forma basis to determine the income-producing potential of the property.

Also, in the case of all types of income-producing properties, reference should be made to state and local tax assessments. These assessments may be reasonably indicative of current values in the area, based on a compilation of actual sales during the preceding year, or may be at a percentage of estimated value based on a survey made some years previous. It is important that the validity of property tax assessments, as a valuation factor, be carefully investigated and explained.

Last but not least, it is highly desirable that appraisals of income-producing properties be made by competent realtors. If substantial value is involved, it is desirable to have as many as three separate appraisals, for experts may differ in their opinions as to value.

Whatever valuations are arrived at for income-producing properties, either by a capitalization of income, by appraisal, or by a combination of these methods, should be subject to the same adjustments for brokerage commissions, fees, capital gains taxes, and discount, as those suggested for non-income-producing properties.

Also, if a real estate holding company has dividend, interest, certain royalties, and other types of "personal holding company income," it will be subject to the undistributed personal holding company tax, unless its adjusted income from rents is 50% or more of adjusted ordinary gross income, and its other personal holding company income, after reduction for dividends actually or constructively paid during the taxable year, is 10% or less of ordinary gross income. Should such a company be a personal holding company, this would be an adverse factor for consideration in a valuation determination.

7

Court Cases

A study by Bosland of 133 Tax Court decisions by 27 different judges during the period from 1944 through 1960 [1] has indicated that 64 of these cases appear to have been finally determined within the compromise area. In two cases, a value was determined exactly midway between the highest value estimated by the taxpayer's witnesses and the lowest value estimated by the Internal Revenue Service witnesses. In 47 cases, the court valuations deviated within 20% of the exact averages, and in the remaining 15 more than 20%. As a matter of interest, the taxpayer was favored in 42 of the 62 Tax Court valuations that deviated from the average.

Bosland went on to mention that the tendency to compromise may be stronger than his figures indicated, because a number of the 69 cases, not considered as settled by compromise, did not involve complex issues. For example, there were some in which the main issue was whether a restrictive contract or agreement to sell stock, or an ownership interest, determined its tax value. In others, there was a question only of whether prices at which market transactions took place were controlling, or, where they were found to be, the size of the discount from market to be applied under the "blockage" theory. Bosland concluded that the number of litigated cases and compromise decisions appeared to be decreasing in recent years.

[1] Bosland, *Tax Value by Compromise,* 19 TAX L. REV. 77 (1963).

In his full report,[2] a study from which the aforementioned article was adopted, Bosland reported that the court cases studied "revealed a strong tendency for the [Internal Revenue] Service to rely on rules of thumb in value determination at the local level. Careful studies of actual market conditions were rarely made until the Service was called on to defend its determinations in court." He also opined that the cases indicated the "Internal Revenue Service has tended to use whatever approach to 'fair market value' will result in a high value and tax liability." On the other hand, "Taxpayers frequently contended for unrealistically low valuations." Also, "some cases seem to have been lost because of inadequate preparation and presentation of the taxpayer's cases."

STUDY OF SELECTED CASES FROM FEDERAL COURTS

Disagreements as to valuation between the taxpayer or his representatives and the Internal Revenue Service continue to be numerous, but it appears that a greater effort is being made to settle them at the administrative level. Unquestionably, when one of the adversaries in a valuation proceeding takes an extreme position, there is a tendency for the other to do likewise, particularly if there appears to be no prospect of settling the controversy short of litigation.

In order to update information on this subject, particularly to determine the application by the courts of Revenue Ruling 59–60 and its companion rulings, an analysis was made of twenty-one selected court decisions on valuations during the period from January 1, 1961, to December 31, 1966, as shown in Table 7–1 (page 155).

BASES OF SELECTION OF CASES

The bases of selection of cases reviewed were that (a) they involved relatively substantial amounts of tax in controversy, (b) they included decisions of the several federal courts trying or re-

---

[2] Bosland, Estate Tax Valuation in the Sale or Merger of Small Firms (1963).

| | | | | | Valuation | | |
Case Ref. No.	Reviewed on Page	Names of Petitioners or Plaintiffs	Type of Tax Case	Federal Court of Jurisdiction	Claimed by Petitioner	Claimed by IRS	Final Adjudication
1	162	Celia Waterman	Gift	Tax Ct.	$ 37,823	$ 126,477	$ 74,750
2	163	Est. of Lida R. Tompkins, et al.	Estate	Tax Ct.	357,120	1,488,000	1,023,000
3	164	Est. of J. Luther Snyder, et al.	Gift	Ct. of Appeals, reversing and remanding Dist. Ct.	396,000	609,840	396,000
4	165	Joseph W. Worthen, et al., Exec.	Estate	Dist. Ct.	84,000	147,000	87,360
5	166	William Hamm, Jr., and Marie H. Hamm	Gift	Tax Ct., aff'd by Ct. of Appeals	26,333	2,240,019	2,240,019
6	168	Lillian M. Daniels	Gift	Dist. Ct.	24,256	191,319	75,800
7	169	The Central Trust Co., et al.	Gift	Ct. of Claims	525,015	1,680,048	1,085,031
8	171	North American Philips Co., Inc.	Income	Tax Ct.	None ascertainable	6,626,250	2,254,320
9	173	F. W. Drybrough, et al., Exrs.	Gift	Dist. Ct.	134,328	526,800	171,452
10	174	Huntington National Bank Co.	Estate	Dist. Ct.	356,095	908,850	671,544
11	176	H. Fort Flowers, et al.	Gift	Tax Ct.	500,000	800,000	800,000
12	178	Est. of Marjorie Gilbert Brush, et al.	Estate	Tax Ct.	188,946	464,492	346,401
13	179	Robert T. Barber, et al.	Gift	Tax Ct.	Not indicated	675,000	407,900
14	181	Nesta Obermer	Estate	Dist. Ct.	357,700	592,167	394,800
15	182	John J. Louis, Jr., et al.	Estate	Dist. Ct., aff'd by Ct. of Appeals	763,750	4,700,000	1,254,900
16	184	James H. Knowles and Gretchen R. Knowles	Income	Tax Ct., aff'd by Ct. of Appeals	1,000	285,000	285,000
17	186	Est. of Matthew I. Heinold, et al.	Estate	Tax Ct., aff'd by Ct. of Appeals	79,250	250,000	200,000
18	187	Albert B. Houghton, et al., Exrs.	Estate	Dist. Ct.	472,900	1,336,500	1,134,300
19	189	Inga Bardahl	Gift	Tax Ct.	286,000	400,400	286,000
20	191	South Carolina National Bank, et al., Exrs.	Estate	Dist. Ct.	184,560	273,420	205,300
21	193	Nellie I. Brown	Gift	Tax Ct.	105,000	258,300	105,000

viewing such cases, i.e., the Tax Court, the Court of Claims, the District Courts, and the Courts of Appeal, and (c) they covered the three principal types of tax valuations—gift, estate, and income. Incidentally, the selected cases constituted a significant segment of valuation cases decided during the period, involving large amounts of tax at controversy.

SOURCE OF CASE MATERIAL

Most of the material shown in Table 7–1 was digested from full texts of the court decisions. In several cases supplemental data were obtained from transcripts of court records. In addition to showing valuations claimed by petitioners and by the Internal Revenue Service, and those adjudicated by the courts, the analyses indicate, for each case, the issues argued, and comments on or excerpts from the court decisions. A short description of the decisive factors considered precedes each case.

PRESUMPTION REGARDING COMMISSIONER'S VALUATIONS

As noted by the authors in reviewing cases listed in Table 7–1, as well as the many others from among which these cases were selected, the Commissioner's determination of value is presumed to be correct, as a general rule, and usually will be sustained by the courts unless the taxpayer proves that such determination is incorrect. If suitable rebuttal evidence is established, the Commissioner's determination will not be sustained, *even though the taxpayer does not establish the correct value.* However, in a proceeding *where suit is brought to recover tax already paid* (District Court or Court of Claims) the taxpayer has a heavier burden of proof to establish the essential facts from which a correct determination of value can be made.[3]

A perusal of the table, in which the cases are reference coded from 1 to 21, shows that the majority of the court decisions continue to reflect valuations that differ from those claimed either by

[3] Walter W. Taylor v. Comm'r, 293 U.S. 507, 55 S. Ct. 287 (1935). Also, Worcester County Trust Co. et al. v. Comm'r, 134 F.2d 578 (1943).

the taxpayer or the Internal Revenue Service. This does not imply that these valuations were arrived at by compromise, for the courts appear to have exercised sounder judgment in their application of valuation techniques, in many cases, than the contestants involved.

CHARACTERISTICS OF CASES REVIEWED

Of the 21 cases reviewed, 10 involved gift taxes, 9 estate taxes, and 2 income taxes. The courts of original jurisdiction were the Tax Court in 11 cases, District Courts in 9, and the Court of Claims in 1. The decisions in two District Court cases were appealed; one was affirmed (case no. 15) and the other reversed (case no. 3) by the Court of Appeals. Three Tax Court cases were appealed and affirmed (cases nos. 5, 16, and 17) by the higher court. Cases nos. 6, 10, and 15 were decided by jury trials, all others were decided by the courts.

Case no. 13 involved the valuation of partnership interests, all others involved stock in corporations. The cases reviewed covered the valuation of companies engaged in various types of manufacturing, real estate holding and operating, investments, department store operations, steamship, dock, and terminal operations, automobile and tractor agencies, newspaper publishing, banking, credit financing, and a Coca-Cola bottling company.

Valuations in Table 7–1 were those shown in federal tax returns filed, and in the Commissioner's notices of deficiencies, except in a few cases where original values claimed were revised prior to or at the outset of the court proceedings.

SOME FINDINGS AND CONCLUSIONS

Represented among the twenty-one case decisions were certain key findings and conclusions which may be summarized as follows.

Fixed Formula Approach Usually Rejected

Although the courts generally recited all of the factors to be considered in valuing stock or interests in closely held or unlisted companies, as set forth in Revenue Ruling 59–60, they recognized, for the most part, which of these were significant in a particular case. They generally rejected a fixed formula approach, although giving weight to several relevant factors, in some instances, to determine valuation. For example, the Commissioner, in case no. 3, valued stock on a special formula for Coca-Cola companies. The Court of Appeals rejected this approach in upholding the petitioner's valuation, on the grounds that earnings of the company had steadily declined over a five-year period.

Upper and Lower Limits

In no case did the court value the stock of a company at a higher figure than that claimed by the Commissioner, or a lower figure than that claimed by the petitioner or plaintiff. An indication that the court might have felt that values should have been higher or lower than those claimed by the litigants could be inferred from the language used in some of the decisions (cases nos. 5, 11, 16, and 19). This language was to the effect that the value of the stock *was not less than* the amount claimed (by the Commissioner), or *not more than* the amount claimed (by the petitioner).

Earnings and Dividends

The greatest weight in valuing the companies involved in the cases reviewed was given to earnings and earnings trends. Dividends were considered to be the next important factor in valuations. It is interesting to note that the courts considered the dividend history of a company, rather than its dividend-paying capacity, where minority interests were being valued. This approach was used on the general premise that a minority stockholder had no control over the dividend policies of a company.

Discounts

This factor was a definite consideration in valuing interests in companies whose stock was closely held. Discounts ranging from 10% to 50% were allowed in computing valuations of minority interests. Such allowances were made in valuing companies involved in manufacturing, real estate holding and operating, and even in a family investment company holding primarily blue chip securities (cases nos. 4, 7, 8, 9, 14, 17, 19, and 20). In some instances where no fixed percentage of discount was shown, this factor was obviously considered in arriving at lower than computed valuations.

Market Values

Where transactions in a company's stock were few and isolated, market prices were disregarded as a factor. Even where transactions were of sufficient frequency to warrant their inclusion as a factor, the courts reviewed the market action of stocks before and subsequent to the critical dates of valuation. In case no. 12 it took into consideration a recent operating loss and cut in dividends, which had not then been fully reflected in a decline in quoted market prices of the company's stock.

In case no. 8 the court recognized that the market price of a stock had increased substantially, during a period of months, while a company was negotiating to take over the subject company. It valued such shares at about one third of the quoted market price at the date of the takeover. This figure was still about 60% higher than the low price for the year, prior to the time negotiations were commenced.

Case no. 17 was also interesting in that the court recognized that a block of shares representing 19% of the total outstanding should be valued at a price lower than the net proceeds per share of a public offering of the stock, due to the disruptive action their sale would have had on the market.

Comparative Statistics

The courts also rejected so-called comparative statistics in cases where the operations of the listed companies whose data were used were not too comparable to those of the company being valued. In case no. 20 the court rejected price–earnings ratios of a number of companies in a similar line of business, except for two companies whose stocks were publicly traded. The ratios derived on the many other companies listed by the Internal Revenue Service in this case were the result primarily of a single transaction involving the sale of all of the capital stock of each such company.

Book Values

These were generally considered of minor significance in arriving at valuations, except in a few cases where a formula approach was used, giving weight to average income, dividends, and "book value."

In case no. 5, a petitioner filed a gift tax return showing the par value of the stock as its "fair market value." This was a large family investment and holding company, and its underlying assets and business were worth many times the figure claimed. In case no. 2 a value approximating book value per share was claimed by the petitioner for a company having substantial interest in improved and unimproved real estate. In each of these cases the court looked through their corporate veils to determine fair market values. Also, the court rejected the Commissioner's valuation in case no. 21 based on discounted book value.

Residual Values

In case no. 6, involving a company owning producing oil land near a large urban area, an expert witness for the Commissioner contended that valuation should be based, in effect, on current and indicated residual asset values, evidential proof of which he failed to establish. The court rejected this approach in favor of the going-concern concept, based on income and dividends. The fact that income was steadily diminishing, with the prospects that dividends (which had exceeded income for a number of years) would likewise be affected, was indicated in the court's charge to the jury.

Alleged "Excess Assets"

In case no. 4 an expert for the government and one for the taxpayer arrived at roughly the same valuation per share (slightly over $100) for the enterprise as a going concern. However, the government witness added $60 to the per-share value thus determined, on the grounds that government securities held represented an "excess investment" in such amount. The court found that the government's position was unjustified. A large part of the securities represented a temporary conversion of cash at the year end, to effect state tax savings. Furthermore, the record proved that the enterprise needed such assets for a regularly followed program of expansion and rehabilitation.

Expert Witnesses

In most of the cases "expert witnesses" were produced by the petitioners or plaintiffs as well as by the Internal Revenue Service. In a number of instances the witnesses for the latter were employees of the Service, but outside experts were sometimes engaged in addition to or in lieu of employees.

In case no. 10 the judge in his charge to the jury gave an excellent presentation of how the evidence offered by expert witnesses in support of the claims of either side in a litigation should be considered. He explained that the rules of evidence ordinarily do not permit the opinion of a witness to be received as evidence. An exception to the rule exists in the case of an expert witness who by education, study, and experience has become an expert in any art, science, or profession, and may give his opinion as to any such matter *in which he is versed and which is material to the case.* He cautioned that the value of the opinion of such a witness *is not the knowledge which he professes but the knowledge he actually possesses.* Also, in judging the weight and credibility of testimony of a witness, consideration should be given to the opportunity he had for observation and learning the facts, what facts he used as bases for his opinion, his ability and experience with respect to the testimony, and his interest, bias, or feelings on the case or his freedom therefrom.

The courts were quite critical of "expert" witnesses who testified in some of the cases reviewed, generally because of their lack of knowledge or disregard of the facts, or their apparent bias in using comparative financial statistics or other data that had little or no bearing on the relative valuations of the subject companies.

DIGEST OF CASES

It would not be practicable to analyze and comment on all of the important facets of the cases summarized in Table 7–1 and reviewed on the following pages. It is suggested that a perusal of the digest of cases should prove rewarding to those having an interest in tax valuations. It is urged, where areas germane to particular problems of the reader are mentioned, that the complete court opinions be obtained and studied. Since they involve many complicated issues, such studies should generally be carried out by legal counsel, assisted by independent public accountants or other experts in required areas.

Case No. 1. Celia Waterman [4]

Issue: Earning power and underlying asset values versus appraised values

Purpose of Valuation: Gift tax

Valuation Claimed by Petitioner	Claimed by IRS	Final Adjudication
$37,823	$126,477	$74,750

Supplementary Information: Maxcell Corporation—a real estate holding company operating seven units of improved rental property

Issues Argued

Maxcell was a Pennsylvania corporation having 571 shares of $50 par value common stock, all of which was owned by the petitioner prior to making gifts of the stock to her daughter and son aggregating 299 shares on September 29, 1955. Petitioner valued the stock in gift tax returns filed at $126.50 per share, an aggregate of $37,823.50, whereas the Commissioner valued it at $423 per share, an aggregate of $126,477. The earnings per share for the five years ended December 31, 1955, averaged $7.95 per share and the latest year's earnings were $7.01. The Commissioner contended that the value of the underlying assets was the proper base for fair valuation and produced a witness who appraised the properties at $277,400. This figure compared with "book value" of such properties of $90,810 and resulted in an adjusted "book value" of $261,209 or $457 per share. Apparently some adjustment was made by the Commissioner to arrive at a fair market value of $423 per share. The petitioner's witness valued the stock on a times-earnings basis, citing as criteria the sale of capital stocks of large industrial corporations.

[4] 20 T.C.M. 1117 (1961).

Decision

The court pointed out that Maxcell was not an industrial corporation, but a real estate corporation which derived its earnings from rentals, and concluded: "Therefore in arriving at our decision, we have weighed the value and nature of the underlying assets in conjunction with the earnings generated by these corporate assets and we find that the stock had a fair market value on the date of the gift of $250 per share."

Case No. 2. Estate of Lida R. Tompkins[5]

Issue: Fair market value of underlying assets governs rather than "book value" of holding company

Purpose of Valuation: Estate tax

Valuation Claimed by Petitioner	Claimed by IRS	Final Adjudication
$357,120	$1,488,000	$1,023,000

Supplementary Information: H Street Building Corporation and its numerous subsidiaries—owners of office buildings and a 50% undivided interest in extensive tracts of unimproved land and some warehouses in process of construction

Issues Argued

H Street Building Corporation, located in Washington, D. C., was incorporated under the laws of Delaware. At the date of her death, on January 28, 1953, Lida R. Tompkins owned 186 shares of no par common and 540 shares of $100 par value 5% preferred stock of the company out of 650 and 1,350 shares respectively outstanding. At one time there had been 3,000 shares of preferred stock of H Street outstanding but this was being redeemed at the rate of 5%, or 150 shares per annum. With minor exceptions the dispute between the Commissioner and the executors of the Estate of Lida R. Tompkins arose over the valuation of the common shares of the corporation held in her estate. Dividends had been paid regularly on the preferred stock of H Street but none had ever been paid on the common stock. In the federal estate tax return filed in 1954 such shares were included at a valuation of approximately $834 per share, whereas the Commissioner valued the shares at $12,725.85. On brief the Commissioner changed his valuation to $8,000 per share, and the petitioner then maintained

[5] 20 T.C.M. 1763 (1961).

that the stock had a fair market value "not in excess of $1,920 per share" which was closely related to "book value" of H Street, the parent company. H Street kept its books and filed its returns on a "cash" basis and reflected relatively nominal "net income" over a ten-year period. The Commissioner contended that fair market value of the underlying assets of H Street and the various other corporations should govern. These values were considerably in excess of the amounts at which they were carried in the books of H Street. Because of the fact that a large part of the underlying assets of H Street and its subsidiaries consisted of a one-half undivided interest in unimproved real estate, and warehouses in process of construction, the petitioner contended that the fair market value of assets should be ignored as an element in the valuation of the corporation's stock.

Decision

After hearing the testimony and mentioning the various factors to be considered, the court concluded that ". . . the fair market value of the corporation's assets is only one factor and not necessarily a controlling factor in determining the value of the stocks" and "To paraphrase the language of Judge Murdock in *Estate of Amy H. Du-Puy* . . . , the evidence does not lead irresistibly to any amount as the obviously correct value, but a finding of the precise amount must be made. It is our best judgment, after considering to the best of our ability all of the evidence in the case and all of the factors suggested by the parties that the value of H Street Building Corporation stock on the valuation date was $5,500 per share."

Case No. 3. *Estate of J. L. Snyder v. United States* [6]

Issue: Weighted average earnings formula rejected where earnings declined

Purpose of Valuation: Gift tax

Valuation Claimed by Petitioner	*Claimed by IRS*	*Final Adjudication*
$396,000	$609,840	$396,000

Supplementary Information: Charlotte Coca-Cola Bottling Company

Issues Argued

The Commissioner valued the stock at $4,620.70 per share based on a "special formula for valuing stocks of Coca-Cola Companies," ten

[6] 285 F.2d 857 (4th Cir. 1961), *reversing and remanding* 182 F. Supp. 71 (W.D.N.C. 1960).

times average annual earnings over a five-year period. The district court reduced this figure to $4,150.00 by using a multiple of nine times average earnings.

Decision

The court of appeals rejected this weighted average, as the earnings of the company had steadily declined during the five-year period ended November 30, 1954, from $599 to $358 per share. In upholding the petitioner's valuation of $3,000 per share the court opined that "Here there was a clearly defined trend to lower earnings. . . . There was no reason to believe that these conditions would disappear. . . . Under these circumstances any computation which presupposes future earnings at levels substantially higher than those realized in 1954 is neither realistic nor reasonable nor should 1954 earnings be projected into the future without adjustments to the capitalization factor to give effect to the probability of continuation of the decline in earnings" (132 shares were involved out of a total of 700 outstanding).

Case No. 4. *Worthen v. United States* [7]

Issue: Addition of so-called excess investment asset values rejected where investments were temporary

Purpose of Valuation: Estate tax

Valuation Claimed by Petitioner	*Claimed by IRS*	*Final Adjudication*
$84,000	$147,000	$87,360

Supplementary Information: Stone and Forsyth Company and its subsidiary—wholesalers of coarse paper products and manufactured paper boxes

Issues Argued

Plaintiff valued the stock for estate tax purposes at $100 per share. Plaintiff's expert witness, giving moderate weight to net assets per share, and yield (annual dividends), gave by far the greatest weight to the factor of earnings and reached a figure of $123 per share as the intrinsic worth of the stock. In the light of the difficulties which would be encountered in selling a minority interest in this "employee owned" company he discounted this figure by "about 10 per cent" to arrive at a fair market value of $104 per share (as a matter of interest the "book value" per share was $295).

[7] 192 F. Supp. 727 (D. Mass. 1961).

The expert for the government arrived at a valuation of $103 per share on a comparable basis of procedure, to which he added $60 per share, the value of government securities held by the companies, which he considered to be an "excess investment."

Decision

The court found that the assumption by the government's witness as to the nature and purpose of holdings of government securities was unjustified. A large part of such holdings was a temporary conversion, at the year end, of cash needed as working capital, to effect state tax savings under the Massachusetts law. Furthermore, the record proved that the companies followed a policy of setting aside earnings for a program of expansion and rehabilitation which was in fact carried out. The court concluded that ". . . when the improper segregation of securities is eliminated, the two experts are found to be in remarkably close agreement as to the value of the stock" which the court found to be $104 per share (840 shares were involved out of a total of 4,328 outstanding).

Case No. 5. William Hamm, Jr.[8]

Issue: Value of underlying assets governs rather than par value of stock

Purpose of Valuation: Gift tax

Valuation Claimed by Petitioner	Claimed by IRS	Final Adjudication
$26,333	$2,240,019	$2,240,019

Supplementary Information: United Properties, Inc.—a family investment and holding company, having business and miscellaneous real estate, a department store, credit companies, automobile agencies, and miscellaneous other investments

Issues Argued

Petitioners valued the stock for gift tax purposes at its par value of $100 per share. The Commissioner valued it at $8,506.40 per share based on fair market value of underlying assets, and amended his claims substantially upward in answer to the petitioner's claims. Each party to the action presented a principal witness for valuing individual parcels of property and investments, including those in operating subsidiaries. The following figures are significant in this case:

[8] 20 T.C.M. 1814 (1961), *aff'd* 325 F.2d 935 (8th Cir. 1963).

Book net worth of United at December 31, 1953		$11,756,708
Par value of 7% cumulative preferred stock $3,500,000	$3,500,000	
Accumulated and unpaid dividends on preferred (not provided for on books)	3,685,500	7,185,500
Applicable to 1,000 shares of common stock		$ 4,571,208
Per share		$ 4,571.21

Decision

Based on the testimony of the experts, the court prepared its valuation of each property and investment. In the case of the real properties, the court accepted total valuations of $7,988,000 computed by the government's witness, against $6,359,000 by the petitioner's witness. Both witnesses substantially agreed on valuations of all properties except one owned by the company and leased to its department store subsidiary. The court found that the rentals received from this property were less than fair, and would not be suitable for capitalization to arrive at fair market value. Investments in two principal subsidiaries, a department store and a credit company, were valued by the court at $1,900,000 and $1,800,000 respectively. Various factors were taken into consideration in such valuations, but in each case the figures were slightly less than 10 times the latest year's earnings. All other investments, assets, and liabilities appeared to be valued alike by stipulation of the litigants. By means of these procedures the court arrived at the following valuation of United:

Net worth	$18,870,456
Less: Equity of preferred shareholders	7,185,500
Fair market value of 1,000 shares of common	$11,684,956
Per share	$11,685

The court concluded on this issue (there was another involving charitable deduction): "By the process of thus considering and weighing all the evidence in the light of our experience and judgment, we have hereinabove found as an ultimate fact, and we here hold, that the fair market value of United's common stock on the material valuation date was not less than $8,506.40 per share; and we further hold that the petitioners have failed to establish error in respondent's determination of value. We decide this first issue in favor of the respondent." As a matter of interest, on the basis of the petitioner's witness a valuation would have been computed in excess of $8,000 per share and the figure based on testimony of the witness for the government approximated $13,000 per share (263⅓ shares were involved out of a total of 1,000 outstanding).

Case No. 6. Daniels v. United States[9]

Issue: Declining earnings of oil-producing company govern, rather than alleged asset values

Purpose of Valuation: Gift tax

		Final
Valuation Claimed by Petitioner	Claimed by IRS	Adjudication
$24,256	$191,319	$75,800

Supplementary Information: Brea Canon Oil Company—a producing oil company

Issues Argued

Lillian M. Daniels made a gift of 6,064 shares of Brea Canon Oil Company capital stock to her relatives, John M. Lynch and Carol J. Lynch, on September 10, 1957. At the date of the gift, she owned 16,754 shares out of a total of 200,000 shares outstanding. The remaining shares were held by about a dozen stockholders, one of whom owned 50,000 shares.

In her gift tax return Lillian M. Daniels reported the value of the stock at $4 per share. The Commissioner appraised the stock at $31.55 per share, and issued her a deficiency assessment based on this valuation. The petitioner paid the deficiency assessment, plus interest, and filed a claim for refund, based on the valuation reported in the gift tax return.

Brea Canon owned 200 acres of land, approximately 18 miles from the city center of Los Angeles, Calif. The corporation was a producing oil company whose property had been leased to Union Oil Company for a number of years. Under the terms of the lease, Brea Canon paid the cost of drilling each well and thereafter Union took the oil at the well and piped it to its own tanks, and thence to its nearby refinery. For all practical purposes the activities of the corporation consisted of the collection of oil royalties under the lease with Union.

A review of the financial statements of Brea Canon for ten years ended in 1960 developed that its income from 1957 to 1960 had declined from approximately $700,000 to $400,000 although annual dividend payments increased from $420,000 to $500,000.

---

[9] 62-2 U.S. Tax Cas. 12,113 (D. Ore. 1961).

The corporation had $1,200,000 cash in bank at the time the gift was made and a valuation expert for the Internal Revenue Service claimed the land had a value of $10,000 per acre, or $2,000,000. Based on these two factors, he arrived at a valuation of $16 per share, before estimated oil reserves. The Internal Revenue Service introduced a summary of financial data of many companies in the United States engaged in oil production, which he attempted to relate to Brea Canon.

Testimony developed that the corporation had made no estimate of its oil reserves, nor was the government prepared to submit any data thereon. However, the secretary-treasurer of Brea Canon testified that, in his opinion, the wells were becoming depleted as evidenced by the amount of gas obtained from the wells which had increased materially in recent years. The testimony of the Internal Revenue expert regarding the value of the land was ruled inadmissible because he was not familiar with land values in the area during 1957.

Decision

The case was tried before a jury and the four experts, who testified, apparently valued the stock of Brea Canon in a range from $10 to $37 per share. The judge in his charge to the jury reviewed the valuation factors to be considered, generally as outlined in Revenue Ruling 59–60. The following excerpt from his charge is of particular interest:

> However, of these factors, earnings reflect most of the other factors listed, and are therefore often the most reliable guide to the value of the stock. The value of the corporate shares is determined more by what income they will bring than by any other single consideration. Of course, it would also depend on other factors such as how long you can expect those dividends to be paid in the future.
>
> In arriving at fair market value, it is not necessary that the figure that you reach is the amount to which any person has testified. All that is necessary is that the figure upon which you agree is within the range of the figures that may be properly deduced from the evidence.

The jury found the fair market value of the stock to be $12.50 a share.

Case No. 7. Central Trust Co., Executor, v. United States [10]

Issue: Valuation based on weighting formula using earnings, dividends, and book value

[10] 305 F.2d 393 (Ct. Cl. 1962).

Purpose of Valuation: Gift tax

		Final
Valuation Claimed by Petitioner	*Claimed by IRS*	*Adjudication*
$525,015	$1,680,048	$1,085,031

Supplementary Information: The Heekin Can Company—a metal container manufacturer of a full line of cans, canisters, and drums

Issues Argued

Gifts were made by members of the Heekin family of 30,000 shares on August 3, 1954, and 40,002 shares on October 21, 1954, to trusts created for benefit of their children. The value of the stock in returns filed was set at $10 a share. Later amended returns and claims for refund were filed asserting a value of $7.50 per share based on private sales involving 44 transactions totalling 13,359 shares between March 22, 1951, and April 16, 1952. Such sales were made by certain minority stockholders to employees and friends of the Heekin family at this prearranged price. The Commissioner contended that the stock had a value of $24 per share based on a study of 11 can and glass container companies' comparatives of earnings, dividend yield, and book value. Two of the companies included in the study were giants and accounted for about 75% of the country's total can sales whereas Heekin did a little less than 1% of the total business. Three expert witnesses testified for the plaintiff, all of whom used a four-factor formula, i.e., book value, earnings, dividends, and prior sales ($7.50 per share). Each gave different weighting to these factors and reduced the resultant formula figures by percentages ranging from 15% to 25% for lack of marketability. One of these witnesses used three years' average earnings and the other two used five years'. Their valuations ranged from $7.88 to $11.76 per share. Two of the witnesses used the unadjusted earnings figures of the company while the third adjusted the figures for certain abnormal and non-recurring items. All witnesses used industry comparatives in their studies. The defendant used an expert witness who made material adjustments to the figures over the period from 1950 to 1954, which showed book earnings for 1954 to be substantially understated. This expert studied eight companies in the industry and concluded that only two could be considered comparable. Correlating the data on such companies with Heekin, and using the latest 12 months' figures because of Heekin's favorable trend and outlook, this witness gave earnings a weight of 50%, dividends 30%, and book value 20%, and arrived at valuations of $21.85 and $21.35 respectively for August 3, 1954, and October 25, 1954.

Decision

The court, in reviewing data submitted, broadened the study of comparatives to give a better base but accepted the formula of the defendant's witness as to weighting and arrived at valuations of $16.67 and $16.54 at the respective dates after a reduction of 12.17% as "the estimated costs that would be involved in marketing the stock." Giving important weight to these figures the court settled on a valuation of $15.50 per share at both dates although the so-called "book value" approximated $33.00 per share.

In reaching its findings, the court considered the age and relative inefficiency of a large part of the company's plant and equipment and its inability to finance a large-scale program of modernization. It concluded: "The fact that the Company was, on the gift dates, a relatively small one competing, with a comparatively old plant, against the giants of the industry, operating at high efficiency with the most modern equipment, makes unwarranted a valuation of this closely held stock representing only a minority interest on any significantly higher basis. For these reasons also the $15.50 valuation [approximately net current asset value] is considered to be fair and just to both plaintiff and defendant."

Case No. 8. North American Philips Co.[11]

Issue: Market value of stock of company negotiating to be acquired rejected because deal affected such value

Purpose of Valuation: Income tax

Valuation Claimed by Petitioner	Claimed by IRS	Final Adjudication
None ascertainable	$6,626,250	$2,254,320

Supplementary Information: Reynolds Spring Company—a manufacturer of cushion springs for the automotive industry

Issues Argued

North American Philips Company (Philips), a Dutch-controlled Delaware corporation, pursuant to an agreement sold the operating

---

[11] 21 T.C.M. 1497 (1962).

assets, patents, trademarks, etc., of its A. W. Haydon Company division, which manufactured precision electrical timing and governing devices to Reynolds in a taxable exchange, for 279,000 shares of newly issued capital stock of the latter in December, 1954.

Philips claimed a capital loss on the transaction whereas the Commissioner computed a capital gain in excess of $5,000,000, by valuing Reynolds shares received at $23.75 per share, which was slightly below the average high–low trading price of Reynolds on the New York Stock Exchange on December 29, 1954. Prior to this transaction there were 280,000 shares of Reynolds outstanding with many public stockholders.

Reynolds' business had been steadily deteriorating since 1951 and substantial losses were sustained by the company in 1952, 1953, and 1954. On the other hand, the Haydon division of Philips had been operating very profitably. The fact that Philips agreed to adjust the purchase price to Reynolds, if the pre-tax profits of the Haydon division would be less than $750,000 for the three years following purchase indicated the prospects of a continuation of profitable operations. In order to gain consent of the New York Stock Exchange for the transaction and listing of the 279,000 Reynolds shares Philips agreed not to divest itself of such shares for a period of three years from December 28, 1954.

Reynolds' stock sold at a low of $5 per share in April 1954, when negotiations were commenced with Philips. Trading in the stock became quite heavy starting in July 1954, but the major increase in its price took place in the last two months of that year. The Commissioner based his valuation on market prices "in accord with the recognized principle that in the absence of clearly proven exceptional circumstances the prices at which shares of stock are traded on an open public market on the valuation date represents the best evidence of fair market value." The court dismissed the testimony of an Internal Revenue employee-witness, who opined that the stock had a fair market value of $16 to $18 per share, "because it appears to have been based on little more than guesswork and erroneous comparisons." A security analyst testified for the Commissioner that the stock had a value of $12.46 per share, and a partner in an investment banking firm testifying for the petitioner valued it at $5 per share.

Decision

In rendering its decision, the court noted that a portion of the rise in market value of Reynolds during the period from April to December was due to the anticipated association with Philips and its Dutch parent. Also, it noted that the Commissioner had not given adequate consideration to the limited market for Philips' holdings of Reynolds, because of the restrictions imposed by the New York Stock Exchange. It then concluded "after considering their testimony [the two expert witnesses], the exhibits presented, and after taking into consideration the various objections to their valuation, we have concluded that the fair market value of the Reynolds stock on December 29, 1954, was $8.08 per share."

Case No. 9. Drybrough v. United States [12]

Issue: Substantial discounts from fair market value of real estate holdings allowed for minority interests

Purpose of Valuation: Gift tax

Valuation Claimed by Petitioner	Claimed by IRS	Final Adjudication
$134,328	$526,800	$171,452

Supplementary Information: Parcel of real estate and four closely held realty corporations holding six parcels of real estate, four parking lots, and two smaller pieces of property

Issues Argued

Although there were other issues involved, the principal one was the valuation of gifts made in May and June 1957, by Mr. and Mrs. F. W. Drybrough to their son. The gifts consisted of an undivided 40% interest in real estate located in Louisville, Kentucky, and 40% of the issued and outstanding capital stock of four real estate holding corporations. The parties agreed that the value of the underlying realty comprising the sole assets of the corporations must be determined and the mortgage indebtedness, if any, should be deducted therefrom, and that 40% of the resulting figure is the "book value" of 40% of issued and outstanding capital stock of the individual corporations. Both sides produced qualified experts and filed briefs summarizing their valuations. The gross valuations of the underlying properties (before deducting mortgage indebtedness of $749,000) of the respective parties and the court were as follows:

	Plaintiff	Defendant	Court
Parcel of land	$ 238,750	$ 238,853	$ 238,800
Properties held by corporations	1,006,400	1,314,220	1,142,000
Total	$1,245,150	$1,553,073	$1,380,800

[12] 208 F. Supp. 279 (W.D. Ky. 1962).

The next and important issue was what discounts, if any, were to be applied to the undivided interest in real estate, and to the minority interests in the corporations. The government contended that no discounts should be allowed, whereas the witnesses for the taxpayer testified to the contrary. They testified that a discount ranging up to 40% should be allowed on the undivided interest in the parcel of land. One witness for the taxpayer testified that a holder of minority interests in Kentucky corporations cannot control policy, dividends, or liquidation, and therefore such interests are not readily marketable. He suggested a discount on the "fair market" value of the 40% interest in the corporations ranging from $33\frac{1}{3}\%$ to 50%. A witness for the government proposed a discount of "approximately 20%."

Decision

From a consideration of all the testimony the court concluded that the value of the undivided interest in the unincorporated real estate should be discounted 15%, and the minority interests in the corporation 35%. The resultant valuations were as follows:

	Gross	Mortgage	Net	40% Interest	Discounted
Parcel of land	$ 238,800	$149,000	$ 89,800	$ 35,920	$ 30,532
Corporations	1,142,000	600,000	542,000	216,800	140,920
	$1,380,800	$749,000	$631,800	$252,720	$171,452

Case No. 10. Huntington National Bank v. United States[13]

Issue: Option prices of stock granted to a relative rejected as conclusive factor

Purpose of Valuation: Estate tax

Valuation Claimed by Petitioner	Claimed by IRS	Final Adjudication
$356,095	$908,650	$671,544

Supplementary Information: Stock investments in Cambria Clay Products, Davis Fire Brick, Ohio Fire Brick, and Oak Hill Savings Bank

Issues Argued

D. D. Davis died on February 14, 1954, and left his estate "exclusively for public, charitable, scientific or educational purposes." At his death the decedent owned the following unlisted stocks in four cor-

---

[13] 62–2 U.S. Tax Cas. 12,088 (S.D. Ohio 1962).

porations: Cambria Clay Products 2,388 shares, Davis Fire Brick 141 shares, Ohio Fire Brick 129 shares, and Oak Hill Savings Bank 664½ shares. With the exception of shares in Oak Hill, all of which were voting, some of the shares in the other three companies were voting and some non-voting. Total outstanding shares of stock of the companies were Cambria 9,000, Davis 402, Ohio 480, and Oak Hill 1,005. In his will, D. D. Davis granted an option to Edward E. Davis, a relative, to purchase the estate's holdings in the four corporations at the following per-share prices: Cambria $61, Davis $320, Ohio $380, and Oak Hill $175. On December 8, 1954, Edward E. Davis exercised the right provided under the will and purchased the shares of stock of the four companies at the prices indicated, except that the price paid for the Oak Hill stock was $155 per share.

The executor elected to value the gross estate on the alternate valuation date and included the shares of stock in the four corporations at the option prices listed in the will. The Commissioner revalued the shares of stock as follows: Cambria $170, Davis $675, Ohio $585, and Oak Hill $500. Additional estate tax was paid based on the deficiency assessment and a suit for refund was filed by the executor, based on the valuations set forth in the estate tax return.

The case was tried before a jury, and the judge, in his charge, explained the usual factors to be considered in valuing the stocks. He further noted that the stocks were to be valued as of December 8, 1954, in accordance with the rule governing property sold or disposed of prior to the alternate valuation date.

The plaintiff produced an expert witness who valued the stocks as follows: Cambria $75 to $80, Davis $400 to $425, Ohio $400 to $425, and Oak Hill $200 to $225. The government had two expert witnesses. One, a Treasury Department engineer, valued the stocks at: Cambria $168, Davis $700, Ohio $590, and Oak Hill $500. The other expert witness arrived at valuations of: Cambria $166, Davis $620, Ohio $447, and Oak Hill $474.

Approximate net income per share of the companies for the year 1954 was: Cambria $35, Davis $100, Ohio $70, and Oak Hill $50. Over a five-year period ended in 1954, only Oak Hill showed a steady improvement in earnings. Earnings of the other three companies were somewhat erratic or static. Relatively substantial dividends had been paid on Cambria, Davis, and Ohio during the period, particularly for 1954. More nominal dividends had been paid on Oak Hill. The approximate "book value" per share of the companies in December 1954, was Cambria $195, Davis $785, Ohio $856, and Oak Hill $568.

The plaintiff claimed that there were contingent matters affecting several of the companies, the settlement of which might involve the payment of large sums of money. These included a claim for back pay by a number of employees who struck and were not rehired, income taxes over a disputed depletion allowance claimed, and damages arising out of a possible patent infringement.

Jury Instructions and Decision

The court instructed the jury as to the following, among other matters:

1. *Option prices of the stocks*—The prices paid for these shares of stock are not conclusive or binding on the jury. "In weighing the value of such evidence you should consider the circumstances surrounding the option, the relationship between the parties and the fact that the option was not at arm's-length. . . . You may nevertheless consider this option price in connection with all the other evidence. . . ."

2. *Contingent liabilities of the companies*—The court explained some conjectural aspects of each of these and implied that the plaintiff's estimates of maximum liability appeared to be high, considering the various remedies available to contest or mitigate the amounts of settlement of the claims.

3. *Testimony of expert witnesses*—"Finally the weight and creditability of the witnesses who have testified in this case is within your sole power to determine, and the weight and credit to be given the testimony of the witnesses is committed to your sound judgment and discretion."

The jury found the fair market value per share at December 8, 1954, of the capital stocks of Cambria, Davis, Ohio, and Oak Hill, respectively, to be $138, $600, $450, and $300.

Case No. 11. H. Fort Flowers [14]

Issue: Price per share of isolated sales to "insiders" and sales to employees under a repurchase plan rejected

Purpose of Valuation: Gift tax

Valuation Claimed by Petitioner	*Claimed by IRS*	*Final Adjudication*
$500,000	$800,000	$800,000

[14] 22 T.C.M. 106 (1963).

Supplementary Information: National Lime and Stone Company Mines —manufacturers and producers of lime and lime products, limestone, and ready-mixed concrete

Issues Argued

On April 1, 1957, members of the Flowers family made taxable gifts, in trust, that included an aggregate of 5,000 shares of National, and H. Fort Flowers, on January 2, 1958, made a taxable gift in trust of certain assets including 5,000 shares of National. In their gift tax returns, petitioners valued National at $50 per share, whereas the Commissioner placed a value of $80 per share on such stock at the dates of gift.

Some interesting financial statistics, per share, on the company for the respective years ended November 30, 1954 to 1958, follow:

Year	Net Earnings	Dividends Paid	"Book Value"	Net Liquid Assets
1954	$10.00	$3.50	$69.84	$45.47
1955	13.32	5.00	78.15	52.76
1956	16.29	6.00	88.45	60.53
1957	14.54	6.00	94.50	58.27
1958	11.51	6.00	99.75	62.04

At November 30, 1958, the company held cash and U. S. Government securities approximating $60 per share of stock. The outstanding shares of National at both gift dates totaled 87,257, which were substantially owned by the Flowers family. There was no market for the stock and the petitioners were relying on a few isolated transactions over a period of some four years, primarily involving insiders, in which small amounts of the stock were priced at $50 per share. The company had a stock purchase plan for the benefit of four key employees, who purchased 2,347 shares of stock at 60% of book value over a period of 6 years ended November 30, 1958. These employees were required under the plan to resell such stock to National, or to certain stockholders, at 60% of book value as determined at the fiscal year-end preceding the date of repurchase. In a series of suits issued between minority and majority shareholders seeking to enjoin or cancel 1,697 shares of stock issued to the four employees during the 1953 fiscal year, H. Fort Flowers had testified that the stock of National, in his opinion had a fair market value ranging from $117.77 to $200 per share on varying bases.

Decision

After hearing all the testimony, the court concluded in this case that "... the evidence clearly establishes that the National stock had a

fair market value of at least $80 per share on the dates of the gifts."
It dismissed the four isolated sales at $50 per share as having no sig-
nificance, as well as the sales to employees under the stock purchase
plan. As to the latter it stated: "Firstly, such stock is restricted as to
its sale. Secondly, even if this did represent the fair market value, the
sales (1,697 shares) in 1953 are too remote."

Case No. 12. Estate of Marjorie Gilbert Brush [15]

Issue: Bid and asked prices of stock for a reasonable period before and
after valuation date considered

Purpose of Valuation: Estate tax

Valuation Claimed by Petitioner	Claimed by IRS	Final Adjudication
$188,946	$464,492	$346,401

Supplementary Information: Seatrain Lines, Inc.—owners and opera-
tors of a fleet of vessels and dock, terminal, and switching facilities
for transporting loaded railroad freight cars

Issues Argued

Included in the Estate of Marjorie Gilbert Brush, deceased, was a
block of 62,982 shares of Seatrain Lines, Inc. Although the company
had approximately 1,200 stockholders, more than two-thirds of the
1,412,891 shares outstanding were owned by three principal groups.

The stock was valued at $3 per share in the estate tax return filed by
the executors at the alternate valuation date of April 6, 1959, although
the mean of the bid and asked quotations published by the National
Quotation Bureau was 7⅜ on that date. The latter valuation was
claimed by the Commissioner in his notice of deficiency. The stock
had fluctuated between a price of 7 and 10⅜ bid and 7⅞ and 11½
asked from January 1, 1959, to April 6, 1959, and the lowest bid price
submitted by a dealer to the National Quotation Bureau for the week
prior to the valuation date was 6½.

Seatrain Lines, Inc. income had declined substantially during the
years 1956, 1957, and 1958, and the company had a loss for the year
1959. Dividends for the year 1959 were reduced to 12½ cents per
share from a rate of 50 cents that had prevailed for a number of years.
The bid price for the stock went as low as 4½ late in 1959.

[15] 22 T.C.M. 900 (1963).

Decision

The court, in its opinion, found the value of the stock to be $5.50 per share and quoted Treasury Regulations 20.2031.–2,(a), (b), and (e). Subsection (e), which reads as follows, is of particular significance: "(e) *where selling prices or bid and asked prices do not reflect fair market value.* If it is established that the value of any bond or share of stock determined on the basis of selling or bid and asked prices as provided under paragraphs (b) . . . of this section does not reflect the fair market value of the stock involved, then some reasonable modification of that basis or other relevant facts and elements of value are considered in determining the fair market value." In reciting the various factors considered in arriving at its decision, the court included the following comment, which indicated it took into account events subsequent to the effective date of valuation: "The bid and ask prices for the shares on the over-the-counter market on and within a reasonable period before and after the applicable valuation date; the extent to which said bid and ask prices may or may not be reasonably regarded to reflect the fair market value of the particular shares of stock here involved; the trend of such prices; and the probability as to the trend of the same over a reasonable period subsequent to the valuation date."

Case No. 13. *Robert T. Barber* [16]

Issue: Valuation included anticipated net profits on construction contracts of partnership

Purpose of Valuation: Gift tax

Valuation Claimed by Petitioner	*Claimed by IRS*	*Final Adjudication*
Not indicated	$675,000	$407,900

Supplementary Information: Barber Brothers Company—a partnership engaged in construction consisting chiefly of paving road, building, and heavy construction work

Issues Argued

Barber Brothers Company, a partnership consisting of five brothers, had operated under various forms of organization for many years prior to May 4, 1956, when they and their respective spouses donated

---

[16] 22 T.C.M. 1025 (1963).

undivided limited or commendam interests in the partnership aggregating 27% to their children, effective as of March 31, 1956. The partnership agreement contained "no restriction on the sale of an interest of a partner in commendam, no option to anyone to purchase the same, no right to insist upon liquidation if such interest of same is not purchased, and no formula with respect to the purchase of any interest."

The principal customer of the firm was the State of Louisiana, its agencies, and subdivisions. Such business was said to account for "at least 85% of their partnership income and was procured through the submission of the lowest competitive bids." The firm, which operated on a fiscal year ending June 30, showed "net" income (presumably before taxes) ranging at the annual rate of $400,000 to $500,000 plus during the recent period through May 31, 1956, and tangible net worth at that date of $921,180. Such income was determined on a completed contract basis.

The parties agreed on brief that the value of the partnership was no less than $921,180. However, the petitioner also contended that its value was no more than this amount. The Commissioner claimed that the fair market value was $2,500,000, arrived at as follows:

Tangible assets, as above	$ 921,180
Gross profit on 31 construction contracts in progress, determined by deducting direct costs incurred from progress payments received, without any allowance for any indirect costs or overhead	466,452
"Tangible assets"	1,387,632
Goodwill (computed at about twice the average net profit earned during an approximate ten-year period)	598,834
Value of work in process	513,534
Total	$2,500,000

Decision

The court rejected the Commissioner's inclusion of both the gross profit on construction projects in progress and the total anticipated net profit on the same contracts. In lieu thereof it computed the anticipated net profit to be realized on such contracts at $500,417, based on the average net profit on construction receipts for a 9¾-year period. The court further rejected the contention that goodwill attached to the greater part of the business: "Since petitioners' contracts obtained through low competitive public bids were the major source of their earnings, and since no expectation of the patronage of the State of Louisiana, or its agencies and subdivisions, could have been conveyed by them to a purchaser of their partnership business, it is clear that to the extent their earnings were dependent upon such contracts they did not own goodwill recognizable for tax purposes."

The court, however, did agree that the firm had goodwill which attached to its private business. Using substantially the method proposed by the Commissioner for this segment of the business, it arrived at a figure of $89,147, which it added to the tangible assets of $921,180 and anticipated net profit of $500,417, for a total valuation of the firm of $1,510,744, or $407,900 for a 27% interest.

Case No. 14. Obermer v. United States [17]

Issue: A 33⅓% discount allowed from fair market value of a 50% interest in a family investment company

Purpose of Valuation: Estate tax

Valuation Claimed by Petitioner	Claimed by IRS	Final Adjudication
$357,700	$592,167	$394,800

Supplementary Information: Austin Page, Inc.—a family investment corporation

Issues Argued

Seymour Obermer died in Honolulu, Hawaii, on February 19, 1957. The bulk of his estate was bequeathed to his wife Nesta, and included 100 shares of Austin Page Inc., a New York investment corporation; the other 100 outstanding shares of Austin were owned by Nesta at the time of Seymour's death. In addition to capital stock, the company had outstanding debentures of $164,405 par value, with accrued interest of $186,170, a total of $350,575. By agreement on October 31, 1955, the company had concluded an arrangement for the retirement of not less than $38,881 par value of debentures plus accrued interest each year. The assets of Austin consisted of blue chip stocks traded on the New York Stock Exchange, marketable bonds, and certificates of deposit, and for tax purposes it was a "personal holding company" subject to the usual penalty tax on undistributed income.

The executor filed the federal estate tax return of the decedent on February 19, 1958, the alternative valuation date, and claimed a value of $4,400 per share for the 100 shares of Austin stock. At this date the "adjusted book value" (presumably valuing Austin's security port-

[17] 238 F. Supp. 29 (D. Hawaii 1964).

folio at market) was $5,921.67 per share. This latter value was claimed by the Internal Revenue Service. Upon the request of the executor, Austin had repurchased 15 shares of its common stock for $4,500 per share on May 16, 1958.

Later, in a conference, the executor and the government representative agreed on a 12½% discount from the $5,921.67 adjusted value per share, and the executor paid the deficiency assessment on this basis, plus interest.

Subsequently the plaintiff, as sole legatee, filed a timely claim for refund, alleging the adjusted value should be discounted 33⅓% and later amended her claim to a 40% discount. On the other hand, the government amended its claim and proposed to disallow any discount.

The government's position was that the corporation was simply an alter ego of the taxpayer and that the blue chip stocks were not in blocks so large that they could not be readily disposed of by her.

Decision

The court in finding for Nesta Obermer, the plaintiff, listed the following factors as adversely affecting the value of the stock:

1. Personal holding company and subject to such penalty taxes, as well as New York State income tax
2. Obligations with respect to redemption of the debentures and interest thereon
3. Built-in capital gains tax (approximately $145,000 at the valuation date) because of substantial market appreciation in portfolio securities
4. Lack of control of a 50% interest in seeking a so-called mythical buyer, since New York State law requires a 66⅔% stock ownership to approve of liquidation
5. Selling expenses which would be involved in disposing of this 50% interest to a mythical buyer

The court concluded its findings to the effect that "the fair market value of the Austin stock on the valuation date in question was a figure determined by deducting 33⅓% of the adjusted book value of $5,921.67 per share" (approximately $3,948 net valuation).

Case No. 15. John J. Louis, Jr., Executor, v. United States [18]

Issue: Low valuation approved for a 5% minority interest, primarily in non-voting stock of company having a poor dividend record.

---

[18] 369 F.2d 263 (7th Cir. 1966), *affirming* 66–1 U.S. Tax Ct. 12,390 (N.D. Ill. 1965).

Purpose of Valuation: Estate tax

		Final
Valuation Claimed by Petitioner	*Claimed by IRS*	*Adjudication*
$763,750	$4,700,000	$1,254,900

Supplementary Information: D. C. Johnson & Son, Inc., Racine, Wis.— manufacturers of a variety of waxes and home care products known as "Johnson's Wax"

Issues Argued

John J. Louis owned 30,000 shares of Class A and 205,000 Class B (non-voting) common stock out of totals outstanding of 479,939 and 3,839,512, respectively at February 19, 1959, the date of his death. In the federal estate tax return filed, his executors valued the 235,000 shares at $3.25 per share as of the date of death. This figure was accepted by the State of Illinois, for inheritance tax purposes.

The stock of the company was closely held and H. F. Johnson and his family owned more than 60% of the outstanding shares. The company also had two classes of preferred stock outstanding on which dividends had been paid regularly. Although the company showed substantial earnings over the five-year period ended June 30, 1958, they were relatively static for the three latest years, being less than $1 per share, after preferred dividend requirements. Only one dividend had been paid on the common stock during this period and that was at the rate of $0.25 per share in 1958; the net book equity per share of common stock was approximately $4.50.

An interesting facet of this case was that the company had relatively substantial balances of marketable securities and cash at December 31, 1958, which had been built up over a period of years. There were transactions in the two classes of common stock during the period from July 1956 to January 1959, aggregating 194,949 shares at prices ranging from $4.49 to $6.68 per share, apparently under a formula and at an ascending scale. All such transactions were among "insiders," including the sale by John J. Louis of 90,000 shares at $4.49 per share to 64 employees during November and December 1956.

On audit of the federal estate tax return, the government proposed to increase the valuation of the shares to $11.50 each. After a conference, the government proposed to value the shares at $5.50 each and the executors paid additional tax and interest on this basis. However, this figure, although approved by the District Office, was rejected by the Regional Office, and a deficiency was assessed against the estate on the basis of $20.00 per share.

The issue was tried before a jury, and two witnesses for the plaintiff testified that the stock was worth $3.25 per share, another valued it at $5.50, and the fourth at $6.00. Three witnesses for the government valued the stock respectively at $17.00, $22.00, and $24.00 per share.

The judge in his charge to the jury mentioned the various factors to be considered, including the testimony of the experts, the sale of stock during a reasonable period of the valuation date at arm's length between an informed buyer and seller, the fact that a portion of the company's consolidated earnings was in foreign countries, the amount of dividends paid over the past five years, the absence of a public market for the stock, and the non-voting status of 205,000 shares of the total of 235,000. He also mentioned that the block of stock to be valued represented a minority interest of approximately 5%. The jury found the value of the shares to be $5.34 per share.

Decision

Upon appeal, the court upheld this figure and stated that "There is no question that the record provides ample support for the jury's verdict. The taxpayers presented an impressive array of expert witnesses . . . who described in detail the manner in which they arrived at their valuations, which varied from $3.25 to $6 together with display of large, easily read charts which simplified the process for the jury. . . . The Government's expert witnesses on the other hand used as 'comparables' a number of prosperous, well-known concerns, whose stock was listed on the stock exchange . . . on the theory that they were in the same or similar line of business, although as the jury must have known many were in the drug or packaged food business." In its appeal, among other things, the government alleged misconduct on the part of counsel for the taxpayers in improperly bringing to attention of the jurors the proposed valuation of $5.50 per share, which was never consummated. The District Court judge had sustained the government's objection to mentioning this figure, and the Appeals Court opined that his flat statement, in sustaining the objection, that the estate claimed a valuation of $3.25 and the government $20.00 a share and anything in between was irrelevant, covered this point adequately.

Case No. 16. *Knowles v. Commissioner* [19]

Issue: Profit on sale of stock sold to officer of company at nominal value deemed compensation for services rather than capital gain

[19] 355 F.2d 931 (3rd Cir. 1966), *affirming* 24 T.C.M. 129 (1965).

Purpose of Valuation: Income tax

		Final
Valuation Claimed by Petitioner	*Claimed by IRS*	*Adjudication*
$1,000	$285,000	$285,000

Supplementary Information: C. H. D. Corporation—a holding company owning all the stock of Hubbard and Company, manufacturer of pole line wire used by electrical utility companies and of other products

Issues Argued

C. H. D. Corporation was organized in July 1954 with an authorized capital stock of 10,000 common shares at a par value of $1 each. All of the authorized stock of the corporation was issued for cash at such par value on July 9, 1954, to Charles H. Dyson, his wife, a trust, and the attorney for Dyson. This corporation was organized to acquire the capital stock of Hubbard and Company, which it did on July 14, 1954, for $4,543,000 which was essentially financed by a dividend from Hubbard to C. H. D., Hubbard using its own funds and a $3,700,000 bank loan to pay the dividend.

James H. Knowles was president of Hubbard at this time and on July 29, 1954, had his first conversation with Dyson regarding continuance of his employment. Dyson agreed to the continuance and on September 23, 1954, he and his wife each sold to Knowles 500 shares of common stock of C. H. D. Corporation for $1 a share or a total of $1,000. Knowles's shares were subject to a written agreement giving Dyson the right to meet any bona fide offer for the sale of such shares and stating that Knowles would join with Dyson if the latter should receive a bona fide offer for the sale of C. H. D. Corporation, on a pro rata basis of the proceeds.

Petitioner's employment by Hubbard ceased on December 1, 1956, and his stock was purchased by Dyson Corporation (formerly C. H. D.) for $285,000 on May 31, 1957.

In his 1957 income tax return the petitioner reported a long-term capital gain on the Dyson stock of $284,000 measured by the difference between the $285,000 proceeds and the $1,000 which had been paid for it. The Commissioner took issue with the petitioner and determined, in his deficiency notice, that the value of the C. H. D. stock on September 23, 1954, was $285,000, and the difference between this amount and the $1,000 paid for the stock was additional compensation for services for the year 1954.

Decision

The court found that the C. H. D. stock, valued on a consolidated basis, had a value of at least $285,000 at the time it was acquired. The price of $285,000 paid for the stock was a compromise figure and represented approximately 10% of Hubbard's earnings for the last three years of petitioner's employment.

It was pointed out by the court that since the purchase price of Hubbard was $4,500,000, petitioner's interest at the date he acquired the C. H. D. stock would appear to have had an immediate value of $450,000. In the court's opinion the government was fair in discounting the value to $285,000 for the purpose of recognizing the minority interest of the petitioner and the changes in circumstances between the C. H. D. purchase of Hubbard stock and petitioner's purchase of C. H. D. stock such as (a) Hubbard's expenditure of $900,000 and the floating of a $3,700,000 bank loan to finance C. H. D.'s purchase, (2) C. H. D.'s acquisition of the Hubbard stock from sellers who had lost interest in the business, and (3) petitioner's acquisition of the C. H. D. stock when it was in the hands of able and aggressive new ownership.

In finding for the Commissioner, the court opined that the Dysons at the time of the sale to Knowles were in no financial difficulty and that "there was no rational economic basis for the sale of a 10 per cent equity in Hubbard for $1,000 other than as a means of compensation to the petitioner for the rendition of services."

Case No. 17. *Estate of Heinold v. Commissioner* [20]

Issue: Fair market value of decedent's stock less than the public offering price for large block being valued

Purpose of Valuation: Estate tax

Valuation Claimed by Petitioner	Claimed by IRS	Final Adjudication
$79,250	$250,000	$200,000

Supplementary Information: Heinold Elevator Company, Inc.—an operator of grain storage facilities and manufacturer of feed

Issues Argued

Matthew I. Heinold died on September 13, 1958, approximately 4½ months after Heinold Elevator Company, Inc. was organized to succeed a predecessor partnership consisting of members of the Hein-

[20] 363 F.2d 329 (7th Cir. 1966), *affirming* 24 T.C.M. 26 (1965).

old family. On May 1, 1958, the four partners, in return for most of the assets of the partnership and the assumption of certain liabilities, each received 25,000 shares of stock in the newly formed corporation.

At that time, close friends and good customers of the predecessor partnership purchased 18,180 shares of stock from the company for $8.50 per share. On July 18, 1958, a public offering of stock was made on a "best efforts" basis at $10 per share, of which 15% was to be paid as underwriting commissions, for net proceeds of $8.50 per share. The public offering was subject to the rights of creditors to apply current indebtedness to the purchase of the corporation's stock at a price of $8.65 per share. During the period of the public offering from July 18, 1958, to June 18, 1959, 38,712 shares of stock were sold to the public, and 4,175 shares to creditors.

The "book value" per share of stock issued to partners of the predecessor partnership was $7.71 per share, based upon the appraised value of the corporate assets, compared with a depreciated original cost basis of $4.81 per share to the predecessor partnership.

In the estate tax return filed, the petitioners claimed a value of $3.21 per share of Heinold stock, which was amended to $3.17 per share. The opinion in the case does not indicate how such values were determined. The Commissioner, on the other hand, contended the stock sales to the public at $10 per share were the best evidence of fair market value.

Decision

The court in finding the fair market value of the decedent's stock to be $8 per share noted that most of the purchases of the stock by the public were in small blocks, and that "the relative size of the purchases when compared with the decedent's holding, indicate that the fair market value of decedent's shares was less than $10 each. In addition, the disruptive effect which the disposition of decedent's shares would have had upon the sales to the public then in progress (and limited number of prospective 'public' purchasers) make it unlikely that decedent's shares would have or could have been sold to the public for $10 per share at the date of decedent's death." At that date, decedent's holdings amounted to approximately 19% of total outstanding stock.

Case No. 18. Houghton, Executor, v. United States [21]

Issue: Stock of closely held manufacturing company valued on low basis in view of dependence on primary customer

[21] 65–1 U. S. TAX CAS. 12,316 (E.D. Wis. 1965).

Purpose of Valuation: Estate tax

		Final
Valuation Claimed by Petitioner	*Claimed by IRS*	*Adjudication*
$472,900	$1,336,500	$1,134,300

Supplementary Information: Drott Manufacturing Corporation—sole supplier of front-end loaders for mounting on tractors manufactured by International Harvester Company, and licensor of another type of front-end loader manufactured by a subsidiary of International; Drott Tractor Company, Inc.—a tractor dealership

Issues Argued

The estate of Edward A. Drott, who died on April 5, 1956, included 1650 shares of Class A voting common stock and 1,046 shares of Class B non-voting common stock of Drott Manufacturing Corporation and 1,367 shares of Class A voting common stock and 3 shares of Class B non-voting common stock of Drott Tractor Company, Inc. Neither the plaintiffs nor the Commissioner considered separate values for the voting and non-voting stock. Accordingly, the estate owned 2,696 shares of Drott Manufacturing out of a total of 6,738 shares outstanding, and 1,370 shares of Drott Tractor out of a total of 7,686 shares.

In the estate tax return filed, the executors had included Drott Manufacturing stock at a value of $195 per share and Drott Tractor at $50 per share. The Commissioner valued Manufacturing at $450 per share and Tractor at $90 per share. The plaintiffs duly paid the additional federal estate tax determined by the Commissioner, with interest, and then filed a claim for refund. In the claim for refund the plaintiffs reduced the value of Manufacturing to $150 per share but retained the original value filed for Tractor.

Manufacturing had shown substantial increases in sales, net profit, and net worth over a five-year period preceding the date of death of the decedent, and for the twelve-month period ending March 31, 1956, showed earnings per share of $160 and "book value" of approximately $292 per share.

Decision

The court did not believe that the decedent's loss to Drott Manufacturing seriously affected the value of the stock even though his inventive ability and management talents were to a large extent responsible for the company's success. He had left an extremely able and experienced management team. Nor did the court feel that the decedent's death would place in jeopardy the agreement with the company's primary customer, which was cancellable on 30 days' notice.

The customer was not in a position to produce the loader because it was not tooled up for such production and because the loader had patented features. The court also felt that the competition between the new model loaders manufactured by International's subsidiary under license from Drott and those manufactured by Drott for International was not of immediate concern. The new model might develop deficiencies that would have to be corrected. International was still promoting the Drott manufactured model; the new model was to supplement, not to replace it.

The court found that the plaintiffs' experts, in arriving at a fair market value per share for manufacturing which closely approximated earnings per share for the twelve-month period preceding death, "at a time when the future of the industry was exceptionally good and Drott Manufacturing evidenced a strong upward trend, unduly stressed Drott Manufacturing's so-called 'vulnerability' with respect to its relationship with International, and failed to properly consider the goodwill of the Drott product and value of its patents." On the other hand the court pointed out that "the defendant's expert did not make sufficient allowance for the fact that while termination of the relationship between Drott Manufacturing and International was not imminent, it was a future possibility, and if it hoped to survive indefinitely, Manufacturing had reached a stage in its growth at which diversification and expenditures incident thereto were necessary."

Earnings of Drott Tractor had been sporadic over a five-year fiscal period ended October 31, 1955, and were $9.16 per share for the latest year. However, the book value per share of Tractor was $132.63 and its net current assets $92.50 per share at that date. Testimony also developed that the decedent had valued Drott Tractor stock at $75 per share in gift tax returns filed in 1954 and 1955.

After weighing all of the facts, the court concluded that the value of Drott Manufacturing stock was $375 per share and that of Drott Tractor was $90 per share.

Case No. 19. Inga Bardahl [22]

Issue: Low valuation approved for minority interest, based on discounts for lack of marketability and one-man management

Purpose of Valuation: Gift tax

Valuation Claimed by Petitioner	Claimed by IRS	Final Adjudication
$286,000	$400,400	$286,000

[22] 24 T.C.M. 841 (1965).

Supplementary Information: Bardahl Manufacturing Corporation—manufacturer and marketer of oil and grease additives

Issues Argued

Ole Bardahl and his wife Inga Bardahl made gifts of Bardahl stock aggregating 2,860 shares to their daughters and grandchildren in 1959. In gift tax returns filed they valued such shares at $100 each. As of December 30, 1959, immediately prior to the gift here involved, there were 20,000 shares of Bardahl stock outstanding, over 85% of which was owned by Ole Bardahl.

The Commissioner, in his notice of deficiency, determined that the fair market value of the Bardahl stock transferred by gift was $140 per share.

Testimony developed that all of Bardahl's operations were under the direct personal supervision of Ole Bardahl, including manufacturing, marketing research, sales, and contacts with distributors.

The petitioners produced an expert witness who valued the Bardahl stock at $68.615 per share. The government's witness, a valuation specialist with the Internal Revenue Service, valued the stock at $132 per share. Incidentally, the book value per share of the stock was $96.57 on December 30, 1959.

Decision

The court found that there were insufficient sales of Bardahl stock to establish its value. Both the petitioner's and the government's experts relied on the price–earnings ratio of two competitor corporations whose stock was publicly traded. The ratio thus derived was applied to the weighted average per-share earnings of Bardahl for the five years ending with the year of gift discounted by the government's expert by 20% for the cost of floating a stock issue to the public and 10% because Bardahl is a "low diversification manufacturer, its products being related in nature and usage, which fact increases the vulnerability to competition and creates a sensitivity to savings in the business cycle." The petitioner's expert used the same 30% discount and "assigned an additional 20 per cent discount because of the one-man management of the corporation and the minority interest being valued."

The court felt that the government's expert should also have discounted his value for "the one-man management of the corporation" and the fact that a prospective buyer would consider anticipated earnings, particularly since available data indicated a decline from the high point achieved for the year of gift.

The court concluded by stating that "the value placed on the stock by respondent's expert witness is too high and that placed by petitioners' expert is too low when all of the relevant factors are considered. However, since petitioners on their gift tax returns used a value of $100 per share and have not claimed an overpayment of gift tax, we do not have to determine a precise fair market value of the stock, but merely that, as we have found as an ultimate fact, the fair market value of the stock on December 30, 1959 was not in excess of $100 per share."

Case No. 20. The South Carolina National Bank, Executor, v. McLeod[23]

Issue: Competitive conditions and poor dividends records major valuation factors

Purpose of Valuation: Estate tax

Valuation Claimed by Petitioner	Claimed by IRS	Final Adjudication
$184,560	$273,420	$205,300

Supplementary Information: The News and Courier Company and The Evening Post Publishing Company—both newspapers published in Charleston, S. C.

Issues Argued

The estate of Julian Mitchell, who died on November 30, 1960, held 100 shares of stock of The News and Courier Company and 179 shares of The Evening Post Publishing Company, out of total outstanding common shares of 1,090 and 1,997 respectively of these newspaper publishing companies at that date. Also, the Evening Post owned 785 shares of common stock of the News and Courier. In the estate tax return filed by the executors, the News and Courier stock was valued at $700 per share and the Evening Post at $640 per share. Upon examination of the return, the Commissioner asserted a value of $980 per share for the stocks of each of these companies and assessed the estate a deficiency tax on such basis. The additional tax and interest was paid by the plaintiffs who then instituted suit for refund of the sum paid. During the period from January 1951 through June 1965, there were only ten transactions involving stock sales in both of the companies. In fact seven such transactions involved

[23] 256 F. Supp. 913 (D. S. Car. 1966).

single share sales, which apparently were qualifying shares sold to officers and directors.

The "book value" per share of the News and Courier at November 30, 1960, was $1,113 per share and that of the Evening Post was $976. Net income per share of the News and Courier averaged $104.03 for the five years ended 1960, and was $120.94 for 1960. That of the Evening Post averaged $54.30 for the five-year period and was $62.14 for 1960. Dividends paid by the companies were low and amounted to approximately 20% of net income for each of them for the year 1960.

Two of the expert witnesses for the plaintiff were well established securities dealers who testified that the values of $700 and $640 per share placed on the stocks were high, because of lack of marketability, low dividend pay-outs, and the fact that such minority interests would have no voice in management. Another witness for the plaintiffs arrived at a fair market value of $632 per share for the News and Courier and $478 for the Evening Post. He arrived at these figures by a formula capitalizing five-year average dividends by 6%, multiplying average earnings for the five-year period by 10, taking 50% of the "book values," and dividing the totals of these factors by three. Another expert witness for the plaintiffs, who was past president of a newspaper company and who had "extensive experience in newspaper appraisal work" arrived at valuations of $642.45 per share for the News and Courier and $503.50 for the Evening Post. His figures were derived by using a formula of five-year per-share dividends capitalized at 4% and 75% of book values, and dividing the sum of these by 2.

The government had only one expert witness, who had many years of substantial newspaper appraisal experience, most if not all as an employee of the Internal Revenue Service. He presented a list of 17 newspapers whose stocks were sold during 1959 and 1960, together with the price–earnings ratios at which they had sold. Two such newspapers had operated at losses. Of the remaining 15 the price–earnings ratios at which they had sold ranged from 9.16 to 33.61. Significantly, however, only two of the companies' stocks were publicly held, and the stock of one traded at a price–earnings ratio of 9.16 and the other at 13.48. The sales of stock of the other companies represented primarily single transactions.

The government's witness "further stated that the Dow Jones public stock quotations (approximately 18 times earnings for 1960) represented a maximum ceiling on the price–earnings ratio at which newspaper stocks are commonly sold." On the basis of his study, this witness concluded that a price–earnings multiple of 16 would result in a conservative estimate of the value of the stock of each newspaper. He further acknowledged that a minority shareholder's interest was subject to some discount, which he proposed to be 35%. On the foregoing basis, adjusting for the value of the Evening Post's holdings in stock of the News Courier, he arrived at a per-share value of $1,250 for the latter and $1,025 for the Evening Post.

Decision

The court noted that there were two television and five radio stations operating in the metropolitan area of Charleston, that were in competition with each other and with the two newspapers for the presentation of news and for advertising. It also noted that, although dollar revenues increased, there was a steady decline in advertising lineage from 1956 through 1960. It also noted that "the dividend factor is a material element in the valuation of a minority stockholder's interest." "For the News and Courier and Evening Post the record of dividends paid is poor for the earnings record. . . ." The court, although agreeing to the relevance of the "price–earnings ratio test," rejected those shown where the market was restricted and concluded. "Nevertheless, the court does rely on the price–earnings ratio and the multiple considered has been between 9.16 and 13.48 established by the publicly held companies. . . ." The court's recognition of the importance of dividends (poor record) was considered of great relevance and "the price–earnings computation must be discounted by this factor."

After considering all of the foregoing factors including the minor and isolated sales of the stock of the two newspapers preceding and following November 30, 1960, which approximated the values claimed by the plaintiffs, the court concluded that "the preponderance of the evidence establishes that the 'fair market value' of the 100 shares of the News and Courier stock and the 179 shares of Evening Post stock . . . did not exceed the per share price of $800 and $700, respectively. . . ."

Case No. 21. *Nellie I. Brown* [24]

Issue: Discounted "book value" rejected as having no relevancy to fair market value

[24] 25 T.C.M. 498 (1966).

Purpose of Valuation: Gift tax

		Final
Valuation Claimed by Petitioner	*Claimed by IRS*	*Adjudication*
$105,000	$258,300	$105,000

Supplementary Information: The Brown and Thomas Automobile Company—automobile sales and service agency for Cadillacs and Oldsmobiles

Issues Argued

Nellie I. Brown made a gift of 42 shares of stock of the Brown and Thomas Automobile Company to her son, Harry H. Brown, Jr. on January 11, 1961. She reported the fair market value of such shares in her 1961 gift tax return to be $2,500 per share, or an aggregate of $105,000. Total outstanding shares of the company at that date were 108, after deducting 12 shares of treasury stock. With these shares and his previous holdings, Harry Jr. owned all but a few outstanding shares of the company. The Commissioner valued the shares at $6,150 each for a total of $258,300 and determined a tax deficiency based on such valuation.

At the time of his death on December 14, 1955, Harry's father, Harry H. Brown, Sr. owned 61 out of 120 shares of the company stock then outstanding and for federal estate tax purposes the value of such shares was "finally determined" to be $2,500 per share as of that date.

In addition to the dealer franchise which was taken over by Harry Jr., the company had a profitable distributor franchise which was terminated by Cadillac in 1956, after the death of Harry Sr. The company's earnings averaged $413.03 per share for the years 1951 through 1955 and showed an average deficit of $0.80 per share from 1956 through 1960. No dividends were paid on the stock of the company after 1955.

During the years 1955, 1956, 1957, 1958, and 1959, Nellie I. Brown made gifts to Harry Jr. aggregating 25 shares and reported them in her gift tax returns at $2,500 per share. Also, the company purchased 12 shares of its stock on January 15, 1958, from the estate of Harry Sr. at $2,500 per share and carried them thereafter as treasury stock.

The Commissioner arrived at his valuation of $6,150 per share by taking the "book value" per share of $6,545 at the close of 1960 and subtracting $395 therefrom "for allowance for nonmarketability." The Commissioner also produced, as a witness, a man employed as a security analyst in the Internal Revenue Service, who valued the shares at $5,890 each. The petitioner called as a witness a man who had been employed by an old established brokerage firm in New Haven, Connecticut, for 12 years, who "described in considerable detail how he had made and checked his valuation of the 42 shares involved herein." This witness concluded that the fair market value of the shares on January 11, 1961, was "2,500 a share, certainly not more."

Decision

The court rejected the Commissioner's method of valuation as having no relevancy to fair market value and was very critical of the lack of objectivity, competence, reasoning, and conclusions of the Commissioner's witness. On the other hand the court found the witness for the petitioner ". . . was most helpful as to fair market value and his opinion is entitled to weight."

The court concluded that the preponderance of evidence supported a fair market value of the stock at $2,500 per share, or $105,000 for the 42 shares.

PART III

BUSINESS COMBINATIONS

8

Basic Considerations, Caveats, and Investigations

In an initial offering of common stock, the prospective purchaser's knowledge of a company is limited to data set forth in the offering prospectus. In the valuation of a business for federal tax purposes, the investigation and review of available data are also somewhat limited, as no arm's-length transaction takes place, and neither the Internal Revenue Service personnel involved nor the experts representing the taxpayer need have a continuing relationship with the company.

However, in the case of an acquisition or merger, a corporate marriage is consummated, and ill considered decisions made prior to and at the time of the transaction may evoke later unpleasant consequences. Fortunately, the several parties to a proposed acquisition or merger usually have sufficient opportunity to investigate each other to a considerable extent, before entering into a definitive agreement.

This is so except in the case of acquisitions via the tender offer route, direct to stockholders, where, for the most part, information on a company will be limited to published data. Only a few years ago this method of acquisition was frowned upon, and those engaged in such activities were termed "corporate raiders." In recent years this method of acquisition, at times with the consent of management of tender offer candidates, became so common as to be considered a normal procedure. Because of its importance, Chapter 11 will be devoted entirely to the procedures and problems surrounding cash tender and direct security offers.

Regardless of the approach taken, acquisitions and mergers present many factors for consideration. Some of these have a direct bearing on valuation; other factors not directly related to valuation also require careful study. Investigative procedures, federal and state income taxes, antitrust laws, and timely disclosure requirements of business combinations will be discussed in this chapter, although only briefly, for the primary purpose of this book is to assist the reader in valuation techniques.[1]

Accounting and Securities and Exchange Commission considerations relating to business combinations are set forth in Chapters 9 and 10, and valuation factors and various studies are discussed in Chapter 12.

VOLUME OF BUSINESS COMBINATIONS

The tide of reported acquisitions and mergers continued to swell, through the year 1969, and fell off during the adverse conditions prevailing in 1970, as indicated by the following statistics:

	Number Reported by	
Year	Federal Trade Commission [2]	W. T. Grimm & Co. [3]
1970	2,916	5,152
1969	4,542	6,107
1968	3,932	4,462
1967	2,384	2,975
1966	1,746	2,377
1965	1,893	2,125
1964	1,797	1,950
1963	1,479	1,361

The Federal Trade Commission figures include merger activity reported by Moody's Industrials, Standard & Poor's Corporation

---

[1] Those interested in these subjects may refer to one or more of the books that give some additional detail. Samuel Depew, a practicing lawyer, reviewed thirteen books on mergers and acquisitions, and particularly recommended a group of four works, including McCARTHY, ACQUISITIONS AND MERGERS (1963). See Depew, "A Readers' Guide to Mergers and Acquisitions," J. CORPORATE VENTURE, Winter 1967.

[2] Federal Trade Commission, "Current Trends in Merger Activity."

[3] W. T. Grimm & Co., "1970 Merger Review."

Records, *The Wall Street Journal, Journal of Commerce,* and *The New York Times.* Partial acquisitions are included in these figures when they comprise whole divisions of other companies. The W. T. Grimm figures of "net announced actions" embrace corporate consolidations of banks and public utilities, as well as the mining, manufacturing, trade, and services groups included in the Federal Trade Commission figures. Undoubtedly, the increase in tender and exchange offers direct to stockholders contributed, in some measure, to the accelerated pace of business combinations during the late 1960's.

HOW TO VIEW ACQUISITIONS

The matter of acquiring or merging companies should be considered as a phase of corporate development. The combination-minded company should ask itself: What is our sales and profit potential with existing facilities and markets? Are we likely to lose markets to larger or more aggressive competitors? Will our principal product or products become obsolete or less in demand because of technological improvements or the introduction of cheaper or more suitable substitute materials? The answers to these questions will help management in determining its overall corporate objectives.

Corporate development may sometimes be achieved solely through the acquisition of outside companies, or through a combination of acquisitions and internal development of products and markets. Often this depends upon size. A medium-sized or smaller company cannot risk a substantial part of its capital if the chances of initially developing and successfully marketing a new product are not overwhelmingly favorable.

Most of today's corporate giants, such as General Motors, duPont, and General Electric, which spend millions annually on research and development, became large and profitable enough to undertake substantial internal development programs primarily because of their earlier growth through acquisitions and mergers. It is very gratifying to be in the position of such large companies and dedicate a portion of profits toward a continuing program of internal development. The average company, however, is not in the fortunate position of the corporate giants because of the limitation of the absolute amounts available for such a purpose.

Internal Expansion Versus Acquisition

Problems that must be weighed in connection with internal expansion include the prospects of developing a commercially marketable product, the cost of building or expanding plant and facilities, the cost at which the new product can be produced, the price at which it can be sold, the cost of penetrating markets (often dominated by others), and the length of time it will take to get a new project "off the ground." How then should management of the average company decide whether to expand from within or through the acquisition of other companies? A reasonable approach to this problem is to investigate the possibility of acquiring other companies in order to accomplish corporate objectives.

During the course of the investigations, a considerable amount of information obtained will be of assistance in estimating the cost of internally developing and marketing comparable products. Otherwise, there are many imponderables to evaluate in a program initiated from scratch to determine product, market research, and starting load costs, without some basic standards for comparison.

INVESTIGATIVE AND EXPLORATORY PROCEDURES

How does management proceed to investigate a candidate company for acquisition? Initially it should decide whether the company merger objectives might best be accomplished through vertical or horizontal integration or through conglomerate acquisitions. If the company is large, or controls a substantial segment of the market of any product, its choice may be limited by antitrust considerations to the conglomerate type of merger, although even some of these will be challenged. Antitrust laws are discussed later in this chapter.

Gathering Preliminary Data

Initially, a screening should be made of published data, such as Thomas' Register of American Manufacturers, Moody's Manuals, Dun & Bradstreet Million Dollar Directory and State Sales Guides, industry publications, company catalogs, stockholders' reports, proxy statements, and prospectuses, to ascertain companies that would appear to be of potential interest. From a perusal of these data, the next step would be to obtain Dun & Bradstreet reports on those companies that qualify as acquisition candidates. Initial screening investigations should be conducted with the utmost discretion to prevent untimely disclosure of interest in a candidate company.

The Initial Overture

When, through a review of data thus obtained, an interest is developed in a company, overtures should be made to its management directly or through an intermediary. The search for acquisition candidates should not be confined to companies whose managements have evinced a desire to sell or merge; many others may be interested in such deals if presented with attractive propositions.

If a candidate company is interested in acquisition, its management should be willing to produce sufficient financial and other information to enable the prospective acquirer to determine a reasonable range of value of the company in terms of cash, securities, or a combination of these. Although some preliminary views may be expressed on the subject, no firm commitment regarding price or the manner of effecting a deal should be made until a reasonable review of such data has been carried out. In other words, the value of a company cannot be determined until the prospective acquirer knows what he is buying.

It is desirable to have a checklist for guidance in conducting investigations of acquisition candidates to assure systematic coverage of the following areas: (a) corporate and financial, (b) management and personnel, (c) sales and marketing, and (d) operations, research, and development. The type of information required in these principal areas will be discussed below.

Concurrently, consideration should be given to the desired form of the acquisition or merger, that is, the relative advantages of a cash or part-cash or debt securities deal versus an exchange of capital stocks, either all common or common and preferred. Also, is it desirable to acquire the net assets and business or the capital stock of a company and the objectives of the proposed sellers? Legal, accounting, tax, and governmental regulatory requirements should be reviewed to the extent that they influence the form of the business combination and the time required to effect it.

The investigatory work may be carried out by company personnel in collaboration with professional advisors, such as lawyers, accountants, and engineers, or may be placed for the most part in the hands of such professionals.

Investment bankers, business brokers, and management consultants often act in a go-between capacity for companies wishing to acquire or sell businesses. If any persons in such organizations are consulted to render assistance, a clear understanding should be obtained of the services to be performed by them and the basis of their compensation. Generally, this understanding should be in writing.

Depending upon the relative importance of the proposed acquisition and the availability of reliable information in the several areas outlined, the study may be completed in a week or two or may require a considerably longer period.

Those carrying out the investigations should cover areas of major importance as expeditiously as possible. Thus, if there are obstacles to the consummation of a deal, these may be given timely consideration and remedied or negotiations dropped. On the other hand, if preliminary investigations confirm the desirability of a business combination, legal counsel of the respective parties at interest may commence drafting the business combination agreement, and consideration be given concurrently to legal, accounting, tax, stock exchange, Securities and Exchange Commission filing requirements, and antitrust aspects of the proposed deal.

PRINCIPAL INVESTIGATIVE AREAS

It is not in order here to go into great detail regarding all of the matters to be covered in investigations of companies proposed to be acquired, but the major areas that should be explored are summarized below.

Corporate Accounting and Financial Background

The corporate history and background of the business enterprise should be written up listing the various corporations involved, if more than one, the date and place of their incorporation, intercorporate relationships, and principal stockholders. These data will be of assistance in determining which stockholders are of importance in conducting negotiations and the methods of effecting a deal for tax and regulatory purposes.

Audited Financial Statements. Audited financial statements should be obtained if available, and the statements of income summarized for a period of three to five years. The latest unaudited financial statements should also be obtained. Any adjustments made to surplus or otherwise affecting prior years should be applied to the particular year they affect. After making such appropriate adjustments, it may be found that a seemingly favorable earnings trend turns out otherwise.

Adjustment to Acquirer's Basis. The income figures used for determining price should, if possible, be based on potential earnings. At the outset, the necessary accounting adjustments should be made to the figures to place them on a basis comparable with those of the prospective acquirer. As mentioned in an earlier chapter, generally accepted accounting principles permit alternative practices in various areas. Inasmuch as the acquired company will presumably adopt the accounting practices of the acquirer, it is essential that earnings for the purposes of establishing valuation should be computed on the latter's basis.

Further adjustments should be made for expected savings (conservatively estimated) as a result of the combination, as well as additional costs which may arise therefrom. Also, if the deal will result in a "purchase" for tax or accounting purposes, consideration should be given to accounting for any goodwill resulting therefrom.

Trend of Costs and Sales by Products

The sales and cost of sales should be summarized, by principal products, for the same period as the summary statements of income, and attention should be directed to any inferences that may be drawn from such figures. The trend of sales and costs by products is particularly significant not only to ascertain what products have been responsible for profits and in what territories, but also for forecasting future operating results.

Rigged Profits

Occasionally, management of a company intending to sell out will deliberately rig profits for a period in an attempt to obtain a better price. For example, unusually large shipments may be made to customers in the latest year, under relaxed credit terms, to the detriment of the subsequent year's earnings. Although investigation may reveal that the sales and gross margins on hitherto profitable products of a company have been declining, this situation may not be reflected as a decrease in net profits because of subnormal expenditures for advertising and sales promotion, and deferring of normal maintenance expenditures. The unwary purchaser of such a company could find himself in a position of starting with a low volume of business and having to spend unusually large amounts, after taking over, to recover a market position or to rehabilitate plant and equipment.

Overall Financial Position

Depending upon their importance, investigations should be carried out and reported on such matters as:

1. The collectibility of accounts and notes receivable. Some companies virtually finance their customers, and a review of bad-debt write-offs does not appropriately reveal their exposed credit position.

2. Methods of taking and pricing physical inventories, procedures with regard to write-offs of obsolete and slow-moving goods, and consignment merchandise practices. The status of inventories in process and uncompleted long-term contracts should be reviewed. Often, substantial potential losses may be concealed in balances of such items carried in inventories. On the other hand, an inventory priced under the LIFO method may be carried substantially below the current value.

3. Unusual amounts of prepaid and deferred items, particularly with respect to preproduction, research and development expense, and prepaid advertising supplies and expense.

4. The age of major items of property, plant, and equipment, and the depreciation practices employed.
5. The nature and apparent evidence, if any, of the value of intangible assets carried on the books. In many cases, such items have no value to the purchaser of a company.
6. Assurance that sufficient provisions have been established for federal and state income taxes, other major liabilities, and possible costs resulting from legal suits instituted or threatened.

Management and Personnel

Some companies have executive talent to spare, but not many. On the other hand, there have been cases where management of an acquiring company was dismayed to find the business they bought going down the drain because they did an executive housecleaning job, after the takeover, before finding out who was responsible for the company's success.

Accordingly, information should be obtained on officers and key personnel including positions, names, ages, family relationships, and ownership interests in the company, as well as their principal duties and responsibilities. (This should also include non-officer directors whose ownership interests are material.) Compensation and benefits received by officers and key executives should be summarized for the same period covered by the income statements.

It is in the area of integrating people at the management and key executive level that many business combinations do not work out successfully. Thus, in addition to obtaining the above background information, the reviewer should try to gain impressions of such persons to determine which of them would fit into the combined organization.

Sales and Marketing

Information in this area should be obtained regarding: (a) channels of marketing the company's products, i.e., through distributors, dealers, manufacturer's agents, or direct to consumers; (b) territories in which the company markets its products and limitations on geographically expanding these territories; (c) any appreciable volume of the company's sales to a few large cus-

tomers or to government agencies; (d) possible effect of technological changes in the industry, price changes, and volume competition, as they may affect the company's future; (e) the company's
advertising and promotion expenses, by product lines and advertising media.

Sales Policies and Credit Terms. It is important to determine
whether a company is customer- or product-oriented; that is, does
it systematically carry out market research to determine customers'
needs and product acceptance, or does it use high-pressure methods to sell products regardless of customer requirements?

The reviewer should determine whether the sales policies and
credit terms of the subject company are compatible with those of
the acquirer. Otherwise, it may be found after consummation of
the deal that the acquirer will be forced to discontinue business
with some customers of the seller because they have been receiving unusually liberal discounts, allowances, and credit terms. This
may result not only in the loss of business but in large losses on
accounts receivable, where credit has been overextended.

Operations, Research, and Development

It is essential to obtain reliable information on the following
points:

1. Facilities owned and leased, and lease terms on major facilities
2. Adequacy or inadequacy of major operating facilities, not only for
   the present but for future needs
3. Evidences of obsolescence of plant or equipment
4. General availability of labor in the area
5. Particulars of the plant work force, wage scales, union contracts,
   and employee benefits

Matters such as good plant housekeeping and a logical layout
to facilitate the work flow are of importance in judging the performance of an engineering department. Effectiveness of research will be indicated by the company's success in improving
the quality of its products, the introduction of new products to

meet changing conditions, and obtaining basic patents or exclusive manufacturing know-how.

TAXABLE TRANSACTIONS

Federal tax aspects are of considerable importance in determining the manner in which acquisitions and mergers are consummated, and also have a bearing on price. Business combination transactions fall into two general categories for federal income tax purposes, i.e., "taxable" and "tax-free." All transactions are taxable except those that are covered under the specific reorganization provisions of the Internal Revenue Code as being "tax-free."

As the terms are used, taxable and tax-free relate to the status of the transaction to the seller; as a general rule, no taxation arises to the buyer when the capital stock or assets of a company are purchased. An exception to this general rule may occur under the so-called recapture provisions of the Internal Revenue Code.

Methods of Effecting Taxable Transactions

There are several methods of arranging a transfer of ownership of a corporate business in a taxable transaction. Principally, these are the sale of the stock by the stockholders, or the sale of the assets of the corporation, pursuant to a plan of liquidation whereby the selling corporation receives cash for the assets and then liquidates such proceeds into the hands of the stockholders.

Where the selling stockholders sell their stock to a corporate purchaser, the purchaser may continue the corporation or liquidate it. Where the corporation is continued, no new tax basis for its assets arises. Where it is liquidated, pursuant to a plan within two years of the purchase, a new tax basis is created, the purchaser allocating the purchase price, whether in cash, securities, debt, or the assumption of liabilities, to the tangible and intangible assets received in liquidation.[4] A new tax basis is also created when the purchaser buys assets of a corporation.

---

[4] I.R.C. § 334(b)(2).

When Taxable Cash Transactions Are Desirable

Taxable cash transactions are generally desirable from the standpoint of the acquirer if his capital stock has no established market. In addition, where his capital stock is selling at a low price–earnings multiple, leverage may be gained by acquiring a company for cash. This is particularly so if a company has excess cash or can borrow whatever other funds are needed at an attractive interest rate. Also, if the fair value of the assets of the selling company has appreciated substantially above the tax basis, the acquirer may allocate the purchase price to such assets and thereby recover, through future tax reductions, part of the price.

The procedure for valuing assets distributed in liquidation of a subsidiary whose capital stock had been purchased for an amount exceeding the tax basis of the seller is outlined on pages 217–26.

Where the fair market values of assets distributed in the liquidation of a subsidiary substantially exceeded the seller's tax basis, a subsequent unexpected income tax liability accrued to the purchaser, in a case reviewed on pages 226–28.

Advantages of Buying Assets

Generally, the purchaser fares better in taxable deals by buying the net assets and business of a company rather than its capital stock. In such deals the federal and state tax liabilities (which may not be precisely determinable) could remain with the seller. Among such federal tax liabilities are those arising out of the depreciation and investment credit recapture provisions when a corporation disposes of its tangible property. Briefly, if depreciation has been deducted for federal income tax purposes after 1961 (1963 for certain real property), to the extent that the fair market value of such assets exceeds the cost (on an item-by-item basis) less accumulated depreciation, ordinary taxable income occurs to the corporation in the year of disposition of the assets.[5] In addition, a tax liability results to the extent of previously utilized

[5] *Ibid.*, §§ 1245 and 1250.

investment credits in the case of early disposition of assets so affected.[6]

Also, the purchase of net assets rather than capital stock may avoid certain income tax consequences to the buyer when the fair market value of assets received exceeds the purchase price. In such a case, the buyer and seller may stipulate by agreement the realistic fair market value of the various classes of current assets, and assign the remainder of the purchase price (including assumed liabilities, if any) to all other assets, tangible and intangible. Customarily, the seller will then retain cash and possibly other liquid assets to equal the amount of liabilities not assumed by the buyer. Also, if there is a dispute regarding the value of accounts receivable, a time limit such as six or nine months may be stipulated for determining their collectibility, and suitable adjustment made in the purchase price for uncollected balances.

TAX-FREE EXCHANGES

Without getting into technicalities, tax-free exchanges may be accomplished through:

1. A statutory merger or consolidation; that is, where one or more companies are absorbed into an existing company or a newly formed company and the shareholders surrender their securities for capital stock and possibly other consideration, pursuant to the applicable statutes of the domiciliary states of the corporations involved

2. An exchange of voting stock for stock of the acquired corporation after which the purchaser owns control (at least 80%) of the stock of the acquired corporation

3. An exchange of voting stock of the purchaser for substantially all of the assets of the seller

Tax-free means that the stockholders of the selling or merged company will not be required, as a result of the transaction, to recognize any gain or loss on the securities received by them from the purchaser or the surviving company. The securities received will have a substituted tax basis equivalent to the basis of the securities surrendered in the transaction.

[6] *Ibid.,* § 47.

A variation of the tax-free exchange is permitted in certain reorganizations where "boot" such as cash or debt securities may be received by the sellers in addition to the stock or securities otherwise permitted by the reorganization sections of the Internal Revenue Code. This boot is usually taxable as ordinary income but not in excess of the gain that would be recognized were the transaction entirely taxable. The securities received in such a partially taxable exchange would have a tax basis equal to the basis of the securities surrendered, increased by the gain recognized and decreased by the cash received in the transaction.

Need To Verify Federal Income Tax Basis

In a tax-free transaction, the federal income tax basis of the assets of the seller should always be verified. It is not safe to assume that the tax basis is the same as the book amounts. In a taxable acquisition of assets this generally is not important, for the purchaser establishes a new tax basis for the assets acquired.

Acquirer's Assumption of Tax Attributes of Seller

The acquirer in a tax-free deal should be aware that he inherits the acquired corporation's tax basis for its assets and takes these assets subject to the disclosed and undisclosed liabilities of the acquired corporation [except possibly in a stock-for-assets transaction as described in (3) above], regardless of whether he is protected by an indemnification agreement. These assets and liabilities have tax attributes which the purchaser should consider before he closes the deal. They may be of such importance as to materially affect the price or even justify killing the deal. Some of the more important tax attributes warranting investigation are the following:

1. Net operating loss carryover
2. Accumulated earnings and profits
3. Capital loss carryover
4. Methods of accounting, i.e., completed contract versus progress reporting and the treatment of bad debts, property taxes, research and development expenses, deferred subscription income, vacation pay, etc.

5. Methods of computing inventories, i.e., first-in, first-out (cost, lower of cost or market on basis of average, moving average, etc.); last-in, first-out (quantity or "dollar value")
6. Methods of computing depreciation, i.e., straight-line, declining balance, sum-of-the-years' digits, machine hours, etc.
7. Installment method of reporting income
8. Methods of reporting exploration and development expenditures
9. Contributions to employees' deferred compensation plans
10. Investment credit for certain depreciable property

CONFLICT IN TAX OBJECTIVES

The tax objectives of the purchaser and seller do not always run parallel. Thus, the price is often affected by the taxability or non-taxability of a deal. For example, the seller may wish to dispose of his business in exchange for capital stock of the purchaser in a tax-free transaction. Thus, he can postpone any recognition of capital gain until it suits his convenience to sell all or part of the securities received. When he sells these securities, he may do so at a time when he establishes capital losses in the disposal of other securities or assets that will reduce or eliminate tax otherwise payable.

Seller's Position

As an illustration, if a sole stockholder whose investment was $100,000 received $4,100,000 in cash for his company, he would pay a tax (capital gains) of $1,400,000 on the transaction, assuming the top marginal rate of 70% applies to one half of such long-term capital gain.[7] If, however, he received capital stock for his company having a fair market value of $4,100,000, no gain would be recognized on the transaction until he disposed of his securities.

Furthermore, if the stockholder were somewhat advanced in years, it could be desirable from an estate tax standpoint to hold the securities until death, *provided they represented a sound investment.*

[7] Without giving effect to the additional tax under I.R.C. § 57 for items of tax preference.

Assuming that the proceeds from the disposal of his company constituted his net estate, it could amount to $2,700,000 in a cash deal and $4,100,000 in an exchange of stock. Upon his demise, applying the maximum marital deduction, the difference in estate tax between a net estate of $4,100,000 and one of $2,700,000 would be about $312,000. Thus, the decedent's estate would be worth $1,088,000 more after all taxes, if the seller received capital stock rather than cash in disposing of his assets.

Purchaser's Position

The purchaser, in the same transaction, may wish to acquire the business for cash. This would be particularly so if the stepped-up basis (i.e., current fair value) of the assets of the business, to which recoverable tax bases could be allocated, substantially approached the purchase price. Thus, through depreciation charges, amortization of certain assets, and disposal of inventories acquired, he would obtain the benefit of income tax deductions. In this situation, however, the seller might be reluctant to effect the deal as a taxable one unless he received a very favorable price adjustment in order to bear directly the possibly substantial tax on the increment in his investment, and indirectly the corporation's tax on the recaptured depreciation and investment tax credits.

INSTALLMENT SALE OF CAPITAL STOCK

The installment method of selling capital stock may offer advantages to both buyer and seller. From the standpoint of the seller, if his company is not too salable, or if for some reason he does not wish to recognize the entire capital gain on the sale in one year for federal income tax purposes, the installment method of reporting gain could benefit him. Similarly, an installment transaction may be very attractive to the buyer, assuming the business purchased will produce profits, so that he would be paying part of the purchase price from the future profits generated by the business.

Qualification of an Installment Sale

In order to qualify as an installment sale, the seller cannot receive more than 30% of the selling price in the year in which the transaction is consummated. Furthermore, under the Internal Revenue Code, a portion of the proceeds may be taxed to the seller as interest income, if interest is not separately stated in the installment agreement, or additional interest may be imputed to the transaction if the contract rate is less than 4% simple interest.

Restrictions Under Tax Reform Act

It had become common in recent years for an acquiring corporation to issue debentures, which were often convertible into common stock, for the assets or common stock of another corporation. The acquirer would have the benefit of interest deductions on the bonds, and the sellers might utilize installment reporting until the bonds were sold or redeemed. The Tax Reform Act of 1969 imposes limitations on interest deductions of acquirers in such deals [8] and disallows installment reporting for the sellers, if bonds or other evidences of indebtedness received from the purchaser are payable on demand or tradable in an established securities market.[9]

Briefly, no deduction shall be allowed for interest paid or incurred by a corporation during a taxable year for corporate acquisition indebtedness where such interest exceeds $5,000,000, except that the latter amount is reduced under certain conditions.

Corporate acquisition indebtedness means any such obligation issued after October 9, 1969, to provide consideration for the acquisition of stock or assets of another corporation. If assets are acquired, they must constitute at least two-thirds of the total assets of the acquired corporation, excluding money. Such obligation must be subordinated to the claims of trade creditors, generally, and in right of payment of any substantial amount of unsecured indebtedness, whether outstanding or subsequently issued. Also, the obligation must either be convertible into stock or include an option to acquire stock in the issuing corporation.

[8] I.R.C. § 279.
[9] *Ibid.*, § 453.

A further test is that either the ratio of debt to equity exceeds 2 to 1, or the projected earnings do not exceed three times the annual interest to be paid or incurred.

The main thrust of this new section of the Internal Revenue Code is to inhibit unsound corporate financing, examples of which are shown in later chapters of this book.

Rules for application of the various tests and further explanatory text are set forth in Section 279 of the Code, reproduced as Appendix I.

CONTINGENT-PRICE TRANSACTIONS

Where a purchaser and seller cannot agree upon the value of a business, this problem may be resolved by having a fixed initial price with an additional pay-out dependent upon future earnings or other contingencies. Deals may be effected in this manner whether they are taxable or non-taxable.

Taxable Transaction

In a taxable transaction, the seller need only recognize the gain based on the initial purchase price and take up additional gains when these are determined to be realized. There would be an exception, however, if at the time of the initial transaction there was a clear indication that the additional contingent purchase price would ultimately be payable and could be valued, or if the buyer's contingent obligation were embodied in a marketable instrument received by the seller.

The installment basis of reporting gain is not available where the price is contingent on future earnings unless there is a maximum price and the seller is willing to compute his installment gains on the basis of this maximum.

Tax-free Transaction

In the case of tax-free transactions, i.e., where the acquirer issues voting capital stock for capital stock or assets of the seller, the latter would not recognize gain to the extent of the shares received at the initial closing. However, if he should sell any shares received, the Internal Revenue Service generally would take the position that the "cost" of his shares used in computing gain should be based on the maximum number of shares he could receive in the transaction, including those under the contingent provision. Interest will also be imputed in this type of transaction unless the contingent shares receivable under the agreement are considered issued and escrowed for the duration of the pay-out period. The agreement will usually provide that, if the corporation's earnings do not reach the prescribed level, a portion of the escrowed shares will be returned by the seller to the acquiring corporation.

VALUING ASSETS IN LIQUIDATION OF PURCHASED SUBSIDIARY

As indicated on page 210, certain acquisitions of capital stock of a company for cash or a combination of cash and securities meeting the test of Section 334(b)(2) of the Internal Revenue Code enable the purchaser to establish new tax bases for the property distributed upon liquidation of the company. The purchaser must adopt a plan to liquidate the acquired company within two years after the date of purchase, in order to avail himself of the privilege of stepping up the tax basis of the assets acquired. The requirements for complete liquidation in such circumstances are strict, as outlined in Revenue Ruling 66–186:

> The retention by a subsidiary corporation of any property, no matter how small in amount, for the purpose of continuing the operation of its present business or for the purpose of engaging in a new business, will prevent the distribution of its remaining property to its parent from qualifying as a distribution in complete liquidation within the meaning of Section 332 of the Internal Revenue Code of 1954.

"Proportional Allocation" of Basis in Liquidations

For years it has been a convenient practice in the liquidation of subsidiaries under Section 334(b)(2) to record assets distributed at 100% of their fair market values, and to record as goodwill any deficiency between net assets so valued and the adjusted purchase price. However, Revenue Ruling 66–290 stated, in effect, that only "cash and its equivalent" (narrowly construed) should be recorded at 100% of fair value. This amount, it is indicated, should be deducted from the basis of the subsidiary's stock and the adjusted purchaser's basis then allocated among various assets received. This method of allocating the basis produces some unusual and unrealistic results, as shown on pages 223 and 224.

Revenue Ruling 66–290 reads as follows:

Basis of property received in liquidations:
On the distribution of property in complete liquidation of a subsidiary corporation, where the requirements of section 334(b)(2) of the Internal Revenue Code of 1954 are met, the basis of the property received by the parent corporation on the distribution will be the adjusted basis of the subsidiary corporation's stock with respect to which the distribution was made as provided in section 1.334–1(c) of the Income Tax Regulations.

Certain adjustments must be made to the basis of the subsidiary's stock. Section 1.334–1(c)(4)(v)(b)(1) of the regulations provides that the adjusted basis of the subsidiary's stock held by the parent with respect to which the distributions in liquidation are made shall be decreased by the amount of any cash and its equivalent received. Section 1.334–1(c)(4)(viii) of the regulations provides that following the adjustments to the basis of the subsidiary's stock as required by section 1.334–1(c) of the regulations, the amount of the adjusted basis shall then be allocated among the various assets received (except cash and its equivalent) both tangible and intangible (whether or not depreciable or amortizable).

The phrase "cash and its equivalent" used in sections 1.334–1(c)(4)(v)(b)(1) and 1.334–1(c)(4)(viii) of the regulations includes cash, currency, bank deposits (including time deposits) whether or not interest bearing, share accounts in savings and loan associations, checks (whether or not certified), drafts, money orders, and any other item of similar nature. It does not include accounts receivable (as the term is commonly used), inventories, marketable securities, and other similar current assets.

Ordinarily, the seller disposes of the capital stock of his company for a price that may have little or no relation to the net book equity or taxable basis of net assets of his company. The purchaser of the stock then is confronted with the problem of establishing new values for the different classes of assets involved if and when he liquidates the company within the prescribed time. This must be done with great care, for the values assigned must be supportable as current fair market values for federal income tax purposes, regardless of whether the purchase price exceeds the tax basis of the seller. If the existing tax basis of the assets exceeds the purchase price of the stock, or if the cost of depreciation recapture and investment credit reversal is excessive, liquidation of the acquired corporation would not be desirable.

Composition of Net Assets Acquired

Assets acquired in such a liquidation may include cash and marketable securities; accounts and notes receivable, inventories of raw materials, work in process, finished goods, and supplies; property, plant, and equipment; miscellaneous investments; prepaid and deferred charges; patents, copyrights, and trademarks; and goodwill on the books of the seller. Also, all liabilities of the liquidated corporation are "assumed" in such a "purchase."

Cash and Marketable Securities. The allocation of the purchase price to cash requires no discussion; marketable securities should be valued at their current market prices.

Accounts and Notes Receivable. Accounts and notes receivable should be valued at their indicated realizable values. To the extent that any reserve for bad debts previously deducted for tax purposes is not utilized in this valuation process, the Internal Revenue Service requires that the unused portion be restored to taxable income by the liquidating corporation.

Inventories. Inventories of raw materials, work in process, finished goods, and supplies ordinarily are included in the financial statements of the seller at the lower of cost or market. However, the purchaser should value usable inventories at their market value, which generally exceeds (often substantially) the seller's aggregate inventory value, whether such inventories are reflected on the books of the seller or have been written off. An exception to this general rule would be where the purchaser intended to discontinue the manufacture or sale of certain lines of the seller and would be required to write down inventories applicable to those lines to their realizable values.

In determining market values for these purposes, raw materials and supplies should be included at current replacement cost, and finished goods at sales values, less the cost of their disposition.

Work in process, depending upon its nature, should be valued at replacement cost (for material, labor, and overhead), or at its sales value, less the cost of completion and disposition, if determinable.

Although the seller may have followed the practice of charging off expendable tools and manufacturing supplies as they were purchased, the purchaser is entitled to inventory them at their current replacement cost.

Properties. Property, plant, and equipment, with rare exceptions, is carried by the seller at cost, less accumulated depreciation. There are various permissible methods of providing for depreciation; also, the prices of fixed assets may have increased since their dates of acquisition. Accordingly, the fair market value of property, plant, and equipment may have little relation to the net carrying amount of such assets on the books of the seller.

A current appraisal is desirable in sustaining a valuation to be allocated from the purchase price to property, plant, and equipment, if the value of such assets is material to the transaction. This may be accomplished through appraisals of machinery and equipment by the purchaser's company engineers, or by having a complete appraisal undertaken by one of a number of professional firms that specialize in this activity. If a professional firm is engaged, it should be advised that the purpose of the appraisal is to establish "net sound values," as there are also appraisals for insurance purposes, on the basis of depreciated replacement cost, and for other special purposes.

Miscellaneous Investments. These may include non-marketable investments in other companies or non-current advances. Needless to say, sufficient underlying data should be obtained on assets in this category to value them realistically.

Prepaid and Deferred Charges. Deferred research and experimental expense, unamortized debt expense, and certain "prepaid" items may have little or no value to a prospective purchaser. Conversely, the purchaser is entitled to inventory advertising and office supplies on hand that will be utilized at their current replacement cost, even though they have been expensed by the seller.

Patents and Copyrights. Patents and copyrights, which generally are written off or carried at a nominal value, may be of considerable value, on a tax basis, to the purchaser. Also, favorable contracts or leases may likewise have value. These items should be carefully investigated to determine what values may be placed on them and the period over which they should be amortized. Purchased trademarks, trade names, and many franchises, even though they have considerable value, may not be amortized for tax purposes because of their indeterminate useful lives.

Goodwill. In an acquisition, goodwill, more appropriately termed "excess of cost over value assigned to net tangible assets acquired," theoretically should be supportable by a calculation indicating a capitalization of excess future earnings. At times, it often is a residual figure remaining after allocating apportionable amounts of the purchase price to tangible assets and intangible assets that have a tax basis. The amount assigned to goodwill is not amortizable for federal income tax purposes.

Liabilities. The purchaser and seller should be very clear on which liabilities of the company are to be covered by a warranty of the latter. In many cases, liabilities for federal and state income taxes may not be finally determined until several years have passed. The seller should take a conservative view regarding his tax liability, particularly if the buy–sell agreement stipulates that the purchaser is only responsible for liabilities disclosed or those for which reserves have been provided in the statement of financial position of the seller.

Other accruals, such as for vacation and holiday pay, royalties, and commissions should be reviewed carefully.

Examples of Assigning "Stepped-up Values"

In the following example, values are assigned to net assets in the liquidation of Company A whose capital stock was purchased by Company B for a cash amount exceeding the tax basis of the former.

	Seller's Basis	Purchaser's Basis Method I— Residual	Purchaser's Basis Method II— Proportional Allocation
Current assets:			
Cash	$ 330,000	$ 330,000	$ 330,000
U. S. Government securities at cost, approximate market value $90,000	100,000	90,000	97,229
Accounts receivable, less allowance of $75,000 for doubtful accounts	1,300,000	1,335,000	1,442,229
Inventories, at cost	2,700,000	3,200,000	3,457,028
Prepaid expenses	35,000	105,000	113,434
	$4,465,000	$5,060,000	$5,439,920
Property, plant, & equipment at cost, less depreciation of $700,000	$1,600,000	$2,250,000	$2,430,723
Patents	—	490,000	529,357
Deferred charges to income	60,000	—	
Goodwill	—	600,000	
Total assets	$6,125,000	$8,400,000	$8,400,000
Liabilities:			
Federal income taxes	$ 700,000	$ 700,000	$ 700,000
Other liabilities	2,100,000	2,100,000	2,100,000
Total liabilities	$2,800,000	$2,800,000	$2,800,000
Net assets	$3,325,000	$5,600,000	$5,600,000
Purchase price	—	$5,600,000	$5,600,000

Method I—Residual. The residual method has been used in many cases in allocating bases to the various classifications of assets distributed upon liquidation of a subsidiary. Briefly, under this method, bases equal to fair market values are assigned to all tangible and intangible assets; the portion of the purchase price remaining, if any, is considered to be goodwill. The amounts shown under Method I—Residual, other than goodwill, are the fair market values, as explained hereinafter.

Method II—Proportional Allocation. Under the proportional allocation method, the fair market values of all assets, including goodwill if any, are first determined. Cash and its equivalent, i.e., cash deposits, are then deducted from the adjusted purchase price of the capital stock, and the remaining portion thereof is allocated to various assets in the ratios that the fair market values of each bear to total fair market value.

For purposes of this example, the following computation is made, which indicates that no goodwill is involved in the purchase:

Net income of Company A prior to its acquisition:		
Latest year		$ 400,000
First preceding year		420,000
Second preceding year		350,000
Total		$1,170,000
Annual average		$ 390,000
Adjust for additional depreciation and amortization, as a result of stepped-up bases:		
Property and plant, etc.	$32,500	
Patents	49,000	
	$81,500	
Less federal income tax	41,500	40,000
Adjusted earnings		$ 350,000
Purchase price of $5,600,000 × 9% (industry average)		504,000
Excess to be capitalized		None

The total basis of assets under Method II is distributed to the various assets pursuant to the following computation:

Fair market value of assets:	
($8,400,000 less goodwill of $600,000)	$7,800,000
Less: Cash	330,000
Adjusted fair market value	$7,470,000
Purchase price	$5,600,000
Liabilities assumed	2,800,000
	$8,400,000
Less: Cash	330,000
Total basis to be distributed	$8,070,000

The fair market value of each classification of assets, except cash, is multiplied by $\frac{8,070,000}{7,470,000}$ or approximately 108%. Although in the above example no goodwill was computed, in many cases there would be computed goodwill, in such liquidations, under the proportional allocation method.

The foregoing example assumes the liquidation of Company A immediately after acquisition of its capital stock. A delay in liquidation could prove costly because of adjustments to the purchase price required as a result of interim transactions. In order to keep the example relatively simple, no consideration has been given to the effect of depreciation recapture, investment credit restoration, or other adjustments attributable to the liquidation.

Some rather peculiar valuations result from using the proportional allocation method. In the above example, marketable securities are valued at some $7,200 in excess of their fair market value and accounts receivable at $67,000 in excess of 100% of their gross value of $1,375,000.

A litigated case is reviewed on pages 226–28, wherein the application of this method of allocation resulted in the assignment of bases to certain current assets in amounts substantially below their fair market values. The results produced under this proportional allocation method leave something to be desired from an equity standpoint in many cases.

Basis of Determining Fair Market Values

In the foregoing example, Company B determined the fair market values of assets distributed in liquidation on the following bases:

1. Marketable securities were at approximate market values.
2. The reserve for doubtful accounts receivable appeared excessive by $35,000 and was, accordingly, reduced by this amount.
3. Inventories of raw materials and supplies, including supplies on hand that had been expensed by the seller, were valued at their current replacement cost; finished goods, at sales values less the estimated cost of their disposition; and work in process, at percentage stages of completion of finished goods.
4. Certain prepaid expenses that had no value to the purchaser were written off, but substantial quantities of advertising materials and office supplies on hand that had been expensed by the seller were valued at replacement cost.
5. Property, plant, and equipment were reflected at their net sound values resulting from an appraisal by one of the major professional appraisal firms. These values included tools, dies, and jigs that had previously been written off the books of the seller.
6. Patents were valued individually by the purchaser's engineers, assisted by outside patent counsel.

7. Deferred charges to income consisted of deferred research and experimental expense that had no value to the purchaser.

8. Goodwill was the residual balance of the purchase price, after assigning values to all other assets and liabilities.

9. Federal income tax liability was covered by the seller's warranty, as the company's tax returns had not been examined for three years. Adjustment of the purchase price was to be made upon final determination of tax liability.

As illustrated in the foregoing example, in a purchase of the capital stock of a company, and its subsequent liquidation, a new basis is established for many of the assets.

Subsequent Accounting for Assets Distributed

Current Assets. *Marketable securities* should be accounted for on the same basis as if they had been purchased in the ordinary course of business.

Accounts and notes receivable should be valued from time to time, the same as any other accounts the purchaser may have had prior to the transaction, and a suitable allowance made for accounts that may become uncollectible. In addition, if receivables are valued in excess of face amount, under the proportional allocation method, a reserve would be required for such excess.

Inventories should be valued on the basis of cost or market, whichever is lower. Cost should be determined on the basis that the purchaser regularly uses in computing inventory valuations, such as first-in, first-out; average; and last-in, first-out. In other words, the purchaser is in no way bound by the method of inventory costing followed by the seller. To the extent that any inventories acquired from the seller remain on hand at the close of subsequent accounting periods, cost and market may be the same. Otherwise, for periods subsequent to acquisition, market is understood to mean current replacement value, either by purchase or by reproduction.

Property, Plant, and Equipment. Provision for depreciation on fair values allocated to machinery and equipment should be based on the estimated remaining useful lives of the assets, in accordance with the regular accounting practice of the purchaser. The depreciation practices of the seller, as to useful lives of assets, need not be followed by the purchaser, although it may be convenient to do so.

Prepaid and Deferred Charges. These should be apportioned over the periods benefited through their use.

Intangible Assets Other Than Goodwill. Amounts capitalized by the purchaser for patents should be amortized over their useful lives or to the date of their expiry, whichever is shorter.

Liabilities, Including Federal Income Taxes. Because of differing employee benefit plans, reserves carried by the seller may not have any relation to the liabilities assumed by the purchaser for such items, either morally or legally. However, if the purchaser is assuming liabilities of the seller, it should be ascertained that provision has been made for all such obligations.

Any tax deficiency assumed by the purchaser becomes an additional tax basis allocable to the assets received, pursuant to the regulations under Section 334(b)(2) of the Internal Revenue Code.

Goodwill. Accounting for goodwill is one of the most troublesome considerations in acquisitions for cash. In the case of other assets acquired that have a tax basis, the purchaser recovers part of his purchase price in the future by means of tax deductions when assets are disposed of, and through periodic charges for depreciation and amortization. Accordingly, it is desirable to establish "recoverable" values to the maximum extent in a purchase.

Inasmuch as accounting for goodwill is discussed at some length in the next chapter, no proposal will be made for its disposition in this section.

Basis of Current Assets—Boise Cascade Case

A somewhat unusual situation resulted in a substantial income tax liability to Boise Cascade Corporation (Boise) upon the disposal of assets in a period following a Section 334(b)(2) liquidation of a subsidiary.

In a U. S. District Court case decided in 1968, Boise sued to recover federal income taxes of $318,264 allegedly erroneously paid, plus interest, resulting from the assignment by the Internal

Revenue Service of values substantially below known fair market value to current assets in the liquidation of a subsidiary.[10]

Boise had purchased the capital stock of Hallack & Howard Lumber Company (H & H) on February 1, 1960, for cash. On November 30, 1960, when H & H was merged into Boise and liquidated, the adjusted purchase price for the company was $6,793,666, and its assets had a fair market value of $9,488,342. Included in the fair market value compilation were the following current assets:

Cash and deposits	$ 202,296
Marketable securities	1,128,068
Accounts receivable	3,424,406
Inventories	1,119,508
Prepaid supplies	30,083

The Internal Revenue Service agreed, in a stipulation of facts, that the fair market values of the current assets were as indicated and that no gain or loss to the taxpayer should be recognized as a result of the liquidation which met the requirements of Section 332. However, the Internal Revenue Service contended that only cash and "equivalents" should be valued at 100% of fair market, and marketable securities, inventories, and prepaid supplies were not equivalents and their bases should be proportionally scaled down. This resulted in these assets being valued at approximately 71% of their acknowledged fair value and involved an income tax liability on their disposition or collection.

Rather inconsistently, the Service agreed that accounts receivable were the equivalent of cash, but later reversed its position. However, the applicable statute of limitations prevented the Service from adjusting its deficiency assessment for this "oversight."

The taxpayer, in contending that cash and its "equivalents" should include the disputed current assets at their fair market value, relied on a broader interpretation than that given by the Internal Revenue Service to the following Regulations:

Sec. 1.334–1(c)(4)(v)(b)(1):
(v) The adjusted basis of the subsidiary's stock held by the parent with respect to which the distributions in liquidation are made . . .

[10] Boise Cascade Corporation et al. v. United States, 288 Fed. Supp. 770 (D.C. Idaho 1968; aff'd C.A. 9, Aug. 31, 1970).

(b) Shall be decreased:

(1) By the amount of any cash and its equivalent received, . . .

✿ ✿ ✿

Sec. 1.334–1(c)(4)(viii): The amount of the adjusted basis of the stock adjusted as provided in this paragraph shall be allocated as basis among the various assets received (except cash and its equivalent) both tangible and intangible. . . . Ordinarily, such allocation shall be made in proportion to the net fair market value of such assets on the date received. . . . The basis of the property received shall be zero if the cash and its equivalent received is equal to or in excess of the adjusted basis of the stock.

The court in upholding the position of the Internal Revenue Service evidently relied on Revenue Ruling 66–290, and summed up its opinion as follows:

In summary, this court is of the opinion that cash and its equivalent as that phrase is used in the regulations under consideration here does not include marketable securities, inventories, prepaid supplies and accounts receivable from third parties. In the opinion of the court there is no merit to taxpayer's contention that the rule of proportionate allocation specified by Section 1.334–1(c)(4)(viii) (1954) of the Treasury Regulations should not be followed in this instance. Taxpayer's intention in regard to what it would have paid for certain assets is not relevant and material to a resolution of the question here and taxpayer's contention in this regard is not meritorious.

STATE TAX CONSIDERATIONS

At the state tax level, characterization of a combination as either taxable or tax-free is not always so evident as it is for federal income tax purposes. There are various types of state taxes whose effect must be considered in connection with any business combination: income taxes (both corporate and personal), franchise taxes (taxes based on capital values, such as net worth or total assets, or on income), sales taxes, and stock transfer or original issue corporation taxes and fees. Moreover, a corporation engaged in other than a strictly local business is probably subject to one or more of these taxes in several states.

State taxes generally are a minor matter relative to potential income tax effects in a business combination. Nevertheless, their consequences must be considered. Because tax statutes vary considerably from state to state, there is no substitute for carefully checking the applicable tax rules of each state to which the constituents to a business combination pay a significant tax, in order to gauge the effect of state taxes on the combination. The discussion that follows presents a broad outline of the points that should be considered in this review.

Corporate Income Taxes

In states such as New York, Pennsylvania, and New Jersey, where taxable income for state purposes is based principally on taxable income reported for federal purposes, an asset transfer on which taxable gain is not recognized for federal purposes should be similarly exempt for state income tax purposes. A number of states have adopted their own detailed income tax statutes, following the general lines of the federal Internal Revenue Code. In many of these states, including California, Minnesota, and Louisiana, the state statutory provisions on reorganization and twelve-month liquidations closely parallel the Internal Revenue Code. Accordingly, in these states, asset transfers, on which gain is not recognized for federal purposes, should also be exempt for state purposes, provided the transaction qualifies under the related statutory provisions of the state. On the other hand, it may be generally assumed that if gain on the sale of the assets of a business is recognized for federal income tax purposes in such states, it will similarly be subject to state taxation.

Greater problems are presented in those states whose income tax laws bear little resemblance to the Internal Revenue Code. State tax laws of this type are often written in broad and general terms, and no specific provisions are made for reorganizations or sales of assets by liquidating corporations. Great discretionary power in prescribing regulations and administering the income tax law is often given the tax commissioner or other officials in such states.

Care must be exercised in checking the rules in these states, to ascertain whether, for example, gain on sale of assets not recognized for federal purposes will be similarly exempted by the state. It may be prudent to request a specific ruling from the state tax authorities in appropriate cases.

Personal Income Taxes

A general personal income tax is imposed in many states and by the District of Columbia. Since most business combinations involve directly or indirectly the exchange of the stocks held by the stockholders of the acquired corporation for stock of the acquiring corporation or for cash or other consideration, the question of possible state income tax liability to the stockholders on such exchanges must be considered. While this is not of direct concern at the corporate level, it could be important if a closely held corporation is involved in a business combination.

Franchise Taxes

Many states and the District of Columbia impose franchise or capital value taxes. These may be divided into two general groups: (a) those that base the tax on stated or nominal capital values, such as par value, or number of shares of stock; and (b) those that base the tax on "real" capital values, such as the market value of outstanding stock, or net worth as shown on the books. Delaware and New Hampshire are examples of the first group, and Pennsylvania, New Jersey, and Texas of the second.

Franchise tax liability in those states basing the tax on nominal or stated capital can be affected by any recapitalization or increase in capitalization incident to a merger, or an acquisition involving issuance of additional shares by the acquiring corporation. It is necessary to check the particular law of each state to which the acquiring corporation pays or will pay a franchise tax in order to evaluate the potential franchise tax effect of the merger. In some cases, credit may be available for taxes previously paid to the state by an acquired corporation absorbed in a merger.

More serious problems can be presented to the acquired corporation in certain of the states that base the franchise tax on actual capital values. For example, in New Jersey the annual franchise tax is ordinarily based, in part, on book net worth. However, in the case of a corporation that sells or transfers its assets and business to an acquiring corporation and then liquidates, the state requires that net worth as reflected on the final return of the liquidating corporation be based on the actual value of the consideration received for its assets.

Sales Taxes

Most states impose some form of sales or gross receipts tax or license tax measured by gross income. Such taxes are also imposed by the District of Columbia and by many municipalities in certain states. In these jurisdictions, a business combination involving a sale of assets must be checked for possible sales tax liability that might attach with respect to the tangible personal property—machinery, equipment, and inventories—included among the assets transferred.

In many states, a transaction involving the sale of all the assets of a business would be exempt from sales tax, either because of the specific exemption of casual sales or by reason of the classifications of taxable transactions prescribed by the state. However, this rule would not hold true in all states. In Colorado, for example, the regulations specifically provide that in the case of the sale of a business ". . . the sales tax must be paid on the purchase price paid for the equipment, furniture, fixtures, supplies and all tangible personal property included in the sale except a stock or inventory of goods acquired for resale in the trade or business."

California is another state in which possible sales tax liability on the sale of a business often proves troublesome, despite an exemption in the law for occasional sales.

Moreover, the fact that assets are transferred to an acquiring corporation for stock in a tax-free reorganization for federal purposes rather than for cash would not necessarily remove the transaction from the definition of a sale in some states.

Stock Transfer and Sundry Taxes

A few states impose stock transfer taxes, and most states impose various qualification and filing fees or fees based on increases in authorized capital stock. Hence, any business combination that requires recapitalization or formation of a new corporation or the qualification of the acquiring corporation in other states will be subject to fees or taxes of this type. In most cases, these may be expected to form a relatively minor part of the cost of effecting a business combination. In a few states, however, certain specialized types of "initial tax" might give rise to an unexpected tax liability.

Pennsylvania imposes an excise tax, which is in addition to the franchise tax, on foreign corporations for the privilege of employing capital in the state. The tax, a so-called "plateau" tax, is assessed only on increases in the amount of capital employed. If a New York corporation having a plant in Pennsylvania sells its assets and business to a Delaware corporation, the tangible property at that plant will be viewed as an increase in the amount of capital employed by the Delaware corporation in Pennsylvania, and accordingly will be subject to excise tax.

State Bulk Sales Laws

In any corporate acquisition involving the purchase of assets, whether for stock or cash, the requirements of the bulk sales laws of the various states should be considered. Bulk sales laws are designed to protect the creditors against the fraudulent sale of business assets, particularly inventories and fixtures. While the laws differ from state to state, the typical requirement is for notice to the creditors in the case of a sale or other disposition in bulk of all or a part of the inventories and fixtures in a transaction not in the ordinary course of business.

Counsel should be consulted on the possible application of the bulk sales laws to any purchase of the assets of a business. Failure to comply may expose the purchaser to possible claims by the creditors of the seller.

TIMELY DISCLOSURE OF BUSINESS COMBINATION DEALS

Until relatively recently, various practices have been followed in the timing of public announcements of business combinations. These have ranged from announcements indicating that a preliminary offer has been made or preliminary negotiations are being conducted, to announcements made only after a formal agreement has been signed. However, due to several landmark decisions in 1968 in actions brought by the Securities and Exchange Commission, such announcements are generally being made at a very early stage of negotiations in a proposed acquisition or merger.

Although these actions, which were against company officials, brokers, and others, did not relate to business combination deals, the principle involved did—the use by "insiders" of information on corporate developments that affected the market price of stock. Unquestionably, a proposed acquisition or merger affects the market movement of the stocks involved.

SEC Position

Section 10(b) of the Securities Exchange Act of 1934 and a general rule, 10 b–5, of that Act, both of which are reproduced below, cover manipulative and deceptive (fraudulent) acts in connection with the "purchase or sale of any security." Up to the close of 1968 the Securities and Exchange Commission had released no formal guidelines on the subject of disclosures (except for tender offers, discussed in Chapter 10).

Section 10. It shall be unlawful for any person, directly or indirectly, by the use of any means or instrumentality of interstate commerce or of the mails, or of any facility of any national securities exchange—
(b) To use or employ, in connection with the purchase or sale of any security registered on a national securities exchange or any security not so registered, any manipulative or deceptive device or contrivance in contravention of such rules and regulations as the Commission may prescribe as necessary or appropriate in the public interest or for the protection of investors.

✻ ✻ ✻

Rule 10 b–5. Employment of Manipulative and Deceptive Devices.
It shall be unlawful for any person, directly or indirectly, by the use of any means or instrumentality of interstate commerce, or of the mails, or of any facility of any national securities exchange
(1) to employ any device, scheme, or artifice to defraud,
(2) to make any untrue statement of a material fact or to omit to state a material fact necessary in order to make the statements made, in the light of the circumstances under which they were made, not misleading, or
(3) to engage in any act, practice, or course of business which operates or would operate as a fraud or deceit upon any person,
in connection with the purchase or sale of any security.

NYSE and Amex Position

The court decisions in 1968 in actions instituted by the Securities and Exchange Commission caused the New York Stock

Exchange to expand its already comprehensive policy for listed companies, on July 18, 1968, to include the following rule on disclosures:

A corporation whose stock is listed on the New York Stock Exchange is expected to release quickly to the public any news or information which might reasonably be expected to materially affect the market for securities. At some point it usually becomes necessary to involve other persons to conduct preliminary studies or assist in other preparations for contemplated transactions, e.g., business appraisals, tentative financing arrangements, attitude of large outside holders, availability of major blocks of stock, engineering studies, market analyses and surveys, etc. Experience has shown that maintaining security at this point is virtually impossible. Accordingly, fairness requires that the Company make an immediate public announcement as soon as confidential disclosures relating to such important matters are made to "outsiders."

On May 20, 1970, the American Stock Exchange revised its disclosure policies as follows:

(1) *Immediate Public Disclosure of Material Information.* A listed company is required to make immediate public disclosure of all material information concerning its affairs, except in exceptional circumstances.

(2) *Thorough Public Dissemination.* A listed company is required to release material information to the public in a manner designed to obtain its fullest possible public dissemination.

(3) *Clarification or Confirmation of Rumors and Reports.* Whenever a listed company becomes aware of a rumor or report, true or false, that contains information that is likely to have, or has had, an effect on the trading in the company's securities or would be likely to have a bearing on investment decisions, the company is required to publicly clarify the rumor or report as promptly as possible.

(4) *Response to Unusual Market Action.* Whenever unusual market action takes place in a listed company's securities, the company is expected to make inquiry to determine whether rumors or other conditions requiring corrective action exist, and, if so, to take whatever action is appropriate. If, after the company's review, the unusual market action remains unexplained, it may be appropriate for the company to announce that there has been no material development in its business and affairs not previously disclosed nor, to its knowledge, any other reason to account for the unusual market action.

(5) *Unwarranted Promotional Disclosure.* A listed company should refrain from promotional disclosure activity which exceeds that necessary to enable the public to make informed investment decisions. Such activity includes inappropriately worded news releases, public announcements not justified by actual developments in a company's affairs, exaggerated reports or predictions, flamboyant wording and other forms of over-stated or over-zealous disclosure activity which may mislead investors and cause unwarranted price movements and activity in a company's securities.

(6) *Insider Trading.* Insiders should not trade on the basis of material information which is not known to the investing public. Moreover, insiders should refrain from trading, even after material information has been released to the press and other media, for a period sufficient to permit thorough public dissemination and evaluation of the information.

ANTITRUST LAWS

Although there are other federal laws that could be pertinent, the basic antitrust laws invoked in business combinations are the Sherman Act and the Clayton Act. The Sherman Act, which was enacted July 2, 1890, and amended several times thereafter, had as its purpose the prevention of monopolistic practices or conspiracies in restraint of trade in interstate trade and foreign commerce.

The Clayton Act, which was enacted October 15, 1914, and amended several times thereafter, contains a specific provision relating to acquisitions and mergers, which enables the enforcing agencies, the Department of Justice and the Federal Trade Commission, *to act to prevent certain business combinations, as well as to petition for their dissolution.* Most of the actions in antitrust cases arising out of business combinations, during recent years, have been instituted under the Clayton Act.

Section 7 of the Clayton Act, which is pertinent to business combinations, contains the following language, enabling the enforcing agencies to act before there is proof of a present monopoly:

. . . no corporation . . . shall acquire the whole or any part of the assets of another corporation . . . where in any line of commerce in any section of the country, the effect of such action *may be* substantially to lessen competition, or to tend to create a monopoly.

The antitrust aspects of a proposed business combination should be carefully considered by legal counsel. During recent years, the Federal Trade Commission and Department of Justice have stepped up their activities and challenged business combination deals that they would have ignored some years ago. Although these law enforcement agencies have contended that bigness, per se, is not evil, many of their major targets have been acquisitions by larger companies.

On April 13, 1969, the Federal Trade Commission announced that, pursuant to a resolution dated April 8, 1969, it will henceforth require firms undertaking large corporate mergers or acquisitions (i.e., involving firms with combined assets of $250 million) to notify the Commission and supply Special Reports within 10 days after any agreement in principle is reached and no less than 60 days prior to the consummation of the transaction. Also, large corporate stock acquisitions will have to be reported to the Commission in those instances in which the acquisition results in a corporation owning at least 10% of the voting stock of another corporation with assets of at least $10 million or more. The Commission has undertaken this action in response to the sharp acceleration in merger activity.

"Mergers and Markets," periodic research studies by the National Industrial Conference Board, point out that of the 26 antitrust complaints filed in the year ended June 30, 1968, 65% of them were against companies having sales of $100 million and over.[11]

Guidelines

A release by the Department of Justice, dated May 30, 1968, outlining its guidelines or standards for determining whether to oppose corporate acquisitions or mergers under Section 7 of the Clayton Act, sheds considerable light on the Department's current enforcement policy. This release, covering twenty-one topical items, outlines the various "standard" percentages of the market for acquiring and acquired firms that ordinarily will lead to a challenge by the Department.

Horizontal, vertical, and conglomerate mergers are covered in the guidelines, as well as the Department's current policy in the acquisition of so-called "failing" companies. The following two paragraphs in the preface to the guidelines indicate their conditional nature:

The Department anticipates that it will amend the guidelines from time to time to reflect changes in enforcement policy that might result from subsequent court decisions, comments of interested parties, or Department reevaluations.

[11] "Mergers and Markets," NICB Studies in Business Economics No. 105 (1969).

Because changes in enforcement policy will be made as the occasion demands and will usually precede the issuance of amended guidelines, the Department said that the existence of unamended guidelines should not be regarded as barring it from taking any action it deems necessary to achieve the purposes of Section 7.

Some of the more important data contained in the release are summarized as Appendix G of this book.

Procedure for Pre-Merger Clearances

The Federal Trade Commission, on May 23, 1969, announced a new procedure for handling of pre-merger clearance requests, and applications for approval of divestitures, acquisitions, or similar transactions.

Under this procedure, the Commission makes public the application for approval together with supporting materials, "except for such information which (a) the applicant has requested to be classified as confidential, showing justification therefor, and (b) the Commission, with due regard to statutory restrictions, its rules, and the public interest has determined should not be made public."

Within thirty days after the date of publication, any interested member of the public may file written objections or comments with the Secretary. If substantial questions of fact are involved which should be resolved before the request or application can be finally approved, the Commission will take appropriate action to resolve the issues presented.

In the event the Commission determines to deny an application for pre-merger clearance, its action is made public by publication of its advisory opinion deleting the names of the applicant and the other company subject to the application and any other confidential information contained in the opinion letter. In the event the disapproval is based upon a request subject to the Commission's review, the Commission's action, with a statement of supporting reasons, will be made public.

With respect to provisional approvals, the new procedure permits interested persons to raise objections to the proposed actions which may not have been considered by the Commission.

Despite constant surveillance by the antitrust enforcement agencies of proposed business combinations, the number of mergers consummated, particularly in the conglomerate category, continues to increase each year, and it is estimated that less than 1% of the business combinations during recent years have been seriously challenged by the government.

GENERAL OR BUSINESS CORPORATION LAWS

The requirements of general or business corporation laws vary from state to state. A statutory merger or consolidation usually requires the approval of the stockholders of all parties to the transaction. A taxable purchase or a tax-free acquisition of assets for capital stock generally requires approval by the stockholders of the selling or transfer corporation but not those of the acquiring corporation.

Where stockholder approval is required, the percentage of assenting voters varies among states from a simple majority to as much as 80%.

Although an acquiring corporation generally is not required by state law to seek approval of its stockholders when it acquires the assets and business of another company, the courts have looked through these transactions in some states and contended that they were de facto mergers and should have had stockholder approval. Furthermore, in sizable transactions the major stock exchanges frequently require stockholder approval.

Rights of Dissenting Stockholders

In the case of a statutory merger or consolidation, states generally grant stockholders who dissent the right to appraisal of their shares and to payment of the appraisal value in cash. Even in the acquisition of assets, such appraisal rights are given dissenting stockholders in a majority of the states. In the case of an acquisition of stock, appraisal rights generally are not granted the dissenting stockholders. However, they do not have to turn in their stock and go along with the deal. Thus, they have the option of selling their shares or remaining as minority stockholders.

Even though stockholders' approval may not be required in some business combinations, particularly on behalf of an acquiring company, it is often prudent to obtain such approval, particularly where the deal is relatively material.

State laws dealing with the rights of dissenting stockholders are discussed at some length in Chapter 14.

Effect of Pre-emptive Rights

Stockholders' pre-emptive rights refer to the right of a present stockholder in a corporation to subscribe to new stock that the corporation may issue, in order to maintain his proportionate share of ownership in the company. Many states have qualified this common-law concept by statute, so that it is often possible for a corporation to limit or entirely eliminate this right by so providing in its articles of incorporation. In fact, in a few states, pre-emptive rights are denied unless the articles specifically provide for them.

To the extent that pre-emptive rights do apply to a corporation, they are not generally considered to extend to the issuance of shares in exchange for specific property or in a merger. In a case where one corporation acquires the assets of another in exchange for its voting stock (a "C" type reorganization) pre-emptive rights could have some application if the acquiring corporation acquires the cash, along with the other assets, of the acquired corporation. The question of possible application of pre-emptive rights is a matter to be considered and discussed with counsel in determining the form that a proposed business combination should take.

BUSINESS COMBINATION AGREEMENTS

The drafting of business combination agreements is in the province of lawyers and should remain so. It is not proposed, therefore, to discuss the many and at times complex problems involved in drawing up such agreements. However, it is recommended that the drafting of written agreements be commenced soon after substantial oral agreement is reached by the several parties to a business combination. Many problems and possible obstacles to a deal may thus be brought to light at an early date, and differences resolved or negotiations dropped without causing undue expense or annoyance to the principals involved.

The prospective acquirer and the seller, each acting in good faith, often have completely different understandings of the terms of a deal, including what is being "bought" and "sold." Accordingly, it should be the objective of legal counsel preparing an agreement to set forth the intent of the several parties to the agreement in language that can have only one meaning to them, to any experts involved in the proceedings, such as independent accountants and professional appraisers, in the event of a dispute, and to a court, if litigation over the deal should unfortunately develop. Obviously, this will require consultation with the various parties at interest and the professionals involved during the course of drafting the agreement.

9

Accounting Aspects

Accounting for business combinations, and the attendant problems of dealing with goodwill, has been the subject of much controversy during a period of years, leading up to the issuance by the Accounting Principles Board of the American Institute of Certified Public Accountants, in August 1970, of Opinions Nos. 16 and 17 revising the accounting rules for such transactions.[1] The accounting treatment available in business combinations is of the utmost importance, and affects the reporting of future earnings of combined enterprises, and therefore the valuation of companies at the time they are acquired or merged.

In view of the many issues raised during the period of gestation and the divergent points of view of board members, these Opinions are very detailed; No. 16, "Business Combinations," contains 99 paragraphs and No. 17, "Intangible Assets," 35 paragraphs. Even the ultimate adoption of the Opinions setting forth the revised rules and procedures was not without dissent, as six of eighteen members of the Board dissented from the Opinion on Business Combinations, and five from the Opinion on Intangible Assets. Provisions of these Opinions which became effective in accounting for business combinations initiated after October 31,

[1] Accounting Principles Board Opinions No. 16, "Business Combinations," and No. 17, "Intangible Assets," August 1970. Copyright 1970 by the American Institute of Certified Public Accountants.

1970, are discussed in this chapter, and examples of some of their applications are given.

In addition, Accounting Principles Board Opinion No. 15, "Earnings Per Share," [2] will be discussed in this chapter, because the issuance, by an acquirer, of securities such as convertible debentures, convertible preferred stock, warrants, and options, in a business combination, has a potentially dilutive effect on earnings, which must be reported when publishing per-share earnings figures.

TYPES OF BUSINESS COMBINATIONS

For accounting purposes, a business combination falls into one of two categories, i.e., a purchase or a pooling of interests.

Purchases

Under the purchase method, one company is deemed to have acquired another. The acquiring corporation records on its books the cost of the acquired assets less liabilities assumed. The difference between the cost of the acquired company and the sum of the fair values assigned to tangible and identifiable intangible assets, less liabilities, is recorded as goodwill. Also, in a purchase the operations of the acquired company are reflected in the accounts and financial statements of the acquirer from the date of acquisition.

Poolings of Interest

The pooling of interests method accounts for a business combination as the uniting of ownership interests of two or more companies by an exchange of equity securities. Accordingly, the shares issued to effect the combination are generally shown at aggregate par or stated value. The capital in excess of par (capital surplus) and accumulated earnings (earned surplus) of each of the constituent companies are respectively combined, subject to appropriate adjustments if the par or stated value of the stock

---

[2] Accounting Principles Board Opinion No. 15, "Earnings per Share," May 1969.

issued differs from the amount at which the capital stock of the disappearing company or companies was carried. In addition, the net book assets of the constituent companies are combined. Since the net book values of assets of the disappearing company or companies are carried forward in the combined enterprise, subject to possible adjustments for purposes of accounting uniformity, no goodwill arises in pooling transactions.

Consistent with the concept that the pooled enterprise is a continuation of all of the constituent companies, their operations are combined for periods prior as well as subsequent to the date of the combination, for accounting and financial statement purposes.

Status of Poolings Prior to Opinion No. 16. Prior to the issuance of Opinion No. 16, the accounting ground rules for business combinations were covered by Bulletin No. 48, as amended, entitled "Business Combinations" and prepared by the Committee on Accounting Procedure of the AICPA.[3] In summary, the factors indicating that a business combination was a pooling of interests, under that bulletin, were:

1. That the consideration given by the acquirer or dominant company in a merger or consolidation be voting capital stock
2. That the interests of the shareholders of each of the constituent companies be substantially proportionate in the combined enterprise to their respective interests in each predecessor company
3. That where all of the capital stock of a constituent company is not being acquired, no significant minority interest remains outstanding
4. That voting rights, as between the constituents, not be materially altered through the issuance of senior equity or debt securities having limited or no voting rights
5. That there be no plan to retire a substantial part of the capital stock issued to owners of one or more of the constituent companies, nor a plan to substantially change ownership interests shortly before or shortly after the business combination
6. That there be a continuity of management or the power to control management; for example, where a constituent company

---

[3] AICPA Committee on Accounting Procedure, "Business Combinations," Bull. No. 48, January 1957, amended by APB Opinion No. 6, December 1965, and APB Opinion No. 10, December 1966.

emerges with less than 5 to 10% of the voting interest in the combined enterprise, its influence on management is presumed to be quite small

After the issuance of Bulletin No. 48, there was a gradual relaxation in adhering to most of the factors indicated in the Bulletin as leading to a presumption of a pooling of interests. During recent years, the only factor rigidly adhered to was that the consideration given by the acquirer, or surviving company in a merger, be voting capital stock (either common or convertible preferred).

There were numerous cases in which the voting rights of constituents had been reduced (usually up to 25%) immediately before or as a result of the business combination, either through the retirement of stock interests, the acceptance of voting senior equity securities, with a consequent reduction in voting power, or at times the sale of equity interests immediately before, simultaneously with, or after a business combination. Furthermore, the criteria of the relative size of the companies involved in a business combination and the continuity of management were ultimately ignored.

Problems Considered in Drafting Opinion No. 16. The greatest controversy in drafting Opinion No. 16, which involved not only the Accounting Principles Board but major elements of the business community, was the question of whether the pooling of interests method was a valid accounting concept. At one extreme, some accountants believed the pooling treatment was inappropriate, or warranted only where two or more companies were substantially equal in size. In all other cases, business combinations, regardless of the fact that equity securities were issued in exchange for equity securities or net assets of acquired companies, would have been treated as purchases by these advocates. This would probably have eliminated 90 to 95% of business combinations from pooling of interests treatment, in the light of merger information developed in recent years.

After considerable discussion, the size criterion was eliminated by the Board as a prerequisite to pooling accounting treatment. However, many restrictive conditions are embodied in Opinion

No. 16 that would proscribe pooling of interests treatment previously acceptable for a substantial number of business combinations. Accordingly, the Opinion also outlines procedures in accounting for such non-qualifying combinations as purchases.

Despite the length of Opinion No. 16, its provisions are so complex that "Unofficial Accounting Interpretations" will be issued from time to time by the staff of the AICPA to resolve intended applications under the Opinion. These will be published in the *Journal of Accountancy* and elsewhere. If desired, a specific problem may be submitted to the AICPA for advice.

Some of the allegedly unsatisfactory accounting practices followed in business combinations, which the revised rules are intended to correct, may be summarized as follows:

1. The failure to amortize goodwill in purchase transactions
2. Crediting so-called "negative goodwill" to income over short periods rather than applying it in reduction of non-current assets acquired
3. Not indicating comparable combined earnings figures in purchase transactions for the year prior to the transaction
4. Giving retroactive effect to a pooling after a company's fiscal year-end
5. Creating "instant earnings" following a pooling transaction by disposing of non-operating assets or investments recorded at low book values
6. Using convertible preferred equity securities in exchange for common stock in a pooling
7. Having part purchase and part pooling transactions where a company initially purchased a capital stock interest in another, and later completed the acquisition by an exchange of capital stock
8. Making disproportionate distributions of capital stock to the same class of stockholders and treating the transaction as a pooling
9. Accounting for a transaction as a pooling where a plan of combination provides for the contingent issuance of securities or other consideration based on future earnings or market price levels

CONDITIONS FOR POOLING-OF-INTERESTS ACCOUNTING

A discussion of conditions, *all* of which should be met to qualify for pooling treatment, is set forth in paragraphs 46 to 48 of Opinion No. 16. Comments on some of the more important conditions follow.

Autonomy and Independence

Each of the combining companies should be autonomous and not have been a subsidiary or division of another corporation within two years before the plan of combination is initiated.

Each of the combining companies should be independent of the other combining companies. This condition means that at the *dates* the plan of combination is *initiated* and *consummated* the combining companies hold as intercorporate investments no more than 10% in total of the outstanding voting stock of any combining company.

The conditions on autonomy and independence automatically eliminate pooling-of-interests accounting treatment where previous ownership interests existed, other than minor holdings. Heretofore, where a company had acquired an interest in another through a cash purchase, and later acquired the remaining interest by a transfer of voting capital stock, the transactions were treated in two steps, the first as a purchase and the second as a pooling of interests.

Relief is granted from the independence condition if a company held as an investment on October 31, 1970, a minority interest in or exactly 50% of the common stock of another company, and it initiated after that date a plan of combination with the latter company calling for an exchange of common stock for common stock. The exchange of stock portion of the business combination in this final step may be accounted for by the pooling-of-interests method, provided the combination is completed within five years after October 31, 1970, and certain other conditions are met.

Time Limitation for Effecting Combination

This condition calls for completion, within one year after the plan is initiated, of a business combination involving an exchange of stock, unless a delay is beyond the control of the combining companies because of governmental proceedings or litigation which prevents completion of the combination. Adjustment in terms of exchange in a plan of combination constitutes initiation of a new plan, unless earlier exchanges of stock are adjusted to new terms.

Medium of Exchange Must Be Common Stock

Only common stock exchanges for substantially all voting common stock interests may qualify for pooling treatment. In recent years, prior to the issuance of APB Opinion No. 16, a significant number of major business combinations were effected by an exchange of convertible preferred stock, or a combination of such stock and common stock, for the common stock or net assets of companies acquired. The issuance of such securities or combinations thereof no longer qualifies for pooling-of-interests treatment.

The plan to issue voting common stock in exchange for voting common stock may include, within limits, provisions to distribute cash or other consideration for fractional shares, for shares held by dissenting stockholders, and the like, but may not include a pro-rata distribution of cash or other consideration. However, a corporation issuing stock to effect the combination may assume the debt securities of the other company or may exchange substantially identical securities or voting stock for other outstanding equity and debt securities of the other combining company. An issuing corporation may also distribute cash to holders of debt and equity securities that either are callable or redeemable and may retire those securities. However, the issuing corporation may exchange only voting common stock for outstanding equity (other than voting common stock) and debt securities of the other combining company that have been issued in exchange for voting common stock of that company during a period beginning two years preceding the date the combination is initiated.

"Substantially All" Voting Common Stock Defined. "Substantially all" of the voting common stock means 90% or more. That is, after the date the plan of combination is initiated, one of the combining companies (issuing corporation) issues voting common stock in exchange for at least 90% of the voting common stock of another combining company that is outstanding at the date the combination is consummated. The number of shares exchanged therefore excludes those shares of the combining company (a) acquired before and held by the issuing corporation and its subsidiaries at the date the plan of combination is initiated, regardless of the form of consideration, (b) acquired by the issuing corporation and its subsidiaries after the date the plan of combination is initiated other than by issuing its own voting common stock, and (c) outstanding after the date the combination is consummated.

In determining the 90% figure, the number of shares of voting common stock exchanged is also reduced for an investment by the combining company in voting common stock of the issuing corporation. The percentage of voting common stock is measured separately for each combining company in determining compliance with the 90% rule, where more than two companies are involved in a combination, including cases where a new company is formed to issue its stock to effect the combination. There are other prohibitions affecting the 90% rule, such as changing equity interests in contemplation of the combination or between the time of its initiation and consummation, except for normal dividend distributions, and requirements of stock option and compensation plans, etc.

Absence of Planned Transactions

Certain transactions after a combination is consummated are considered to be inconsistent with combining interests in a pooling transaction. These include agreement or intention by the issuer to (a) retire or reacquire all or part of the common stock issued to effect the combination, (b) guarantee loans of former stockholders of the absorbed company which are secured by stock issued in the combination, and (c) dispose of a significant part of the assets of the combining companies within two years after the combination, except to eliminate duplicate facilities or excess capacity.

Application of Pooling Method

The accounting application of the pooling-of-interests method remains substantially the same under Opinion No. 16 as it did under Bulletin No. 48, as amended, which is briefed on pages

243–44. However, Opinion No. 16 contains detailed instructions covering certain matters that were previously treated in alternative ways. These include expenses related to effecting a business combination which were at times treated as additions to assets or reductions of stockholders' equity. These, and losses or estimated losses on disposal of duplicate or excess facilities, must now be deducted from combined income as incurred.

Retroactive Application in Annual Reports. Heretofore, if a business combination was consummated between the end of the fiscal year and the time a company issued its annual report, retroactive effect was given to the combination and a single report was issued containing combined financial statements of the companies. Under the revised rules, a company in such a position is required to issue its pre-combination financial statements and disclose as supplemental information, in notes to financial statements or otherwise, the financial effects of the combination. The acquiring company, issuing financial statements in such a case, should record as an investment any common stock of the other combining company held at its fiscal year-end. However, if a company involved in a business combination files a registration or proxy statement with the Securities and Exchange Commission, after its fiscal year-end but before issuance of its annual report to stockholders, the Commission will require financial statements included therein to give retroactive effect to a pooling.

All financial statements issued, for periods after the combination is consummated, should be restated on a combined basis, for periods prior as well as subsequent to the date of combination, subject to suitable adjustments.

Notes to financial statements of a combined company, for the period in which a business combination occurs and is accounted for as a pooling of interests, have not always been fully informative. Opinion No. 16 contains detailed instructions of data to be disclosed in such notes.

PURCHASE ACCOUNTING

Prior to the issuance of Opinion No. 16, business combinations that qualified as purchases fell into one of two general categories: (a) acquisitions of the net assets and business or voting capital stock of a company for cash or a combination of cash and securities, and (b) acquisitions of voting capital stock of a company in a statutory merger involving the issuance, wholly or in part, of securities other than voting stock, as permitted under laws of certain states. Under the purchase method of accounting the fair value of the consideration given was determined—whether in cash or securities or a combination thereof, or the assumption of liabilities—and was allocated to tangible and identifiable intangible assets. To the extent such purchased cost was not allocable to such identifiable assets goodwill arose. If, however, the fair value of property acquired was more clearly evident than the value of consideration given, such value was utilized.

Purchases Under Opinion No. 16

In addition to transactions considered as purchases prior to Opinion No. 16, some business combinations that previously would have qualified for pooling treatment henceforth will be considered purchases. These include deals involving the issuance of convertible preferred stock, and those in which one or the other company involved in a combination, where common stock is exchanged, had more than a minimal amount of voting common stock of the other prior to the combination. Such transactions will still qualify as "tax-free" exchanges under the Internal Revenue Code, so that the surviving company in a deal will not be able to avail itself of stepped-up tax bases, with resultant savings in income taxes.

Although the same general principles of accounting apply as heretofore for a business combination qualifying as a purchase, the determination of the total purchase cost and its allocation will present difficulties where voting capital stock, either common or preferred, constitutes the principal medium of exchange. Also, in such cases the determination of the acquirer and the acquired company may not always be clearly evident.

Determining the Cost of an Acquired Company. Opinion No. 16, as excerpted below, suggests various alternatives for determining the cost of an acquisition:

Principles of Historical-Cost Accounting. Accounting for a business combination by the purchase method follows principles normally applicable under historical-cost accounting to recording acquisitions of assets and issuances of stock and to accounting for assets and liabilities after acquisition.

Acquiring assets. The general principles to apply the historical-cost basis of accounting to an acquisition of an asset depend on the nature of the transaction:

a. An asset acquired by exchanging cash or other assets is recorded at cost—that is, at the amount of cash disbursed or the fair value of other assets distributed.
b. An asset acquired by incurring liabilities is recorded at cost—that is, at the present value of the amounts to be paid.
c. An asset acquired by issuing shares of stock of the acquiring corporation is recorded at the fair value of the asset—that is, shares of stock issued are recorded at the fair value of the consideration received for the stock.

General principles must be supplemented to apply them in certain transactions. For example, the fair value of an asset received for stock issued may not be reliably determinable, or the fair value of an asset acquired in an exchange may be more reliably determinable than the fair value of a noncash asset given up. Restraints on measurement have led to the practical rule that assets acquired for other than cash, including shares of stock issued, should be stated at "cost" when they are acquired and "cost may be determined either by the fair value of the consideration given or by the fair value of the property acquired, whichever is the more clearly evident." "Cost" in accounting often means the amount at which an entity records an asset at the date it is acquired whatever its manner of acquisition, and that "cost" forms the basis for historical-cost accounting.

The same accounting principles apply to determining the cost of assets acquired individually, those acquired in a group, and those acquired in a business combination. A cash payment by a corporation measures the cost of acquired assets less liabilities assumed. Similarly, the fair values of other assets distributed, such as marketable securities or properties, and the fair value of liabilities incurred by an acquiring corporation measure the cost of an acquired company. The present value of a debt security represents the fair value of the liability, and a premium or discount should be recorded for a debt security issued with an interest rate fixed materially above or below the effective rate or current yield for an otherwise comparable security.

The distinctive attributes of preferred stocks make some issues similar to a debt security while others possess common stock characteristics, with many gradations between the extremes. Determining cost of an acquired company may be affected by those characteristics. For example, the fair value of a nonvoting, nonconvertible preferred stock which lacks characteristics of common stock may be determined by comparing the specified dividend and redemption terms with comparable securities and by assessing market factors. Thus although the principle of recording the fair value of consideration received for stock issued applies to all equity securities, senior as well as common stock, the cost of a company acquired by issuing senior equity securities may be determined in practice on the same basis as for debt securities.

The fair value of securities traded in the market is normally more clearly evident than the fair value of an acquired company. Thus, the quoted market price of an equity security issued to effect a business combination may usually be used to approximate the fair value of an acquired company after recognizing possible effects of price fluctuations, quantities traded, issue costs, etc. The market price for a reasonable period before and after the date the terms of the acquisition are agreed to and announced should be considered in determining the fair value of securities issued.

If the quoted market price is not the fair value of stock, either preferred or common, the consideration received should be estimated even though measuring directly the fair values of assets received is difficult. Both the consideration received, including goodwill, and the extent of the adjustment of the quoted market price of the stock issued should be weighed to determine the amount to be recorded. All aspects of the acquisition, including the negotiations, should be studied, and independent appraisals may be used as an aid in determining the fair value of securities issued. Consideration other than stock distributed to effect an acquisition may provide evidence of the total fair value received.

Costs of acquisition. The cost of a company acquired in a business combination accounted for by the purchase method includes the direct costs of acquisition. Costs of registering and issuing equity securities are a reduction of the otherwise determinable fair value of the securities. However, indirect and general expenses related to acquisitions are deducted as incurred in determining net income.

Contingent Consideration. Opinion No. 16 is quite detailed as to the accounting for contingent consideration. However, the principles involved are summarized in the following paragraphs:

Contingency based on security prices. Additional consideration may be contingent on the market price of a specified security issued to effect a business combination. Unless the price of the security at least equals the specified amount on a specified date or dates, the acquiring corporation is required to issue additional equity or debt securities or transfer cash or other assets sufficient to make the current value of the total consideration equal to the specified amount. The securities issued unconditionally at the date the combination is consummated should be recorded at that date at the specified amount.

The cost of an acquired company recorded at the date of acquisition represents the entire payment including contingent consideration. Therefore, the issuance of additional securities or distribution of other consideration does not affect the cost of the acquired company, regardless of whether the amount specified is a security price to be maintained or a higher security price to be achieved. On a later date when the contingency is resolved and additional consideration is distributable, the acquiring corporation should record the current fair value of the additional consideration issued or issuable. However, the amount previously recorded for securities issued at the date of acquisition should simultaneously be reduced to the lower current value of those securities. Reducing the value of debt securities previously issued to their later fair value results in recording a discount on debt securities. The discount should be amortized from the date the additional securities are issued.

Recording Assets Acquired and Liabilities Assumed. The following general comments are made in Opinion No. 16 covering the allocation of the cost of an acquired company to the assets acquired and the liabilities assumed:

First, all identifiable assets acquired, either individually or by type, and liabilities assumed in a business combination, whether or not shown in the financial statements of the acquired company, should be assigned a portion of the cost of the acquired company, normally equal to their fair values at date of acquisition.

Second, the excess of the cost of the acquired company over the sum of the amounts assigned to identifiable assets acquired less liabilities assumed should be recorded as goodwill. The sum of the market or appraisal values of identifiable assets acquired less liabilities assumed may sometimes exceed the cost of the acquired company. If so, the values otherwise assignable to noncurrent assets acquired (except long-term investments in marketable securities) should be reduced by a proportionate part of the excess to determine the assigned values. A deferred credit for an excess of assigned value of identifiable assets over cost of an acquired company (sometimes called "negative goodwill") should not be recorded unless those assets are reduced to zero value.

The word "goodwill" connotes something of value in a business sense; "negative goodwill" is an anomalous term. Generally, when a company buys another at a substantial discount from its net assets, it is because of the low or negative earning power of the acquired company.

Independent appraisals may be used as an aid in determining the fair values of some assets and liabilities. Subsequent sales of assets may also provide evidence of values. The effect of taxes may be a factor in assigning amounts to identifiable assets and liabilities.

Effect of Taxes.

The market or appraisal values of specific assets and liabilities . . . may differ from the income tax bases of those items. Estimated future tax effects of differences between the tax bases and amounts otherwise appropriate to assign to an asset or a liability are one of the variables in estimating fair value. Amounts assigned to identifiable assets and liabilities should, for example, recognize that the fair value of an asset to an acquirer is less than its market or appraisal value if all or a portion of the market or appraisal value is not deductible for income taxes. The impact of tax effects on amounts assigned to individual assets and liabilities depends on numerous factors, including imminence or delay of realization of the asset value and the possible timing of tax consequences. Since differences between amounts assigned and tax bases are not timing differences (APB Opinion No. 11, *Accounting for Income Taxes*), the acquiring corporation should not record deferred tax accounts at the date of acquisition.

Excess of Acquired Net Assets Over Cost.

The value assigned to net assets acquired should not exceed the cost of an acquired company because the general presumption in historical-cost based accounting is that net assets acquired should be recorded at not more than cost. The total market or appraisal values of identifiable assets acquired less liabilities assumed in a few business combinations may exceed the cost of the acquired company. An excess over cost should be allocated to reduce proportionately the values assigned to noncurrent assets (except long-term investments in marketable securities) in determining their fair values. If the allocation reduces the noncurrent assets to zero value, the remainder of the excess over cost should be classified as a deferred credit and should be amortized systematically to income over the period estimated to be benefited but not in excess of forty years. The method and period of amortization should be disclosed.

No part of the excess of acquired net assets over cost should be added directly to stockholders' equity at the date of acquisition.

Disclosure in Financial Statements.
Opinion No. 16 contains instructions as to disclosure in the financial statements of an acquiring corporation. Included in such instructions are the following:

Notes to the financial statements of the acquiring corporation for the period in which a business combination occurs and is accounted for by the purchase method should include as supplemental information the following results of operations on a pro forma basis:

a. Results of operations for the current period as though the companies had combined at the beginning of the period, unless the acquisition was at or near the beginning of the period.

b. Results of operations for the immediately preceding period as though the companies had combined at the beginning of that period if comparative financial statements are presented.

ACCOUNTING FOR GOODWILL

Goodwill recorded in a business combination accounted for by the purchase method should be amortized in accordance with the provisions of Opinion No. 17 of the Accounting Principles Board.[4]

---

[4] *Op. cit.*

Status of Goodwill Prior to Opinion No. 17

Prior to the issuance of Opinion No. 17 there were two acceptable methods of accounting for purchased goodwill, as outlined in Accounting Research Bulletin No. 43, as amended, entitled "Intangible Assets."[5] The first was by systematically amortizing it over the period expected to be benefited, and the second by carrying it at full value until there was evidence that its term of existence had become limited.

In concept, these methods of handling goodwill were appropriate if objective criteria were used in determining the nature of the purchased goodwill. Where consumer products were involved and a brand name or trade name had wide acceptance, or a company had exclusive manufacturing know-how that could not be readily duplicated, carrying goodwill at full value was a reasonable procedure. However, with rare exceptions, all companies followed the non-amortization method of dealing with goodwill in recent years, regardless of its characteristics. This has resulted, in some cases, in the payment of high prices for acquisitions, the probable overstatement of earnings subsequent to acquisitions, and the accumulation of substantial amounts of intangible "assets" of indeterminate and sometimes dubious value.

The principal problem in accounting for purchased goodwill that led to much controversy over the years is that no tax benefit can be obtained from its amortization, although it is often the most valuable "asset" a company purchases. For many years recommendations have been made by various tax experts to Congress and the Treasury Department to revise the Internal Revenue Code in order to permit systematic amortization of goodwill for tax purposes. With the newly adopted accounting requirement to amortize such intangibles, as explained hereinafter, it now seems appropriate for Congress to amend the Code to permit similar treatment for tax purposes, with a specified minimum period for such write-offs.

[5] AICPA, "Restatement and Revision of Accounting Research," Bull. No. 43, September 1961, Chap. 5.

Goodwill Under Opinion No. 17

Opinion No. 17 deals with two types of intangible assets, i.e., those which are specifically identifiable, such as contracts, patents, franchises, and supplier lists, and those which are not specifically identifiable but are related to the enterprise as a whole—goodwill.

A company should record the costs of intangible assets *acquired from other enterprises or individuals.* The cost of identifiable intangible assets is an assigned part of the total cost of the enterprise or group assets acquired. The cost of unidentifiable intangible assets, goodwill, is a residual figure, being the difference between the total purchase price and the costs assigned to all other assets, less liabilities assumed.

Subsequent to a business combination, the costs of developing, maintaining, or restoring intangible assets which are not specifically identifiable, have indeterminate lives, or are inherent in a continuing business and are related to the enterprise as a whole —such as goodwill—should be deducted from income when incurred.

Amortization of Intangible Assets. In arriving at Opinion No. 17, the Board stated:

The Board believes that the value of intangible assets at any one date eventually disappears and that the recorded costs of intangible assets should be amortized by systematic charges to income over the periods estimated to be benefited. Factors which should be considered in estimating the useful lives of intangible assets:

a. Legal, regulatory, or contractual provisions may limit the maximum useful life.
b. Provisions for renewal or extension may alter a specified limit on useful life.
c. Effects of obsolescence, demand, competition, and other economic factors may reduce a useful life.
d. A useful life may parallel the service life expectancies of individuals or groups of employees.
e. Expected actions of competitors and others may restrict present competitive advantages.
f. An apparently unlimited useful life may in fact be indefinite and benefits cannot be reasonably projected.
g. An intangible asset may be a composite of many individual factors with varying effective lives.

The period of amortization of intangible assets should be determined from the pertinent factors.

The cost of each type of intangible asset should be amortized on the basis of the estimated life of that specific asset and should not be written off in the period of acquisition. Analysis of all factors should result in a reasonable estimate of the useful life of most intangible assets. A reasonable estimate of the useful life may often be based on upper and lower limits even though a fixed existence is not determinable.

The period of amortization should not, however, exceed forty years. Analysis at the time of acquisition may indicate that the indeterminate lives of some intangible assets are likely to exceed forty years and the cost of those assets should be amortized over the maximum period of forty years, not an arbitrary shorter period.

Method of amortization. The Board concludes that the straight-line method of amortization—equal annual amounts—should be applied unless a company demonstrates that another systematic method is more appropriate. The financial statements should disclose the method and period of amortization. Amortization of acquired goodwill and of other acquired intangible assets not deductible in computing income taxes payable does not create a timing difference, and allocation of income taxes is inappropriate.

Subsequent review of amortization. A company should evaluate the periods of amortization continually to determine whether later events and circumstances warrant revised estimates of useful lives. If estimates are changed, the unamortized cost should be allocated to the increased or reduced number of remaining periods in the revised useful life but not to exceed forty years after acquisition. Estimation of value and future benefits of an intangible asset may indicate that the unamortized cost should be reduced significantly by a deduction in determining net income. However, a single loss year or even a few loss years together do not necessarily justify an extraordinary charge to income for all or a large part of the unamortized cost of intangible assets. The reason for an extraordinary deduction should be disclosed.

Disposal of Goodwill. Ordinarily goodwill and similar intangible assets cannot be disposed of apart from the enterprise as a whole. However, a large segment or separable group of assets of an acquired company or the entire acquired company may be sold or otherwise liquidated, and all or a portion of the unamortized cost of the goodwill recognized in the acquisition should be included in the cost of the assets sold.

PRICE AFFECTED BY ACCOUNTING CONSIDERATIONS—ILLUSTRATIONS

Somewhat different results are obtained in accounting for business combinations under the three general methods discussed in Accounting Principles Board Opinions Nos. 16 and 17. Such differing results generally will have an effect on the valuation to be established for an acquisition. To recapitulate, these types of transactions may be described as follows:

1. A *pooling of interests*—where substantially all of the common stock of a company is acquired in exchange for common stock of the issuer in compliance with the 90% rule and the conditions discussed earlier in this chapter.

2. A *purchase*—where the net assets or capital stock of a company are acquired in a "taxable" transaction for cash or its equivalent. In such a case the purchaser is required to restate the assets acquired to fair market values and establish a new federal income tax basis for them.

3. A *purchase*—where the net assets or capital stock of a company are acquired in exchange for voting preferred stock or a combination of such stock and common stock, or where the acquirer, although using common stock as consideration, fails to obtain the requisite 90% of the common stock of the seller under prescribed conditions. It is assumed that such an acquisition will be a non-taxable reorganization for federal tax purposes and stepped-up tax values would not be available to the acquirer.

The following hypothetical illustrations show the results obtained using the three different methods of consideration by the Alpha Company in acquiring the Beta Company. The common stocks of both companies are assumed to have been traded on the New York Stock Exchange and the transactions in such cases were effected in February 1971, based on figures as of December 31, 1970, their common fiscal year-end.

These illustrations have been kept reasonably free of complicating conditions in order to assist the reader in understanding the basic accounting, tax, and economic conditions involved in the transactions. It is believed that the valuations used for illustrative purposes in "acquiring" Beta are reasonable under conditions existing at the time of the transactions. However, it should be appreciated that, in a business combination, the price or shares exchanged is a matter of negotiation as there are no precise standards of values.

It will be assumed, in each case, that cash has been retained by Beta in the amount of $100,000 to pay expenses arising out of the business combination, including delivery of Alpha securities to the stockholders and the dissolution of Beta. Such expenses were considered extraordinary and Beta's income for purposes of the business combination was not penalized as a result thereof.

Pooling of Interests

In this first illustration, Alpha is deemed to have exchanged 1,200,000 shares of its $1 par value common stock for the net assets and business of Beta. This is considered as a non-taxable reorganization for federal income tax purposes because the acquirer exchanged voting capital stock "for substantially all of the assets" of the seller. (See Chapter 8, page 211.) The following statistics at the latest fiscal year-end are pertinent to the business combination of the two companies:

Pre-Merger.

	Alpha	Beta
Shares outstanding	2,500,000	1,500,000
Market price per share	$15.50	$11.00
Total market values	$38,750,000	$16,500,000
Sales	$46,000,000	$30,000,000
Net income	$ 2,750,000	$ 1,500,000
Net income as percentage of sales	6%	5%
Net income per share	$1.10	$1.00
Price–earnings ratios	14	11
Dividends per share	$0.60	$0.40
Net worth (book value)	$21,000,000	$14,700,000
Return on net worth (approx.)	13%	10%

Post-Merger. The following statistics illustrate the results to Beta stockholders of this exchange involving 0.8 of a share of Alpha stock for each of the 1,500,000 shares of Beta stock:

	Per Share		Premium or
	Pre-Merger	Post-Merger	Discount
Market value	$11.00	* $12.40	13%
Dividends	0.40	0.48	20%
Earnings	1.00	0.92	(8%)
Book value	9.80	7.72	21%

* The 1,200,000 Alpha shares received by Beta stockholders had a total market value of $18,600,000, based on a price of $15.50 per share.

Based on the 3,700,000 shares (2,500,000 plus 1,200,000) of Alpha common stock outstanding after the pooling, and combined

Fig. 9–1. Pro Forma

	Alpha	Beta	Pro Forma Adjust- ments	Pro Forma Combined
Assets		*(000's omitted)*		
Cash	$ 1,300	$ 900		$ 2,200
Accounts receivable	6,000	3,200		9,200
Inventories	9,700	5,600		15,300
Prepaid expenses, etc.	700	500		1,200
Total current assets	17,700	10,200		27,900
Investments in partially owned companies	900	1,200		2,100
Property, plant, and equipment	16,600	12,600		29,200
Less: Depreciation and amortization	5,500	4,100		9,600
	11,100	8,500		19,600
Total assets	$29,700	$19,900		$49,600

*The following adjustment has been made in effecting the pooling of interests: elimination increase in capital surplus necessitated by the exchange.

earnings of $4,250,000, earnings per share would be approximately $1.15.

The pro forma balance sheet in Fig. 9–1 illustrates the accounting effects, as a pooling of interests, of the business combination of Alpha and Beta companies.

Purchase in a "Taxable" Transaction

In this second illustration, Alpha is deemed to have exchanged $20,000,000 of its 6½% Convertible Subordinated Debentures due April 1, 1996, for all of the assets and business of Beta and to assume the latter's liabilities. This would be a taxable transaction for federal income tax purposes, as the debentures issued are considered to be a "cash equivalent."

Balance Sheet.

	Alpha	Beta	Pro Forma Adjust- ments	Pro Forma Combined
Liabilities and Stockholders' Equity		*(000's omitted)*		
Notes payable, due within one year	$ 500	$ 700		$ 1,200
Accounts payable and accruals	5,400	2,600		8,000
Federal income tax	700	400		1,100
Total current liabilities	6,600	3,700		10,300
Notes payable, due after one year..	1,600	1,000		2,600
Deferred federal income tax	500	500		1,000
Stockholders' equity:				
Alpha Company common stock, authorized 5,000,000 shares, par value $1 per share, issued and outstanding	2,500		$1,200 *	3,700
Beta Company common stock, par value $1 per share, issued and outstanding		1,500	(1,500)*	—
Capital surplus	4,500	3,900	300 *	8,700
Retained earnings	14,000	9,300		23,300
	$29,700	$19,900	—	$49,600

of the par value of Beta stock and the issuance of additional shares of Alpha stock and the

The debentures are subject to redemption under a mandatory sinking fund, commencing in 1981, and the company will be required to pay to the trustee prior to April 1 each year an amount of cash sufficient to redeem $1,000,000 principal amount of debentures and may make an optional additional payment each year up to but not exceeding a sum sufficient to redeem $1,000,000 principal amount. The right to make such optional payment is non-cumulative.

The holders of the debentures will be entitled at any time prior to April 1, 1996, to convert each $1,000 principal amount of debentures into 58.823 shares of common stock subject to adjustment in certain events, including stock dividends, stock splits, etc., of common stock of Alpha (equivalent to $17 per share). The debentures at the time of their issuance are deemed to be worth

100% of their principal amount. Beta stockholders will receive an aggregate of $20,000,000 market value of debentures for the net assets and business of their company compared with $18,600,000 in market value of Alpha stock in the first illustration. Customarily, a larger cash offer would be required to effect this kind of deal than one involving an exchange of common stock, because the stockholders of the acquired company must recognize in the year of the transaction any capital gains resulting therefrom, for federal tax purposes. Also, Alpha stockholders would receive more benefits from the standpoint of increased net income (before conversion of debentures) and market value per share than they would have in the pooling transaction above.

As indicated in the pro forma balance sheet in Fig. 9–2 (pages 264–65) the combined assets of Alpha and Beta were $49,600,000 before restating the net assets of Beta at fair market values, and $55,400,000 after such restatement.

The transaction will have the following effect on the net income of Alpha, assuming the same level of operations of the combined enterprise, as in the latest fiscal year:

Net income of Alpha		$2,750,000
Net income of Beta (pre-acquisition)		1,500,000
		$4,250,000
Adjustments resulting from restatement of assets acquired from Beta:		
Interest on debentures	$1,300,000	
Additional depreciation on properties	250,000	
Amortization of patents	12,000	
	$1,562,000	
Less federal income tax (estimated)	781,000	
	$ 781,000	
Amortization of goodwill	50,000	831,000
Revised net income		$3,419,000

The above tabulation does not show the adverse result on net income of the write-up of inventories (of approximately $410,000), because this will probably affect only the initial year of post-acquisition operations.

The results of this transaction, as it affects former stockholders of Beta, follow:

Per Share

	Pre-Acquisition	Post-Acquisition	Premium
Market value	$11.00	$13.33	21%
Dividends	0.40	—	} 116
Interest		0.866	
Book value	9.80	13.33	36

Upon conversion of their debentures the former stockholders of Beta would receive a maximum of 1,176,460 shares of Alpha common stock.

The results of this transaction, as it affects Alpha stockholders, follow:

Per Share

	Pre-Acquisition	Post-Acquisition
Net income	$ 1.10	$ 1.37
Dividends	$ 0.60	$ 0.60
Book value	$ 8.40	$ 8.40 *
Market value	$15.50	$17.125
Price—earnings ratios	14	12.5 **

     * Book value includes intangible assets.
     ** It is assumed that the market price of the Alpha stock would reflect increased earnings per share, but at a lower price—earnings multiple, because of the greatly increased ratio of debt to total capitalization, the cost of servicing the debt, and the potentially dilutive effect on earnings of conversion of the debentures into common stock.

Based on full conversion of the $20,000,000 debentures into Alpha common stock, the earnings of the company would be approximately $1.11 instead of $1.37 per share computed as follows:

$$\frac{\text{Net income \$3,419,000 plus net debenture interest cost of \$650,000}}{\text{2,500,000 shares outstanding plus 1,176,460 converted shares}}$$

However, it is unlikely that debenture holders would wish to convert until such time as the dividends on Alpha stock exceed the equivalent interest received on the debentures. In any case, should the market value of the common stock increase beyond the conversion parity, this would increase the market price of the bonds.

Fig. 9–2. Pro Forma

	Alpha	Beta	Pro Forma Adjust- ments	Alpha, After Purchase
Assets			*(000's omitted)*	
Cash	$ 1,300	$ 900		$ 2,200
Accounts receivable	6,000	3,200	$ 30[1]	9,230
Inventories	9,700	5,600	820[2]	16,120
Prepaid expenses, etc.	700	500	30[3]	1,230
Total current assets	17,700	10,200	880	28,780
Investments in partially owned companies	900	1,200	300[4]	2,400
Property, plant, and equipment	16,600	12,600	(1,600)[5]	27,600
Less: Depreciation and amortization	5,500	4,100	(4,100)[5]	5,500
	11,100	8,500	2,500	22,100
Patents			120[6]	120
Excess of cost over net assets received in business acquisition			2,000[7]	2,000
Total assets	$29,700	$19,900	$5,800	$55,400

Notes: The following adjustments have been made in effecting the "taxable" purchase of Beta by Alpha:

1. Accounts receivable reserve was in excess of requirements.

2. Finished goods were valued at estimated selling prices, less costs of disposal and a reasonable profit allowance for the selling effort of the acquiring corporation; work in process was on the same basis as finished goods, with an additional allowance for costs to complete; and raw materials were at current replacement costs.

3. Certain prepaid items that had little value to the purchaser were written off, but advertising and other supplies that had been expensed by the seller were inventoried at replacement value, resulting in a net increase in this asset.

4. Investments in partially owned companies were written up to reflect the underlying equity in such companies applicable to the investments.

5. Property, plant, and equipment was restated on the basis of appraisals at "net sound values."

6. Patents were stated at their appraised values with an average ten-year remaining life.

Balance Sheet.

	Alpha	Beta	Pro Forma Adjust- ments	Alpha, After Purchase
Liabilities and Stockholders' Equity		(000's omitted)		
Notes payable, due within one year	$ 500	$ 700		$ 1,200
Accounts payable and accruals	5,400	2,600		8,000
Federal income tax	700	400	$ 1,000[8]	2,100
Total current liabilities	6,600	3,700	1,000	11,300
Alpha Company, 6½ convertible subordinated debentures, due April 1, 1995			20,000[9]	20,000
Other debt due after one year	1,600	1,000		2,600
Deferred federal income tax	500	500	(500)[10]	500
Stockholders' equity:				
Alpha Company, common stock: Authorized—5,000,000 shares, par value $1 per share, issued and outstanding	2,500			2,500
Beta Company, common stock: Par value $1 per share, issued and outstanding		1,500	(1,500)[11]	
Capital surplus	4,500	3,900	(3,900)[11]	4,500
Retained earnings	14,000	9,300	(9,300)[11]	14,000
	$29,700	$19,900	$ 5,800	$55,400

7. This represents a residual figure remaining after valuing net assets at fair values and deducting the aggregate thereof from total cost of the acquisition. This amount is to be amortized over 40 years because the Beta Company makes a standard household item in common use.

8. This additional income tax liability arises as a result of restating property, plant, and equipment at fair market values. To the extent that such fair market values exceed cost less depreciation, on an item-by-item basis, ordinary taxable income occurs as a "recapture" of depreciation previously claimed (Chapter 8, page 214).

9. This reflects the issuance of the debentures to purchase the net assets of Beta.

10. Deferred federal income tax of Beta arose primarily as a result of using accelerated methods of depreciation for tax purposes and the straight-line method for book purposes. Inasmuch as a new basis of depreciable property values has been established upon its revaluation, this liability no longer exists.

11. The equity of Beta stockholders was eliminated upon the sale of that company's net assets and business.

Purchase in a "Non-taxable" Transaction

In this third illustration, Alpha is deemed to have exchanged 360,000 shares of $3 cumulative convertible preferred stock having a par value of $10 per share for all of the assets and business of Beta and to assume its liabilities. Each share of convertible preferred stock is convertible into 3 shares of common stock, subject to adjustment in certain events, including stock dividends, stock splits, etc.

Holders of the $3 cumulative convertible preferred stock are entitled to one vote per share on all matters presented to holders of the common stock, and are entitled to preferential voting treatment only in the event of failure of the company to pay six or more quarterly dividends. The transaction is considered a non-taxable reorganization for federal tax purposes because the acquirer exchanged voting capital stock for "substantially all of the assets" of the seller (Chapter 8, page 211).

All or any part of the shares of $3 cumulative convertible preferred stock are redeemable at any time after April 1, 1976, at $62 per share during the first year of redemption, reduced annually thereafter at the rate of $1 per share, to a redemption price of $55, together in each instance with all cumulative and unpaid dividends to the date of redemption. In the event of voluntary liquidation, dissolution, or winding up of the company, the holders of the $3 cumulative convertible preferred stock shall be entitled to receive $55 per share or the then current redemption price, whichever is higher, plus all accrued and unpaid dividends thereon, before any distribution of assets is made to holders of common stock of the company.

The $3 cumulative convertible preferred stock is deemed to be worth $50 per share at the time of its issuance. Beta stockholders therefore would receive an aggregate of $18,000,000 market value of this stock, compared with $18,600,000 in market value of common stock in the first illustration and $20,000,000 in market value of debentures in the second illustration.

As indicated, this combination involving the exchange of voting preferred stock of Alpha for the net assets and business of Beta is a non-taxable reorganization, and no federal tax liability results to Beta stockholders as a result of the transaction. Additional justification for assuming a lower price for this type of acquisition would be the preferred position that the former Beta stockholders would enjoy from the standpoint of dividends and liquidation (than if they received common stock of Alpha) while still having an opportunity to share in the growth of the enterprise through conversion of their preferred stock.

Accounting Principles Board Opinion No. 16 states that ". . . assets acquired for other than cash, including shares of stock issued, should be stated at 'cost' when they are acquired, and 'cost' may be determined either by the fair value of the consideration given or by the fair value of the property acquired, whichever is the more clearly evident. . . ."

In this illustration it has been assumed that the consideration given was more readily determinable than the property acquired. In allocating the total cost of this acquisition amounts assigned to identifiable assets in Fig. 9–3 (pages 268–69) were lower than the appraisal values shown in Fig. 9–2, recognizing that no portion of the stepped-up appraisal values was available as a deduction for federal income tax purposes.

A similar procedure of valuation would obtain if a deal were consummated whereby Alpha, through an exchange of its common stock, acquired from the stockholders of Beta 80% or more, but less than 90%, of their common stock. Such a transaction would be non-taxable for federal income tax purposes (Chapter 8, page 211), but would not qualify for pooling-of-interests accounting treatment. In such a case the minority interest of remaining Beta stockholders would be shown in Alpha's balance sheet and in the statement of income.

The transaction will affect the net income of Alpha as shown on page 270, assuming the same level of operations of the combined enterprise as in the latest fiscal year.

The tabulation does not show the adverse result on net income of the write-up of inventories in the amount of $410,000, as this will probably affect only the initial year of post-acquisition operations.

Fig. 9–3.   Pro Forma

	Alpha	Beta	Pro Forma Adjust- ments	Alpha, After Purchase
Assets		*(000's omitted)*		
Cash	$ 1,300	$ 900		$ 2,200
Accounts receivable	6,000	3,200	$ 15[1]	9,215
Inventories	9,700	5,600	410[2]	15,710
Prepaid expenses, etc.	700	500	15[3]	1,215
Total current assets	17,700	10,200	440	28,340
Investments in partially owned companies	900	1,200	300[4]	2,400
Property, plant, and equipment	16,600	12,600	(2,480)[5]	26,720
Less: Depreciation and amortization	5,500	4,100	(4,100)[5]	5,500
	11,100	8,500	1,620	21,220
Patents			60[6]	60
Excess of cost over net assets received in business combination			380[7]	380
Total assets	$29,700	$19,900	$2,800	$52,400

Notes: The following adjustments have been made in effecting the "nontaxable" purchase of Beta by Alpha. It will be noted that the market or appraisal levels of assets generally are lower than those shown in Fig. 9–2, because the appraisal write-ups are not deductible for income tax purposes.

1. Accounts receivable reserve was in excess of requirements.

2. Inventories were valued on the same basis as in Fig. 9–2, less tax benefits which will not be available.

3. There was a net increase in the value of prepaid items.

4. Investments in partially owned companies were restated to the underlying equity basis. There is no present intention to sell, therefore no estimated future tax effect was considered.

5. Property, plant, and equipment was restated on the basis of appraisals at "net sound values" adjusted for federal income tax basis not available. The present value of future cash flow, which would have been returned to Alpha in the form of reduced federal taxes if a step-up in tax basis were available, was determined by computing

Balance Sheet.

	Alpha	Beta	Pro Forma Adjust- ments	Alpha, After Purchase
Liabilities and Stockholders' Equity			*(000's omitted)*	
Notes payable, due within one year	$ 500	$ 700		$ 1,200
Accounts payable and accruals	5,400	2,600		8,000
Federal income tax	700	400		1,100
Total current liabilities	6,600	3,700		10,300
Notes payable due after one year ..	1,600	1,000		2,600
Deferred federal income tax	500	500	$ (500)[8]	500
Stockholders' equity:				
Alpha Company:				
$3 cumulative convertible preferred stock, authorized 1,000,000 shares, par value $10 per share, issued and outstanding, 360,000 shares.			3,600[9]	3,600
Common stock, authorized 5,000,000 shares, par value $1 per share, issued and outstanding	2,500			2,500
Beta Company, common stock:				
Par value $1 per share, issued and outstanding		1,500	(1,500)[10]	
Capital surplus	4,500	3,900	14,400[9] (3,900)[10]	18,900
Retained earnings	14,000	9,300	(9,300)[10]	14,000
	$29,700	$19,900	$2,800	$52,400

the present worth of $1 per period for ten years (remaining depreciable life) at 7% interest.

6. Patents were stated at their appraised values, less tax benefits not available. The item was too small to refine to the present value of tax benefits.

7. This represents a residual figure after valuing net assets at their "adjusted fair values" and deducting the aggregate thereof from the total cost of the acquisition. This amount is to be amortized over 40 years as the goodwill is deemed to have an indefinite life of over 40 years. APB Opinion No. 17, paragraph 30, prohibits giving tax effect to amortization of acquired goodwill.

8. Liability for deferred federal income tax was eliminated upon the establishment of a new basis for depreciable property value.

9. This reflects the issuance of the cumulative convertible stock to purchase the net assets of Beta.

10. Equity of Beta stockholders was eliminated upon the sale of that company's net assets and business.

Net income of Alpha		$2,750,000
Net income of Beta (pre-acquisition)		1,500,000
		$4,250,000
Adjustments resulting from restatement of net assets:		
Additional depreciation on properties	$162,000	
Amortization of patents	6,000	
Amortization of goodwill	9,500	177,500
Revised net income		$4,072,500
Less: Annual dividends payable on preferred stock		1,080,000
Net income available for common stock		$2,992,500

The results of this "non-taxable purchase" as it affected former stockholders of Beta follow:

	Per Share		Premium
	Pre-Acquisition	Post-Acquisition	Discount
Market value	$11.00	$12.00	9%
Dividends	0.40	0.72	80
Earnings	1.00	0.72	(28)
Equity in capitalization	9.80	* 13.20	35

* Based on lowest voluntary redemption value of $55 per share for the preferred stock.

Upon conversion of their preferred stock, the former stockholders of Beta would receive an aggregate of 1,080,000 shares of Alpha common stock.

The results of this transaction as it affects Alpha stockholders follow:

	Per Share	
	Pre-Acquisition	Post-Acquisition
Net income	$1.10	$ 1.20
Dividends	0.60	0.60
Book value	8.40	7.68 *
Book value	8.40	10.90 **

* Based on deducting $55 per preferred share outstanding.
** Based on full conversion of the preferred stock into 1,080,000 shares of common.

Based on full conversion of the 360,000 shares of cumulative convertible preferred stock into common stock of Alpha, the earnings of the company would be approximately $1.14 instead of $1.20 per share computed as follows:

$$\frac{\text{Net income } \$2,992,500 \text{ plus preferred dividends of } 1,080,000}{2,500,000 \text{ shares outstanding plus } 1,080,000 \text{ converted shares}}$$

However, it is unlikely that preferred stockholders would wish to convert until such time as the dividends on Alpha stock exceeded dividends received on the preferred stock. In any case, should the market value of the common stock increase beyond the conversion parity, this would increase the market price of the preferred stock.

EARNINGS PER SHARE

In light of the overwhelming importance of "earnings per share" in valuing companies, the methods of determining such figures should be explained.

The increasingly complex capital structures of many companies, which include securities such as convertible debentures, convertible preferred stock, warrants, and options, all of which have a potentially dilutive effect on earnings, has complicated the reporting of earnings per share of common stock. An endeavor was made to solve the problem by the Accounting Principles Board of the American Institute of Certified Public Accountants in Part II of its Opinion No. 9, issued in December 1966, which was revised and expanded in Opinion No. 15, dated May 1969.

Opinion No. 15 embodies arbitrary criteria, and in context is as complicated as the problem is complex. It would be impossible to explain all of the ramifications of this Opinion in a short space, but a digest of some of its salient features follows.

A company that has a simple capital structure requires only a single presentation of earnings per common share on the face of the income statement. Companies with complex capital structures should present two types of earnings-per-share data with equal prominence on the face of the income statement. The first presentation should be based on the outstanding common shares and those securities that are in substance equivalent to common shares and have a dilutive effect (termed "primary" earnings per share). The second should be a pro forma presentation that reflects the dilution of earnings per share that would have occurred if all contingent issuances of common stock that would individually reduce earnings per share had taken place at the beginning of the period, or the time of issuance of the convertible security, etc., if later (termed "fully diluted earnings" per share).

Primary Earnings per Share

Common stock equivalents include certain convertible preferred stocks, convertible debt securities, shares to be issued in the future for little or no consideration upon satisfaction of certain conditions, options, and warrants.

A *convertible security* (either preferred stock or debenture) is considered a common stock equivalent at the time of issuance if, based on its market price, it *has a cash yield of less than 66⅔% of the then current bank prime interest rate*. This determination is made only at the time of issuance and should not be changed thereafter.

Options and warrants and their equivalents should be treated as if they had been exercised and earnings-per-share data computed under the "treasury stock" method. Under this method, earnings-per-share data are computed as if the option or warrant were exercised at the beginning of the period or the time of issuance, if later, and the funds obtained were used to purchase common stock at the average market price during the period. It is recommended, under Opinion No. 15, that the assumption of exercise not be reflected until the market price of the common stock obtainable has been in excess of the exercise price for substantially all of the three consecutive months ending with the period to which earnings per share relate.

In cases where (a) debt may or must be tendered in payment of the exercise price, (b) the proceeds from exercise must be applied toward the retirement of debt, (c) convertible securities require cash payments upon conversion, and (d) the number of shares of common stock obtainable upon exercise of outstanding options or warrants exceeds 20% of the number of common shares outstanding at the end of the period, the Opinion limits the application of the "treasury stock" method and prescribes other methods of applying the proceeds from the assumed exercise of the options and warrants.

In no case where the assumed conversion of securities or the exercise of options or warrants would have an antidilutive effect on earnings should they be included in the computation.

Fully Diluted Earnings per Share

The purpose of the fully diluted earnings-per-share presentation is to show the maximum potential dilution of current earnings per share on a prospective basis. The computation should include outstanding common stock, securities which are common stock equivalents and, also, those which are not common stock equivalents but which would reduce primary earnings per share had their conversion, issuance, or exercise taken place at the beginning of the period.

Also, the computation should give weighted effect to securities converted or exercised during the period. As in the case of primary earnings per share, securities whose subsequent conversion, exercise, or other contingent issuance would have an antidilutive effect should be excluded from the computation of fully diluted earnings per share. The market price of the common stock at the end of the period should be used in applying the treasury stock method if it is higher than the average price used in the computation of primary earnings per share. The provisions of Opinion No. 15 for the computation of fully diluted earnings per share are generally the same as those for computing pro forma earnings per share under Opinion No. 9.

Supplementary Earnings per Share

Opinion No. 15 includes a requirement for a "supplementary" earnings-per-share amount in certain cases. The purpose of this disclosure is to show what primary earnings per share would have been if conversions during the current period had taken place at the beginning of the period.

Effective Date of Opinion No. 15

The Opinion is effective for fiscal periods beginning after December 31, 1968. However, in the case of securities issued prior to June 1, 1969, for the purposes of computing primary earnings per share, the issuer has the option to classify all securities under the provisions of Opinion No. 15, or to continue to classify as common stock equivalents those securities termed "residual" under Opinion No. 9. The latter Opinion excluded options and warrants from residual securities, and convertible securities that did not "clearly derive" a major portion of their value from conversion rights or common stock characteristics.

10

SEC and Stock Exchange
Requirements

SEC REGISTRATION AND FILING REQUIREMENTS

Prior to the Securities Acts Amendments of 1964,[1] generally only (a) companies whose securities were listed on a national exchange and (b) those others that had filed a registration statement under the Securities Act of 1933, where the market value of the total outstanding securities of the class offered exceeded a certain amount, were subject to the periodic and other reporting requirements under the Securities Exchange Act of 1934. Pursuant to these 1964 amendments, issuers have been required to register under Section 12 of the 1934 Act, if and when they have total assets exceeding $1,000,000 and a class of equity security (other than an exempted security) held of record by five hundred persons. Upon registration such companies also become subject to the proxy rules under Regulation 14A of the 1934 Act and other reporting requirements under that Act.

By the latter part of 1968, as a result of the 1964 Amendments, approximately 3,200 additional companies became subject to the Commission's proxy rules under Regulation 14A of the 1934 Act, and the periodic and other reporting requirements under that Act.

---

[1] Securities Acts Amendments, August 20, 1964.

In addition to the many companies already subject to the filing and reporting requirements of the Securities and Exchange Commission, companies may initially become subject to its filing requirements as a result of the issuance of securities pursuant to an acquisition or merger plan. It is essential to investigate carefully, through legal counsel, what requirements, if any, should be complied with. It is often desirable to confer with SEC personnel, where any doubt exists as to the necessity for filing.

Where a corporate acquisition or merger requires a filing under the federal securities laws, it may be (a) a proxy statement under Regulation 14A of the Securities Exchange Act of 1934, or (b) a registration statement (generally Form S–1 or S–14) under the Securities Act of 1933. Even though a proxy statement or a registration statement may not be required, a current report (generally Form 8–K) under the Securities Exchange Act of 1934 may be needed. The general requirements of these forms will be summarized after a discussions of exemptions from filing under certain circumstances.

Exemptions from Filing

There are two types of exemptions from the registration requirements of the 1933 Act that have been most frequently relied upon for acquisition and merger transactions. These are known as the "no sale" rule and the "private offering" exemptions.

"No Sale" Aspects of Certain Business Combinations

The Securities and Exchange Commission decided a number of years ago, as a matter of administrative policy, that no sale was involved when a plan of consolidation or merger for a transfer of corporate assets to another corporation for securities of the latter was submitted to security holders, and the affirmative vote of the majority bound the minority holders.

Rule 133

To afford companies relying on its administrative policy the protection embodied in a rule, the Securities and Exchange Commission in 1951 adopted Rule 133 under the Securities Act of 1933.

Section (1) of this rule, as amended January 9, 1968, which describes the conditions where no sale is deemed to be involved, reads as follows (amended portion in italics):

(a) For purposes only of Section 5 of the Act no "sale," "offer," "offer to sell," or "offer for sale" shall be deemed to be involved so far as the stockholders of a corporation are concerned where, pursuant to statutory provisions in the state of incorporation or provisions contained in the certificate of incorporation, there is submitted to the vote of such stockholders a plan or agreement for a statutory merger or consolidation or reclassification of securities, or a proposal for the transfer of assets of such corporation to another person in consideration of the issuance of securities of such other person or securities of a corporation which *owns stock possessing at least 80 percent of the total combined voting power of all classes of stock entitled to vote and at least 80 percent of the total number of shares of all other classes of stock* of such other person, under such circumstances that the vote of a required favorable majority (1) will operate to authorize the proposed transaction so far as concerns the corporation whose stockholders are voting (except for the taking of action by the directors of the corporation involved and for compliance with such statutory provisions as the filing of the plan or agreement with the appropriate State authority), and (2) will bind all stockholders of such corporation except to the extent that dissenting stockholders may be entitled, under statutory provisions or provisions contained in the certificate of incorporation, to receive the appraised or fair value of their holdings.

The fact that a business combination fulfills the conditions of Section (a) of Rule 133 and therefore does not require the filing of a registration statement under the Securities Act of 1933 does not mean that the recipients of such securities may, without exception, dispose of them at will. The remaining Sections (b) to (f) of this rule (which were not amended) deal with the applicability of registration requirements where recipients of securities in such a transaction receive them with a view to offering them publicly or later to dispose of them under circumstances that would constitute a public offering. Thus, Rule 133 should be read in its entirety.

Private Sale Exemption

Another type of transaction not requiring the filing of a registration statement in a business combination is one exempted under

Section 4(2) of the Securities Act of 1933, which relates to "private" offerings and transactions. This type of exemption is discussed more fully in Chapter 3.

It is important to recognize that the determination as to whether a transaction involves any public offering is essentially a question of fact, in which all surrounding circumstances must be given consideration, and no one factor is in itself conclusive. It is good practice for a company's legal counsel to consult with the staff of the Commission in many cases where there is a question as to the availability of the exemption under Section 4(2). Although the staff will not rule authoritatively on the question, it may issue a "no action" letter if the facts presented so warrant.

PROXY STATEMENTS

Where a filing with the Securities and Exchange Commission is required in an acquisition or merger transaction (other than a current report form), a proxy statement is most frequently used. Regulation 14 adopted in 1938 and amended several times thereafter [2] contains rules regulating the solicitation of proxies with respect to securities registered pursuant to Section 12 of the 1934 Act, except for certain specified exceptions.[3] The purpose of the proxy rules is to provide sufficient information to enable a stockholder intelligently to exercise his right upon the corporate matters presented to him for approval.

Included in Regulation 14 is Schedule 14A, which specifies, in twenty-two items, the information required in a proxy statement. Item 14 of Schedule 14A outlines the information to be furnished if action is taken with respect to a merger, consolidation, or acquisition of the securities or business of another issuer.

Financial Statement Requirements

The financial statements required in a proxy statement soliciting stockholder approval of a business combination are the same as those in an original registration (generally Form 10) under

[2] Securities Exchange Act of 1934, Regulation 14.
[3] Rule 14a–2, "Solicitations to which Rules Apply."

the 1934 Act and apply to all parties to the transaction. However, all schedules required for a registration statement, other than schedules of supplementary profit and loss information, may be omitted in a proxy statement.[4]

Certified balance sheets are required as of the close of the latest fiscal years unless such fiscal years have ended within 90 days prior to the date of filing the proxy statement, in which case the balance sheets may be as of the close of the preceding fiscal year. Certified profit and loss and source and application of funds statements are required for each of the three fiscal years preceding the dates of the balance sheets.[5]

Item 15(c) of Schedule 14A provides that any or all of the financial statements "not material for the exercise of prudent judgment in regard to the matter to be acted upon may be omitted if the reasons for omission are stated" in the proxy statement. However, the Commission has consistently taken the position that all the required financial statements are material for the exercise of prudent judgment in cases involving the issuance of securities in a merger or acquisition.

The annual report to stockholders may be incorporated in a proxy statement. Item 15(d) of Schedule 14A permits incorporation by reference, in a proxy statement, of financial statements contained in an annual report to stockholders, provided the financial statements substantially meet the requirements of the schedule. Although this seems an expeditious means of meeting the financial statement requirements of the regulation, very few companies have availed themselves of this provision. The probable reason for this is that all required financial information is seldom embodied in the annual reports.

A summary of earnings, or an income statement in its entirety, is required in a proxy statement for the last five years of the operations of each company that is a party to a business combination, except where the life of a company or its immediate predecessor is less. In addition, statements are required for any period between the latest fiscal year and the latest balance sheet furnished, and the corresponding interim period of the preceding fiscal year.

---

[4] Securities Exchange Act of 1934, Regulation 14, Item 15 of Schedule 14A.
[5] *Ibid.*, Items 14 and 15 of Schedule 14A.

Earnings and dividends per share are required for each year or part thereof included in the summary or statement.

Market Prices of Stocks of Constituent Companies

As to each issue of securities of the issuer, or of those of any person involved in a merger, consolidation, or acquisition, admitted to dealing on a national securities exchange, or with respect to which a market otherwise exists, and which will be materially affected by the plan, the high and low sales prices (or in the absence of trading in a particular period, the range of the bid and asked prices) is required for each quarterly period within two years.

Pro Forma Financial Statements

Pro forma financial statements in a proxy statement soliciting stockholder approval of a merger or acquisition consist of a combined pro forma balance sheet, and combined pro forma statements of income for the same periods as those covered by the historical statements. However, if the transaction establishes a new basis of accounting for assets of any of the constituent companies, a pro forma summary of earnings is required only for the most recent fiscal year and interim period, and should reflect appropriate pro forma adjustments resulting from the new basis of accounting.

The principal objective of pro forma statements is to present the necessary financial data in the most useful and informative manner to enable the investor to arrive at an intelligent decision regarding the merits of the proposed exchange. Such financial statements in an exchange offer would ordinarily represent both companies' historical financial statements combined on a retroactive basis to give effect to the proposed terms of the offer. The circumstances governing adjustments made to properly present pro forma statements will vary, but there are guides that should be followed in their preparation.

Pro Forma vs. Historical Statements

Statement headings should describe the financial statements as "Pro Forma Balance Sheet" or "Pro Forma Income Statement (or summary of earnings)" and include references to footnotes or comments describing the basis on which such statements are prepared. If the pro forma statements are based principally on historical statements with only a few easily understandable assumptions, it may be sufficient to describe the assumptions in a footnote.

However, if the assumed transactions are numerous or complicated, it is advisable to have a balance sheet in columnar form showing (a) the historical figures for each company, (b) the adjustments arising from the assumed transactions, and (c) the pro forma amounts resulting from such adjustments. It is desirable to have a notation to the pro forma statements to the effect that, "These pro forma statements should be read in conjunction with the other financial statements appearing elsewhere in this Proxy Statement." Incidentally, pro forma financial statements are not audited and sometimes contain a statement to the effect that, "The combined pro forma net earnings are not necessarily indicative of results to be expected after the merger."

Forecasts Generally Not Acceptable

Pro forma statements should be based on completed transactions or on proposed transactions expected to occur in the near future. Except for certain real estate companies, as described in Item 6(2) of Form S–11, financial statements or earnings summaries that give effect to forecasts and projections are not permitted in filings with the Securities and Exchange Commission. Generally, it is also unacceptable to adjust historical statements for estimated reductions in expenses resulting from proposed mergers and acquisitions. This does not preclude giving pro forma effect to a reduction in expenses if the amount can be fairly determined, and it is clearly evident that the expenses so eliminated will not be replaced by other expenses.

It should be noted that the 1934 Act regulations specify certain types of information that, if included in a proxy statement, may be misleading, depending upon the particular facts and circumstances. Prominent among these are "predictions as to specific future market values, earnings, or dividends." [6]

---

[6] *Ibid.*, Rule 14a–9, as amended to January 26, 1956.

Need To Reflect All Transactions

Pro forma statements should reflect proposed transactions as well as all changed conditions during the period that materially affect the presentation. It would be misleading to give effect to certain proposed transactions, while at the same time ignoring other conditions affecting the pro forma statements. When, for example, one company proposes to purchase another and intends to revise the operations of the acquired business to such an extent that they will no longer be comparable to those of prior years, a pro forma combination of both companies' past income statements to show the effect on operations and earnings of the business combination would not be appropriate. If the effect of all changed conditions of significance cannot be properly reflected on a pro forma basis, the appropriate course may be to present the historical financial statements only, together with a footnote describing the changed conditions and explaining the impracticability of determining their pro forma effect.

Rules Governing Pro Forma Statements

There are few published rules on decisions of the Securities and Exchange Commission regarding pro forma statements. Rule 15c1–9 under the 1934 Act states in part:

> The term manipulative, deceptive, or other fraudulent device or contrivance . . . is defined to include the use of (pro forma) financial statements purporting to give effect to the receipt and application of any part of the proceeds from the sale or exchange of securities unless the assumptions upon which each such financial statement is based are clearly set forth as part of the caption to each such statement in type at least as large as that used generally in the body of the statement.[7]

A similar requirement is contained in Rule 170 under the 1933 Act.[8] Although these rules require that the assumed conditions be set forth in the heading captions, in practice an acceptable alternative is to describe such assumptions in a footnote with reference thereto being made in the statement heading. The types of pro forma financial statements to be included in a proxy state-

---

[7] *Ibid.*, Rule 15c1–9, as amended to June 28, 1938.
[8] Securities Act of 1933, Rule 170, as amended to October 20, 1956.

ment will depend largely on the accounting treatment of the transaction.

Timely Filing for Proxy Material

Five preliminary copies of a proxy statement and form of proxy and any other soliciting material to be furnished security holders concurrently shall be filed with the Securities and Exchange Commission at least 10 days prior to the date definitive copies of such material are first sent or given to security holders, or such shorter period prior to that date as the Commission may authorize upon a showing of good cause therefor. If additional solicitation material relating to the same meeting or subject matter is to be furnished to security holders subsequent to the proxy statement, such material shall be filed with the Commission at least two days prior to the date copies thereof are first sent or given to security holders, unless a shorter period is authorized by the Commission.[9] This rule applies whether the proxy is being solicited by the issuer or by an opposition stockholders group.

If action is to be taken with respect to an acquisition or merger transaction, the material features of the plan must be outlined, including the reasons therefor and the general effect upon the rights of existing security holders. If the plan is set forth in a written document, three copies must be filed with the Commission at the time preliminary copies of the proxy statement and form of proxy are filed. Also, information is required as to the issuer and each person to be merged with or acquired by the issuer relative to the nature of their businesses and a description of their plants and properties from an economic and business standpoint.

Contested Proxy Solicitations

An attempt to gain control of a company without the cooperation of its board of directors will often result in a proxy contest between the incumbent management and the opposition shareholders group. When faced with an increasing number of such proxy contests in the early 1950's, the Securities and Exchange

[9] Proxy Rules—14a–6.

Commission, in 1956, issued a rule governing proxy contests for the election of directors. This rule was designed to "aid public investors in the exercise of their voting rights" by furnishing them with a proxy statement containing certain information called for by Schedule 14B of Regulation 14.

Information Required by Schedule 14B. The data in Schedule 14B fall into three general categories. The first is information as to the identity and background of each participant [as defined in 14(a)–11(b) of the Act], the second, information as to each participant's interest in the securities of the issuer, and the third, information as to the circumstances surrounding the individual participant's becoming involved in the contest.

In an effort to facilitate compliance with Rule 133, the Securities and Exchange Commission, in 1959, adopted a simplified registration statement, S–14 (consisting of a proxy statement with certain additional limited information) to be used for securities acquired in acquisitions and mergers. This form may be used only where the issuer was subject to, and solicited proxies from its stockholders with respect to the transaction, pursuant to the Commission's proxy rules.

In substance, Form S–14 requires that a prospectus include the same information contained in the proxy statement of the successor corporation and permits it to be in the form of the proxy statement if supplemented by certain additional information, as follows:

1. The form states that "the information . . . shall be current in terms of the requirements of the appropriate registration form, other than Form S–14, at the time the registration statement is filed." [10] This means, in effect, that the financial statements must be as timely as if they were to be included in a filing by the registrant on Form S–1. However, the Commission may, upon showing of good cause, permit the furnishing of other financial statements in a particular case.

2. If not contained in the proxy statement, the prospectus must contain the information called for by item 7 of Schedule 14A of Regulation 14A under the Securities Exchange Act of 1934. Item 7 calls for information regarding remuneration and other transactions with officers, directors, and other specified persons.

[10] Securities Act of 1933, Form S–14, Part 1, item 1(a), July, 1959.

3. The prospectus must contain the required information as to (a) the persons on whose behalf the securities are to be offered, and (b) the underwriting and distribution of the securities, which would be required in a filing by the registrant on Form S–1.

4. The prospectus must contain information with respect to the consummation of the Rule 133 transaction and any material developments in the business or affairs of the registrant subsequent thereto that would be required in a filing by the registrant on Form S–1.

5. Certain other matters in compliance with rules and regulations under the Securities Act of 1933, relating to the form and content of prospectuses must be fulfilled.

FORM S–1 OF THE SECURITIES ACT OF 1933

Form S–1, which is most frequently used in public offerings of securities for cash, is required to be filed in business combination transactions where voluntary exchange offers of securities are made by one person or corporation directly to security holders of another company. The use of Form S–1 in business combinations has accelerated recently due to the increasing number of exchange offers of securities being made directly to security holders. The general requirements of S–1 are outlined in Chapter 3. More specific requirements relating to exchange offers are discussed below.

Direct Offers to Stockholders To Exchange Securities

During recent years, a number of offers have been made directly to stockholders of other companies to exchange their securities for those of the offering companies. Frequently, these offers have had the consent of the management of the companies whose stock is solicited, although in some cases they have not.

The initial announcement or notice to security holders of such other issuer made in accordance with Rule 135 does not constitute an offer but merely advises them of the intention of the would-be acquirer to propose an offer. Such notices may be sent not more than 60 days prior to the proposed offering of the securities, and may only state the name of the issuer, the title of the securities to be surrendered in exchange for the securities to be offered, the basis upon which the exchange is proposed, and the period during which the exchange may be made. Furthermore, the notice shall state that the offering will be made only by means of a prospectus, filed with the Securities and Exchange Commission, which will be furnished to the security holders.[11] Where a list of stockholders to be solicited is not available, notice may be given in a newspaper or other publication.

Special Filing Requirements in an Exchange Offer

Form S–1 contains certain requirements for additional information to be provided in a prospectus, when it is being used to register securities to be issued in an exchange offer. The most important of these requirements is general instruction F to the form, which reads as follows:

> F. *Exchange Offers—*
> If any of the securities being registered are to be offered in exchange for securities of any other issuer, the prospectus shall include the information which would be required by Items 6 to 10 inclusive and Item 12 if the securities of such other issuer were being registered on this form. Item 11 should be included if any promoter of such other issuer is a promoter, officer or director of the registrant or a security holder named in answer to Item 19(a). There shall also be included the information concerning such securities of such other issuer which would be called for by Items 13, 14 or 15 if such securities were being registered. In connection with this instruction, reference is made to Rule 409.

Item 19(a) relates to persons owning more than 10% of any such class of securities. Rule 409 reads as follows:

> Information required need be given only insofar as it is known or reasonably available to the registrant. If any required information is unknown and not reasonably available to the registrant, either because the obtaining thereof would involve unreasonable effort or expense, or because it rests peculiarly within the knowledge of another person not affiliated with the registrant, the information may be omitted, subject to the following conditions:
>
> (a) The registrant shall give such information on the subject as it possesses or can acquire without unreasonable effort or expense, together with the sources thereof.
> (b) The registrant shall include a statement either showing that unreasonable effort or expense would be involved or indicating the absence of any affiliation with the person within whose knowledge the information rests and stating the result of a request made to such person for the information.

[11] Securities Act of 1933, Rule 135.

This rule is intended, among other things, to deal with the situation that confronts a registrant when the management of the company to whose stockholders the exchange offer is made does not approve of the offer or the terms thereof and, accordingly, declines to cooperate in the preparation of the registration statement. In situations such as these, the Commission has permitted the registration statement to become effective containing only that information regarding the offeree corporation that is available from public sources.

Items 6 through 15 referred to above deal with the following subjects:

Item 6. Summary of earnings
Item 7. Organization of registrant
Item 8. Parents of registrant
Item 9. Description of business
Item 10. Description of property
Item 11. Organization within five years
Item 12. Pending legal proceedings
Item 13. Capital stock being registered
Item 14. Long-term debt being registered
Item 15. Other securities being registered

"RELIEF" FROM CERTIFICATION REQUIREMENTS

A release in 1969 by the Securities and Exchange Commission indicates that relief may be requested from the three-year certification requirements of financial statements of companies acquired or to be acquired under certain conditions.[12] Instruction 13 of Form S–1 permits the Commission to grant relief from this requirement of certification where it is consistent with the protection of investors. Generally, relief has been requested in the past because no independent accountant has observed the taking of inventory of the acquired company necessary for certification of financial statements for those years and no alternative methods of verification have been available.

---

[12] Securities Act of 1933, Release No. 4950, February 20, 1969.

The release, which is reproduced as Appendix E, contains a formula approach for determining whether relief will be considered by the Commission. This formula consists of evaluations of gross sales and operating revenues, net income, total assets, total stockholders' equity, and total purchase price compared to total assets of the registrant. These evaluations compare such data, on a percentage basis, with those of the registrant on a consolidated basis (without the acquired company). Depending upon the relative magnitude of such data of acquired companies, the certification requirements may be relaxed, if agreed to by the Commission, from the point of no certified statements up to full certification requirements.

The release states, "Income statements for periods not certified shall not be combined with the certified statements if to do so would result in a qualification by the auditors on the grounds of materiality." This statement would appear to stop an independent accountant from requesting relief in any cases involving other than relatively small acquisitions, because of the requirement to retroactively "pool" operating and income figures of all constituent companies. For this reason, the release does not appear to provide any real relief where acquisitions are accounted for as poolings of interest.

DISCLOSURE PROPOSALS—THE WHEAT REPORT

On April 14, 1969, a report prepared by a study group under the direction of Commissioner Francis M. Wheat was submitted to the Securities and Exchange Commission. The report dealt with registration requirements under the Securities Act of 1933, principal exemptions from registration under that Act, and reporting requirements under the Securities Exchange Act of 1934. A number of the suggestions and recommendations of the group were adopted by the Commission during 1970 and 1971, and several others were still in the proposal stage early in 1971.

Form of Combination Governs Filing Requirements

Of particular interest in the study is the section on business combinations and the present varying filing requirements because of the form in which such transactions take place. Under present requirements, only a voluntary exchange of securities (direct offers to stockholders by the acquiring company) requires a registration statement under the 1933 Act. Under a statutory merger or sale of assets to the acquiring company in exchange for its securities, no sale is deemed to be involved where the transaction requires the approval of the stockholders of the acquiring company.

Problem Posed by Rule 133

The study points up one of the principal problems created by Rule 133 (the no-sale rule):

If Corporation A (a publicly held corporation) wishes to acquire Corporation B (a non-public corporation) through a voluntary exchange of shares, the former shareholders of B must take their new shares subject to severe restrictions on resale if A is to claim the "private offering" exemption from registration. If the structure of the transaction can be changed, however, to a merger or sale of assets and Rule 133 applies, then restrictions on resale affect only the controlling stockholders of B and those restrictions permit immediate public resale in brokerage transactions of substantial quantities of the newly-acquired stock.

Assuming that Corporation B's outstanding shares are held by 400 shareholders of record (so that the requirement of registration under Section 12 of the '34 Act is inapplicable) then, if Corporation A wishes to offer its shares in a voluntary exchange for the outstanding shares of B, it must register the shares to be offered under the '33 Act and deliver a prospectus to the offerees. If the transaction can be structured as a merger or sale of assets and Rule 133 applies, however, not only is registration under the '33 Act avoided but, under the laws of many states, the only document which must be sent the shareholders of B in advance of their vote on the transaction is a bare notice of meeting.

The Study questions whether these important distinctions between the Securities Act consequences of different methods of business combination—differences which affect not only the choice of the method to be used but also the interest of public investors—can be justified.

Proposed Solution

Several possible alternative solutions to the problem were examined. The most promising of these involves the replacement of Rule 133 with a special kind of '33 Act registration procedure adapted to mergers and sales of assets. The new procedure would be consistent with the proposition that where an acquired company is publicly held, a proxy statement under the Commission's rules is both an appropriate and an adequate form of disclosure; nothing additional, by way of a prospectus, is needed. Such a solution would substantially eliminate all distinctions under the '33 Act between the three types of business combinations.

There are, of course, certain practical difficulties in applying the '33 Act registration process to transactions now covered by Rule 133. The Study does not minimize these practical difficulties. It believes, however, that they are surmountable. Under the proposed procedure, one document would serve both as a '34 Act proxy statement (where the acquired company is subject to the proxy rules) and as the '33 Act prospectus.

CURRENT REPORTS—FORM 8-K

Even though a company entering into a business combination may not be required to register shares to be issued under the Securities Act of 1933, or to comply with the proxy regulations under the Securities and Exchange Act of 1934, it may nonetheless be required to file a current report, usually Form 8–K, under the latter act. Upon the occurrence of certain events, a company subject to the reporting requirements of Sections 12(g), 13, or 15(d) of the 1934 Act must file a report on Form 8–K within ten days after the close of the month in which the specified event occurs. The form itself specifies the events to be reported on and provides relief from filing in the event the same information has previously been reported by the issuer. There is also provision for incorporating by reference material contained in proxy statements filed with the Commission or annual reports to stockholders.

Business Combinations

Item 2 of Form 8–K entitled "Acquisition or Disposition of Assets" reads, in part, as follows:

If the registrant or any of its majority-owned subsidiaries has acquired or disposed of a significant amount of assets, otherwise than in the ordinary course of business, furnish the following information:

(a) The date and manner of acquisition or disposition and a brief description of the assets involved, the nature and amount of consideration given or received therefor, the principle followed in determining the amount of such consideration, the identity of persons from whom the assets were acquired or to whom they were sold and the nature of any material relationship between such persons and the registrant or any of its affiliates, any director or officer of the registrant, or any associate of such director or officer.

(b) If any assets so acquired by the registrant or its subsidiaries constituted plant, equipment or other physical property, state the nature of the business in which the assets were used by the persons from whom acquired and whether the registrant intends to continue such use or intends to devote the assets to other purposes, indicating such other purposes.

Instructions [1 and 6 are omitted; italics added]

2. The term "acquisition" includes every purchase, acquisition by lease, exchange, merger, consolidation, succession or other acquisition; provided that such term does not include the construction or development of property by or for the registrant or its subsidiaries or the acquisition of materials for such purpose. The term "disposition" includes every sale, disposition by lease, exchange, merger, consolidation, mortgage, or hypothecation of assets, assignment, whether for the benefit of creditors or otherwise, abandonment, destruction, or other disposition.

3. The information called for by this item is to be given as to each transaction or series of related transactions of the size indicated. The acquisition or disposition of securities shall be deemed the indirect acquisition or disposition of the assets represented by such securities if it results in the acquisition or disposition of control of such assets.

4. An acquisition or disposition shall be deemed to involve a significant amount of assets (i) *if the net book value of such assets or the amount paid or received therefor upon such acquisition or disposition exceeded 15 percent of the total assets of the registrant and its consolidated subsidiaries,* or (ii) if it involved the acquisition or disposition of a business whose gross revenues for its last fiscal year exceeded 15 percent of the aggregate gross revenues of the registrant and its consolidated subsidiaries for the registrant's last fiscal year.

5. Where assets are acquired or disposed of through the acquisition or disposition of control of a person, the person from whom such control was acquired or to whom it was disposed of shall be deemed the person from whom the assets were acquired or to whom they were disposed of, for the purposes of this item. Where such control was acquired from or disposed of to not more than five persons, their names shall be given, otherwise it will suffice to identify in an appropriate manner the class of such persons.

Increase in Amount of Securities Outstanding

Item 7 of Form 8–K requires that a report be filed if the aggregate amount of previously unreported increases in any class of securities of the issuer exceeds 5% of the outstanding securities of the class. No report need be made, however, if the aggregate amount unreported does not exceed $50,000 face value or 1,000 shares or other units. The item has application to reissued treasury shares and indebtedness for which the maturity date has been extended.

A company that has been involved in a corporate acquisition or other business combination that does not meet the "significance test" set forth in Item 2 of Form 8–K may still have to file the form if the number of shares or principal amount of the securities issued in this and other unreported transactions, in the aggregate exceed 5% of the outstanding securities of the class.

Item 11 of Form 8–K requires that a report be filed if any matter has been submitted to a stockholders' vote.

Financial Statements

The only financial statements required in a Form 8–K filing are those of businesses acquired by the issuer, as described in Item 2 of the form. Such required statements are as follows:

1. There shall be filed a balance sheet of the business as of a date reasonably close to the date of acquisition. This balance sheet need not be certified, but if it is not certified, there shall also be filed a certified balance sheet as of the close of the preceding fiscal year.

2. Profit and loss statements of the business shall be filed for each of the last three full fiscal years and for the period, if any, between the close of the latest of such fiscal years and the date of the latest balance sheet filed. These profit and loss statements shall be certified up to the date of the certified balance sheet.

3. If the business was in insolvency proceedings immediately prior to its acquisition, the balance sheets required above need not be certified. The profit and loss statements required shall be certified to the close of the latest full fiscal year.

4. Except as otherwise provided in this instruction, the principles applicable to a registrant and its subsidiaries with respect to the filing of individual, consolidated, and group statements in an original application or annual report shall be applicable to the statements required by this instruction.

Regulation S–X governs the certification, form, and content of the balance sheets and profit and loss statements required by the preceding instructions, specifies the basis of consolidation thereof, and prescribes the statements of surplus to be filed in support thereof. No supporting schedules need be filed.

STOCK EXCHANGE REQUIREMENTS FOR LISTING ADDITIONAL SECURITIES

Companies entering into business combinations will occasionally have an original listing of the securities of the combined enterprise on a securities exchange shortly after a merger or consolidation, particularly where neither company prior to the combination was of sufficient size by itself to meet the necessary listing qualifications. However, since the vast majority of acquisitions and mergers involving stock exchange listings are by companies who already have their shares listed, the requirements discussed in this chapter will be those relating to applications for listing additional amounts of securities. The original listing qualifications of the New York and American Stock Exchanges are discussed in Chapters 2 and 3.

New York Stock Exchange

The New York Stock Exchange requires a company, already having securities listed on the Exchange, to file a listing application subsequent to original listing in the event:

1. The company proposes to issue an additional amount of a listed class, issue, or series.
2. The company desires listing of a class, issue, or series different from the securities already listed.
3. The company proposes to make a change in a listed class, issue, or series, which in effect creates a new security or which alters any of its rights, preferences, privileges, or terms.
4. The company desires to have a previously granted listing authorization changed.

Even though the aggregate amount of shares of stock or debt securities issued in a business combination is less than the minimum that would require the filing of a Form 8–K with the Securities and Exchange Commission, a company whose securities are listed on the Exchange must make timely disclosure of the transaction and file a subsequent listing application. Furthermore, where a company has to file a Form 8–K report in a business combination (a copy of which is filed with the Exchange), this does not satisfy the timely disclosure requirement of the Exchange, since such report is not filed with the Commission until the month after the transaction.

A company creating a new class of security, such as preferred stock, for issuance in a business combination could list the new class merely by filing a subsequent listing application with the Exchange. A simplified registration, Form 8–A, would also have to be filed with the Securities and Exchange Commission in such cases. No financial statements are required with Form 8–A. Form S–1 under the 1933 Act, or a proxy statement under the 1934 Act, relating to the business combination and filed with the Commission, may be incorporated into the subsequent listing application.

In certain instances involving the issuance of securities, the Exchange feels that stockholder approval is essential and requires it to be secured through the solicitation of proxies pursuant to Regulation 14 of the Securities Exchange Act of 1934 as a condition of the listing.

Solicitation of Proxies. Among situations requiring solicitation of proxies are the following:

1. The acquisition of a company or property in which directors, officers, or substantial security holders have an interest
2. Acquisition of a company or property where:
   a. The amount of stock to be so issued represents an increase in outstanding shares of 20% or more, or
   b. The combined value of stock (including securities convertible into common stock) and all other consideration approximates 20% or more of the market value of the outstanding common stock
3. Actions resulting in a change in the control of the company

In any proposed listing involving a business combination, the Exchange will not approve of a transaction that would have the effect of circumventing its standards for original listing and result in a so-called "backdoor listing." By this is meant that an unlisted company that proposes to combine with, and into, a listed company under circumstances that, in the opinion of the Exchange, constitute an acquisition of a listed company by an unlisted company, the resulting company must meet the standards for original listing. If the resulting company would not qualify for original listing, the Exchange will ordinarily refuse to list the additional shares for that purpose.

In deciding whether a proposed transaction constitutes a "backdoor listing," the Exchange states that "consideration will be given to all applicable factors, including changes in ownership of the listed company, changes in management, whether the size of the company being acquired is larger than the listed company, and if the two businesses are related on a horizontal or a vertical basis. All circumstances will be considered collectively and weight given to compensating factors." As a precautionary measure, it is recommended that any plan of this nature be submitted for an informal opinion prior to filing a listing application, particularly where the stockholders of the listed company emerge with less than 50% of the voting power of the combined enterprise.

Time Required To Clear Applications.   Basically, subsequent (additional) listing applications are designed to provide the Exchange and the investor with pertinent information regarding the proposed use of the securities and to update information previously filed.

To allow time for preliminary examination and revision, four draft copies of the application should be submitted to the Department of Stock List at least two weeks in advance of the date on which it is desired to have the application acted upon.

Final approval of the listing application rests with the Board of Governors of the Exchange, and action is usually taken as soon as practicable after all the information and other requirements are complied with. As soon as the listing has been authorized, the Exchange distributes copies of the final listing application, which becomes a public document, to all member firms and to all others requesting a copy.

Accordingly, if a company has followed the practice of disclosing to the public through its annual reports to stockholders, or otherwise, the data required in the application, a simplified form may generally be used with only the following information.

1. Heading
2. Description of transaction
3. Recent developments
4. Authority for issuance
5. Opinion of counsel

If the securities being listed are to be issued in connection with the acquisition of a controlling interest in or the net assets of another company, the latest available balance sheet and statements of income and surplus of such company must be included in the application.

The financial statements of the issuer are seldom included in a subsequent listing application for acquisition of another company, even though the Stock Exchange Company Manual indicates that such statements are required. It is understood that the Exchange waives this requirement because it feels its regular reporting procedures for listed companies are adequate for the investor, and the inclusion of the issuer's financial statements in a listing application for the acquisition of another company would involve unnecessary expense.

If the securities being listed are to be issued in connection with a transaction that was fully described in a prospectus under the Securities Act of 1933 or a proxy statement under Regulation 14 of the Securities Exchange Act of 1934, either of these documents may be used as a part of the listing application. Any additional data required by the application would be furnished with either document.

Description of Transaction.   Since the subsequent listing application is designed to provide the exchange and the investor with information regarding the proposed use of the securities, in a business combination, certain of the instructions included under "Description of Transaction" are of particular interest:

If the securities are to be issued in connection with the acquisition of a controlling interest in, or a major part of the business and assets of, another company, describe briefly the history and business of such other company. Appropriate financial statements, usually the most recent annual financial statements, supplemented by the latest available interim earnings statement, should be included. A recent balance sheet and/or pro forma or combined statements may be considered appropriate in some circumstances.

Independently audited annual statements are preferred but where these are not available company statements may be accepted. Interim statements would usually be unaudited company statements. The foregoing data should be appended as an exhibit and reference made to it under the caption "Description of Transaction."

If the securities are to be issued for property, securities, or for any form of consideration other than cash, describe such properties, securities or consideration in detail sufficient to indicate the relative values of the securities to be issued and the consideration to be received. A statement should be made as to why the company regards the acquisition as a favorable one from the standpoint of the company. Indicate whether or not any officer, director or principal stockholder of the company (or any of its affiliates) has any direct or indirect beneficial interest in the property, securities, or other consideration to be received and, if such interest does exist, describe it.

Describe the accounting treatment to be accorded the transaction on the books of the company. State the policy to be followed with respect to amortization whenever intangible assets are acquired or created. State the treatment to be given in consolidation where it differs from the method followed in recording the transactions on the books. Where other than routine transactions such as issue of securities for cash, stock dividends, stock splits, etc., are involved, the accounting treatment should be reviewed with the company's independent accountants and mention of their review and approval included under this heading.

American Stock Exchange

The American Stock Exchange has adopted procedures substantially similar to those of the New York Stock Exchange for listing additional securities, or a new class of securities, in an acquisition or merger. Its general policy regarding "backdoor listings" is also similar.

Time Schedule. The additional listing application must be filed with and approved by the Exchange prior to the issuance of the additional securities. Accordingly, applications should be filed at least one to two weeks in advance of the date by which the applicant wishes action taken. In any case where it is essential that the securities be fully qualified for admission to trading by a certain date, the Securities Division of the Exchange should be consulted at an early date so that a satisfactory time schedule may be arranged. This is particularly important in the case of rights or exchange offers.

Short Form with Prospectus or Proxy Statement. If a prospectus relating to the additional securities to be listed (or if a proxy statement describing the transaction in which such securities are to be issued) has recently been declared effective or cleared by the Securities and Exchange Commission, the applicant may, at its option, attach it to the listing application. (A preliminary prospectus may be used with the proof copies for the Exchange's consideration, but a final prospectus must be used with the final application.)

If so attached, the listing application is usually limited to:

(a) Items 1 to 6, inclusive, and 8 and 9 of the simplified application, and

(b) For Item 7 of the simplified form, substitute an item entitled "Prospectus" or "Proxy Statement," as the case may be, referring to and incorporating same by reference and indexing the information contained therein. If an index is contained in the prospectus or proxy statement, a reference to such index will suffice.

Simplified Application Form. Where a company has disclosed to the public through its annual reports or otherwise the data required to be set forth in the application, a simplified form (three typewritten copies of which should be submitted) may generally be used that includes the following information:

1. Title page
2. Capitalization
3. Funded or long-term debt
4. Authority for and purpose of issuance
5. Opinion of counsel
6. Registration under Securities Act of 1933
7. Recent developments
8. General information
9. Certificate and signature of duly authorized officer of the applicant

Under item 4, "Authority for and purpose of issue" are the following instructions relating to mergers and acquisitions:

In the case of acquisitions refer (by date and names of parties thereto) to the contract pursuant to which the securities will be issued and state that a copy of such contract has been submitted in support of the listing application.

(a) *Mergers, consolidations, modifications of previously listed securities, etc.:* Ordinarily these transactions are covered by a proxy statement to be attached to the listing application, so that only a statement of the dates of authorization by directors and shareholders is required . . . , with a reference to the proxy statement for further details, if modification of a previously listed security is not covered by a proxy statement attached to the listing application, describe the nature and effect of the proposed modification, and the basis of exchange.

❖   ❖   ❖

(d) *Acquisitions:* If the securities applied for are to be issued as the total or part of the consideration for the acquisition of a controlling interest in, or the major part of the business and assets of, another company, or specific assets or properties,

(1) Describe the transaction, and the assets or business to be acquired, in sufficient detail to indicate the relative value thereof in relationship to the consideration to be paid;

(2) State the principle followed, and the factors considered in determining the consideration to be paid in the acquisition, and identify the persons making the determination and their relationship to the applicant.

(3) State why the management of the applicant regards the acquisition as a favorable one from its viewpoint.

State whether or not any officer, director or principal shareholder of the applicant (or any of its affiliates) has any direct or indirect beneficial interest in the assets to be acquired or the consideration to be paid and, if such interest does exist, describe it.

If a controlling interest in, or the major part of the business and assets of, another company is being acquired, describe briefly the history and business of such other company, and furnish financial statements of such other company as called for under Paper A(1).

If any engineering, geological or appraisal reports, etc. were obtained in connection with the proposed acquisition, refer to and include appropriate excerpts from such reports in the application.

Accounting Treatment: Describe the accounting treatment to be accorded the transaction on the books of the Company, and in consolidation. In the case of acquisitions state whether the transaction will be treated as a "purchase" or a "pooling of interests." State the policy to be followed with respect to amortization whenever intangible assets are acquired or created. Where other than routine transactions such as issue of securities for cash, etc. are involved, the accounting treatment should be reviewed with the Company's independent accountants and a statement should be made that they have reviewed and approved such accounting treatment as being in accordance with generally accepted accounting principles. Any variations from pronouncements of the AICPA should be specified.

Financial Statement Papers To Be Filed. The following are the financial statement requirements in business combinations:

Paper A. (1) Acquired Company:
If the securities to be listed are to be issued in connection with the ac-

quisition of a controlling interest in, or of all assets subject to the liabilities of, another company, there shall be submitted, *in duplicate*, the balance sheet of such company at recent date and its income account and surplus account to the date of such balance sheet. Usually these are the most recent annual financial statements, supplemented by the latest available interim statements. Such statements should be accompanied by the report or opinion of independent auditors, but in cases where independently audited financial statements are not available, statements certified to by the chief accounting officer of such other company may be accepted. The financial statements of acquired companies are printed at the end of the listing application.

Paper A. (2) Applicant Company:
Applicants which use the short or simplified form listing application are not, in ordinary circumstances, required to submit additional financial statements unless those in the prospectus, proxy statement or annual and quarterly reports were prepared as of and to a date more than six months prior to the date of the listing application. In such event the supplementary financial statements referred to below should be submitted.

Supplementary Financial Statements:
Statements, similar in form, content, and degree of consolidation to the last independently audited financial statements, as of and to a date not more than six months prior to the date of the listing application, which supplementary financial statements will, in ordinary cases, be accepted either (a) independently audited, or (b) certified by the chief accounting officer of the applicant. Such interim statements should be submitted *in duplicate*.

The interim statements should carry appropriate footnotes generally equivalent, if applicable, to the footnotes to the independently audited statements as of and to the previous fiscal year end, but revised and amplified to cover any changes therein since the last fiscal year end. If desired, a statement may be made referring to and incorporating by reference the notes to the audited financial statements for the previous fiscal year end, and specifying that such notes are applicable to the interim statements "subject to" (specify any changes or additions therein since the date of the last fiscal year end).

Although financial statements of acquired companies are printed in the listing application, the Exchange will determine in each case whether it is necessary to print the financial statements of the applicant therein.

BLUE SKY LAWS

As explained in Chapter 3, the majority of states have comprehensive laws governing the issuance of securities. Some states exempt from provisions of their blue sky laws, transactions in securities resulting from mergers and reorganizations; others require the filing of an application for permission to issue securities in a merger, consolidation, or reorganization, including the furnishing of financial data on constituent companies, and copies of all documents used in soliciting security holders.

The requirements for obtaining negotiating permits, or permits for the issuance of securities, should be ascertained by legal counsel, for the states of domicile of the several constituent companies involved in such transactions, and for other states in which they have security holders or property.

11

Tender Offers

ADVANTAGES AND LIMITATIONS OF TENDER OFFERS

Usually a company is interested in acquiring another because the acquisition will increase the combined earnings per share, or it believes that there are values, either present or potential, not reflected in the market price of the stock of the company proposed to be acquired. This is so whether the would-be acquirer makes his move via the tender offer route or by approaching the management for negotiating purposes. The difference between some companies that are the targets of tender offers, and those approached for negotiation, may be that the undervaluation of the capital stock of the former seems more apparent.

The cash tender offer, i.e., direct solicitation by a company, individual, or group, to stockholders of another company, to purchase all or part of their capital stock, usually at a fixed cash price, became increasingly important in the merger movement during the late 1960's despite certain inherent disadvantages on the side of the acquirer and the acquired. An obvious disadvantage to tendering stockholders is the necessity to pay a federal capital gains tax which could be postponed if the combination were effected through an exchange of capital stock. For the acquiring company there is danger because of the lack of opportunity to investigate a proposed acquisition other than through published sources.

An Efficient Acquisition Method

Nevertheless, the tender offer remains a viable acquisition method. It is still cheaper and faster to obtain effective or full control of a company via the tender offer route than through negotiated deals, because of the limited amount of information required under the Tender Offer Disclosure Act, as explained below. Furthermore, there is considerable flexibility in the use of the tender offer, if a would-be acquirer does not wish to undertake complete acquisition for cash, which might strain his resources or borrowing power.

In some cases companies established a substantial position in a stock through market purchases or from institutional or other large holders. They then make a public tender offer for additional shares to establish a controlling interest and finally offer an exchange of capital stock or other securities, with remaining stockholders, to complete the acquisition. However, two factors could adversely affect such a method of acquisition: (a) under Accounting Principles Board Opinion No. 16, the entire transaction in such a case must be treated as a purchase for accounting purposes, and (b) there are limitations on the interest deductible for federal tax purposes on debt incurred to acquire the stock or assets of another company.

BACKGROUND AND REGULATION

Hayes and Taussig, in a study published in 1967,[1] estimated that cash tender offers had increased from 25 at a value at $186 million in 1960 to 75 at $951 million in 1965. In contrast, direct offers to stockholders to exchange capital stocks increased modestly during this period from $435 million to $558 million.

This situation changed several times during subsequent years. A disclosure requirement law relating to cash tender offers, enacted shortly after midyear in 1968, caused a change in tactics by would-be acquirers, and a number of substantial offers to ex-

---

[1] Hayes and Taussig, *Tactics of Cash Takeover Bids*, HARV. BUS. REV., March–Apr., 1967.

change securities, some of which involved debt securities and warrants, were made directly to stockholders. However, the Tax Reform Act of 1969 imposed limitations on interest deductions on corporate indebtedness incurred after October 9, 1969, for the purpose of acquiring the stock or assets of another corporation (Chapter 8, page 215). This factor and general economic conditions during 1970 slowed the pace of cash tender offers as well as direct offers to stockholders to exchange equity and other securities.

In a number of cases, incumbent management of companies whose shares were solicited have cooperated with would-be acquirers, or at least maintained a neutral position regarding offers. However, contested tender solicitations have brought this means of acquisition to the forefront of public notice, and resulted in a number of articles on the subject in various periodicals and house organs of investment firms.

Cash tender offers may or may not be in the best interests of the stockholders of a company whose stock is solicited. At times it is quite evident that an offer is of significant advantage to them, but at others it is not so apparent.

Despite certain drawbacks, the cash tender offer has advantages for the would-be acquirer in that it does not involve the detailed SEC filing requirements of a registration statement nor a long waiting period for clearance from the Securities and Exchange Commission.

As explained in Chapter 10, offers direct to stockholders of other companies to exchange their securities for those of the offerers have different announcement, timing, and filing requirements than cash tender offers. However, some of the offensive and defensive measures for cash tender offers have equal application to such security exchange offers. Direct offers to stockholders to exchange securities are discussed in the final section of this chapter.

Tender Offer Disclosure Act

On July 29, 1968, *amendments to the Securities Exchange Act of 1934* were enacted to provide for full disclosure of corporate ownership of securities. These amendments, together with further revisions through December 22, 1970, are set forth in Sections 13(d) and (e), and Sections 14 (d), (e) and (f) of the Act. The law provided for the Securities and Exchange Commission to adopt rules and regulations, and issue the necessary orders to implement the amendments to the Act. Pursuant to this authority the Commission adopted Rules 13D and 14D, with subsections, and Schedules 13D and 14D outlining information to be filed pursuant to such rules.

On December 22, 1970, the Commission also adopted Rule 434B *under the Securities Act of 1933* which reads as follows:

Additional Information Required to be Included in Prospectuses Relating to Tender Offers:
Notwithstanding the provisions of any form for the registration of securities under the Act, any prospectus relating to securities to be offered in connection with a tender offer for, or a request or invitation for tenders of, securities which is subject to Section 14(d) of the Securities Exchange Act of 1934 shall, if used after January 28, 1971, include all of the information, not otherwise required to be included therein, required by Rule 14d–1(c) under such Act to be included in all such tender offers, requests or invitations, published, sent or given to the holders of such securities.

The law and rules relate to the acquisition of more than 5% of a class of securities registered under applicable sections of the 1934 Act and the Investment Company Act of 1940, the purchase of securities by the issuer thereof during the period of an outside tender offer, the making of tender offers or solicitations in favor of, or in opposition to, such tender offers, and the replacement of a majority of the directors of the issuer in connection with an acquisition or a tender offer, and fraudulent, manipulative, and deceptive practices.

Any person acquiring any equity security so registered, who becomes directly or indirectly the 5% owner of such class of stock, is required to send to the issuer of such securities a statement containing specified information, and to file copies with each exchange where the security is traded, and eight copies with the Securities and Exchange Commission, *within ten days* after such acquisition. The Commission may require any additional information necessary and appropriate in the public interest, or for the protection of investors.

Any person making a tender offer for more than 5% of such class of registered securities is required to file a statement containing similar information with the Commission at the time copies of the offer or request or invitation are first published or sent or given to securities holders.

Information Required Under Disclosure Act. The information required to be filed, under the Act, is somewhat similar, but more extensive than that which is required in Schedule 14B of Regulation 14A of the 1934 Act, in proxy solicitations other than by the issuer.

The matters covered include, among other things, the identity and background of principals involved, covering a ten-year period; source and amount of funds to be used in making purchases; purpose of the transaction, i.e., plans to acquire control, sell assets, liquidate, merge with other persons, or effect any major change in its business or corporate structure. Information is also required with respect to the rights of security holders to withdraw their securities, and the pro rata acceptance of tenders, where all securities tendered are not accepted.

The law relating to the disclosure of the acquisition of corporate equity securities and the making of tender offers (as amended through December 22, 1970) is set forth in Appendix J.

Other Regulation of Cash Tender Offers

In addition to that exercised under the aforementioned Disclosure Act, authority of the Securities and Exchange Commission may be exercised in cash tender offer transactions under Rules 10b–5 and 10b–4 of the Securities and Exchange Act of 1934. Rule 10b–5 does not apply solely to tender offer transactions, but covers manipulative and deceptive (fraudulent) acts in connection with the "purchase or sale of any security," and is discussed on page 233 in Chapter 8.

Rule 10b–4, which was adopted July 1, 1968, prohibits the practice of "short tendering" in connection with a request or invitation for tenders of any security. Under the previously existing practice, brokers tendered securities which, in effect, they did not own.

Tender offers commonly provide that stock certificates need not be deposited if a bank or a member firm of a stock exchange guarantees that they will be delivered on demand, or at a specified time, if accepted. This procedure was originally introduced to permit acceptance on behalf of stockholders who were out of town or otherwise not in a position to deposit their certificates. However, it resulted in abuses. For example, if a broker estimated that only half of the shares tendered would be accepted, on a pro rata basis, he could tender without depositing, twice as many shares as he owned. As a result, all of the shares which he actually owned would be accepted, and the number of shares purchased from other investors would be correspondingly reduced.

Rule 10b–4 proscribes the practice of short tendering as constituting a manipulative or deceptive device or contrivance. It thus prohibits a person from tendering any security for his own account unless he owns the security. It also prohibits a person from tendering or giving a guarantee of a tender of a security on behalf of another person unless the security is in the possession of the person making the tender or giving the guarantee, or unless that person, acting in good faith, has reason to believe that the other person owns the tendered security and will deliver it for the purpose of the tender to the person making the tender or giving the guarantee. Accordingly, although the rule prohibits short tendering, a broker or a bank may still guarantee delivery of securities *actually owned by customers* and, in this way, accommodate those who are unable to deposit their securities before the termination of the tender offer. The rule sets forth criteria for determining when a person owns a security being tendered.

PROCEDURES IN EXTENDING THE TENDER OFFER

While in many instances prospective acquirers approach management or other large shareholders of a company whose stock they propose to solicit, in the majority of cases they do not. Accordingly, the first rule in a campaign to acquire stock in this manner is to maintain the utmost secrecy prior to the public announcement.

Pursuit of Available Information

Before coming to a decision regarding a tender offer, all available public information should be discreetly obtained regarding the company proposed to be acquired, along the lines suggested in Chapter 8. The same criteria should be used in appraising the value of a tender offer target as in a negotiated acquisition or merger.

Desirability of Prior Stock Acquisitions

As demonstrated later in this chapter, it is often desirable to acquire shares through open market purchases prior to making a tender offer to stockholders of the sought-after company. This may be done through broker nominees. If the shares being acquired are those of a company required to file annual reports with the Securities and Exchange Commission, the beneficial owner must send statements containing appropriate information, under the disclosure provisions of the 1934 Act, to the Commission, to the issuer of the securities, and to each exchange where the security is traded, when his holdings aggregate 5% or more of the class of equity securities outstanding. A person shall be deemed to be the beneficial owner of securities which he has the right to acquire through the exercise of presently exercisable options, warrants, or rights or through the conversion of presently exercisable convertible securities.[2]

Tender Offer Announcements

Tender offers are customarily made through newspaper announcements, and must contain certain information required under the Disclosure Act. In addition to this required information, many announcements show the price range of the sought-after stock for a considerable period, together with its recently published closing price. Some announcements have the offer instructions, and the letter of transmittal which may be clipped from the announcement and used by the solicited stockholder. Other an-

---

[2] Securities Exchange Act of 1934, Rule 16a–2(b).

nouncements contain a coupon which may be used to obtain a letter of transmittal for forwarding the stock.

Fees or Commissions on Stock Tendered

All announcements indicate the fee or commission that will be paid to any member of a national securities exchange or of the National Association of Securities Dealers, soliciting shares pursuant to the offer, whose name appears on the letter of transmittal. The two major stock exchanges require that brokers be paid at least two full stock exchange commissions on shares tendered. This furnishes an incentive to such brokers to assist the tender offerer, in addition to which they will receive a commission, in many cases, for reinvesting the proceeds for their customers.

Varying Terms of Tender Offers

A cash tender offer is invariably at a fixed price and stipulates that it will expire at the close of business on a specified date, unless extended. Otherwise the terms of offers may vary considerably.

For example, the initial period in which stockholders may tender their shares could be as short as ten days, and as long as thirty. In some few cases longer or shorter periods are specified.

The relative number of outstanding shares requested may vary in accordance with the objectives of the would-be acquirer, and the number of shares of stock of a company held prior to the tender solicitation. Some of the variations of share requests follow:

1. *A fixed number*—in some cases the soliciting company may reserve the right to rescind or accept the offer, if fewer shares are submitted. Another feature may be an election to purchase any and all shares tendered in excess of the specified amount. In rare cases companies following this procedure may specify minimum and maximum amounts.

2. *A maximum number*—if shares are submitted in excess of the amount requested, those tendered prior to a certain date are accepted on a pro-rata basis.

3. *A specified minimum*—if tenders are not received for the minimum, the soliciting company reserves the right to reject shares offered. Conversely, it will accept additional amounts, if tendered. Usually the specified minimum shares, if tendered, will give the soliciting company at least working control.

4. *All or a specified minimum*—companies making offers on this basis are, in fact, disclosing their intention to acquire substantially all (at least 80%) of the capital stock of the company whose shares are solicited. Usually, the specified minimum will give them a majority interest, or at least what is deemed effective working control.

5. *All*—companies soliciting all the outstanding shares may have many modifying conditions, as it is virtually impossible to obtain all voting stock by means of a tender offer, if a substantial number of shares are outstanding in the hands of many stockholders. Usually they will try to obtain stock representing at least 80% of the voting power of all classes of stock, and the same percentage of non-voting. Such an interest will enable them to include the company, whose stock is requested, in a consolidated federal income tax return and give them legal freedom of action, for most corporate purposes. Accordingly, companies requesting all shares generally reserve the right to accept any lesser number of shares tendered that will accomplish their purpose.

How Tender Offers Are Financed

Chapter 12 (page 370) shows how companies have financed the purchase of shares of capital stock of others. Although the initial financing of cash requirements to purchase stock through tenders was often obtained by means of short-term bank loans, more permanent, or long-term refinancing was generally required when such loans fell due.

In some cases, tendering companies were able to cover temporary financing costs through dividends received on stock they acquired. As a general rule, dividends received from a domestic corporation by another corporation are subject to a credit of 85%. In other words, such dividends would be subject to federal income tax at only 15% of the effective rate of tax. On the other hand, interest on money borrowed to finance a tender offer is deductible from income at the effective tax rate subject to certain limitations as to the amount thereof.

RESISTING THE TENDER OFFER

As mentioned, management of many companies whose stock is solicited by tender offers either cooperate with the would-be acquirers or maintain a neutral position. However, there are a number of cases where management or substantial stockholders of sought-after companies actively resist tender offers. Usually this is done by means of newspaper announcements urging stockholders to reject the offer, followed up by letters to stockholders, legal actions, or finding a more compatible merger partner.

Newspaper Announcements

Resistance announcements vary considerably in form and content, from restrained statements showing that the stock has sold at a higher price during recent years than that offered, or that the net asset value per share exceeds the offering price, to more contentious statements. The latter may attack the good faith of the tender offerer, its financial record, the fact that the amount of money borrowed to finance the deal will impair its future borrowing power, or similar adverse comments.

Generally, where management does not control too much of the sought-after stock, and the earnings record and stock market action have been static or poor for a period, management's resistance, if any, necessarily is restrained. The chances of a successful conclusion to an offer in these cases is overwhelming, and a belligerent attitude could lead to the speedy unemployment of incumbent management of the companies being taken over.

Letters to Stockholders

If management resisting a tender offer has a good case, and sufficiently large blocks of shares are lined up in its support, letters to stockholders containing information similar to that shown in newspaper announcements may be desirable. Otherwise, such a procedure may redound to the benefit of the tender offerer by notifying many stockholders who had not become aware of the deal via the newspaper announcement.

Legal Actions

Often legal actions are used to resist tender offers with the company management alleging that (a) the terms of the offer are unfair and do not reflect the real value of the sought-after company, (b) the combination of the two companies would violate the antitrust laws, (c) a conflict of interest would exist because of interlocking directorates, or (d) the acquirer would be subject to the public utility or other regulatory acts, thus hampering its operations or forcing divestment of important income-producing properties.

There have been reverse legal actions by would-be acquirers, where incumbent management attempted to sell or exchange additional shares of unissued stock to third parties, to reduce the relative interest of tendered shares. Also, in some instances allegations have been made that incumbent management was engaged in manipulative transactions to drive the price of the stock above that offered in the tender.

Repurchase of Shares for Treasury

Subject to restrictions under the Tender Offer Disclosure Act, a company may make a counter offer to stockholders to repurchase its own shares, up to a certain amount, at a higher price than the tender offer. This would have the effect of driving the market price up, and may be justified on the grounds that the company's earnings per share will be increased because of the reduced number of shares outstanding. However, the mathematics of such a gambit should be weighed because the tender offerer could end up with the same interest in a company by increasing his price per share beyond that offered by the company, for very little, if any, additional overall cost, because of the reduced number of shares outstanding. Furthermore, in such cases, directors may run the risk of stockholder suits for wasting corporate assets.

Finding a More Compatible Merger Partner

This may be the best defense that management has against a seemingly undesirable cash tender offer. However, timing is a matter of great importance, and if no discussions on this subject have been held with others prior to the tender offer, it may be difficult to obtain immediate action from eligible partners. If there are any grounds for legal action to restrain or delay the consummation of the tender offer or a concomitant merger plan, this will often afford the additional time required for merger negotiations with others.

Other Defensive Measures

In many instances, control of a simple majority of the voting stock of a company will permit persons in that position to elect the entire slate of directors. There are several ways to inhibit such action by seeking stockholder approval to (a) increase the percentage of assenting votes required to effect a merger, consolidation, or disposal of substantial amounts of corporate assets, (b) adopt a cumulative voting system for electing directors, and (c) stagger the election of directors (say, elect one third of the board each year for a three-year period). However, the latter action is not favorably regarded by the major stock exchanges because it could perpetuate incompetent management in office.

Other procedures used to resist tender offers include the acquisition of a company that competes with the bidder to such an extent that the acquisition by the tender offerer would be in violation of antitrust laws. Increases in cash dividends or the declaration of a stock dividend or split are defensive techniques which have been used from time to time by incumbent management. Also, lending institutions often have a provision in loan agreements indicating a condition of default if there is a change in control of the borrowing company.

STUDY OF SELECTED CASH TENDER OFFERS

As indicated by the following study covering selected cash tender offers, many of the companies approached would not fit into the category of "raid bait," but are the same types of companies generally involved in negotiated mergers. Undoubtedly, a number of these tender deals were effected with the consent of management of companies whose stocks were solicited.

Table 11-1 (pages 322–25) shows data relating to 74 cash tender requests for capital stock involving companies listed on the New York Stock Exchange, during the period from January 1, 1965, to April 28, 1967. These tender offers were made to the security holders of 70 companies. One of the offers was made concurrently to two companies that were affiliated, offers were made by three different companies to acquire the stock of one company, and two offers each were made to three other companies. Four of the tender offers were made by individuals or groups rather than companies.

Data used for the study were obtained generally from Moody's Manuals, Standard & Poor's Stock Guide, *The New York Times*, and *The Wall Street Journal*.

The premiums over the approximate market prices of the securities prior to the tender offers ranged from 2% to 53%. There was one premium offered of 71% which, however, was made concurrently with a 10% premium offer to stockholders of an affiliated company of the former. The median premium of all offers was 21%. That is to say, there were approximately the same number of offers above and below this figure.

In determining the approximate market prior to offers, published prices a day or two before the announcements were used generally, except where there was indication that the news of the offer may have leaked before public solicitation. In the latter cases published prices of earlier periods were used.

Results of Tender Offers

The 74 selected cash tender requests during the period from January 1, 1965, to April 28, 1967, were reviewed through December 31, 1967, to determine the results to that date of the offers and further related actions, as summarized below:

Offer successful and acquired all or substantial control (generally 80% or more) of shares of company solicited 20
Offer successful for partial acquisition, and merger or control later effected by exchange of capital stocks or additional cash purchases 24
Acquired shares as a result of these or subsequent tender offers, generally insufficient for consolidation or merger—still held at December 31, 1967 10
Acquired shares as a result of these or subsequent tender offers, but later sold them, or exchanged them in merger with third party (7 sold, 4 exchanged) 11
Tender offers failed and shares obtained, if any, returned to tendering shareholders 9
   Total 74

Financial Characteristics of Subject Companies

Earnings and net book equity figures shown in the study tabulation were as of the latest fiscal year-end prior to the offer of the company solicited, except where the offer date was close to the subsequent fiscal year-end, when figures as of the latter date were used.

Earnings Pattern. The 70 companies whose stocks were solicited showed the following earnings history or trend in the most recent year or several recent years prior to solicitation:

Improved (in 27 cases, substantially)	44
Static or sporadic	14
Unfavorable (in 9 cases, substantially)	12
Total companies	70

This would indicate that offerers via the tender route are not too anxious to acquire companies showing adverse earnings trends, because of the administrative time and the expenditures generally required to revitalize such companies.

Price–Earnings Ratios. Any company whose common stock is selling at a low price–earnings ratio is a prime target for a takeover bid. This fact was evident in the case of the companies included in the study. Immediately prior to the tender offers, their common stocks were selling at a median price–earnings ratio of 12, based on the closing market prices at that time and their latest estimated twelve-months' earnings per share shown in Standard & Poor's Monthly Stock Guides.

Net Book Equity per Share. There is a general view that companies whose capital stocks are selling below net book equity per share are particularly vulnerable to tender offers. This supposition has some merit, as market prices of 29 of the 70 companies were below their net book equity per share prior to the tender offers. Of these 16 had net book equity per share in excess of the tender offers. As might be expected, 9 of the 16 companies, where tender offers were below net book equity per share, were among those showing unfavorable earnings trends.

Liquidity of Companies Solicited. Unquestionably, any company having substantial liquid assets (cash and marketable securities) beyond the reasonable needs of the business is vulnerable to a cash tender offer. The standard ploy is to make a cash tender offer for a portion of the stock, and if successful, effect a merger through an exchange of capital stocks, for shares outstanding after the initial acquisition. The acquirer then makes use of the excess cash to liquidate, in whole or in part, the loan incurred for the initial acquisition. Thus, part of the company is purchased with its own cash.

Evidently, there were not many acquirable companies still in this vulnerable position. There were only 5 cases out of the 70 companies whose stock was sought, where excess liquid assets (cash and marketable securities) would be significant relative to the total cost of the stock solicited by tenders. However, other of the companies had not fully utilized their borrowing power, which proved a boon to the acquirers.

Some view a high ratio of current assets to current liabilities as a sign of liquidity. However, if the substantial portion of "current assets" is represented by accounts and notes receivable and inventories, a company may be in a non-liquid state. A relatively large amount of receivables could be the result of financing customers by extending overly liberal credit terms, and inventories could be unbalanced or considerably in excess of desirable levels, thus raising a question as to the real value of such "assets."

Stock Interest in Companies Prior to Solicitation. In 24 instances, companies owned stock in those companies whose stock they solicited prior to the tender offer; in 15 of these, their interests were substantial. In 20 of these cases, they acquired all or substantially all of the stock of sought-after companies immediately or through subsequent merger or purchases. Of the four other cases, two companies acquired shares which they still held at December 31, 1967, one acquired shares which were later sold, together with its previous interest, and only one company's offer failed and shares tendered were returned. In the latter instance, another company made a higher tender offer which was successful and ultimately effected a merger between it and the company whose stock was acquired as a result of the tender.

Status of Uncompleted Deals

Of the ten acquirers that still held tendered shares at December 31, 1967, market prices were lower than their cost per share in six instances and higher in four. Where shares were acquired and later sold or exchanged for securities in mergers with third parties, acquirers profited by such deals in nine of the eleven cases. Such information was not readily available in the two other cases.

It should be noted that any person or company becoming the beneficial owner of more than 10% of any class of equity security of an issuer of securities registered under the Securities Exchange Act of 1934 is regarded as an "insider" under Section 16(b) of that Act. Accordingly, if securities are sold within a period of less than six months from the date of purchase, any profit realized therefrom may be recovered by the issuer of the securities regardless of the intention of the beneficial owner in entering into the transaction.

As indicated, only nine out of 74 tender offers could be considered to have "failed." Four of the sought-after companies later merged with others, and in two cases the tenderers withdrew their offers, even though they had approval for the deals from the opposite managements. In the cases where such companies were still operating as entities at December 31, 1967, the market price of their stock was higher at that date than the tender offers in three out of five, including the two where the would-be acquirers had withdrawn their offers.

Conclusions

The evidence indicates that companies contemplating acquisition by use wholly or in part of cash tender offers fare better if they first establish a position in the sought-after stock through open market or private purchases from large stockholders. As a corollary to the desirability of obtaining a stock interest in a company prior to a tender solicitation to its stockholders, it would be generally unwise to attempt a tender takeover of a company whose management, or other large stockholders, hold a substantial voting stock interest, without first gaining their approval.

From the stockholder's standpoint, one often wonders whether it is better to accept what appears to be an attractive cash tender offer or to hold out in the hope of a higher offer, either through a further tender or an exchange of capital stock in a subsequent merger. The study of the 24 companies whose offers were successful for partial acquisition, which later effected control through subsequent purchases or merger, indicated that in 16 cases the solicited stockholders who originally held out fared better.

Publicized Opposition and Legal Action. Publicized opposition to tender offers either by the management or stockholders of sought-after companies was noted in 20 cases, although there probably were more. Notice of legal action was found in 15 cases (some involved several actions), including 12 of the 20 cases where public opposition had been expressed to offers. In addition to actions arising through opposition to the offers or later merger proposals, others were instituted by antitrust or other governmental regulatory agencies.

The publicized opposition alone did not contribute significantly to the record of failures. However, when coupled with legal action, it appeared to be the reason that the majority that acquired shares and later sold or exchanged them had taken such steps. In other words, unless valid and often legally provable reasons were produced in opposing a tender offer, at a good premium above market, opposing factions have not been too successful in their endeavors.

Good Offense Is Best Defense. As previously mentioned, a good defensive measure to employ against a tender takeover attempt is to find a more compatible merger partner, or for the hunted to become the hunter. In at least eight cases included in the study, sought-after companies were able to effect mergers with companies other than those making the original tenders. In others, companies whose stock was sought resisted possible takeover attempts by acquiring other companies.

Among these was Famous Artists Schools, which substantially increased its volume and earnings through a series of acquisitions. As a result, the market price of the stock was 77⅞ at December 31, 1967, compared with 18⅞ in July, 1965, when Crowell Collier made a tender offer of 24, and acquired about 15% of the then outstanding shares.

Size No Deterrent to Would-be Acquirers. A noted phenomenon in the tender offer field is the takeover of companies by those that are smaller from the standpoint of net assets and earnings. Among these was Colorado Milling & Elevator, which acquired a 42% voting interest in Great Western Sugar through a tender offer, which yielded approximately 110,000 preferred and 200,000 common shares of the latter, out of total outstanding shares, respectively, of 200,000 and 1,800,000. The peculiar twist in this deal was that each share of the preferred stock of Great Western was entitled to twelve times the voting power of each common share. Colorado Milling later effected a merger with Great Western, which was a number of times its size. This deal resulted in stockholders' litigation, which is discussed in Chapter 14.

Amount of Premium To Offer. There can be no hard and fast rule about the percentage premium to be offered solicited stockholders in a company whose stock is publicly traded. Under ordinary circumstances a premium in the area of 20% or so should be attractive to most stockholders. This figure may be adjusted downward, if there has been little movement in the price of the stock, or it has been declining during a recent period. Conversely, if the market price of the stock has been moving upward, but does not fully reflect the results of a recently improved earnings trend, a higher premium may be required for a successful offer.

Overriding these obvious conditions are the objectives of the would-be acquirer, and the estimated total cost of a completed deal, whether it be in one or more steps leading to a complete acquisition or merger. The tendering company must weigh the benefits to be gained by the deal, against the cost thereof, before making an offer at a premium believed attractive to solicited stockholders.

DIRECT OFFERS TO EXCHANGE SECURITIES

As explained in Chapter 10, direct offers to stockholders to exchange their securities for those of the offerers have different announcement, timing, and filing requirements than cash tender offers. Nevertheless, many of the offensive and defensive measures pertinent to cash tender offers have equal application to offers to acquire capital stocks through the exchange of securities.

There is nothing new about direct offers to stockholders to exchange their securities. Many business combinations effected on a friendly basis have been accomplished through this medium. In fact, a number of the combinations reviewed in Chapter 12 were effected in this manner. What is unique about some recent direct offers to stockholders to exchange their securities is (a) the apparent lack of an earnings record or financial stature of some of the companies making the offers, and (b) the types of securities they offer for exchange.

Although some of these direct offers to exchange debt securities and warrants for capital stock have been made by substantial companies, the ones of particular interest have involved combinations where the sought-after company would furnish the principal financial substance and earnings potential to the combined enterprise.

Advantages and Hazards to Offerer

A company making an announcement of a proposed offer to exchange securities does not incur any obligation to go through with a deal. The announcement merely signifies an intention, at that point, to make an offer which becomes valid only after a registration statement (generally Form S–1) filed with the Securities and Exchange Commission becomes effective. Meantime, the company making the announcement of a proposed offer has an opportunity to contact substantial security holders of the target company and otherwise survey its chances of gaining effective control of the latter. Also, the original proposal may be amended one or more times if it is found that solicited stockholders' interest has been generated but a better offer is desired.

However, because of the informal nature of these proposals and the lack of any initial firm commitment on the part of the would-be acquirer, the original proposer often finds himself engaged in a bidding contest with one or more competitors before the definitive offer is made by means of an effective prospectus.

Some Proposals To Exchange Securities

Among announcements during the latter part of 1968 of proposals to exchange debt securities, or common stock and purchase warrants for capital stock of sought-after companies were the following:

Offerer	Sought-after Company	Type of Consideration Offered
N.V.F. Co.	Sharon Steel Corp.	Debentures and warrants
Haven Industries Inc.	National Sugar Refining Co.	Convertible debentures, common stock, and warrants
D.W.G. Corp.	Southeastern Public Service Co.	Convertible debentures

The warrant—which is a right or option to purchase stock, generally common, at a price or at varying prices over a period, terminating at a fixed date—is explained more fully in Chapter 12.

In each of the above cases, the offering companies were inconsequential from an earnings or net assets standpoint, or both, relative to the companies they sought to acquire. Further, none of these companies could be classed as a conglomerate, at the time of their exchange offers, although D.W.G. acquired interests in several companies in 1966 and 1967, pursuant to a plan to sell its cigar business and diversify. In order to illustrate some of the features of this type of exchange proposal, particulars of the N.V.F.–Sharon deal are set forth below.

N.V.F.–Sharon Steel Exchange

On September 20, 1968, N.V.F. announced a proposed offer to acquire all of the outstanding common shares of Sharon, approximately 1,656,000 at that time, in exchange for a package of $50 principal amount of 5% subordinated debentures and warrants to purchase 1.5 shares of common stock at $33 per share. This proposal was vigorously opposed by the management of Sharon.

TABLE 11-1 Selected Cash Tender Requests for Capital Stock Involving New York Stock Exchange Companies
(January 1, 1965, to April 28, 1967)

Company Making Offer	Date of Initial Tender	Company Whose Stock Was Requested	Shares* Outstanding at Offer Date	Number of Shares* Requested	Offer Price	Approx. Market Price Prior to Tender Offer	Per Cent of Tender Offer in Excess of Market Price	Results of Offers— Notes†
Management and Capital	1/11/65	American Metal Prod.	1,379	400 max.	$ 24	$ 20$\frac{3}{8}$	18%	5
Consolidated Paper	2/11/65	Doeskin Products	1,380	All	5$\frac{1}{4}$	4$\frac{1}{4}$	24	3
C. I. T. Financial	2/24/65	Meadowbrook Nat'l Bk.	3,718	All	31$\frac{3}{4}$	24$\frac{1}{2}$	30	2
U. S. Smelting & Ref.	3/29/65	Mueller Brass	570	All	42	32$\frac{3}{4}$	28	3
Eltra Corp.	3/21/65	Mueller Brass	570	All	40	32$\frac{1}{2}$	23	1 and 6
May Dept. Store	4/ 1/65	Meier & Frank	920	All	56	51	10	3
A. B. C. Consolidated	4/ 2/65	Nedicks Stores	512	All	12$\frac{1}{2}$	12$\frac{1}{4}$	2	2
Diebold, Inc.	4/22/65	Lamson Corp.	275	141	31$\frac{1}{2}$	23$\frac{1}{2}$	34	3
Baldwin–Montrose Chem.	5/14/65	Paramount Pictures	1,565	125	64	56$\frac{3}{4}$	14	5
Nat'l. Union Elec.	6/ 5/65	Emerson Radio–Phon.	2,214	1,158 min.	18	16$\frac{1}{8}$	12	3
Chicago & Northwestern	7/ 2/65	Michigan Chemical	779	230 min.	33	24$\frac{7}{8}$	33	1 and 3
Husky Oil	7/ 6/65	Rimrock Tidelands	1,540	400	7$\frac{1}{2}$	5$\frac{1}{4}$	43	1 and 2
Glen Alden Corp.	7/12/65	McKesson & Robbins	4,260	1,000	49	37	32	5
Phila. & Reading Corp.	7/16/65	Lone Star Steel	3,899	All or 2,000 min.				
American Steel & Pump	7/18/65 amended 7/31/65	Standard Products	741	400	22 / 15	17$\frac{1}{8}$ / 11	28 / 36	3 / 6
Continental Grain	7/28/65	Allied Mills	823	413	50	42$\frac{3}{4}$	17	4
Crowell Collier	7/28/65	Famous Artists Schools	1,240	200	24	18$\frac{7}{8}$	27	4
United Utilities	8/ 2/65	Inter–Mountain Tel.	2,118	106	32$\frac{1}{2}$	30	8	1 and 3

	Date	Acquired	Shares*					Ref†
Simmonds Precision	8/ 9/65	Liquidometer Corp.	512	187	$9\frac{1}{2}$	$6\frac{1}{4}$	50	1 and 2
Castle & Cooke	8/18/65	Standard Fruit & SS	1,057	200 min.	26	$21\frac{1}{2}$	21	1 and 2
Wm. White & Associates	8/25/65	Colo. Milling & Elev.	523	50	25	$21\frac{1}{2}$	16	5
Combustion Engineering	9/10/65	National Tank	1,515	818	35	32	9	2
Nortruk	9/23/65	Norwalk Truck	373	373	$21\frac{1}{2}$	19	13	2
Electric Bond & Share	9/27/65	American & Foreign Power	7,204	400	$19\frac{3}{8}$	$17\frac{7}{8}$	16	1 and 3
Bangor Punta Alegre	10/ 6/65	Smith & Wesson	282	All	80	63	27	2
Greatamerica Corp.	11/ 9/65	Braniff Airways	2,948	400 min. 525 max.	75	$67\frac{5}{8}$	11	1 and 2
Kewanee Oil	11/14/65	North Penn Gas	450	200	$18\frac{1}{4}$	14	30	1 and 4
Pennzoil Co.	11/22/65	United Gas Corp.	12,869	1,000 min.	41	$35\frac{7}{8}$	14	1 and 3
Giannini Controls	11/29/65	Veeder-Root, Inc.	1,111	370 min.	38	$30\frac{5}{8}$	24	6
Wallace Murray	12/ 1/65	Simonds Saw & Steel	1,500	All	$43\frac{1}{2}$	$33\frac{1}{2}$	26	2
Eltra Corp.	12/19/65	No. Amer. Refractories	340	All	34	$28\frac{1}{2}$	19	1 and 2
Brown Co.	12/21/65	K.V.P. Sutherland Paper	2,218	1,109	33	$29\frac{1}{8}$	13	3
Stewart–Warner	1/10/66	Thor Power Tool	728	All or 200 min.	19	$16\frac{3}{8}$	16	4
Montgomery Ward	1/25/66	Pioneer Tr. & Sav. Bk.	120	All	165	108	53	2
Foremost Dairies	2/ 8/66	McKesson & Robbins	4,626	1,000	51	$47\frac{7}{8}$	7	1 and 3
George W. Murphy	2/ 8/66	Studebaker Corp.	2,820	500	30	$25\frac{3}{8}$	18	6
H. K. Porter Co.	2/ 8/66	Philip Carey Mfg.	1,014	300	38	$31\frac{1}{2}$	21	6
B.V.D. Co.	2/10/66 amended 2/18/66	Timely Clothes, Inc.	152	All	20	16	25	1 and 2
Glen Alden Corp.	2/14/66	Philip Carey Mfg.	1,014	300	40	37	8	3
Consolidated Foods	2/16/66	E. J. Brach & Sons	2,281	400 min.	48	40	20	6
W. R. Grace & Co.	2/17/66	The Ruberoid Co.	1,857	700	50	$40\frac{1}{8}$	25	5
Eltra Corp.	2/23/66	Burrus Mills, Inc.	394 com. 40 pfd.	Any or All	$15\frac{3}{4}$ 80	$10\frac{1}{2}$ 71	50 13	1 and 2

* 000's omitted.
† See page 325.

TABLE 11-1 (cont.) Selected Cash Tender Requests for Capital Stock Involving New York Stock Exchange Companies (January 1, 1965, to April 28, 1967)

Company Making Offer	Company Whose Stock Was Requested	Date of Initial Tender	Shares* Outstanding at Offer Date	Number of Shares* Requested	Offer Price	Approx. Market Price Prior to Tender Offer	Per Cent of Tender Offer in Excess of Market Price	Results of Offers— Notes
Total American	Leonard Refineries	2/23/66	1,247	300	$17\frac{1}{8}$	$14\frac{3}{4}$	12%	4
Wean Engineering	McKay Machine	3/ 7/66	245	70	55	$46\frac{1}{4}$	19	1 and 3
Genesco Inc.	Julius Garfinckel & Co.	3/10/66 amended 3/21/66	1,075	Any or all	$43\frac{1}{2}$	$34\frac{1}{2}$	26	4
Colo. Milling & Elev.	Great Western Sugar	4/ 4/66	1,800 com. 150 pfd.	100 110	44 190	$38\frac{1}{2}$ 159	14 19	3
Crane Co.	Sawhill Tubular Prod.	4/12/66	663	250	20	$16\frac{1}{2}$	21	5
Liggett & Meyers	Star Industries Inc.	4/14/66	995	All	55	$32\frac{1}{4}$	71	2
	Paddington Corp.		2,666	All	35	$31\frac{1}{4}$	10	
Amer. Bosch Arma	Bacharach Industrial	5/12/66	125	All	25	$20\frac{3}{4}$	20	1 and 2
Amer. Elec. Pow. Co.	Michigan Gas & Elec.	5/17/66	204	103 min.	100	$74\frac{1}{2}$	34	3
Tung-Sol Elec.	Wagner Elec. Corp.	5/31/66	2,057	954 min.	35	$27\frac{1}{4}$	28	1 and 3
Gamble–Skogmo	First Nat'l. Stores	6/12/66	1,655	500	35	34	3	6
Victoreen Instruments	North & Judd Mfg.	6/27/66	252	At least 100	34	$25\frac{3}{4}$	32	1 and 5
S. T. Scheinman	Art Metal	7/13/66	894	125	25	$21\frac{1}{4}$	18	5
Sun Chemical Co.	Harshaw Chemical	7/22/66	1,047	350	40	$33\frac{3}{8}$	20	5
Foremost Dairies	McKesson & Robbins	9/ 2/66	4,620	550	53	$44\frac{1}{2}$	29	1 and 3
United Fruit	Winchell Donut	9/14/66	750	All	25	21	19	6
General Dynamics	United Elec. Coal	10/ 5/66	674	170 min.	50	42	19	1 and 2
Allied Products	Dayco Corp.	10/24/66	1,408	854	26	21	14	6

324

	Date		Shares					Notes
AMK Corp.	11/14/66	John Morrell & Co.	1,254	200	$27\frac{1}{2}$	$21\frac{1}{2}$	28	1 and 3
Fifth Ave. Coach	12/ 7/66	Austin Nichols	518	260 min.	20	$17\frac{1}{2}$	14	4
American Tobacco	12/ 9/66	James B. Beam Distill.	2,620	All	$42\frac{1}{2}$	32	33	2
Ling-Temco	12/21/66	Wilson & Co.	2,426	750	$62\frac{1}{2}$	$49\frac{1}{2}$	26	3
Sperry & Hutchinson	2/ 7/67	Bigelow Sanford	2,810	1,360 min.	27	$22\frac{1}{8}$	22	2
Carborundum Co.	1/20/67	Commercial Filters	641	All or min. of 80%	15	$11\frac{1}{4}$	33	2
Paul Revere Corp.	2/ 3/67	Avco Corporation	13,964	4,000	33	$26\frac{1}{4}$	26	3
Condec Corp.	2/ 6/67	Lunkenheimer Co.	414	209	36	31	16	4
General Instrument	2/ 6/67	Universal Controls	10,979	1,500	$6\frac{1}{4}$	$5\frac{7}{8}$	6	1 and 3
Houston Oil Field	2/17/67	Holly Sugar	1,250	100 (7)	24	$17\frac{3}{4}$	35	1 and 5
Bucyrus-Erie	2/28/67 amended 3/ /67	Racine Hydraulics	408	All (7)	26	$21\frac{1}{4}$	22	1 and 4
Rockwell-Standard	3/ 1/67	Draper Corp.	2,450	1,050	30	24	25	1 and 3
Dresser Industries	3/ 1/67 amended 3/10/67	Link Belt Co.	2,865	1,300	52	42	24	5
FMC Corp.	3/13/67	Link Belt Co.	2,865	All	58	42	38	3
Private Group	4/ 4/67	Metro-Goldwyn-Mayer	5,314	250 max.	43	41	5	4

* 000's omitted.

Notes:

1. Owned stock in companies solicited prior to tender offer.
2. Offer successful and acquired all or substantial control of shares of company solicited.
3. Offer successful for partial acquisition, and merger or control later effected by exchange of capital stocks or additional cash purchases.
4. Acquired shares as a result of these or subsequent tender offers, generally insufficient for consolidation or merger—still held at December 31, 1967.
5. Acquired shares as a result of these or subsequent tender offers, but later sold them or exchanged them in merger with third party.
6. Tender offers failed and shares obtained, if any, returned to tendering shareholders.
7. Offers also included all outstanding convertible debentures of solicited companies.

325

Competitive Proposals and Counter-Proposal. Shortly after the N.V.F. announcement, Sharon received a proposal from Alloys Unlimited. The merger talks with Alloys, who were offering a convertible preferred stock on a share-for-share basis for Sharon common, were terminated in November 1968, because of failure of the parties to reach agreement.

After the Alloys talks were terminated, a proposal was received from Cyclops Corporation to exchange a package of $30 principal amount of 6¾% subordinated debentures and one-fourth share of $4.00 convertible preferred stock for each share of Sharon common. This offer, which had the approval of the Sharon management, was evidenced by a registration statement filed with the SEC which became effective on January 22, 1969. However, early in February, the Department of Justice advised that it would oppose the merger on the grounds that Cyclops and Sharon were substantial competitors in the production of various steel products. The president of Cyclops, shortly after receiving this information, announced that this left Cyclops with no alternative but to withdraw its exchange offer.

Meantime, N.V.F. improved its initial exchange offer twice, as evidenced by an originally effective prospectus dated January 24, 1969, and an amended one dated February 3, 1969. Under the amended offer, N.V.F. proposed to exchange, for each share of Sharon common stock, $70 principal amount of 5% subordinated debentures of N.V.F. due 1994, and warrants exercisable through January 31, 1979, to purchase 1.5 shares of N.V.F. common stock at $22 per share. Another feature of this offer was that the debentures, *valued at the principal amount thereof,* could be applied to the payment of the exercise price of the warrants until January 31, 1979.

The N.V.F. prospectus stated that "N.V.F. was advised on October 4, 1968 by Sharon management that Sharon declined to furnish information for the purpose of preparing the registration statement of which this Prospectus is a part. N.V.F. understands that the reaction of the management of Sharon to the Exchange Offer is unfavorable." Sharon's financial statements and the notes thereto were included in the N.V.F. prospectus on the basis of information taken from Sharon's annual reports on Form 10–K to the SEC, a registration statement prepared by Sharon in 1966, published interim reports, and the registration statement of Cyclops Corporation, which contained information furnished by Sharon to Cyclops. The Cyclops exchange offer was subsequently withdrawn, as indicated previously.

Federal Income Tax Status of Exchange. Under the caption "Federal Income Tax Status" N.V.F. stated it had received an opinion from counsel that Sharon stockholders exchanging their shares of common stock for debentures and warrants of N.V.F. would realize gain or loss (on the exchange) for federal income tax purposes. The opinion further indicated that any stockholder, in whose hands the Sharon common stock was a capital asset, who realized gain on the exchange might, under certain conditions, postpone such gain and treat it on the installment basis, under Section 453 of the Internal Revenue Code. The opinion was qualified in this and other respects and concluded with a statement that, "The opinions set forth above are included herein for informational purposes only, and it is recommended that each holder of Sharon common stock obtain independent tax advice as to the Federal income tax consequences of an exchange hereunder and related matters."

Financial Data Re Exchange. The data extracted from the N.V.F. February 3, 1969, prospectus and from other published sources are of interest; they are compiled on page 328.

Pro Forma Financial Data. Pro forma (unaudited) statements of earnings (loss) in total and per share, based on the assumption that N.V.F. acquired 49%, 51%, 80%, or 100% of the common stock of Sharon, were included in the prospectus. These statements combined figures of N.V.F. *for the year ended September 29, 1968,* and the consolidated statement of income of Sharon *for the year 1967,* "as it was historically more representative of Sharon's operations than the consolidated statement of income for the year ended September 30, 1968." (The Board of Directors of Sharon anticipated a substantial loss for the fourth quarter of 1968, which

	N.V.F.	Sharon
Earnings for 1967, before extraordinary items ... $	63,840	$ 3,088,000
Extraordinary items	279,781[1]	—
Net earnings ....$	343,621	$ 3,088,000

	N.V.F.	Sharon
Earnings (loss) nine months ended September 30, 1968, before extraordinary items ....$	(39,107)	$ 5,549,000[2]
Extraordinary items	374,360[1]	—
Net earnings ....$	335,253	$ 5,549,000

Net earnings per common share:

Year 1967	0.52	1.87
Nine months ended September 30, 1968	0.48	3.35
Net assets—September 30, 1968 ....$	16,812,828	$104,051,000
Per share	$22.98	$62.81

Quoted market prices:

Common stock—September 19, 1968 (prior to first announcement)	$32⅞–35¼	$43½–44⅜
Common stock—October 15, 1968 (prior to revised offer)	$24¼–27⅝	$49⅝–51¾
Common stock—February 3, 1969 (date of prospectus)	$25⅝	$49⅜
Common stock—April 30, 1969	$19¼	

Securities offered in exchange:
February 3, 1969 (quote per prospectus on
when-issued basis) .... Bid $50.40
                                         Asked $59.00
April 30, 1969 (over-the-counter quote) ..... Bid $54.00
                                               Asked $55.75

March 10, 1969:
Common shares of Sharon received for exchange (approximate)   1,491,000
Equivalent securities to be issued:
Principal amount of debentures $104,370,000
Warrants 2,236,500

Notes:
1. Extraordinary items (credits) to income included in "net earnings" of N.V.F. consist of net proceeds of $279,781 from the sale of unimproved land and investments in 1967, and an increase of $374, 360 resulting from a change in accounting for the investment tax credit in the nine months ended September 30, 1968.
2. Sharon's income for the nine months ended September 30, 1968, was increased by $496,000 as the result of a change in accounting practices.

would reduce reported nine months' earnings to the approximate level of 1967 for the full year.) The pro forma figures shown below, based on 80% and 100% ownership, give effect to certain assumptions relative to the business combination as described in the notes:

	Condensed Pro Forma Statements of Earnings (Loss) Assuming	
	80% Ownership	100% Ownership
	(Thousands Omitted)	
Net sales	$214,110	$214,110
Cost of products sold, selling and administrative expenses	206,358	206,358
	$ 7,752	$ 7,752
Other charges:		
Interest on long-term debt of Sharon and N.V.F.	$ 3,605	$ 3,605
Pro forma interest on 5% debentures to be issued	4,639	5,798
Pro forma amortization of deferred debt expense on 5% debentures	1,764[1]	2,233[1]
	$ 10,008	$ 11,636
Other credits:		
Pro forma amortization of excess of equity over cost of investment in Sharon	(491)[2]	(644)[2]
Interest and other income (net)	(948)	(949)
Net charges	$ 8,569	$ 10,043
Loss before taxes on income and minority interest	$ (817)	$ (2,291)
Provision for income taxes, without benefit of operating loss carryback	(1,780)[3]	(1,780)[3]
Minority interest in net earnings of Sharon	(617)	—
Pro forma (loss) without operating loss carryback	$ (3,214)[3]	$ (4,071)[3]
Assumed operating loss carryback	2,406	2,574
Pro forma (loss) assuming benefit of operating loss carryback	$ (808)[3, 4]	$ (1,497)[3, 4]

Notes: The captions of some of the above items are self-explanatory. The following additional explanatory data are based on the notes to the several pro forma statements in the prospectus:

[1] "The value assigned to warrants and deferred debt expense is based on the company's estimate and reflects current market conditions." The value assigned to

Per-Share Statistics Assuming

	80% Ownership	100% Ownership
(Loss) per N.V.F. common share outstanding, assuming no exercise of N.V.F. and Sharon stock options and no exercise of warrants included in exchange offer:		
Without recognition of operating loss carryback	$ (4.72)	$ (5.99)
With recognition of operating loss carryback	$ (1.19)	$ (2.20)
Net earnings per Sharon common share outstanding assuming exercise of N.V.F. and Sharon stock options and exercise of warrants included in the exchange offer:		
Without recognition of operating loss carryback	$ 1.80	$ 1.77
With recognition of operating loss carryback	$ 2.30	$ 2.38

Pertinent Pro Forma Balance Sheet
Items Assuming

	80% Ownership	100% Ownership
	(Thousands Omitted)	
Deferred debt expense	$ 41,085[1]	$ 51,356[1]
Notes payable	9,000	9,000
Long-term debt outstanding:		
Prior (including current portion)	58,507	58,507
5% subordinated debentures	92,773	115,966
Stockholders' equity	41,749[5]	47,713[5]
Excess of equity over cost of investment in Sharon	4,908[2]	6,445[2]

the warrants is $12 for the purchase of one share of N.V.F. common for $22 per share, or an aggregate of $24,935, 814, based on 80% ownership, and $30,899, 772, based on 100% ownership. In each case this includes values assigned to 90,000 warrants to be issued to the investment bankers for services.

Deferred debt expense amounts to $41,085,013, based on 80% ownership, and $51,356,274, based on 100% ownership. Such deferred debt expense is to be amortized on the "bonds-outstanding method." The debentures bear a January 1, 1994, maturity date, but there are sinking fund payment requirements to retire stipulated amounts thereof commencing January 1, 1989. In addition to the deferred debt expense, fees and expenses incurred with respect to the tender offer estimated at $1,709,000, based on 80% ownership, and $2,097,000, based on 100% ownership, have been recorded as a cost of the investment in Sharon.

[2] Represents the excess of equity over the cost of the N.V.F. investment in Sharon amortizable over a ten-year period. [This later turned out to be a much more substantial figure.]

Report to Stockholders for 1969. In its report to stockholders for the year ended December 31, 1969, issued in 1970, N.V.F. announced that it had "acquired as of March 1, 1969, 1,415,235 common shares of Sharon Steel Corporation (approximately 86%) in exchange for $99,066,000 principal amount of 5% subordinated debentures due 1994, and 2,122,852 common stock purchase warrants. Deferred debt expense of $56,609,000 attributable to the 5% subordinated debentures was recorded and is being amortized on the 'bonds outstanding' method. The value of $22,129,000 assigned to the warrants issued with respect to the exchange has been reflected as part of the cost of the investment in Sharon."

Consolidated net income of N.V.F. and subsidiaries for 1969 was $8,058,000 (*after provision for federal and state income taxes of $4,682,000*) before minority interest and $6,878,000, after such interest, equivalent to $8 per primary common share of N.V.F. and $4 per fully diluted share. However, the N.V.F. income statement, the consolidated statement of earnings of Sharon, which was also shown separately in the N.V.F. report to stockholders, and the letter of the chairman of N.V.F. to stockholders had some revealing information on these figures.

Sharon's net earnings for the year were $7,713,000, *after provision of $6,049,000* for federal and state taxes on income. Approximately ten-twelfths of such income (from March 1) would be includable in N.V.F.'s consolidated figures. Also, N.V.F.'s consolidated statement of income included a credit of $1,653,000 rep-

---

3 The assumed operating loss carryback for federal income tax purposes would result primarily from pro forma interest and debt expense relating to the 5% subordinated debentures. Presumably, pro forma net earnings (losses) were computed with and without this deduction, because there was no assurance that the combined enterprise would realize sufficient income in future years to avail itself of such net operating loss carryovers (income available for carryback losses is not too substantial).

4 The statement of earnings of N.V.F. included in the pro forma combined statement reflects changes in pension actuarial assumptions and in methods of accounting for depreciation and the investment tax credit. If such changes, which increased income by $895,000, had not been made, N.V.F. would have shown a loss of $454,684 instead of $440,316 net earnings.

5 There are restrictions on the payment of cash dividends on N.V.F. common stock resulting from its own prior indebtedness and the outstanding debt obligations of Sharon.

resenting ten months' amortization of the excess of equity over cost of investment in subsidiary (Sharon). The total of such excess equity amounted to $19,835,000, and is being amortized over a ten-year period. The following comment appeared in the chairman's letter, after mention of Sharon's net earnings:

N.V.F.'s 1969 operating profit (exclusive of Sharon and *before debenture interest, deferred debt expense, Sharon dividends and taxes*) was $3.4 million, almost four times greater than operating profit in 1968.

An analysis of this statement indicates that the so-called profit was before debenture interest of $4,000,000 and debt expense of $1,795,000. In other words, N.V.F.'s operations, exclusive of Sharon, resulted in a loss of several million dollars.

1970 Transactions. As of January 6, 1970, the company purchased and retired 650,000 of its outstanding warrants from N.G.C. Capital Management Corporation, a non-affiliated company, and some of the latter's customers, for $9.375 each, an aggregate of $6,093,750. The funds were obtained for this purpose from short-term borrowing and the cost thereof was charged to capital in excess of par value and the warrants retired.

Consolidated net income of N.V.F. and subsidiaries for 1970 was $2,530,000 (after provision for federal and state income taxes of $1,110,000) before minority interest, and $1,996,000 after such interest, equivalent to $2.03 per primary share and $1.80 per fully diluted share. The retirement of the 650,000 warrants early in 1970 is the reason for the relatively smaller difference between the primary and fully diluted share figures in 1970 versus 1969.

Sharon's net earnings were $3,673,000, over $3,000,000 of which was included in N.V.F.'s consolidated net income. Also, N.V.F.'s consolidated statement of income included a full year's credit of $1,984,000 for amortization of the excess of equity over the cost of the investment in Sharon. Without this credit, N.V.F. broke about even on a consolidated basis, and again had a loss of several million dollars, excluding Sharon's operations.

As of December 31, 1970, the last sale price of N.V.F. common stock on the New York Stock Exchange was 8¾. The bonds and warrants, both of which are listed on the Pacific Coast Exchange, were quoted at 32½ and 4½ respectively as of that date.

SEC Action Filed Against Officers in 1971. A Complaint for Preliminary and Final Injunction was filed on May 20, 1971, against certain officers of Sharon, who with the exception of Wilbur T. Blair succeeded to such positions pursuant to the takeover of that company. The following excerpt from the Securities and Exchange Commission News Digest release of May 21, 1971, summarizes such action:

Complaint Cites Sharon Steel Co., Others. The Commission yesterday filed a complaint in Federal court in New York against the following alleging violations of the antifraud and stock acquisition provisions of the Federal securities laws: Sharon Steel Company, DWG Corporation, NVF Corporation, Victor Posner, board chairman and president of Sharon as well as chairman of NVF and DWG, Bernard Krakower, vice president of Sharon Steel and officer of DWG and NVF, William [sic] T. Blair, general counsel and vice president of Sharon Steel.

In its complaint the Commission alleged that the defendants in violation of the above cited provisions of the Federal securities laws, from on or about January 1, 1969 to the present time, have caused the assets of the pension funds of the Sharon Steel Corporation, Trumbull County, Ohio, to be invested in securities issued by corporations in which the defendants had a substantial beneficial interest. In addition, the complaint alleged that the defendants caused these assets to be used to meet certain corporate obligations of companies with which the defendants are affiliated and to assist certain of these affiliated companies in their takeovers of other corporations.

Those named in the complaint denied any wrongdoing and *The Wall Street Journal* of May 26, 1971, attributed the following statement to Posner:

All investments were made with a view to improve the performance of the pension fund, ... None of the actions taken by the trustees or those named in the complaint were improper.

12

Valuation Factors and Studies—Selected Acquisitions and Mergers

In Chapter 8 various investigations were suggested to a would-be acquirer prior to making overtures and during the course of negotiations. It should be emphasized that these investigations are germane to arriving at an appropriate valuation. Without them it is difficult to determine, with any degree of confidence, the profit potential of the acquisition prospect, the most suitable manner of effecting the deal, and whether it will be compatible from a personnel standpoint.

There are many factors that enter into the valuation of a company to be acquired through an exchange of capital stock or other securities, or via the purchase route for cash or cash equivalent. In the latter case the method of financing the acquisition is also important. These matters will be discussed in this chapter, as well as pertinent data developed in an extensive study of business combinations during a seven-year period.

PRIMARY FACTORS IN VALUING COMPANIES

Potential earnings and dividend-paying capacity generally are the most important factors in valuing a company. This holds true except for companies with substantial holdings of disposable assets such as securities of real estate, or companies which have been sustaining losses, when valuation would be more closely related to fair market or liquidating values.

Use of Latest Earnings

As illustrated in Chapter 4, it has become accepted practice for investment bankers and other experts to value companies for purposes of security offerings at a certain number of times the latest year's earnings, or to use an even shorter period, annualized for this purpose. This is particularly true where a company has been showing a favorable earnings trend over a period of years. If the reverse is the case, although the latest annual earnings might be used for such a purpose, the price–earnings multiple generally would be at a lower rate.

Return on Net Worth in Cash Deals

It is not an easy matter to arrive at a fair valuation of a company for acquisition or merger purposes. Generally speaking, a price should be considered fair if both the acquirer and seller benefit as a result of the transaction. Some companies that include acquisitions and mergers in their permanent growth plan have general yardsticks for price determination. That is, in cash deals, they expect a return on their investment either equivalent to the company's present rate on net worth or its customary return on an investment in a new plant complete with facilities.

As a general indication of value on this basis, 2,068 of the leading manufacturing corporations had a return of 12.5% on net worth for the year 1969.[1] However, this rate varied by industries, with the high returns registering in the soap, cosmetics, drugs and medicine, soft drinks, office and computing equipment, instruments, and photographic goods industries, and the low in sugar, building, heating and plumbing equipment, iron and steel, and the cement industries. The return was down to 10% for 1970 due to adverse business conditions.

Some companies have announced general guidelines for return on net worth. For example, duPont has endeavored to obtain a

[1] First National City Bank, Monthly Economic Letter, April 1970.

minimum rate of 10% after taxes, and Textron, 25% before taxes. They may not have always been successful in consummating acquisitions on these bases, but it is well to have some goals to strive for.

In exchanges of capital stock, most successful acquirers, as a guideline, endeavor not to dilute their earnings per share by reason of an acquisition or merger. This computation may be based, to the extent practicable, on prospective rather than historical earnings. However, where long-range prospects are unusually favorable, some dilution is acceptable.

Net Assets in Support of Earnings

Even though earnings per share may be the dominant factor in determining price, either in cash or capital stock, they normally should be supported by sufficient net assets to continue to produce such earnings. If a company is in a tight position for liquid assets, as the result of having had large losses, or having been milked, or otherwise overextended, the prospective purchaser should consider that any additional capital he must furnish beyond the purchase price, in order to operate the company properly, adds to the cost of his investment. Accordingly, he should measure his expected return in future earnings against this total investment and not the purchase price alone.

Importance of Usable Assets

At times a prospective acquirer may find the seller has certain assets he does not want, such as:

1. Manufacturing plants or warehouses that would not be of use because the acquirer intends to consolidate such operations into his own or new facilities
2. Non-operating assets, such as excess cash and investment securities and real estate, insurance policies on officers' lives, personal automobiles, etc.

Excluding such assets from the deal often will greatly reduce the purchase price and eliminate controversy between the buyer and seller regarding the disposable value of assets not desired by the former.

Also, it makes no sense to give long-term compensation contracts and related benefits to principals of selling companies, if they will not be working executives in the combined enterprise, unless a suitable reduction is made in the purchase price of the selling company.

Other Factors and Intangibles

Factors that are susceptible to evaluation and enter into price consideration are (a) tax benefits that may accrue to the purchaser or seller, and (b) compensation, stock option, and royalty agreements to be made to principal selling stockholders.

In addition to factors which may be deduced from figures, there are intangible factors to be considered in negotiations for a business combination, some of which are favorable and some adverse.

The favorable factors include the acquisition of:

1. Needed management and technical personnel
2. Newly developed products whose effects on profits has not yet been realized
3. Sales outlets or sources of raw materials for the acquirer's products
4. Manufacturing or warehouse facilities in strategic geographic areas
5. Profits to utilize tax-loss carryovers, or
6. Products to utilize excess plant capacity

Adverse factors to consider are:

1. Impending expiration of patents
2. Loss of hitherto exclusive manufacturing know-how
3. Possible loss of competent top management
4. Possible loss of major customers
5. Effect of cutback in government contracts
6. Possible requirement for renewed advertising and sales promotion efforts
7. Possible inventory obsolescence resulting from new inventions or discoveries

MISCELLANEOUS CONSIDERATIONS

A number of other considerations of a broad nature must be weighed in addition to the factors dealt with above.

Cash Acquisitions Versus Exchange of Capital Stock

Management should always weigh carefully the advantages of cash equivalent acquisitions versus those involving the issuance of capital stock. If the acquirer's stock is selling at a high price–earnings ratio, it is usually to his advantage to acquire by an exchange of capital stock. Conversely, if the acquirer's stock is selling at a low price–earnings ratio, or the net tangible assets of the seller are above the purchase price, considerable leverage in per-share earnings may be gained in a cash or cash equivalent deal.

Certainty That All Shares To Be Exchanged Are Considered

Upon entering into a deal involving the exchange of capital stocks, both sides should carefully determine the total number of shares that will be involved in the exchange by each company. This will include shares under stock options, stock warrants, employee stock purchase plans, and shares issuable upon conversion of debentures or preferred stock. Otherwise, agreement may be reached on per-share exchange ratios, based on shares outstanding at the time of negotiation, but additional shares may be issued before closing, without receipt of equivalent value by the issuing company.

Market Indexes and Price–Earnings Ratios

The general level of the stock market, and price–earnings ratios, in particular industries, will have an important bearing on the price paid to acquire a company. Statistics on Standard & Poor's composite market index on 500 stocks listed on the New York Stock Exchange, as well as the composite index of the Exchange of all of its listed stocks, are shown for a number of years in Chapter 2. Price–earnings ratios, as compiled by Standard & Poor's and Dow Jones over a period of recent years, follow:

	Standard & Poor's 425 Industrials			Dow Jones 30 Industrials
	High	Low	Year-End	Year-End
1970	17.7	12.9	17.7	16.4
1969	18.0	16.0	17.3	13.4
1968	18.0	16.9	17.8	16.3
1967	18.2	17.4	17.8	16.8
1966	16.4	14.0	14.8	13.6
1965	17.7	15.7	17.7	18.1
1964	18.8	17.5	18.8	18.8
1963	17.9	17.0	17.7	18.5
1962	19.7	15.1	15.8	17.9
1961	22.9	20.2	20.6	22.9
1960	18.9	16.3	18.9	19.1

The high and low ratios are based on figures shown by Standard & Poor's at the end of each quarter during the respective years. At the close of the first six months of 1970, the Standard & Poor's industrial price–earnings ratio took a significant drop to 13.7, and the Dow Jones to 12.8. It is interesting to note that the "blue chip" stocks included in the Dow Jones industrial averages were generally selling at lower price–earnings ratios than other industrials on the New York Stock Exchange during the most recent years.

Optimism of Seller Regarding Value

Seasoned New York Stock Exchange industrials have been selling at composite averages ranging from 14 to 18 times earnings during the five and a half years ended June 30, 1970, and some top companies that have shown good earnings and dividend pay-outs have sold at even less attractive price–earnings ratios. Despite this fact, the principals of some companies wishing to sell seem to feel they should obtain a price of 20 to 30 times earnings. Accordingly, the prospective acquirer often has his work cut out to convince an optimistic seller of the real value of his business and should be fortified with industry and stock market statistics to support his offering price.

Prices of Initial Public Offering

Valuation criteria and information on 200 initial public offerings, discussed in Chapter 4, are pertinent to the valuation of companies for purposes of acquisition or merger. During the late 1950's and until the stock market decline in May 1962, an unprecedented number of companies had their first public stock offerings. Many of these issues sold at prices that were in no way supported by current or reasonably foreseeable earnings or other fundamental indexes of value. The offering prices of such stocks, during this period, influenced asking prices of companies for acquisition purposes, and many acquirers later found that they had greatly overpaid for what they received. A similar situation built up during the years 1967 to 1969 to an even greater extent.

Arriving at a Fair Price

Ideally, an acquisition or merger price in terms of cash or securities is fair if both acquirer and seller benefit from the transaction. As some experts have put it, in a successful business combination there should be synergism. That is to say, the resultant effect of the combination should be greater than that of the two companies taken independently. Implicit in this statement is the view that a combination of managerial skills, marketing techniques, production facilities, and research and development will produce exceptional results. However, on the basis of such purported synergism, a number of mergers have not worked out very well. In fact, one of the principal reasons for the increase in conglomerate mergers during the late 1960's is that a combination of financial resources of companies in itself appears to have been the main criterion for a so-called "successful" merger.

As indicated, a purchase price in terms of cash or cash equivalent (notes or bonds), or an exchange of securities in a business combination, is dependent upon a number of factors, some susceptible to evaluation and some not. As an illustration of the breadth of this problem, different prices could be offered for the same company, and each be fair in the following varying circumstances:

1. A *cash offer* could be higher than that proposed in an exchange of securities because the purchaser would recover part of the price paid through reductions in federal income taxes resulting from a stepped-up tax basis of assets acquired. Also, a seller generally would require a higher price in a cash deal than in an exchange of securities because of the immediate income tax consequences.

2. An *exchange of securities offer* of a company in a glamour industry whose stock was selling at a very high price–earnings ratio could be much more generous than one whose stock was selling on a conservative basis relative to earnings and dividend yield.

3. A *company in an industry allied with that of the prospective seller,* whose management knew the value and potential of a company's products, might be willing to pay a top price because of the ability to integrate operations of the seller and increase sales and profits with the combined existing manufacturing and marketing facilities. Conversely, duplicate facilities may be eliminated in such a deal with resultant savings.

4. An *offer of an investor solely for the purpose of putting his funds to work* without any intention of exercising influence on the management of the company would ordinarily be conservative, as he would expect a return on such an investment to be better than in a blue chip stock or mutual fund.

5. Last but not least, the accounting treatment required to be followed in a business combination, which treatment depends upon the type of consideration offered by the acquirer, and his success in obtaining the requisite number of shares of the sought-after company, will affect the offering price. This matter is discussed and illustrated in Chapter 9.

Additional Contingent Price for Acquisition

At times companies cannot agree on a fixed price in cash or capital stock. This problem may arise where a company being acquired has an unstable earnings history, or an operating loss carryover, which may be available for federal tax purposes, or where benefit has not yet been realized from recent additions to product lines or changes in operations or marketing. This problem may be solved by agreeing on a basic price, with additional contingent amounts to be paid over a period upon the fulfillment of certain conditions. However, under current accounting rules, additional contingent consideration would negate pooling-of-interests accounting treatment of a business combination.

COMPARATIVE STUDY OF BUSINESS COMBINATIONS

As indicated in Chapter 8, the number of acquisitions and mergers consummated in recent years generally has been accelerating. Also, there have been relatively more transactions involving substantial consideration, in terms of capital stock or cash and debt securities.

In order to determine valuation and other related data on acquisitions and mergers, a study was made of selected transactions consummated from January 1, 1962, to December 31, 1968. The data thus obtained are summarized in Tables 12–1 through 12–3 on pages 346–59. These data generally are in chronological order, by the months in which the transactions were announced, and are coded numerically with the notes and names of the companies listed on pages 360–69, following the tables.

The initial screening in the study covered over 10,000 business combinations reported during the period in "Announcements of Mergers and Acquisitions" published monthly by the National Industrial Conference Board. Based on the initial review, approximately 1,700 acquisitions and mergers, in which the seller's total assets were over $5,000,000, were segregated for further study into groups ranging in size by tens of millions up to $100,000,000. The final group covered combinations where the seller's total assets exceeded $10,000,000.

A random selection was made from each group. For the 500 business combinations remaining, a comprehensive review of available information was made. Published data utilized for this purpose included Moody's Investors Service, Standard & Poor's Corporation Record, published annual reports to stockholders, proxy statements and prospectuses, listing applications to the several stock exchanges, *The New York Times, The Wall Street Journal*, National Stock Summary, Standard & Poor's Stock Guide, Bank and Quotation Record, and Moody's and Standard & Poor's Dividend Records. Also, the record of business combinations consummated during 1968 shown in *Mergers and Acquisitions* was utilized for that year.

In addition to the 204 business combinations listed in Tables 12–1 to 12–3, information was developed on 88 transactions involving the issuance of convertible preferred stock in whole or in part by the acquirers. These qualified as poolings of interest for accounting purposes during the period of the study but would not do so under the rules applying to business combinations initiated after October 31, 1970. While these combinations involving the issuance of preferred stock will not be individually listed, statistics derived from them are of interest and are commented on in this chapter.

From the sources given above, sufficient information was developed for reporting on the 204 business combinations listed in the following tables:

Table		Number
12–1	Statistics on Selected Business Combinations involving the issuance of voting capital stock of the acquirer, or surviving company in the case of merger	142
12–2	Statistics on selected corporate purchases for cash or cash equivalent	37
12–3	Statistics on Selected Business Combinations involving a partial purchase for cash, and subsequent acquisition of remaining interest by exchange of voting capital stock	25
	Total	204

Business Combinations Involving Common Stock

Among other things, Table 12–1 shows per-share premium or discount paid by the acquirer relative to equivalent figures of the seller, for market values, earnings, dividends, and net assets. In making these statistical comparisons, it is not intended to imply that they show the entire "cause and effect" of the acquisitions and mergers, because in many cases they were consummated because of expected future benefits to be derived as a result of the combinations.

For purposes of comparison of market values of the seller's stock with that of the acquirer's, prices were used at dates approximately two months prior to the first public announcements of the combinations, as it was evident that market prices subsequent to announcements were generally influenced by the proposed transactions. Where market prices were not available two months prior to announcements, quotations were used at dates closest thereto. For the other statistics in the tables, the figures used generally were those reported for the latest fiscal year prior to the business combination.

Market Values. As might be expected, in the 142 deals involving the issuance of capital stock, the acquiring company generally paid a premium in terms of market value of the seller's stock as follows: premiums 120, discounts 20, even exchange 2.

The general pattern of premiums above market values, paid by the acquirers, was not as clearly discernible as in the case of cash tender offers. Although a number were in excess of 50% the median premium above market of the 120 companies was 22%. Discounts were generally modest, the median being 12%, and undoubtedly resulted from using the arbitrary pre-merger time period for determining market prices, as described above.

Earnings. The acquirer generally benefited consolidated earnings as a result of the 142 acquisitions. In 85 cases earnings were acquired at discounts, in 56 at premiums, and in 1 at an even exchange.

Included in the totals were some companies operating at a loss. This situation applied to acquired companies in 6 cases, to acquirers in 3, and in 1 case to both the acquirer and the acquired company.

Dividends. Increased dividends appeared to be a definite inducement to stockholders of the 142 acquired companies to enter into such deals. In 82 cases the sellers received higher dividends, in 44 lower, and in 16 an even exchange.

Included in the increased dividend group were 25 cases where sellers had not been on a dividend-paying basis, and, in the "even exchange" category, generally neither the acquirer nor the seller had been paying dividends.

Net Assets. Net assets do not generally have significance in valuing a going industrial or commercial enterprise where business combinations are effected by an exchange of capital stocks, and accounted for under the "pooling of interests" concept. However, there are cases where an acquiring company may not be too strong financially, and the business combination will give it the use of funds not fully employed, or make available additional borrowing power of the absorbed company. For any persons who may be interested, comparative per-share figures of net assets are shown in Table 12–1.

Corporate Purchases

Table 12–2 contains statistics on 37 corporate purchases, 35 of which were for cash and 2 for convertible debentures. In all but 3 cases, the purchasers acquired all or substantially all of the net assets of the companies "taken over." In 26 cases the price paid for the acquisition exceeded the net assets of the company acquired, as reported for the latest fiscal year-end. In 6, the net assets acquired exceeded the purchase price, and in 5 they were substantially the same. The relationship of the cash, or equivalent consideration given, to net tangible assets acquired is important in a purchase. To the extent that the purchased cost cannot be allocated to tangible assets, or intangible assets such as patents, trademarks, copyrights and franchises, which have a definite tax life, goodwill arises. The technical aspects of accounting for goodwill are discussed in Chapter 9.

The acquiring companies showed return on net worth, based on their latest fiscal year reports prior to the purchase, ranging from 2% to 38%. In only 6 cases did these companies purchase companies or interests therein for a better return on the purchase price than they were obtaining in their own operations, and in 30 cases at a lesser return. In 1 case, the return was the same.

The percentage of net income of the acquired companies applicable to the purchase prices ranged from 2% to 13% with a median of 6%. One company acquired was operating at a loss.

Acquisitions for Cash and Capital Stock

Table 12–3 contains statistics on 25 business combinations involving partial purchases for cash, of the sought-after companies, and a subsequent acquisition of remaining interests by an exchange of capital stocks. The initial acquisitions, which may have been made in one or more transactions, ranged from a low of a 5% interest up to a high of 90%, the median figure being 47%. In 14 cases, the relative cost of the remaining interest acquired, based on the market value of securities issued on or about the effective date of the merger, was higher, and in 11 cases lower.

TABLE 12-1 Statistics on Selected Business Combinations Involving the Issua◼
(January 1, 1962,◼

Acq. or Merger	First Public Announcement	Market Price per Share Two Months Prior to First Public Announcement		Ratio of Common Shares of Acquirer for Shares of Seller	Earnings per Share— Latest Fiscal Year	
		Acquirer	Seller		Acquirer	Selle◼
1	Dec. 1961	59¼	20 (d)	0.525 for 1	2.64	.0◼
2	Feb. 1962	25¼	20⅝	5 for 7	1.20	1.1◼
3	Apr. 1962	28½	13	0.68 for 1	1.01	(.1◼
4	July 1962	39⅝	10	35 for 100	2.14	1.1
5	Aug. 1962	38¼	17½	7 for 8	1.63	(.2◼
6	Jan. 1963	26⅞	27	1 for 1	2.16	2.4◼
7	Nov. 1962	37⅞	27¾ (d)	$\frac{9}{10}$ for 1	2.01	2.1◼
8	Oct. 1962	34⅞	4¾ (d)	1.02 for 4	3.62	.5◼
9	May 1963	21¾	15⅞ (d)	1 for 1	1.37	2.9◼
10	Sept. 1963	74⅜	13⅜	0.17 for 1	3.36	.6◼
11	July 1963	70	31⅜	1 for 1.75	3.29	1.4◼
12	July 1963	44½	30⅝	6 for 10	2.04	1.1◼
13 (b)	Nov. 1963	50¼	31¾	7 for 10	4.56	1.0◼
14 (b)	Sept. 1963	51½	13¾	1 for 4.5	1.92	.2◼
15	Aug. 1963	23⅜	26⅜	1$\frac{3}{10}$ for 1	1.06	1.5◼
16	Nov. 1963	45¼	5⅛	1 for 9	2.60	.3◼
17	Sept. 1963	35	9¾	1 for 4.335 (c)	1.90	.3◼
18	Jan. 1964	103	18	1 for 5.5	3.78	1.2◼
19 (b)	Mar. 1964	6	12½	4½ for 1	(.19)	(.7◼
20	Sept. 1963	45¾	18⅝	1 for 2	1.97	1.1◼
21	Apr. 1964	44¼	47	1 for 1	3.89	3.0◼
22 (b)	Nov. 1963	5⅜	9⅝	1½ for 1	.29	(2.4◼
23	Aug. 1964	45	9½	1 for 4	1.85	.7◼
24	Oct. 1964	72⅜	41⅛	2 for 3	3.26	2.4◼
25	Aug. 1964	45	5⅞	1 for 7.514	2.56	.7◼
26	July 1964	12⅛	10⅞	1 for 1	.57	.7◼
27	June 1964	43½	2⅜	1 for 10	1.40	(.64
28	Sept. 1964	62⅜	8¾	1 for 5.66	2.81	.6◼
29	Nov. 1964	29½	20	7 for 10	2.55	1.5◼
30	Dec. 1964	55	21	0.51988 for 1	3.22	2.1◼
31	Jan. 1964	28¾	1⅜ (d)	1 for 7.53	1.79	.03
32	Dec. 1963	453¾	29	1 for 13.814	10.45	.74
33	Jan. 1965	31⅜	29⅞	9 for 10	2.75	7.93
34	Feb. 1965	42½	16¼	1 for 2.25	3.35	1.31
35	Nov. 1964	22¾	5⅞	1 for 4	1.60	.49
36	July 1965	45⅞	30⅞	1 for 1	2.26	2.77

NA = not available.

* See Notes and Key to Corporate Identities, pp. 360–69.

346

of Voting Capital Stock of the Acquirer, or Surviving Company, in the Case of a Merger
December 31, 1968)*

Annual Rate of Dividends per Share		Net Assets per Share—Latest Fiscal Year		Per Cent of Premium or (Discount) Paid by Acquirer per Share Relative to Equivalent Figures of Seller				
				Market Price Prior to Public Announce-	Latest Fiscal Year			Acq. or
Acquirer	Seller	Acquirer	Seller	ment	Earnings	Dividends	Net Assets	Merger
.50 (e)	.80	29.17	44.77	56	6,830	(67)	(66)	1
.40 (e)	.40	15.16	8.89	(13)	(26)	(27)	22	2
.40	.10	62.28	16.43	49	—	170	158	3
1.60	.20	24.11	12.21	39	(32)	180	(31)	4
.74	— (e)	10.58	7.59	91	—	—	22	5
1.00 (e)	1.02½	12.01	29.30	—	(11)	(2)	(59)	6
1.00 (e)	1.25	19.87	34.10	23	(17)	(28)	(48)	7
1.60	.20	50.87	6.59	87	77	105	97	8
.90	.50	9.33	20.82	37	(54)	80	(55)	9
—	—	20.69	4.04	(5)	(12)	—	(13)	10
3.10	.40 (e)	37.90	13.43	27	29	343	61	11
1.00 (e)	.60	15.18	11.62	(13)	6	—	(22)	12
2.50	.50	90.76	73.95	11	196	250	(14)	13
.95	— (e)	12.36	5.27	(17)	87	—	(48)	14
.36	— (e)	2.86	9.81	15	(9)	—	(62)	15
2.00	—	39.83	2.79	(2)	(4)	—	59	16
1.20	.28	19.75	3.94	(17)	12	(1)	16	17
2.70	—	18.72	7.03	4	(45)	—	(52)	18
—	—	3.44	28.96	108	(8)	—	(47)	19
1.30 (e)	.55	26.09	4.33	23	(14)	18	201	20
1.80 (e)	1.80 (e)	35.81	37.63	(6)	26	—	(5)	21
—	— (e)	1.78	4.51	(16)	—	—	(41)	22
.40	.52	16.14	8.94	18	(41)	(81)	(55)	23
1.60	1.20	28.07	21.67	17	(11)	(11)	(14)	24
.50 (e)	.31	21.05	3.58	2	(53)	(77)	(22)	25
1.00	.25	9.91	9.15	11	(26)	300	8	26
—	—	5.75	1.84	83	—	—	(69)	27
1.45	— (e)	24.87	6.67	26	(26)	—	(34)	28
1.60	.55	39.34	24.58	3	17	104	12	29
1.85	.90	41.78	31.05	36	(23)	7	(30)	30
.80 (e)	.03½	12.88	2.20	178	692	204	(22)	31
4.25	.10	57.27	3.11	13	2	210	33	32
1.20	4.75	30.10	116.94	(5)	(69)	(77)	(77)	33
1.80	.75 (e)	18.98	13.08	16	14	7	(36)	34
.80	.20	27.44	3.95	(3)	(18)	—	74	35
1.10	.90	9.46	15.26	49	(18)	22	(38)	36

TABLE 12-1 (cont.) Statistics on Selected Business Combinations Involving the Issuance
(January 1, 1962, to

Acq. or Merger	First Public Announcement	Market Price per Share Two Months Prior to First Public Announcement		Ratio of Common Shares of Acquirer for Shares of Seller	Earnings per Share— Latest Fiscal Year	
		Acquirer	Seller		Acquirer	Seller
37	June 1965	$28\frac{1}{4}$	$32\frac{5}{8}$	1 for 1	1.66	2.02
38	July 1965	$76\frac{7}{8}$	$32\frac{7}{8}$	46 for 100	2.18	1.15
39	Apr. 1965	$15\frac{1}{8}$	$5\frac{1}{2}$	1 for 2	(.26)	.32
40	Dec. 1961	82	15	$\frac{4}{13}$ for 1	4.55	1.45
41	July 1963	$35\frac{3}{4}$	$33\frac{1}{8}$	1 for 1	4.24	1.16
42	June 1964	$19\frac{1}{8}$	$3\frac{7}{8}$ (d)	1 for 4.9	1.46	.10
43	Nov. 1963	$56\frac{1}{2}$	20	4 for 10	2.84	1.31
44	Oct. 1964	$41\frac{3}{8}$	$20\frac{1}{4}$	0.4616 for 1 (c)	1.86	1.78
45	May 1964	$5\frac{3}{4}$	$7\frac{7}{8}$	$1\frac{3}{8}$ for 1	(.43)	.69
46	May 1965	$43\frac{3}{4}$	11	0.3543 for 1	3.67	.95
47 (b)	June 1965	$12\frac{5}{8}$	$2\frac{3}{4}$	1 for 4	1.29	.29 (a)
48	Aug. 1965	$35\frac{3}{8}$	13	1 for 2.5	3.31	1.25
49	June 1965	$41\frac{3}{4}$	$8\frac{1}{4}$	1 for 3	2.83	.84 (a)
50	Sept. 1965	29	11 (d)	1 for 2.5	2.89	1.30
51	Oct. 1965	$35\frac{3}{8}$	24	2 for 3	1.66	1.44
52	Oct. 1965	50	17 (d)	0.3535 for 1	2.49	1.21
53	June 1965	$53\frac{7}{8}$	$16\frac{1}{4}$	0.3308 for 1	2.49	.83
54	Jan. 1966	$76\frac{1}{2}$	4	1 for 8	2.61	.27
55	Jan. 1966	$30\frac{3}{8}$	48	2 for 1	1.71	3.40
56	Aug. 1965	27	$3\frac{1}{2}$	0.1883 for 1	1.62	.13
57	Jan. 1966	41	$29\frac{1}{2}$	$\frac{7}{10}$ for 1	2.42	2.00
58	June 1966	$35\frac{1}{4}$	$29\frac{3}{4}$	1 for 1.04	.72	1.25
59	July 1966	$48\frac{1}{2}$	9	0.2325 for 1	2.49	.72
60	May 1966	$90\frac{1}{4}$	$12\frac{7}{8}$	1 for 6.0382 (c)	4.22	.88
61	Aug. 1966	$38\frac{7}{8}$	24	$\frac{3}{4}$ for 1	1.87	2.58
62	June 1966	$71\frac{1}{4}$	$19\frac{3}{4}$	0.3845 for 1	3.02	1.48
63	Sept. 1966	$28\frac{7}{8}$	$7\frac{7}{8}$	1 for 2.5	2.51	1.25
64	July 1966	$49\frac{3}{4}$	$32\frac{1}{2}$	1 for 1	3.25	3.63
65	June 1966	$18\frac{3}{4}$	$17\frac{1}{4}$	$\frac{9}{10}$ for 1	.98	1.30
66	Sept. 1966	$46\frac{1}{4}$	$14\frac{1}{4}$	0.442 for 1	2.79	1.56
67	Apr. 1967	$18\frac{5}{8}$	$13\frac{1}{2}$	0.8688 Class B for 1 (c)	1.42	1.47 (a)
68	May 1967	36	15	$\frac{1}{2}$ for 1	2.08	1.23 (a)
69	Mar. 1967	$32\frac{3}{8}$	$10\frac{3}{4}$	0.4347 for 1	2.14	1.17
70	May 1967	$17\frac{3}{4}$	11	0.4953 for 1	2.11	1.60
71	Apr. 1967	$58\frac{5}{8}$	$12\frac{1}{8}$	1 for $3\frac{7}{16}$	2.21	1.81
72	July 1967	16 (d)	$12\frac{1}{4}$ (d)	$2\frac{1}{4}$ for 1	1.51	2.23

NA = not available.

* See Notes and Key to Corporate Identities, pp. 360-69.

of Voting Capital Stock of the Acquirer, or Surviving Company, in the Case of a Merger December 31, 1968)*

Annual Rate of Dividends per Share		Net Assets per Share—Latest Fiscal Year		Per Cent of Premium or (Discount) Paid by Acquirer per Share Relative to Equivalent Figures of Seller				
				Market Price Prior to Public Announce-	Latest Fiscal Year			Acq. or
Acquirer	Seller	Acquirer	Seller	ment	Earnings	Dividends	Net Assets	Merger
.75	.85	14.18	16.95	(13)	(18)	(12)	(16)	37
1.05	.67$\frac{1}{2}$ (e)	7.97	3.62	8	(13)	28	1	38
—	—	14.17	6.57	38	—	—	8	39
2.20	1.00	50.88	32.90	68	(3)	(32)	(52)	40
1.20	1.62$\frac{1}{2}$	27.89	36.99	8	266	(26)	(25)	41
—	.05	7.73	3.62	1	198	(100)	(56)	42
1.60	.60 (e)	22.08	10.07	13	(13)	7	(12)	43
1.20	—	37.90	9.94	(5)	(52)	—	76	44
—	—	10.91	5.34	—	—	—	181	45
2.00	.40	29.35	4.51	28	37	78	131	46
.30	—	9.93	1.19 (a)	15	10	—	108	47
1.25	.15	30.69	12.01	9	6	233	2	48
1.50	— (e)	31.17	8.62 (a)	69	12	—	21	49
1.60	.38	20.17	NA	5	(11)	68	NA	50
.52$\frac{1}{2}$ (e)	.12$\frac{1}{2}$	11.61	3.81	(2)	(23)	180	103	51
1.35	.60	19.84	9.16	4	(27)	(20)	(23)	52
1.35	—	19.84	5.32	10	(1)	—	19	53
1.10	—	20.07	6.06	139	22	—	(59)	54
.57$\frac{1}{2}$	1.20 (e)	11.10	NA	27	1	(4)	NA	55
.30	—	7.24	4.27	45	138	—	(68)	56
1.20	.78	18.29	11.44	(3)	(15)	8	12	57
—	— (e)	13.47	7.55	14	(45)	—	72	58
1.15	.30	16.57	1.18	25	(20)	(11)	226	59
1.77$\frac{1}{2}$	— (e)	31.85	6.66	16	(21)	—	(21)	60
.95	1.20	12.33	38.29	22	(46)	(41)	(76)	61
1.20	.40 (e)	23.77	4.99	39	(22)	15	83	62
1.30 (e)	.20	33.09	NA	47	(20)	160	NA	63
1.60	1.75	39.88	33.17	53	(10)	(9)	20	64
.20	.40	21.72	NA	(2)	(32)	(55)	NA	65
1.17$\frac{1}{2}$	.24 (e)	26.34	6.19	44	(21)	117	88	66
.40 (e)	.65	8.48	5.54 (a)	20	(16)	(47)	33	67
—	.30	13.57	NA	20	(15)	(100)	NA	68
1.20	.60	17.07	5.72	31	(21)	(13)	30	69
.60	.60	14.64	4.97	(20)	(35)	(50)	46	70
.47$\frac{1}{2}$	—	18.80	5.08	31	(67)	—	—	71
.33	.50	6.70	21.79	194	52	50	(31)	72

TABLE 12-1 (cont.)   Statistics on Selected Business Combinations Involving the Issuance
(January 1, 1962, to

Acq. or Merger	First Public Announcement	Market Price per Share Two Months Prior to First Public Announcement		Ratio of Common Shares of Acquirer for Shares of Seller	Earnings per Share— Latest Fiscal Year	
		Acquirer	Seller		Acquirer	Seller
73	Apr. 1967	75	23 (d)	1 for $2\frac{1}{4}$	5.52	2.31
74	Sept. 1967	54	$21\frac{5}{8}$	0.4583 for 1	3.26	2.36
75	Aug. 1967	55	$10\frac{3}{4}$	0.28 for 1	2.01	.67
76	Sept. 1967	$77\frac{1}{4}$	18	0.33 for 1	2.74	.69
77	Sept. 1967	$46\frac{1}{2}$	$15\frac{3}{8}$	1 for 2	2.06	1.16
78	July 1967	$29\frac{5}{8}$	$3\frac{1}{8}$ (d)	1 for 7	.97	.22
79 (b)	Sept. 1965	28	$31\frac{3}{4}$	1 for 1	2.20	3.00
80	Sept. 1965	$5\frac{3}{8}$	$17\frac{1}{8}$	5 for 2	.50	1.25
81	Nov. 1965	$23\frac{1}{4}$	$7\frac{1}{2}$	1 for 3	1.52	.44
82	Mar. 1966	$38\frac{3}{4}$	$42\frac{3}{4}$	$1\frac{4}{10}$ for 1	3.05	1.92
83	Jan. 1966	45	$17\frac{1}{2}$	0.62 for 1	1.73	.76
84	Mar. 1966	74	14	1 for $3\frac{1}{2}$	2.61	.32
85	Apr. 1966	$51\frac{1}{4}$	$10\frac{1}{8}$	1 for 3	1.42	1.13
86 (b)	Apr. 1966	$5\frac{1}{4}$	$4\frac{1}{4}$	0.85 for 1	(2.87)	.32 (a)
87	July 1966	$29\frac{1}{2}$	$21\frac{1}{4}$	1 for 1	4.28	2.72
88	June 1966	$23\frac{5}{8}$	$18\frac{7}{8}$	1 Class A for 1	1.95	1.41
89	July 1966	$24\frac{1}{2}$	21	$\frac{9}{10}$ for 1	1.10	1.34
90	Dec. 1966	$41\frac{1}{4}$	$25\frac{3}{8}$	1 for 1	2.14	1.74
91	Jan. 1967	$24\frac{7}{8}$	$34\frac{7}{8}$	$1\frac{3}{4}$ for 1	2.66	(5.23)
92	Mar. 1967	$27\frac{5}{8}$	$38\frac{1}{4}$	2.05 for 1	1.53	4.16
93	Jan. 1967	$35\frac{1}{4}$	43	$1\frac{3}{10}$ for 1	5.84	5.30
94	Nov. 1966	$34\frac{1}{4}$	58	$2\frac{1}{10}$ for 1	1.78	4.46
95	Feb. 1967	$44\frac{7}{8}$	18	0.4325 for 1	2.49	1.35
96	Mar. 1967	$20\frac{1}{8}$	$5\frac{3}{4}$	1 for 4	2.45	(.39)
97	May 1967	$47\frac{3}{4}$	$33\frac{3}{4}$	0.8411 for 1	1.42	1.94
98	May 1967	38	$13\frac{3}{4}$	0.495 for 1	4.39	3.07
99	Mar. 1967	48	27	1 for 1.4	5.75	3.61
100	May 1967	$22\frac{3}{8}$	$10\frac{7}{8}$	$\frac{7}{10}$ for 1	.93	1.52
101	Mar. 1967	$35\frac{1}{4}$	$23\frac{3}{8}$	1 for 2	1.76	1.35
102 (b)	Feb. 1967	$17\frac{1}{4}$	$11\frac{1}{8}$	4 for 5	1.65	2.02
103	Aug. 1967	$62\frac{1}{4}$	33	$\frac{7}{10}$ for 1	2.16	1.85
104	May 1967	$124\frac{1}{2}$	$32\frac{1}{4}$	0.43 for 1	2.05	.84
105	Dec. 1967	$44\frac{1}{2}$	20	1 for 2	.65	.23
106	Jan. 1968	$48\frac{1}{8}$	25 (d)	0.55 for 1	3.29	1.69
107	Jan. 1968	$39\frac{3}{8}$	$28\frac{1}{2}$ (d)	0.785 for 1	2.62	1.77

NA = not available.
* See Notes and Key to Corporate Identities, pp. 360-69.

350

of Voting Capital Stock of the Acquirer, or Surviving Company, in the Case of a Merger December 31, 1968)*

Annual Rate of Dividends per Share		Net Assets per Share—Latest Fiscal Year		Per Cent of Premium or (Discount) Paid by Acquirer per Share Relative to Equivalent Figures of Seller				
				Market Price Prior to Public Announce-	Latest Fiscal Year			Acq. or
Acquirer	Seller	Acquirer	Seller	ment	Earnings	Dividends	Net Assets	Merger
5.00	1.00	56.01	33.41	45	6	122	(26)	73
1.50	.50	20.29	5.64	14	(37)	37	65	74
.71½ (e)	.10	12.20	3.57	48	(16)	100	(4)	75
1.27½	.10	9.76	6.83	42	30	320	(53)	76
.40	—	12.93	7.19	51	(11)	—	(10)	77
—	—	4.29	2.19	35	(36)	—	(72)	78
2.10	2.10	14.00	23.39	(12)	(27)	50	(40)	79
.10	.40	8.64	22.81	(22)	—	(37)	(5)	80
1.00	—	12.44	5.08	6	15	—	(18)	81
1.65	2.28	22.85	33.93	27	122	1	(6)	82
.70 (e)	.10	9.75	9.27	59	41	334	(35)	83
1.10	—	20.07	4.99	51	133	—	15	84
— (e)	.20	18.00	6.39	69	(58)	(100)	(6)	85
—	—	1.58	.98 (a)	5	—	—	37	86
1.70	1.00	14.93	22.03	40	57	70	(32)	87
—	.22½	11.75	6.46	25	38	(100)	79	88
.30	.25	14.85	7.96	5	(26)	8	68	89
1.16	.91	15.62	13.90	62	23	27	12	90
.60	.75 (e)	11.25	33.18	25	—	40	(41)	91
1.00	1.35 (e)	13.21	27.35	48	(25)	52	(1)	92
.25	.90	24.95	31.21	6	43	(64)	4	93
.95	1.25 (e)	6.84	34.15	24	(16)	60	(58)	94
1.15	.26	16.60	9.79	8	(20)	91	(27)	95
.60	—	18.06	4.69	(12)	—	—	(4)	96
.43	.20	8.33	10.14	20	(39)	81	(31)	97
1.45 (e)	.64	17.45	13.28	41	(29)	12	(35)	98
2.80	1.50	40.63	17.17	27	14	33	69	99
.64 (e)	—	7.63	10.07	44	(57)	—	(47)	100
.60	—	12.60	6.14	(25)	(35)	—	3	101
1.00	.75	12.51	20.61	24	(35)	7	(51)	102
— (e)	— (e)	16.64	7.27	32	(18)	—	60	103
—	—	14.07	2.51	66	5	—	141	104
—	—	9.29	3.49	10	41	—	33	105
2.20	—	35.93	6.53	5	7	—	203	106
1.60	.40	16.08	13.94	8	10	214	(9)	107

TABLE 12-1 (cont.) Statistics on Selected Business Combinations Involving the Issuance

(January 1, 1962, to

Acq. or Merger	First Public Announcement	Market Price per Share Two Months Prior to First Public Announcement		Ratio of Common Shares of Acquirer for Shares of Seller	Earnings per Share— Latest Fiscal Year	
		Acquirer	Seller		Acquirer	Seller
108	Jan. 1968	86	56 (d)	0.76 for 1	2.97	3.30
109	Mar. 1968	$53\frac{1}{2}$	$16\frac{1}{2}$ (d)	$\frac{1}{3}$ for 1	2.76	1.41
110	Feb. 1968	119	30	0.285 for 1	4.06	1.06
111	Dec. 1967	109	$36\frac{1}{4}$	0.39266 for 1	2.50	1.27
112	Dec. 1967	109	$10\frac{1}{8}$	1 for 9	2.50	.55
113	Apr. 1968	$78\frac{1}{2}$	43 (d)	0.715 for 1	1.34	1.94
114	Feb. 1968	$33\frac{1}{4}$	$25\frac{5}{8}$	0.875 for 1	3.45	1.50
115	Apr. 1968	$30\frac{1}{2}$	$13\frac{3}{4}$ (d)	1 for 2	2.27	.32
116	Feb. 1968	88	39	0.6 for 1	3.45	3.16
117	Jan. 1968	$46\frac{1}{4}$	10 (d)	1 for 4	1.92	.56
118	June 1968 (p)	$40\frac{3}{8}$	$24\frac{1}{2}$ (d)	1 for 1.4	3.65	2.65
119	May 1968	$51\frac{5}{8}$	$14\frac{3}{4}$	0.28 for 1	2.49	1.26
120	Apr. 1968	$78\frac{1}{2}$	$21\frac{1}{2}$ (d)	0.43 for 1 (q)	4.06	2.54
121	Feb. 1968	$54\frac{5}{8}$	30	0.62 for 1	2.12	2.86
122	Feb. 1968	$30\frac{1}{2}$	$10\frac{1}{2}$	0.3 for 1	1.34	.70
123	Feb. 1968	30	23	0.825 for 1	1.92	1.16
124	Apr. 1968	$30\frac{1}{4}$ (d)	$8\frac{7}{8}$	1 for 3	2.40	.87
125	Apr. 1968	$49\frac{7}{8}$	$15\frac{3}{4}$ (d)	0.386 for 1	2.11	1.01
126	May 1968	$26\frac{3}{4}$	$18\frac{1}{4}$	0.9 for 1	1.19	1.04
127	Oct. 1967	$38\frac{7}{8}$	35 (d)	1 for 1	2.12	1.37
128	Aug. 1968	$44\frac{1}{2}$	$31\frac{3}{4}$ (d)	0.7875 for 1	3.27	1.24
129	July 1968	27	$12\frac{3}{4}$	1 for 2	1.61	.90
130	Mar. 1968	$52\frac{1}{2}$	$20\frac{1}{4}$	0.495 for 1	4.14	1.91
131	Mar. 1968	$295\frac{1}{4}$	$32\frac{1}{2}$	0.1525 for 1	4.43	.95
132	June 1968	39	70 (d)	2 for 1	2.16	3.45
133	June 1968	46	32 (d)	1.22138 for 1	3.04	4.04
134	Sept. 1968	$135\frac{5}{8}$	$62\frac{3}{8}$	1 for 2	3.96	2.35
135	June 1968	62	58	1 for 1	5.22	3.16
136	Sept. 1968	59	$40\frac{3}{4}$	0.76923 for 1	3.05	5.04
137	Oct. 1968	$29\frac{1}{4}$	29	1 for 1	1.79	1.27
138	Dec. 1968	$48\frac{1}{4}$	$20\frac{7}{8}$	1 for 2	4.40	(1.12)
139	Dec. 1968	$61\frac{1}{2}$	$21\frac{3}{4}$	0.44 for 1	3.02	.60
140	Apr. 1968	$40\frac{1}{4}$	$21\frac{5}{8}$ (d)	1 for 1.7	3.65	1.02
141	July 1968	$51\frac{1}{8}$	48 (d)	1.1 for 1	2.35	1.92
142	July 1968	$41\frac{3}{8}$	25	$\frac{2}{3}$ for 1	1.46	1.74

NA = not available.

* See Notes and Key to Corporate Identities, pp. 360–69.

of Voting Capital Stock of the Acquirer, or Surviving Company, in the Case of a Merger
December 31, 1968)*

					Per Cent of Premium or (Discount) Paid by Acquirer per Share Relative to Equivalent Figures of Seller			
Annual Rate of Dividends per Share		Net Assets per Share—Latest Fiscal Year		Market Price Prior to Public Announce-	Latest Fiscal Year			Acq. or
Acquirer	Seller	Acquirer	Seller	ment	Earnings	Dividends	Net Assets	Merger
1.335	2.10	16.23	12.17	17	(32)	52	1	108
−	.20	22.63	4.47	7	(35)	(100)	69	109
1.35	.50	33.68	7.64	13	9	(23)	26	110
(e)	(e)	14.52	5.45	18	(23)	−	5	111
(e)	.15	14.52	7.29	34	(50)	(100)	(78)	112
.425	.925	9.07	21.22	30	(51)	(67)	(69)	113
1.80	.66	19.27	6.78	14	101	139	149	114
.24	−	17.99	3.83	11	255	−	135	115
1.40	1.10	24.31	28.92	35	(34)	(24)	(50)	116
−	−	12.16	4.51	16	(14)	−	(30)	117
1.60	.575	18.02	16.31	18	(2)	99	(20)	118
1.66	.52	16.60	4.92	5	(45)	(11)	(6)	119
1.00	1.44	26.96	17.11	57	(31)	(70)	(32)	120
1.10	.69	13.81	14.58	12	(54)	(2)	(41)	121
.70	.12 (e)	6.26	7.72	(13)	(43)	75	(76)	122
.30	.60	7.46	6.37	8	37	(59)	(3)	123
1.20	.20	7.38	4.91	14	(8)	100	(50)	124
1.60	.60	15.61	16.77	22	(19)	3	(64)	125
−	.25	36.89	13.89	32	3	(100)	140	126
1.31	.65	16.50	7.76	11	55	102	113	127
.85	−	13.89	10.05	10	108	−	9	128
.63¾	−	16.81	5.21	7	(11)	−	61	129
2.25	1.00	61.41	19.81	28	7	11	53	130
1.10	.72	16.76	10.51	39	(29)	(77)	(76)	131
1.70	2.60	23.98	42.42	11	25	30	13	132
1.25	1.85	15.13	24.11	76	(8)	(17)	(23)	133
1.20	.20	43.90	15.35	9	(16)	200	43	134
4.00	1.35	36.01	40.12	7	65	196	(11)	135
−	.30	16.13	16.98	11	(43)	(100)	(27)	136
−	.60	9.46	13.87	1	41	(100)	(32)	137
2.50	.10	48.40	13.12	16	−	115 (o)	84	138
1.10	−	39.96	6.26	24	121	−	181	139
1.60	.10	18.44	4.90	9	110	(6)	121	140
1.00	.40	36.78	18.92	17	35	175	114	141
.40	.60	5.69	9.08	10	(44)	(56)	(58)	142

TABLE 12-2 Statistics on Selected
(January 1, 1962, to

		Acquirer			Seller
Acquisition or Merger	Date	Earnings per Share— Latest Fiscal Year Prior to Purchase	Net Assets per Share— Latest Fiscal Year Prior to Purchase	Per Cent Return on Net Assets	Net Assets at Latest Fiscal Year Prior to Purchase
143	Apr. 1963	.15	8.58	2%	$ 47,087,234
144	May 1963	1.84	15.86	12	4,780,347
145	Aug. 1964	.75	4.64	16	NA
146	Oct. 1965	3.06	22.95	13	12,392,251
147	Sept. 1965	2.58	31.71	8	28,032,401
148	Feb. 1966	4.47	36.93	12	49,174,212
149	Apr. 1965	1.41	9.13	15	1,803,536
150	Oct. 1965	1.37	32.35	4	6,152,358 (a)
151	Dec. 1965	.60	24.65	2	10,001,179
152	Feb. 1966	3.10	30.12	10	6,227,881
153	Apr. 1966	1.62	7.24	22	4,713,347 (a)
154	Mar. 1966	2.15	15.31	14	8,085,282
155	Apr. 1966	.97	6.53	15	1,845,831
156	Aug. 1966	1.49	21.67	7	5,852,934
157	Sept. 1966	2.03	5.73	35	4,711,514
158	Mar. 1967	3.01	26.05	12	4,778,692
159	June 1967	1.21	13.89	9	7,293,469
160	Aug. 1967	.75	22.13	3	3,710,601
161	Aug. 1967	2.10	15.13	14	7,388,627
162	Nov. 1967	1.94	17.35	11	9,459,209
163	Dec. 1967	1.91	5.08	38	5,578,220 (a)
164	Jan. 1968	1.23	7.78	16	3,813,526
165	Mar. 1966	2.42	12.92	20	13,330,193 (a)
166	Sept. 1966	3.08	14.37	21	20,221,091
167	Apr. 1967	2.33	9.71	24	46,807,564
168	May 1967	1.01	25.37	4	27,487,300
169	July 1967	2.84	16.54	17	68,495,375
170	Nov. 1967	2.51	17.77	14	60,195,345
171	Mar. 1968	1.56	9.68	16	6,273,806
172	Mar. 1968	3.78	27.75	14	179,460,000
173	Mar. 1968	1.08	9.20	12	22,056,022
174	June 1968	3.24	30.72	10	10,462,580
175	Sept. 1968	1.31	6.44	20	11,825,914
176	Aug. 1968	1.74	10.30	17	17,718,296
177	Dec. 1968	2.66	18.07	15	50,482,832
178	Oct. 1968	1.36	13.78	10	14,380,383
179	July 1968	3.17	25.13	8	24,330,489

NA = not available.
* See Notes and Key to Corporate Identities, pp. 360-69.

Corporate Purchases for Cash
December 31, 1968)*

		Seller				
Approx. Price Paid for Acquisition	Per Cent Acquired	Net Income—Latest Fiscal Year Prior to Purchase	Per Cent of Net Income to Acquisition Price	Per Cent Return on Net Assets	Acquisition or Merger	
$ 90,000,000	100%	$ 3,917,195	4%	8%	143	
15,000,000	100	743,436	5	16	144	
2,400,000	100	187,087	8	NA	145	
22,000,000	100	1,513,717	7	12	146	
51,000,000	97	3,986,453	8	14	147	
63,000,000	95	5,481,211	8	10	148	
5,800,000	100	471,919	8	26	149	
18,600,000	100	1,298,228 (a)	7	20	150	
4,200,000	90	221,039	5	2	151	
11,900,000	100	679,628	6	11	152	
2,900,000	100	43,924 (a)	2	2	153	
9,000,000	100	452,222	5	6	154	
1,100,000	100	(43,782)	—	—	155	
4,000,000	100	329,487	8	6	156	
8,900,000	100	856,392	10	18	157	
8,800,000	100	675,702	8	14	158	
7,100,000	90	593,709	6	8	159	
4,400,000	100	573,074	13	14	160	
6,000,000	100	466,715	8	6	161	
11,900,000	100	770,138	6	8	162	
5,700,000	100	505,065 (a)	9	9	163	
4,600,000	66	641,214	9	17	164	
19,200,000†	100	1,826,395 (a)	10	14	165	
32,900,000	59	3,483,173	6	17	166	
70,000,000	96	5,082,141	7	11	167	
78,000,000	100	4,358,036	6	18	168	
52,700,000‡	100	4,994,616	9	7	169	
82,000,000	63	7,465,521	6	12	170	
18,130,064	90	1,043,125	6	17	171	
622,000,000	100	26,280,000	4	15	172	
46,900,000	95	2,884,015	6	13	173	
10,000,000	100	804,345	8	8	174	
42,117,560	98	2,584,316	6	22	175	
18,600,000	97	1,567,198	5	5	176	
123,800,000	96	8,357,901	7	16	177	
21,057,420	84	1,040,345	5	7	178	
24,893,280	72	1,578,963	6	6	179	

† Principal amount of 5% convertible debentures.
‡ Principal amount of $5\frac{1}{4}$% convertible debentures.

TABLE 12-3   Statistics on Selected Business Combination
Offer and Subsequent Acquisition
(January 1, 1962,

| Acq. or Merger | Date | Acquirer | | | Seller | | |
		Earnings per Share— Latest Fiscal Year Prior to Purchase	Net Assets per Share— Latest Fiscal Year Prior to Purchase	Per Cent Return on Net Assets	Approx. Price Paid for Initial Acquisition†	Per Cent Acquired	Net Assets— Latest Fiscal Year Prior to Purchase
180	11/65	(.46)	7.05	(7)%	$ 4,900	61%	$ 3,994,169
181	12/65	.60	2.60	23	5,900	59	6,033,038
182	10/67	1.40	7.55	19	7,200	44	4,525,961
183	11/67	.33	6.37	5	8,100	55	9,572,214
184	1/66	.70	19.86	4	36,600	50	83,697,817
185	1/67	6.47	28.66	23	81,500	53	121,983,033
186	1/67	.91	3.78	24	1,500	33	1,348,556
187	5/67	1.21	13.89	9	30,000	26	81,187,512
188	3/67	2.07	12.54	17	71,200	40	112,770,494
189	5/67	2.60	19.08	14	66,900	30	122,787,308
190	12/65	3.01	17.66	17	225,600	42	324,300,930
191	2/66	1.36	13.81	10	11,800	28	38,848,194
192 (f)	3/66	1.83	12.79	14	2,300 (g)	17 (g)	13,603,485
193	6/66	1.85	29.15	6	36,000	50	64,826,048

* See Notes and Key to Corporate Identities, pp. 360–69.
† 000's omitted.

volving Two-Step Transactions by Means of a Partial Cash
maining Interest by Exchange of Stock
cember 31, 1967)*

	Seller		Subsequent Acquisition of Remaining Interest				
et Income— Latest Fiscal Year Prior to Purchase	Net Income as Per Cent of Acq. Price	Eff. Date of Merger	Ratio of Common Shares of Acquirer for Shares of Seller	Approx. Market Value of Securities Issued†	Per Cent Acquired	Premium or (Discount) as Per Cent of Initial Acquisition Price	Acq. or Merger
715,797	9%	6/66	$1\frac{9}{10}$ for 1	$ 3,300	39%	5%	228
917,150	9	5/66	0.7248 $.50 Conv. pfd. for 1	3,200	41	(22)	229
1,400,009	9	10/67	0.7709 for 1	9,000	56	(2)	230
1,683,372	11	7/68	$\frac{4}{10}$ $.60 Conv. pfd. for 1	8,600	45	30	231
3,183,695	4	5/66	1 $1.50 Conv. pfd. for 1	34,100	50	(7)	232
2,904,752	8	6/67	1 $5.00 Conv. pfd. for 1.5	144,200	47	100	233
9,199	0	4/67	$\frac{7}{10}$ for 1	5,900	67	97	234
8,496,459	7	5/67	1 $1.20 Conv. pfd. for 1	90,900	74	6	235
2,058,534	7	6/67	1 $2.25 Conv. pfd. for 1	94,900	60	(11)	236
2,410,605	6	9/67	0.46 for 1	125,300	70	(20)	237
1,897,841	6	4/68	1 $4.00 Conv. pfd. for 2	618,000	58	98	238
2,892,002	7	6/67	1 $2.25 Conv. pfd. for 1	37,800	72	25	239
1,123,694	8	5/67	$2\frac{1}{3}$ $1.26 Conv. pfd. for 1	5,400	46	(13)	240
4,528,546	6	9/66	$\frac{1}{2}$ 1.66\frac{1}{4}$ Conv. pfd. plus $17.50 principal amount of $6\frac{7}{8}$% debentures for 1	15,500 18,100	50	(9)	241

TABLE 12-3 (cont.)   Statistics on Selected Business Combination
Offer and Subsequent Acquisition
(January 1, 1962,

		Acquirer			Seller		
Acq. or Merger	Date	Earnings per Share— Latest Fiscal Year Prior to Purchase	Net Assets per Share— Latest Fiscal Year Prior to Purchase	Per Cent Return on Net Assets	Approx. Price Paid for Initial Acquisition†	Per Cent Acquired	Net Assets— Latest Fiscal Year Prior to Purchase
194	9/66	1.10	9.75	11%	$ 124,000 (h)	51% (h)	$160,773,955
195	11/66	.88	11.75	7	11,200	33	53,397,381
196 (f)	3/67	3.51	17.12	21	10,900	15	60,024,885
197	3/65	4.40 (i)	98.22	4	20,300 (j)	82 (j)	29,140,431
198	6/65	2.84	18.29	16	7,800	90	6,251,510
199	6/65	1.56	12.95	12	25,000 (k)	62 (k)	36,669,944
200	8/65	3.33	28.82	12	64,000	73	79,195,387
201	12/63	1.71	12.56	14	23,000 (l)	50 (l)	22,495,578
202 (m)	10/65	1.39	27.99	5	7,800	5	308,192,107
203 (n)	4/66	3.52	40.85	9	36,600 (r)	47 (r)	89,819,533
204	8/67	2.16	16.64	13	21,000 (o)	30 (o)	31,255,918

* See Notes and Key to Corporate Identities, pp. 360–69.
† 000's omitted.

olving Two-Step Transactions by Means of a Partial Cash
naining Interest by Exchange of Stock
ember 31, 1967)*

t Income— Latest scal Year Prior to Purchase	Net Income as Per Cent of Acq. Price	Eff. Date of Merger	Ratio of Common Shares of Acquirer for Shares of Seller	Approx. Market Value of Securities Issued†	Per Cent Acquired	Premium or (Discount) as Per Cent of Initial Acquisition Price	Acq. or Merger
			Seller	**Subsequent Acquisition of Remaining Interest**			
,083,193	6%	7/67	$\frac{3}{4}$ common plus 1 $1.80 Conv. pfd. for 1	$ 48,400 / 107,300	49%	31%	242
695,899	2	12/67	$\frac{1}{2}$ common plus $\frac{1}{4}$ $3.20 Conv. pfd. for 1	29,700 / 29,700	67	161	243
,165,846	7	9/67	1 $4.75 Conv. pfd. for 3	50,700	76	(8)	244
262,353	1	9/65	$\frac{42}{100}$ $5.50 Pfd. for 1	3,700	18	(17)	245
485,112	6	7/65	1 for 1	600	10	(31)	246
2,077,269	4	5/66	1 for 1	28,000	38	83	247
7,349,880	8	4/66	1 5% Class A Pfd. for 4	17,900	27	(24)	248
1,003,839	4	5/66	$1\frac{1}{4}$ for 1	35,600	50	55	249
5,385,618	10	12/67	$\frac{6}{10}$ for 1	110,100	44	60	250
9,276,222	12	1/68	$\frac{1}{3}$ common plus 1 $1.88 Pfd. for 1 $190. prin. amt. of 6% debenture for 1 share of pfd.	45,100 / 35,500 / 6,700	53	112	251
4,839,095	7	8/67	0.08 common plus $\frac{1}{15}$ $3.00 Conv. pfd. for 1	77,500 / 35,200	70	130	252

Notes and Key to Corporate Identities—
Tables 12-1, 12-2, and 12-3

Notes

a. Latest fiscal year amounts not available. Amounts are shown for year previous.

b. Acquirer purchased a portion of the seller for an undisclosed amount prior to this transaction, as follows:

Acquisition or Merger	Per Cent Owned at Time of Transaction	Acquisition or Merger	Per Cent Owned at Time of Transaction
13	74	86	24
14	77		
19	85	102	34
22	62		
47	49		
79	26		

c. Represents weighted average as follows:

Acquisition or Merger	
17	Acquirer issued one common share for each 4 shares held by the public (727,508 shares—33%) and one common share for each 4.5 held by a family group (1,477,062 shares—67%).
44	Acquirer issued 4 common shares for each 9 shares held by the chairman of the board and major stockholder, and 4 common shares for each 8.5 shares publicly owned.
60	Acquirer issued one common share for each 6.2295 shares owned by the seller's management group, and one common share for each 5 shares publicly owned.
67	Acquirer issued $\frac{8}{10}$ Class B shares for each share owned by the seller's management group, and one Class B share for each share publicly owned.

d. Market price two months prior to announcement not available. Represents closest quoted date.

e. Stock dividend also paid.

f. Acquirer purchased a portion of the seller for an undisclosed amount prior to the tender offer, as follows:

Acquisition or Merger	Tender Offer
192	27
196	9

g. Includes 2% purchased on the open market between July and December 1966. In addition, the Wean Family and the Raymond J. Wean Foundation exchanged their 10% holding in McKay Machine Co. for Wean Industries preferred stock in July 1966.

h. Includes 23% purchased in October 1965 from Glen Alden Corp. for approximately $51,000,000; less than 1% purchased shortly before on the open market for approximately $3,100,000; 16% purchased through a tender offer in February 1966, for approximately $40,000,000; and 12% purchased through the tender offer of September 1966 for approximately $29,900,000.

i. Earnings per share is before special item. Earnings per share after special item was $6.71.

j. Includes 72% purchased through the tender offer of April 1965 for approximately $18,000,000 and 10% purchased shortly thereafter for approximately $2,300,000.

k. Includes 52% purchased through the tender offer of June 1965 for approximately $20,900,000 and 10% purchased by exercising an option in December 1965 for approximately $4,100,000.

l. Includes 45% of the common stock purchased from the Bell System companies in March 1964 for approximately $19,600,000 and 5% of the common stock purchased through the tender offer of August 1965 for approximately $3,400,000. In addition, 100% of the preferred stock was purchased from the Bell System companies in March 1964.

m. Acquirer owned 55% of the seller as a result of the latter's recapitalization in February 1952. Subsequent purchases and sales, including the purchase of 5% in October 1965, resulted in the acquirer's owning 56% of the seller at the time of the merger.

n. Concurrent with the tender offer of May 1966, the acquirer tendered 76% of the preferred stock of the seller for approximately $22,100,000. Due to the preferred stock's superior voting power, the acquirer held a 45% voting interest in the seller after the tender offer.

o. Includes 9% purchased in July 1966 for approximately $1,000,000 cash and $5,000,000 4% notes payable over 5 years, 2% purchased in November

1966 for approximately $1,500,000 cash and notes, and 12% purchased through the tender offer of February 1967 for approximately $8,700,000. In addition, 7% was acquired in November 1966 by an exchange of common stock on a ratio of approximately 0.16 for 1.

p. The acquisition was first announced in 1966 but was delayed pending final approval by the Interstate Commerce Commission. Market prices two months prior to June 1968 were used.

q. In the actual exchange ratio, the seller received .86 share of the new common stock for each of its shares and the acquirer received 2 shares of the new stock for each of its shares.

r. In addition, the acquirer issued $190 principal amount subordinated sinking fund debentures at 6% due 1987 for each share of the acquired company's 7% preferred. The 6% debentures are carried in the accounts at a value of $6,668,000.

Key to Corporate Identities in Mergers and Acquisitions

1. Hunt Foods & Industries Inc.—W. P. Fuller & Co. (February 1962)*
2. Siegler Corp.—Lear Inc. (Lear Siegler Inc.) (June 1962)
3. Sharon Steel Corp.—Macomber Inc. (August 1962)
4. Genesco Inc.—Flagg Utica Corp. (September 1962)
5. Upjohn Co.—Carwin Co. (October 1962)
6. Swingline Inc.—Wilson Jones Co. (March 1963)
7. Georgia Pacific Corp.—St. Croix Paper Co. (March 1963)
8. W. R. Grace & Co.—Zonolite Co. (April 1963)
9. American Machine & Foundry Co.—Western Tool & Stamping Co. (July 1963)
10. Litton Industries Inc.—Adler Electronics Inc. (September 1963)
11. Singer Co.—Friden Inc. (October 1963)
12. Addressograph-Multigraph Corp.—Charles Bruning Co. (November 1963)
13. Anaconda Co.—Anaconda Wire & Cable Co. (December 1963)
14. Chas. Pfizer & Co. Inc.—Coty Inc. (December 1963)
15. Lanvin-Parfums Inc.—Charles of The Ritz Inc. (Lanvin-Charles of The Ritz Inc.) (January 1964)
16. United Aircraft Corp.—Vector Manufacturing Co. Inc. (January 1964)
17. General Mills Inc.—Morton Foods Inc. (February 1964)

* Effective dates of combinations are shown parenthetically throughout.

18. Coca-Cola Co.–Duncan Foods Co. (May 1964)
19. Fairbanks Whitney Corp.–Fairbanks Morse & Co. (Colt Industries Inc.) (May 1964)
20. W. R. Grace & Co.–DuBois Chemicals Inc. (May 1964)
21. American Hardware Corp.–Emhart Manufacturing Co. (Emhart Corp.) (June 1964)
22. Lestoil Products Inc.–Bon Ami Co. (Standard International Corp.) (July 1964)
23. Boise Cascade Corp.–Associated Stationers Supply Co., Inc. (September 1964)
24. Celanese Corp. of America–Champlin Oil & Refinery Co. (October 1964)
25. Rexall Drug & Chemical Co.–Colorite Plastics Inc. (October 1964)
26. Arden Farms Co.–Mayfair Markets (Arden–Mayfair Inc.) (November 1964)
27. Teledyne Inc.–Servomechanisms Inc. (November 1964)
28. Beatrice Foods Co.–Bloomfield Industries Inc. (November 1964)
29. Interlake Iron Corp.–Acme Steel Co. (Interlake Steel Corp.) (December 1964)
30. Rex Chainbelt Inc.–Mathews Conveyor Co. (December 1964)
31. Ritter Corp.–Kerr Manufacturing Co. (January 1964)
32. International Business Machines Corp.–Science Research Associates Inc. (February 1964)
33. West Point Manufacturing Co.–Pepperell Manufacturing Co. (West Point–Pepperell Inc.) (March 1965)
34. Federal-Mogul Bowes Bearings, Inc.–Sterling Aluminum Products Inc. (Federal-Mogul Corp.) (April 1965)
35. Amphenol-Borg Electronics Corp.–Cadre Industries Corp. (Amphenol Corp.) (May 1965)
36. Caterpillar Tractor Co.–Towmotor Corp. (November 1965)
37. Pfaudler Permutit Inc.–Ritter Corp. (Ritter Pfaudler Corp.) (November 1965)
38. Bristol-Myers Co.–Drackett Co. (August 1965)
39. Varian Associates–Eitel-McCullough Inc. (August 1965)
40. Gimbel Bros. Inc.–Ed Schuster & Co. Inc. (April 1962)
41. Gamble-Skogmo Inc.–General Outdoor Advertising Co. Inc. (October 1963)

42. Albertson's Inc.—Greater All American Markets Inc. (July 1964)

43. Jewel Tea Co., Inc.—Star Market Co. (Jewel Companies Inc.) (February 1964)

44. S. S. Kresge Co.—Holly Stores Inc. (February 1965)

45. Waldorf System Inc.—Restaurant Associates Inc. (Restaurant & Waldorf Associates Inc.) (January 1966)

46. Borden Co.—Henderson's Portion Pak, Inc. (October 1965)

47. Hess Oil & Chemical Corp.—Billups Eastern Petroleum Co. (October 1965)

48. American Chain & Cable Co. Inc.—Mechanical Handling Systems Inc. (October 1965)

49. Westinghouse Air Brake Co.—Wilcox Electric Co. Inc. (September 1965)

50. Bliss & Laughlin Industries Inc.—Waco-Porter Corp. (January 1966)

51. Rexall Drug & Chemical Co.—Ralph Wilson Plastics Inc. (January 1966)

52. Beatrice Foods Co.—Colorado By-Products Co. (November 1965)

53. Beatrice Foods Co.—Inland Underground Facilities Inc. (June 1965)

54. Honeywell Inc.—Electro Instruments Inc. (April 1966)

55. Mosler Safe Co.—American Bank Stationery Co. (April 1966)

56. B.V.D. Co. Inc.—Almar Rainwear Corp. (June 1966)

57. Jewel Tea Co., Inc.—Buttrey Foods Inc. (Jewel Companies Inc.) (June 1966)

58. Varian Associates—Applied Physics Corp. (July 1966)

59. Consolidated Foods Corp.—Oxford Chemical Corp. (December 1966)

60. Carnation Co.—Trenton Foods Inc. (September 1966)

61. Abbott Laboratories—Faultless Rubber Co. (October 1966)

62. Universal Oil Products Co.—Norplex Corp. (October 1966)

63. Castle & Cooke, Inc.—Ames Mercantile Co. (December 1966)

64. Ruberoid Co.—American Felt Co. (October 1966)

65. Bates Manufacturing Co. Inc.—Martinall Industries Inc. (December 1966)

66. W. R. Grace & Co.—Seapak Corp. (March 1967)

67. Brown-Forman Distillers Corp.—Quality Importers Inc. (July 1967)

68. Colt Industries Inc.—Elox Corp. of Michigan (July 1967)

69. McGraw-Edison Co.—Halo Lighting Inc. (June 1967)

70. U. S. Industries Inc.—Georgia Shoe Manufacturing Co., Inc. (July 1967)

71. Bell & Howell Co.—Wilding Inc. (August 1967)

72. Mid-Continent Manufacturing Co.—Huber Corp. (September 1967)
73. Liggett & Meyers Tobacco Co.—National Oats Co. (September 1967)
74. Beatrice Foods Co.—Airstream Inc. (December 1967)
75. Max Factor & Co.—Denver Chemical Manufacturing Co. (November 1967)
76. Norwich Pharmacal Co.—Texize Chemicals Inc. (November 1967)
77. Smith Industries International Inc.—Drilco Oil Tools Inc. (December 1967)
78. Whittaker Corp.—American Petrochemical Corp. (November 1967)
79. Rockwell-Standard Corp.—Murray Co. of Texas Inc. (December 1965)
80. Associated Brewing Co.—Drewrys, Ltd. U.S.A. Inc. (December 1965)
81. Tennessee Gas Transmission Inc.—Nixon-Baldwin Chemicals Inc. (Tenneco Inc.) (January 1966)
82. American Tobacco Co.—Sunshine Biscuits Inc. (May 1966)
83. Radio Corp. of America—Random House Inc. (May 1966)
84. Honeywell Inc.—Computer Control Co. Inc. (May 1966)
85. SCM Corp.—Proctor-Silex Corp. (June 1966)
86. United Whelan Corp.—Perfect Photo Inc. (Perfect Film & Chemical Corp.) (June 1966)
87. Household Finance Corp.—White Stores Inc. (November 1966)
88. E. J. Korvette Inc.—Spartans Industries Inc. (Spartans Industries Inc.) (September 1966)
89. General Aniline & Film Corp.—Sawyer's Inc. (October 1966)
90. General Telephone & Electronics Corp.—Hawaiian Telephone Co. (May 1967)
91. McDonnell Co.—Douglas Aircraft Co., Inc. (McDonnell-Douglas Corp.) (April 1967)
92. Scott Paper Co.—S. D. Warren Co. (May 1967)
93. Studebaker Corp.—Wagner Electric Corp. (Studebaker Worthington Corp.) (May 1967)
94. Warner-Lambert Pharmaceutical Co.—American Optical Co. (April 1967)
95. Consolidated Foods Corp.—Abbey Rents (June 1967)
96. American Bosch Arma Corp.—Packard Instrument Co. Inc. (June 1967)
97. Will Ross Inc.—Matheson Co. Inc. (July 1967)
98. Hayes Industries Inc.—Albion Malleable Iron Co. (Hayes-Albion Corp.) (August 1967)

99. North American Aviation Inc.—Rockwell Standard Corp. (North American Rockwell Corp.) (September 1967)

100. Purex Corp. Ltd.—Pacific Airmotive Corp. (September 1967)

101 Sundstrand Corp.—United Control Corp. (June 1967)

102. El Paso Natural Gas Co.—Beaunit Corp. (October 1967)

103. General Instrument Corp.—Jerrold Corp. (December 1967)

104. Itek Corp.—Applied Technology Inc. (September 1967)

105. Electronic Memories, Inc.—Wems, Inc. (December 1967)

106. American Can Co.—Butterick Co. (January 1968)

107. Corn Products Co.—S. B. Penick & Co. (January 1968)

108. Emerson Electric Co.—Therm-o-Disc, Inc. (January 1968)

109. MCA Inc.—Spencer Gifts, Inc. (May 1968)

110. ITT—Levitt & Sons, Inc. (February 1968)

111. Teledyne Inc.—Rodney Metals Inc. (February 1968)

112. Teledyne, Inc.—Firth Sterling, Inc. (December 1967)

113. American Hospital Supply Co.—Hamilton Manufacturing Co. (April 1968)

114. Eaton, Yale & Towne, Inc.—Fawick Corp. (March 1968)

115. Fisher Scientific Co.—Jarrell-Ash Co. (April 1968)

116. Universal Oil Products Co.—Calumet & Hecla Inc. (April 1968)

117. Ward Foods Inc.—Food Corp. of America, Inc. (March 1968)

118. PepsiCo, Inc.—North American Van Lines, Inc. (June 1968)

119. Consolidated Foods Corp.—Country Set, Inc. (May 1968)

120. ITE Circuit Breaker Co.—Imperial-Eastman Corp. (April 1968)

121. Pitney-Bowes Inc.—Monarch Marking System Co. (May 1968)

122. Purex Corp., Ltd.—Airwork Corp. (June 1968)

123. Rexall Drug & Chemical Co.—Beauty Counselors, Inc. (May 1968)

124. Scott & Fetzer Co.—Kingston Products Corp. (April 1968)

125. Upjohn Co.—Asgrow Seed Co. (April 1968)

126. General Host Corp.—Li'l General Stores, Inc. (July 1968)

127. General Telephone & Electronics Corp.—Northern Ohio Telephone Co. (August 1968)

128. Milton Bradley Co.—Playskool Manufacturing Co. (August 1968)

129. Sola Basic Industries, Inc.—Dielectric Products Eng. Co. (July 1968)

130. J. P. Stevens & Co.—United Elastic Corp. (June 1968)

131. Xerox Corp.—Ginn & Co. (July 1968)

132. Hartford Gas Co.—New Britain Gas Light Co. (September 1968)

133. Houdaille Industries, Inc.—Viking Pump Co. (September 1968)
134. National Cash Register Co.—Electronic Communications, Inc. (September 1963)
135. Standard Oil Co. (Ohio)—Old Ben Coal Corp. (August 1968)
136. Colt Industries Inc.—Central Transformer Corp. (November 1968)
137. Kawecki Chemical Co.—Beryllium Corp. (October 1968)
138. National Steel Corp.—Republic Foil Inc. (December 1968)
139. Potlatch Forests Inc.—Swanee Paper Corp. (December 1968)
140. PepsiCo, Inc.—Chandler Leasing Corp. (July 1968)
141. Amfac, Inc.—Fred Harvey Co. (July 1968)
142. Coronet Industries, Inc.—Shelby Williams Industries, Inc. (July 1968)
143. American Petrofina Inc.—Cosden Petroleum Corp. (April 1963)
144. American Metal Climax Inc.—Hunter Engineering Corp. (May 1963)
145. Avnet Electronics Corp.—Valley Forge Products Inc. (Avnet Inc.) (August 1964)
146. Bangor Punta Alegre Sugar Corp.—Smith & Wesson Inc. (Bangor Punta Corp.) (October 1965)
147. Combustion Engineering Inc.—National Tank Co. (November 1965)
148. Wallace-Murray Corp.—Simonds Saw & Steel Co. (June 1966)
149. ABC Consolidated Corp.—Nedick's Stores Inc. (April 1965)
150. Allis-Chalmers Manufacturing Co.—Simplicity Manufacturing Co. Inc. (October 1965)
151. Coplay Cement Manufacturing Co.—Nazareth Cement Co. (December 1965)
152. International Telephone & Telegraph Corp.—Wakefield Corp. (February 1966)
153. B.V.D. Co. Inc.—Timely Clothes Inc. (April 1966)
154. Consolidated Foods Corp.—E. Kahn's Sons Co. (March 1966)
155. Crescent Corp.—Royal School Laboratories Inc. (April 1966)
156. City Stores Co.—Wolf & Dressauer Co. (August 1966)
157. Swank Inc.—Prince Gardner Co. (September 1966)
158. Ferro Corp.—Electro Refractories & Abrasives Corp. (March 1967)
159. General Aniline & Film Corp.—Shelby Business Forms Inc. (June 1967)
160. Penn-Dixie Cement Corp.—Hausman Corp. (August 1967)
161. Weyenberg Shoe Manufacturing Co.—Nunn-Bush Co. (August 1967)
162. American Pipe & Construction Co.—H. C. & D. Ltd. (November 1967)

163. Koret of California Inc.—Byer-Rolnick Corp. (Koracorp. Industries, Inc.) (December 1967)

164. Automation Industries Inc.—Consolidated American Services Inc. (January 1968)

165. Spartans Industries Inc.—Atlantic Thrift Centers Inc. (March 1966)

166. Whirlpool Corp.—Warwick Electronics Inc. (September 1966)

167. Sperry & Hutchinson Co.—Bigelow-Sanford Inc. (April 1967)

168. American Standard Inc.—Mosler Safe Corp. (May 1967)

169. Gulf & Western Industries Inc.—South Puerto Rico Sugar Co. (July 1967)

170. City Investing Co.—Rheem Manufacturing Co. (November 1967)

171. General Cinema Corp.—American Beverage Corp. (March 1968)

172. Kennecott Copper Co.—Peabody Coal Co. (March 1968)

173. National General Corp.—Grosset & Dunlap, Inc. (March 1968)

174. Union Camp. Corp.—Moore-Handley, Inc. (June 1968)

175. Saturn Industries, Inc.—Tyler Pipe Industries, Inc. (September 1968)

176. U. S. Finance Co.—Rhodes, Inc. (August 1968)

177. Teledyne, Inc.—Ryan Aeronautical Co. (December 1968)

178. Wyle Laboratories—Curtis Manufacturing Co. (October 1968)

179. American Tobacco Co.—Duffy-Mott Co. (July 1968)

180. United Whelan Corp.—Hudson National Inc. (Perfect Film & Chemical Corp.) (June 1966)

181. APL Corp.—U. S. Consumer Products Corp. (May 1966)

182. Cenco Instruments Corp.—Jackes-Evans Manufacturing Co. (October 1967)

183. National Industries Inc.—Cott Corp. (July 1968)

184. Brown Co.—KVP Sutherland Paper Co. (May 1966)

185. Ling-Temco-Vought Inc.—Wilson & Co., Inc. (June 1967)

186. LTV Electrosystems Inc.—Memcor Inc. (April 1967)

187. General Aniline & Film Corp.—Ruberoid Co. (May 1967)

188. FMC Corp.—Link Belt Co. (June 1967)

189. SCM Corp.—Glidden Corp. (September 1967)

190. Pennzoil Co.—United Gas Corp. (Pennzoil United Corp.) (April 1968)

191. Glen Alden Corp.—Phillip Carey Manufacturing Co. (June 1967)

192. Wean Industries Inc.—McKay Machine Co. (Wean United Inc.) (May 1967)

193. Tung-Sol Electric Inc.—Wagner Electric Corp. (Wagner Electric Corp.) (September 1966)

194. Foremost Dairies Inc.—McKesson & Robbins Inc. (Foremost-McKesson Inc.) (July 1967)

195. AMK Corp.—John Morrell & Co. (December 1967)

196. Rockwell-Standard Corp.—Draper Corp. (September 1967)

197. U. S. Smelting, Refining & Mining Co.—Mueller Brass Co. (September 1965)

198. Diebold Inc.—Lamson Corp. (July 1965)

199. National Union Electric Corp.—Emerson Radio and Phonograph Corp. (May 1966)

200. Philadelphia & Reading Corp.—Lone Star Steel Co. (April 1966)

201. United Utilities Inc.—Inter-Mountain Telephone Co. (May 1966)

202. Electric Bond & Share Co.—American & Foreign Power Co. (December 1967)

203. Colorado Milling & Elevator Co.—Great Western Sugar Co. (Great Western United Corp.) (January 1968)

204. General Instrument Corp.—Universal Controls Inc. (August 1967)

In one case the information was not available. Where the market price was lower, it was appreciably so in only 3 cases. By contrast, in 12 out of the 14 cases, where market values were higher, they were substantially so.

The acquiring companies showed return on net worth, based on their latest fiscal year reports prior to initial purchases, ranging from 4% to 24%. In 1 case the acquirer showed a negative return. In 4 cases, acquiring companies purchased initial interests on a better return on net worth than they were obtaining on their own operations, in 2 the return was the same, and in the other 12 it was lower, generally substantially.

As discussed in Chapter 9, such deals will no longer qualify as part purchase and part pooling transactions, except that if a company owned a minority interest (up to 50%) in common stock of another at October 31, 1970, and initiated a plan for an exchange of common stock with the latter after that date, this final transaction may be accounted for as a pooling if completed within five years after October 31, 1970, and if certain other conditions are met. Otherwise such transactions, consummated in two or more steps, shall be treated in entirety as purchases.

The percentage of net income of the acquired companies applicable to the initial purchased interests ranged from less than 1% to 12% with a median of 7%.

Financing Arrangements

A study was made of 35 purchases, wholly or partially for cash, each of which involved an outlay of $10,000,000 or more, listed in Tables 12–2 and 12–3. In a number of cases, cash requirements were temporarily financed by short-term bank loans. However, where this was the case, such loans were refinanced. The following summary shows the major methods of financing ultimately carried out by the purchasers:

Insurance company and bank term loans	12
Combination of long-term borrowing and sale of capital stock	6
Sale of debentures	9
Sale of debentures and bank term loan	2
Use of working capital	4
Use of working capital and bank term loan	1
Other	1
	35

Accounting Treatment of Goodwill

In 29 business combinations included in the study where companies acquired all or a major interest in others, totally or partially for cash (Tables 12–2 and 12–3), the difference between the purchase price and the proportionate net tangible assets acquired was approximately $5,000,000 or more. The net assets acquired in two of these purchases exceeded their cost. One of the latter companies allocated the credit to reduce property, plant, and equipment. The other handled part of the credit in this manner and indicated it would credit the remaining portion to income over a period of eight years.

In the 27 acquisitions where the purchase price exceeded net tangible assets acquired, all of the difference was allocated to various assets in two cases, and part of the difference was allocated to various assets and the remainder to goodwill in six. All of the difference was allocated to goodwill in 18 other cases, and in one a 59% interest purchased was carried as an investment at cost to be adjusted for subsequent changes in equity. In two of the 24 cases, where goodwill arose as a result of business combinations, it was included in bulk charges to retained earnings and/or capital surplus and capital stock upon the subsequent mergers of the companies involved. In the 22 cases where goodwill remained on the books of the acquirers they indicated no present intention of amortizing it. As discussed in Chapter 9, the current accounting rules now require amortization of goodwill acquired after October 31, 1970, except for business combinations initiated on or before that date and consummated subsequent thereto.

Data on Acquisitions for Convertible Preferred Stock

In 88 single-step transactions treated as poolings of interest and involving the issuance of convertible preferred stock in whole or in part, the following statistics are pertinent, in terms of premiums (or discounts) accruing to the absorbed companies' stockholders:

	Market Value	Earnings	Dividends
Premiums	79	14	74
Discounts	8	74	12
Even exchange	1	—	2
	88	88	88

One of the disclosures of the study was the increased use of convertible preferred stock by acquirers during the period. Such stock was issued in whole, or in part, in 88 transactions included in the study (but not listed) as poolings of interests under the then existing rules, and in 14 out of 25 two-step transactions listed in Table 12–3. Considering the random basis of selection followed in the study, these results indicated what was then a major trend toward the use of convertible preferred stock in business combinations. Incidentally, in 73% of these acquisitions the acquiring companies' earnings attributable to common stock would be adversely affected by conversion, and substantially so in a number of such cases.

Under the revised accounting rules the use of convertible preferred stock as consideration for the acquisition of the capital stock or net assets of another company no longer qualifies for pooling-of-interests treatment. However, convertible preferred stock still may be used to purchase companies either by direct exchange or sale to the public and use of the cash proceeds, and is of interest from that standpoint.

Convertible preferred stock may offer advantages to the issuer as well as to erstwhile investors. It is desirable from the standpoint of the issuer, if the value of each share of such stock is substantially above the market value of the issuers' common stock. In such a case, the purchasers will emerge with less voting power (assuming the typical case where each class of stock is entitled to one vote per share), than if common stock had been issued.

From the standpoint of the investor, convertible preferred stock will offer a safer investment, a generally higher dividend yield than on common stock, and still provide an opportunity to share in the growth of a company through the conversion feature. The latter factor is valid provided the conversion ratio of preferred into common is reasonably attractive, based on the current market price of the common.

Conversion Value of Convertible Preferred Stocks. The conversion value of a preferred stock is measured by the number of shares of common stock receivable on conversion multiplied by the market price of the common stock. Generally, the conversion feature of a convertible preferred stock is not considered to have much value, at the time of issuance, if the premium at which it is selling is more than, say, 15 to 25% over the conversion value of the common. The following statistics on the convertible preferred stocks included in the study bear out this view based on relative market prices shortly after issuance of the preferred:

	Number of Issues
Conversion parity immediately available	26
Premium under 15%	38
Premium 15% to 25%	17
Premium over 25%	21
Total	102

Convertible Debentures and Stock Purchase Warrants

During the late 1960's, because of accelerating interest rates, many companies issued convertible debentures to raise borrowed capital. Whereas a company would have had to issue a nonconvertible bond to yield annual interest at the rate of 8 to 9% or greater, a convertible debenture would be priced to yield, say, 5 to 6%, depending upon current economic conditions. This was so because of the purchaser's opportunity to share in the growth of the company through converting his debenture holdings into common stock at some future date, should the company prosper. Usually convertible debentures are subordinate to other senior debt securities and bank loans. However, as explained in Chapter 8, page 215, there is a limitation on the amount of annual interest deductible on subordinated corporate indebtedness used to acquire the stock or assets of another corporation.[2]

An extension of the practice of issuing convertible debentures took place in business combinations during 1968, when a number of offers were made involving the issuance of such securities to offerees in exchange for capital stock by the would-be acquirers. In some cases, offers included, in a package, debentures and stock purchase warrants.

In a number of cases, companies that issued bonds for cash, or borrowed from insurance companies, included stock purchase warrants in the "package" to make the deal salable where they might otherwise have had difficulty in disposing of bonds or obtaining a term loan because of their unattractive credit rating. Warrants, in effect, are options to buy unissued stock, generally common, at a fixed price for a stated period, or at changing prices at varying intervals. The option may be exercised for cash, or, at times, by surrendering the bonds with which they were concurrently issued at face value. Inasmuch as warrants are a "call" on the stock for a long period, they generally sell at a premium. That is to say, if one were to purchase a warrant and pay the option price to acquire the common stock, it would generally cost more than buying the stock outright on the market.

The feature of being able to utilize bonds at face amount in exercising warrants also tends to increase the market price of war-

[2] I.R.C. § 279.

rants. Thus, the current price of warrants usually has no relation to their exercise value but reflects the degree of optimism of the investing public in the earnings potential of the company which, if realized, will be reflected in the increased value of its common stock at some future time.

The market status of twenty stock purchase warrants at April 30, 1969, is illustrated in the tabulation below. Fifteen of the warrants were traded on the American Stock Exchange, four in the over-the-counter market, and one on the Pacific Coast Exchange. The Amex listed warrants represented most of those traded on that exchange on April 30, 1969, after eliminating warrants scheduled to expire in the next year or two, and those issued by investment companies which tend to maintain reasonable exercise parity of exchange with the price of the common stock.

| | | Each Warrant Entitled To Purchase* | | | | Market |
	Year of Expiration	No. of Common Shares	Price per Share	Market Price of Warrant	Together	Price of Common Stock
AMK Corporation	1979	1	$ 46.00	$10.75	$ 56.75	$37.25
Allied Products Corp.	1983	1	58.00	14.00	72.00	47.25
Atlas Corp.	Perpetual	1	6.25	4.38	10.63	6.88
Avco Corp.	1978	1	56.00	10.50	66.50	34.63
Bangor Punta Corp.	1981	1	55.00	10.50	65.50	35.38
Braniff Airways	1986	3	73.00	21.13	94.13	51.00
Daylin Inc.	1989	1	45.00	19.25	64.25	44.13
Elgin National Inds.	1973	0.4	8.75	3.88	12.63	5.60
Gulf & Western	1978	1	55.00	10.63	65.63	33.50
Jones & Laughlin	1979	1	37.50	6.25	43.75	18.00
Ling-Temco-Vought	1978	1.13	115.00	19.25	134.25	59.04
Loew's Theatres	1980**	1	35.00	26.13	61.13	48.38
McCrory Corp.	1981	1	20.00	11.63	31.63	28.75
N.V.F.	1979	1	22.00	9.25	31.25	19.25
Northwest Industries	1979	1	110.00	18.00	128.00	77.50
Pacific S.W. Airlines	1977	1	23.40	11.63	35.03	20.75
Rapid American	1994	1	35.00	12.00	47.00	31.50
Transworld Airlines	1973	1	22.00	24.63	46.63	40.38
U. S. Smelting	1979**	1	66.00	13.25	79.25	49.25
Ward Foods	1979**	1	60.00	9.50	69.50	36.25

* All data, including market prices of common stock, have been computed on the number of shares or fraction thereof purchasable upon exercise of warrants.

** The terms of these warrants change during the period prior to their expiration.

SMALL PROFESSIONAL AND PERSONAL SERVICE ORGANIZATIONS

The valuation of small professional and personal service organizations, such as accounting and legal firms, advertising, insurance, and real estate agencies, pose more than the usual run of problems for the valuer.

Difficulty of Determining What Is Being Purchased

In the first place, such practices or businesses are operated on a personalized basis and the prospective purchaser generally will have difficulty in determining exactly what he will acquire and how enduring it will be. In the merger of such organizations the principal or principals of the absorbed firms generally continue in the surviving organization, whereas a sale usually transpires because of the imminent retirement or the demise of such principals. Larger service organizations do not pose the same problems, because the accounts of their clients or customers are, in effect, institutionalized and it is quite common to change the executives handling them.

A valuation for purposes of the sale by a retiring partner or principal, or his estate, of an interest in a personal service organization to others in that organization, requires the same approach in valuing the business as though it were being sold to an outsider. However, it does not require the same investigative procedures or as much general concern about losing accounts, because of the familiarity of the remaining principals with the business and clients.

The principles and problems regarding the valuation of small professional and personal service organizations have general application to other small businesses, such as automobile agencies, laundries, service stations, drug stores, etc.

General Investigative Procedures

Certain investigative procedures on the part of the prospective purchaser will be common in the case of any of the above types of personal service organizations and should be carried out before an agreement is reached on a purchase price.

A review of financial statements should be made for a period of three to five years to determine the profitability of the business, the trend of gross and net income, and the assets and liabilities as of a current date.

Information should be obtained on personnel, including duties, capabilities, salary scales, and fringe benefits. Such matters should be discussed with key personnel to ascertain their satisfaction with existing or proposed revised arrangements, and their willingness to remain with the purchaser. The purchaser should not ordinarily assume obligations of the seller to superannuated employees, or for unfunded pension costs for services to date, unless suitable adjustment is made for such matters in the purchase price.

Visits should be made by the prospective purchaser and seller, or their representatives, to important clients or customers to ascertain that they intend to continue to do business with the successor owner or owners. Alternatively, where customers attend at the premises of the business, they should be informed of its contemplated sale and reactions gained regarding their willingness to continue doing business with the successor owner.

Agreements, leases, copies of federal and state tax returns, and insurance policies should be reviewed to determine what potential liabilities of the business exist and what protection is afforded by insurance coverage.

Valuation Procedures

The valuation of small professional and personal service organizations is generally determined on a two-step basis. First, the tangible assets to be acquired are valued, and then goodwill representing the capitalized value of future earnings is computed.

Such tangible assets may include furniture, fixtures, office equipment and supplies, accounts receivable, unbilled work for services rendered, and at times real property. If not significant, tangible assets may be accepted on a book basis of valuation. Otherwise, if purchased, they should be currently valued with particular attention to long outstanding accounts receivable and relatively large amounts of unbilled work.

In some cases furniture, fixtures, and equipment may have little value to the purchaser because he can adequately handle the seller's business with his existing facilities, or such assets had not been replaced in recent years in anticipation of a sale of the business. Also, the purchaser may not wish to acquire accounts receivable but agree to remit collections of such accounts outstanding to the seller so that relations with continuing clients or customers will not be disrupted.

Agreement may be reached by the purchaser and seller on how to split the profit on work in progress at the time of sale, which will be completed by the purchaser.

It is generally unwise to assume liabilities, in the purchase of a small business, except for unexpired terms of leases, and contracts for goods and services necessary and desirable for the conduct of the business. Also, it should be determined that any assets to be acquired are free and clear of encumbrances, or that proper adjustment is made in the purchase price for any liens against them. Furthermore, the purchaser, even if he does not assume them, should be aware of the principal liabilities of the seller to be assured that he is not buying a de facto bankrupt business and hence becoming accountable to creditors of the seller for assets acquired by him.

The valuation of capitalized future earnings presents problems that are peculiar to the different types of small professional and service organizations and requires a knowledge on the part of the purchaser of the particular type of business being offered for sale. It is obviously risky to purchase such a business if the buyer does not have reasonable experience and knowledge of its ramifications.

Gross Revenues Not a Valuation Base. One myth should be laid to rest under this section on valuations, that is, a so-called "rule of thumb" for valuing such businesses based on gross revenues. Contentions are frequently made, usually by the prospective sellers of such businesses, that they are worth one or two times the gross revenues of the latest completed or projected current year.

Obviously, a business that grosses $100,000 a year in revenues or fees and nets $30,000 a year is far more valuable than one with a similar gross, with a net of $10,000 a year. As in the case of other operating businesses, the purchaser of a professional or service organization is interested in its potential *net* income.

Computing Value of Goodwill

Also, the prospective purchaser in valuing future earnings should bear in mind that his own services have a value, assuming he intends to work in the business to be acquired. Such value should be roughly equivalent to what he would expect as compensation as an employee, based on his competence and the volume of work he intends to handle. Any computation of goodwill, representing the capitalized value of future earnings, should take this into consideration as a modifying factor.

In computing capitalized earnings, the purchaser should review the composition of business of the seller and eliminate (a) business that it is apparent he will not retain, and (b) business that he does not wish to retain, i.e., of an unprofitable nature, or requiring a particular skill that he does not possess. With these eliminations he should then estimate the net income on such business proposed to be retained.

Usually, the price paid for goodwill of a small professional, personal service, or other small business is low relative to valuations of large businesses, and may be two to three times adjusted annual net income, before federal income taxes. Such evaluations may be modified downward if the seller is under compulsion to dispose of his business because of illness, or other reasons, and upward if the purchaser is able to absorb the business without replacing the retiring owner-manager.

In support of a relatively low valuation of goodwill of small professional and personal service organizations, the tax courts have generally held that no goodwill accrues to a business depending solely on the skill and ability of the person or persons operating it. In one case, a court ruled that the business of a small advertising agency had no goodwill, but placed a value on certain profitable unexpired contracts the agency had with advertisers.

Method of Payment for a Small Business

Another policy that should be observed generally in purchasing a small professional or other personal service organization is not to pay for the business in a lump sum, or to make too large a down payment. It is impossible to predict that all the clients or customers of the seller will remain with the purchaser after the transaction is consummated.

A reasonable procedure would be to make a down payment equivalent to tangible assets acquired, plus one third to one half of the goodwill purchased. The balance of the purchase price could be paid in installments over a period. In fairness to the seller, this period might be two to three years, but not more than five years. In general, a provision of the agreement should be that the total purchase price is contingent upon retention of accounts or a certain volume of business for the period of the pay-out. Adjustment, if any, could be made under an agreed-upon formula for any business not retained during this period.

13

Conglomerates

The merger movement at the turn of the century was characterized by the combination of many companies in the same industries into single enterprises. These horizontal mergers resulted in large concentrations of particular industries in the top companies thus created.

The next merger movement, from 1925 to 1931, gave rise to more vertical acquisitions leading to the integration of manufacturers, suppliers, and distributors. DuPont was one of the few companies during this period to embark on a conglomerate acquisitions program, to broaden its growth potential, which had been limited primarily to the manufacture of explosives and munitions.

The latest movement, commencing after the termination of World War II, continued at an accelerated pace through the 1960's. What is unique about this movement is the number of so-called conglomerate companies that have emerged via business combinations during recent years.

There are many multimarket or diversified manufacturing companies. However, the term "conglomerate" as applied to a business enterprise generally refers to a company whose operations became diversified through the acquisition of other companies in completely different lines of business. Perhaps size should also be a consideration in applying this term to an enterprise. Generally a company's volume of business should run several hundred million dollars before it is deemed a conglomerate.

SUPPORT AND CRITICISM OF THE CONGLOMERATE MOVEMENT

The conglomerate merger movement has its proponents as well as critics. The proponents claim that they are benefiting stockholders of many companies taken over by shaking up or dispensing with complacent or moribund management. Whether they acquire for cash or securities, the stockholders of the absorbed companies supposedly wind up with a higher price for their stock. This situation has not held true in most acquisitions or mergers effected in recent years, particularly if the recipient stockholder retained such securities, which included bonds and stock purchase warrants, as well as common and preferred stock.

Other claims made by proponents are to the effect that conglomerates, because of diversification, are not subject to violent earnings fluctuations, exercise better financial management over their various components, and are able to raise capital on more advantageous terms than individual companies could. Also, they maintain that top management costs are minimized because each division head deals only with his own business problems and is not involved in financing, stockholders, and other general corporate activities.

The critics of the conglomerate movement contend that the mere act of embarking on an aggressive acquisitions program expands stock market prices without increasing economic values on which such prices should depend. They scoff at the claims made regarding financial benefits and efficiencies allegedly effected as a result of conglomerate management as not being susceptible to proof. After a company has been acquired by a conglomerate, it is virtually impossible to determine how it would have fared had it not been acquired. Some of the most vocal critics of the recent conglomerate movement are the management of older conglomerates who claim that the sheer mathematics of such business combinations give the appearance of growth where none exists.

A STUDY OF TWENTY-ONE CONGLOMERATE MERGERS

Table 13–1 lists some of the larger companies traded on the New York Stock Exchange, which reached conglomerate status during recent years, together with pertinent statistics thereon for 1969 and 1968. These statistics, with the exception of market prices of common stocks, were extracted primarily from annual reports to stockholders for 1969 fiscal years, which include restated figures for 1968, where applicable, to reflect pooling-of-interest transactions in fiscal 1969.

As shown in Table 13–1, all of the companies but Olin Corporation had convertible securities, and twelve of them had stock purchase warrants outstanding, indicating the popularity prior to 1970 of these forms of securities in package deals for acquisitions and financing by conglomerates. Of the sixteen companies carrying goodwill on their balance sheets, only three—W. R. Grace, Tenneco, and Textron—mentioned amortization of such intangibles. AMK Corporation had net negative goodwill which was being amortized by credits to income over a ten-year period. However, the revised accounting rules discussed in Chapter 9 and adopted in 1970, which permit pooling-of-interest accounting treatment with common stock only, and require amortization of purchased goodwill, should tend to reduce the number of acquisitions by conglomerates in the future.

Mention was made in Chapter 12 of additional contingent payments in cases where the buyer and seller cannot agree on the potential value of a business. Five of the conglomerates under discussion—City Investing, W. R. Grace, Walter Kidde, Litton, and U. S. Industries—indicated that they may be required, under acquisition agreements, to make additional payments to the sellers, usually in capital stock. These contingent payments are in accordance with prescribed formulas and are generally dependent upon future earnings of the acquired businesses and the future market value of the acquirer's stock.

Most of the conglomerates listed did well from the standpoint of profits (largely as the result of acquisitions) and market action in 1967. The year 1968, however, told a different story. Primary earnings per common share, before extraordinary items, were off for seven of the companies and market prices were down for ten. This contrasts with an increase in Standard & Poor's composite index of 500 stocks from 96.47 to 103.86 for the year 1968.

Until the stock market slump in 1969 and 1970, conglomerates showed no discernible market pattern as a group, as industry groups do. Their market action was based on individual performances. In fact, their price–earnings ratios at December 31, 1968, varied from less than 10 times to as high as 60 times earnings. Most of the stocks whose market prices showed relative decreases during 1968 had poor earnings records for their latest fiscal year. Several others, showing similar adverse action, had substantial deals pending that may not have been too favorably regarded by investors.

However, the years 1969 and 1970 told a different story. With increasing pressure from the antitrust enforcement agencies to prevent or challenge massive takeovers by larger conglomerates, the enactment of a provision in the Internal Revenue Code limiting interest deductions on money borrowed to acquire businesses, and the general tightness of credit, conglomerate securities declined substantially more than the average. Whereas Standard & Poor's composite index of 500 stocks declined 36% from a high of 108.37 at the close of business on November 29, 1968, to a closing low of 69.29 on May 26, 1970, when the market bottomed out, the study group of 21 stocks showed an average decline of 74%, as shown on page 385.

Excessive borrowing at high interest costs not only affected the operating results of several of the conglomerates but placed them in a financial squeeze with creditors. During 1970 and 1971 many of the companies acquired by conglomerates in preceding years were offered for sale as lending institutions exerted pressure on the conglomerates to reduce their loan balances. This situation contributed further to the general disenchantment of the investing public in conglomerate securities.

It would not be practicable in this book to discuss the statistics shown in Table 13–1 for all of the twenty-one conglomerates listed, nor to analyze the factors that contributed to their market action. Comments on a selected few and highlights from their annual reports are set forth below. In addition, a study of Walter

TABLE 13-1 Pertinent Statistics on "Conglomerate" Combinations

		Fiscal Years Ending in 1969 (or as Indicated)					
		Thousands of Dollars					
		Indebtedness		Stock-holders' Equity	Net Income		
Companies*	Goodwill	Long-Term	Short-Term		(1)	(2)	Fully Diluted
AMK Corp. (Dec.)	$385,968	$ 314,615	$ 87,239	$ 459,026	$2.69	$ 3.89	$ 2.96
A-T-O, Inc. (Dec.)	2,089	70,684	22,580	94,033	.81	1.07	1.06
Avco (Nov.)	—	414,427	263,939	420,038	3.12	3.12	2.33
Bangor Punta (Sept.)	42,758	163,918	13,735	137,320	1.44	(2.83)	NR
City Investing (Apr. 1970)	122,306	347,369	99,781	641,797	1.33	2.35	1.96
General Tire (Nov.)	—	197,803	61,979	404,193	2.08	1.90	1.90
W. R. Grace (Dec.)	42,422	405,928	123,513	658,210	1.58	2.31	2.25
Gulf & Western (July)	76,344	962,400	226,179	590,066	3.15	2.15	2.00
International Tel. & Tel. (Dec.)	NR	1,145,383	658,067	2,081,309	2.90	2.90	2.80
Walter Kidde (Dec.)	30,761	238,620	87,963	256,151	3.54	3.54	3.30
Ling-Temco (Dec.)	31,659	1,500,792	389,302	502,593	(.05)	(10.15)	(10.59)
Litton Industries (July)	102,728	352,420	219,543	704,308	2.43	2.43	2.43
Martin Marietta (Dec.)	67,619	285,591	39,620	447,506	2.21	2.21	2.10
National Distillers (Dec.)	15,199	269,772	29,274	455,157	1.31	.99	.95
Northwest Indus. (Dec.)	33,549	486,537	26,632	667,925	(.23)	(.23)	(.23)
Olin Corp. (Dec.)	—	198,649	112,867	612,663	2.10	2.10	2.10
Signal Companies (Dec.)	20,263	243,476	257,366	662,062	2.52	2.52	2.52
Teledyne Inc. (Oct.)	23,861	206,155	30,809	518,437	2.00	2.00	1.94
Tenneco (Dec.)	40,480	1,840,549	282,546	1,476,820	2.31	2.31	2.06
Textron (Jan. 3, 1970)	34,911	135,238	17,506	485,258	2.14	2.14	2.14
U. S. Industries (Dec.)	72,135	184,742	58,865	329,854	2.23	2.12	2.12

Fiscal Years Ending in 1968 (or as Indicated)

Companies*	Goodwill	Thousands of Dollars — Indebtedness Long-Term	Short-Term	Stock-holders' Equity	Net Income (1)	(2)	Fully Diluted
AMK Corp. (Dec.)	–	$ 45,339	$ 46,502	$ 81,237	$1.32	$ 1.43	$ 1.42
A–T–O, Inc. (Dec.)	$ 548	98,313	20,812	90,981	.36	.36	.36
Avco (Nov.)	–	229,710	149,426	354,427	3.76	3.76	2.69
Bangor Punta (Sept.)	38,039	134,906	6,789	114,270	2.40	2.71	2.55
City Investing (Apr. 1969)	113,797	296,464	66,168	580,538	1.02	1.95	1.78
General Tire (Nov.)	–	188,317	60,105	385,002	2.36	2.39	2.39
W. R. Grace (Dec.)	39,079	470,700	199,927	677,471	2.76	1.62	1.60
Gulf & Western (July)	51,840	917,912	166,851	541,144	3.13	3.00	2.64
International Tel. & Tel. (Dec.)	80,400	961,646	388,900	1,896,756	2.62	2.79	2.68
Walter Kidde (Dec.)	14,861	94,401	57,998	169,312	3.04	3.04	2.87
Ling–Temco (Dec.)	51,034	1,236,693	419,805	654,002	3.88	5.01	3.43
Litton Industries (July)	46,223	241,552	81,824	624,739	1.82	1.82	1.82
Martin Marietta (Dec.)	–	203,198	8,341	343,756	2.08	2.08	2.05
National Distillers (Dec.)	15,199	227,107	11,048	434,850	1.26	1.26	1.19
Northwest Indus. (Dec.)	33,457	402,352	24,972	636,156	2.64	4.64	3.06
Olin Corp. (Dec.)	–	189,562	93,688	604,322	2.30	3.11	3.11
Signal Companies (Dec.)	15,128	158,837	180,235	612,662	2.50	4.30	4.30
Teledyne Inc. (Oct.)	22,319	159,599	18,786	367,087	1.63	1.63	1.58
Tenneco (Dec.)	37,731	1,739,288	208,362	1,504,342	2.21	2.39	2.10
Textron (Dec. 28, 1968)	35,205	145,713	15,575	468,889	2.11	2.11	2.11
U. S. Industries (Dec.)	41,300	89,805	55,954	252,211	1.80	1.80	1.80

NR = not reported.

* With the exception of Olin Corp. all companies had debentures or preferred stock outstanding, either directly or through subsidiaries, which were convertible into common shares. In addition, twelve of them had stock purchase warrants outstanding at December 31, 1969.

(1) Net income per common and common share equivalent, before extraordinary items.

(2) Net income per common and common share equivalent, after extraordinary items.

385

DECLINE IN MARKET PRICES OF SELECTED CONGLOMERATE
COMMON STOCKS FROM BULL MARKET HIGHS IN 1967
AND 1968 TO MARKET CLOSE ON MAY 26, 1970

| | Bull Market Highs | | Close | |
	Price	Year	May 26, 1970	Percentage of Decline
AMK Corporation	58⅜	1968	12⅛	79.2%
ATO Inc.	74	1968	6⅝	91.0
Avco	65⅜	1967	12¾	80.5
Bangor Punta	61⅛	1968	7¼	88.1
City Investing	39¼	1968	12½	68.2
General Tire	38¼	1967	13¼	61.3
W. R. Grace	61⅜	*	21¾	64.6
Gulf & Western	64¼	1968	9¾	84.8
International Tel. & Tel.	62½	1968	33⅛	47.0
Walter Kidde	82¾	1968	18½	77.6
Ling-Temco	169½	1967	8	95.3
Litton Industries	112¼	1967	17⅛	84.7
Martin Marietta	31⅜	1968	12⅛	61.4
National Distillers	49⅛	1967	14½	70.5
Northwest Indus.	60⅝	1968	9	85.2
Olin Corp.	81¾	1967	14	82.9
Signal Companies	56½	*	14⅜	74.6
Teledyne Inc.	65¾	1968	14⅜	78.1
Tenneco	32¾	1968	17½	46.6
Textron	57⅞	1968	15⅝	73.0
U. S. Industries	36¾	1968	12⅝	65.6
Average				74.0%

* Prior to 1967.

Kidde from the inception of that company's acquisitive program
through the year 1968 illustrates how earnings per share may be
steadily improved through acquisitions.

TEXTRON AND LITTON

With few exceptions, among which were Textron and Litton,
most of the companies included in this study reached conglomerate status in relatively recent years. Textron was one of the earli-
est of the modern-day giants to seek diversification of operations.
This was done to escape the cyclical pattern of the textile busi-

ness. Starting its acquisitions move in 1953, it acquired American Woolen Company in 1955 with its substantial tax-loss carryovers. The funds generated by using these carryovers, and by selling off American Woolen's plants, contributed capital that gave impetus to Textron's acquisition program.

The company divested itself of its last textile operation in 1963. It now operates over thirty divisions that may be combined into four basic industry groups, i.e., aerospace, consumer products, industrial, and metal products. Each division has a profit goal of 25% before taxes, based on its invested capital.

Although Textron showed substantial increases in earnings during the early and middle 1960's its earnings per common share remained relatively static for the years 1967, 1968, and 1969.

Litton Industries, founded in 1953, had a spectacular history as a conglomerate. Through numerous acquisitions it penetrated markets in many diverse industries both here and abroad. Its common stock sold at a high price–earnings ratio for many years, thus facilitating its acquisitions program through the exchange of capital stock. Through the period covered by this study to December 31, 1969, Litton had yet to pay a cash dividend on its common stock, but had issued annual stock dividends for a period of years. Its common stock was selling at approximately 40 times estimated earnings at December 31, 1968, despite a decrease in earnings per share of over 20% for that fiscal year. However, the conglomerate syndrome caught up with it in the 1969–1970 bear market, and although its earnings recovered in fiscal 1969, its common stock was selling at only 8 times earnings in May 1970.

The fact that no dividends had been paid on Litton's common stock may have accounted for an offer to its shareholders, in 1966, which resulted in an exchange of a substantial number of common shares into a $2.50 convertible preference stock. Also, in recent years, this and another class of convertible preferred stock has been used in making acquisitions.

Over the years a number of Litton management executives moved on to top executive positions in other companies and have instituted extensive diversified acquisition programs for those companies.

A-T-O INC.

Sales volume for A-T-O Inc. (formerly Automatic Sprinkler) had grown from $22,000,000 in 1963 to $325,000,000 in 1968 (increased to $379,000,000 in 1969) by means of numerous acquisitions over that period. There was a substantial drop in primary earnings per share for the year 1968 compared with 1967—$0.10 versus $1.45. The 1968 earnings per share were restated in 1969 to $0.36 per share as the result of poolings, and earnings for 1969 recovered to $0.81 per share before a net extraordinary gain on the sale of securities. The following explanation in its 1968 annual report to stockholders, although expressive, was far from specific regarding the reasons for the drastic reduction in 1968 earnings:

In many ways by 1968, we had laid the foundation for a great U. S. growth company. In 1968, however, our earnings took a terrific tumble—we took a real shellacking—and the prophets of doom forecast dire results for our future. Certainly, we are not proud of our 1968 earnings, but our earnings drop was largely attributable to situations which had their seeds in contracts and situations which existed before we bought the companies involved. But we bought those companies in accordance with a program of growth dedicated to certain growth industries, sound companies and good managements. Therefore, we regard this earnings setback as temporary.

The decline in earnings during 1968 apparently was due to a combination of factors, as outlined in notes to Automatic's consolidated unaudited statement of income for the six months ended June 30, 1968, shown in a prospectus effective September 26, 1968, pursuant to an exchange offer to shareholders of United States Pipe and Foundry Company. Pertinent excerpts from the notes follow (italics added):

Earnings during the six month period ended June 30, 1968, were adversely affected by several circumstances, including principally a $4.5 million before-tax writeoff in connection with a Government contract for production of 105 mm. armor-piercing cartridge cases awarded in early 1966 to Baifield Industries, Inc. prior to its acquisition by "Automatic." This writeoff was largely necessitated by the failure of vendors to supply satisfactory materials and included unexpectedly high costs for installing and renovating equipment furnished by the Government, heavy start-up costs, and other expenses anticipated but not yet incurred. Because of the concentration of the Baifield Division's management on the 105mm. cartridge case program, a decline in new contracts (also experienced by the defense industry generally) and high start-up costs in certain programs, *operating results of the Division may be further adversely affected for the balance of the year.*

Earnings during the six month period were also adversely affected by strikes at the American La France and Fee & Mason Division plants, the writeoff of certain development expenses related to the activity of the Interstate Engineering Division as a subcontractor in connection with the C–5A aircraft being built for the Defense Department, continued reduction in home vacuum cleaner and fire alarm sales as a consequence of the change in marketing program, and substantially increased interest expenses in connection with the 4⅞% Convertible Subordinated Debentures issued June 29, 1967, and increased bank borrowings. Also for the period ended June 30, 1968, provision has been made to reflect the Federal income tax surcharge retroactive to January 1, 1968. During the early part of the period, since "Automatic" accounts on a "completed contract" basis with respect to sprinkler system installations, earnings were adversely affected by completion of relatively high-cost contracts performed largely during the transfer of the "Automatic" Sprinkler Division's operations from Youngstown, Ohio to Swainsboro, Georgia.

For the year 1969 A-T-O had net income of $10,695,000 including a net-of-tax gain of $2,068,000 on the sale of securities, less loss on the sale of fixed assets. This was equivalent to $1.06 per common share on a fully diluted basis.

Transactions in 1970

For the year 1970 A-T-O reported net income of $7,499,000 including a net-of-tax gain of $555,000 upon disposal of certain intangible and fixed assets. This was equivalent to $0.68 per common share on a fully diluted basis.

CITY INVESTING

Until early in 1967, City was engaged primarily in real estate operations, ranging from management of developed properties to development of large land areas. During the earlier years and through its fiscal year ended April 30, 1968, a substantial portion of its earnings was derived from realized gains on dispositions of real estate investments. Commencing in 1967, City acquired substantial ownership in companies engaged in manufacturing, real estate development, savings and loan activities, and fire and casualty insurance. Comments on some of the major transactions effected by City follow.

Late in 1967, City acquired for cash approximately 64% of the stock of Rheem Manufacturing Company, engaged in the manufacture of a wide variety of metal products and acquired the remaining Rheem stock for cash pursuant to an agreement in November 1968. The total cost of this acquisition was in the area of $120,000,000.

City acquired approximately 96.8% of the outstanding common stock of The Home Insurance Company pursuant to an exchange offer in August 1968, which was later extended. Under the offer, City exchanged one share of $2 cumulative convertible preference stock and 4/10 of a share of common for each share of Home common stock. Although this transaction was consummated as an exchange of voting capital stocks, City treated it as a purchase for accounting purposes and valued the capital stock issued to Home stockholders at $448,040,000. On June 30, 1970, City acquired the remaining interest in Home.

In February 1969, City acquired approximately 53.8% of the common stock of Guerdon Industries, Inc., a manufacturer of mobile homes and modern home units, for $13,657,852 in cash and $38,608,819 principal amount of 7% installment notes.

During the fiscal years ended April 30, 1969 and 1970, City increased its investment in General Development Corporation, a real estate development, building, and management company, and had an approximate 50% interest in that company at the latter date, which was carried at $67,712,000.

City acquired for $12,857,000, during the two fiscal years ended April 30, 1969, some 400,000 shares of Moore and Mc-Cormack Co., Inc., a steamship company, with an agreement to acquire the remaining 2,000,000 shares for a package of City common stock and convertible debentures. However, the agreement to complete the acquisition was terminated because of a material adverse change in the financial position of the steamship company. At April 30, 1970, this investment, which was still carried by City at $12,857,000, had a market value of $4,200,000.

At April 30, 1970, City had goodwill in the amount of $122,-306,000, in addition to which the carrying amount of its investments in unconsolidated subsidiaries exceeded its equity in their net assets by $268,391,000. The larger part of this difference, $210,165,000, applied to its investment in Home Insurance Company. City's investments in unconsolidated subsidiaries are carried at cost, plus undistributed earnings since acquisition.

During the fiscal years ended April 30, 1969 and 1970, a substantial portion of the net income of City was derived from net gains on sales of securities and real estate. This net gain, which was primarily from sales of securities by Home Insurance, amounted to $0.66 in fiscal 1970 and $0.65 in 1969, per common share, assuming full dilution.

LING-TEMCO-VOUGHT

Ling-Temco, the surviving corporation resulting from a series of mergers and acquisitions, reorganized its business and operations in December 1964, and formed three subsidiary corporations, LTV Aerospace, LTV Electrosystems, and LTV Ling Altec, to take over the business and operations of three of its principal divisions. The deal was effected by the issuance to Ling-Temco of common and convertible preferred shares of each of the subsidiaries, some debentures of two of the subsidiaries, and the assumption of certain indebtedness by one of them.

Besides the avowed purpose of decentralizing management, this reorganization placed the subsidiaries in a position to borrow money, make public offerings of securities, or acquire other companies for cash and securities, thereby increasing Ling-Temco's flexibility of action in such areas.

In the ensuing years, through exchanges of stock with Ling-Temco's stockholders and public offerings, the subsidiaries emerged with public interests. Also, Ling-Temco and its subsidiaries acquired a number of companies during the next several years through its existing subsidiaries or others newly organized for this purpose. The major consideration for such deals was cash, a large part of which was raised through loans subsequently assumed by the subsidiaries or liquidated, in part, by public offerings of stock of the subsidiaries.

The company showed spectacular earnings growth in 1966 and 1967, primarily as the result of acquisitions during those years. The Ling-Temco annual report to stockholders for 1967 indicated that the successor companies to Wilson & Co., acquired in 1967, and the Okonite Company, acquired in 1966, together with the latter's acquisitions in 1967, contributed approximately 63% of consolidated net income for 1967. This did not take into account the earnings contributions of companies acquired by Electrosystems and Ling Altec during 1967.

In 1968, Ling-Temco's financial position and earnings were adversely affected as the result of several large acquisitions during that year. Whereas, at December 31, 1967, Ling-Temco had consolidated long-term debt of $205,100,000 and short-term debt of $170,063,000, an aggregate of $375,163,000, such figures had increased at December 31, 1968, to $1,236,693,000 for long-term and $413,970,000 for short-term debt, an aggregate of $1,650,-663,000. Combined long- and short-term debt further increased to $1,859,186,000 at December 31, 1969. In comparison, stockholders' equity amounted to only $268,174,000 at the latter date.

More than $1,000,000,000 of the increase in long- and short-term debt was the result of indebtedness incurred or assumed in acquisitions by Ling-Temco of major interests in Greatamerica Corporation and Jones & Laughlin Steel Corporation. Substantial additional indebtedness was also incurred by Ling-Temco and its subsidiaries, part of which resulted from the issuance of subordinated debentures, with common stock purchase warrants, in an exchange offer for Ling-Temco common stock.

A comparison of 1969 and 1968 figures taken from the statement of consolidated income in the company's 1969 annual report is of interest:

	(Thousands Omitted)	
	1969	1968
Income before federal, state, and foreign income taxes and other charges and credits	$ (1,369)	$ 38,196
Federal, etc., taxes (credit)	(15,227)	9,710
	$ 13,858	$ 28,486
Equity in earnings of unconsolidated subsidiaries	3,214	8,899
Minority interest in income of subsidiaries	(14,736)	(13,832)
Income before extraordinary items	2,336	23,553
Extraordinary items	(40,630)	5,846
Net income (loss)	$(38,294)	$ 29,399

The extraordinary items in 1969 consisted of a reserve of $30,-000,000 for possible losses in anticipated sales of Ling-Temco's investments in Braniff and Okonite, and net losses on sales of other interests during the year. In 1968 such items consisted of gain on retirement of debt and on the sale of property.

The unusually large increase in consolidated indebtedness with a resultant increase in interest expense (before federal tax effect) from $19,567,000 in 1967 to $122,642,000 in 1969 appears to be a primary reason for the rapid decline of the Ling-Temco empire.

As indicated on pages 384 and 386, Ling-Temco had a loss per common share, assuming full dilution, of $10.59 for 1969, and a decline in market value per share of 95% from its bull market high in 1967 to the close of business May 26, 1970, when the market bottomed out.

As a result of settlement of an anti-trust suit, Ling-Temco was ordered to divest itself of its interests in Braniff and Okonite, or in the alternative, Jones & Laughlin, within three years. The company, in its 1969 report to stockholders, indicated its intention to dispose of Braniff and Okonite.

Transactions in 1970

For the year 1970, Ling-Temco reported a loss of $69,619,000, after a net extraordinary charge of $18,468,000. Such loss was equivalent to $17.18 per share, on a fully diluted basis. Particulars of the net extraordinary charge follow:

Additional provision for possible loss on disposition of subsidiaries, principally Okonite and Braniff	$36,735,000
Loss of L-T-V Ling Altec, Inc., on disposal of subsidiaries and a division	5,051,000*
Losses of L-T-V Aerospace Corp., on sale of interest in subsidiary and discontinuance of certain operations	3,402,000*
Loss on shutdown and abandonment of facilities by Jones & Laughlin Steel Corp.	4,478,000*
Provision for loss on investment in unconsolidated real estate subsidiary	1,440,000
Loss on sales of investments and real estate by subsidiaries, etc.	1,179,000*
	$52,285,000
Gain on sale of interests in certain subsidiaries, principally Wilson Sporting Goods Co. (less applicable income tax of $11,646,000)	33,817,000
Net total	$18,468,000

* Net of applicable federal income tax benefits.

WALTER KIDDE & COMPANY

This company, which basically manufactured fire detection and extinguishing equipment, was relatively small and showed modest profits through December 31, 1963. With the association of new management, early in 1964, the company commenced a series of acquisitions. For the years 1964 and 1965 these were made by the issuance of Kidde common stock. In 1966 and 1967 some acquisitions were made with a new class of $2.20 cumulative convertible preferred stock, some with common, and others with a combination of such stocks. In 1968 all stock acquisitions were made with common stock. As mentioned later, Kidde also made two substantial partial acquisitions for cash in 1968.

Table 13–2 shows the earnings contribution per share of companies acquired by Kidde during the years 1964 to 1968, inclusive. The cumulative earnings contribution of the companies to consolidated earnings were over and above earnings applicable to shares issued by Kidde to acquire such companies. Such contributions were based on the latest year's net income figures, reported for the companies in listing applications filed at the time of acquisition, or other public sources. In some cases, net income reported for part of a year has been annualized. Also, as indicated in the notes to the table, the income figures of two acquisitions have been omitted because of the lack of available data on them. An illustration of the method of computing the earnings contribution of acquired companies follows:

	Net Income	Total Common Shares Outstanding	Earnings per Share	Contribution per Share Earnings
Walter Kidde & Company, Inc. and acquired companies prior to acquisition of Weber Showcase & Fixture Co., Inc.	$1,098,000	1,330,629*	$ .83	
Acquisition of Weber Showcase & Furniture Co., Inc., 1965; net income of acquired company	810,000			
Original shares issued 375,642				
Original shares adjusted for stock dividends through December 31, 1968 422,778		422,778		
Combined	$1,908,000	1,753,407	$1.09	$.26

* Adjusted for stock dividends through December 31, 1968.

At December 31, 1968, Kidde had 6,978,199 shares of common stock outstanding, and, assuming the immediate conversion of preference stock and convertible subordinated notes (adjusted for stock dividends) into common stock, would have had 8,019,503 shares outstanding. Of this total, 7,586,781 shares consisted of the 721,993 Kidde shares outstanding at December 31, 1963, plus 6,864,788 shares issued or to be issued assuming conversion for acquisitions during the years 1964 through 1968. The earnings contribution of companies acquired during the five-year period based on their earnings reported for the latest year prior to acquisition, as described above, amounted to $23,495,000 or $2.75 per share which when added to Kidde's 1963 earnings of $275,000 or $.38 per share of Kidde totaled $3.13 per share applicable to the 7,586,781 shares. Shares totaling 432,722 also were issued or issuable, assuming conversion, for stock options, conversion of subordinated notes, and for acquisitions where income information was not available, making the total of 8,019,503 residual shares outstanding at December 31, 1968. Consolidated net income applicable to such shares amounted to $24,687,000 or $3.11 per share for 1968.

In other words, the company dramatically improved its earnings per share by the sheer economics of acquiring other companies at price–earnings ratios which were below, in some cases substantially, those at which Kidde stock was selling. This, of course, is the general objective of a conglomerate in its acquisitive program.

Whereas Kidde acquisitions through 1967 had been made primarily by the use of capital stock, in 1968 it acquired, for cash, approximately 45% of the outstanding capital stock of United States Lines for $50,292,455, and a number of common and preferred shares of Crum & Forster for $27,485,819 during 1968 and 1969.

On January 10, 1969, Kidde acquired the remaining 55% interest in United States Lines in exchange for 483,867 common shares and 285,736 Series B Convertible Cumulative Preference shares. Since the transaction was accounted for as a purchase, the accounts of United States Lines were not included in Kidde's financial statements until 1969.

TABLE 13-2 Walter Kidde & Company, Inc.—Earnings Contribution per Share of Companies Acquired, 1963-1968*

	Kidde Shares Issued[1]				Income of Acquired Companies[2] ($000)	Earnings Contrib. per Share to Total Kidde Outstanding[3]
		Common				
	Preferred	Common	Assuming Conv. of Preferred	Total Common		
Walter Kidde & Co. Inc., 12/31/63		721,993		721,993	$ 275	$ .38
1964 Acquisitions:						
Cocker Machine & Foundry Co.		91,722		91,722	96	.08
Associated Testing Lab., Inc.		187,081		187,081	189	.10
1965 Acquisitions:						
Audio Equipment Co., Inc.		48,477		48,477	92	.06
Air–Tech Industries, Inc.		9,609		9,609	16	.01
Fyre Safety, Inc.; Fyre Safety Sales Co.; Graphic Guaranty Co., Inc.; Triumph Accept. Corp.		22,881		22,881	24	.01
Pathé Equipment Co., Inc.		112,048		112,048	203	.11
Columbian Bronze Corp.		136,818		136,818	203	.08
Weber Showcase & Fixture Co., Inc.		422,778		422,778	810	.26
Park Products Co.		18,960		18,960	159	.08
M & D Store Fixtures, Inc.		153,567		153,567	358	.09
Morris Manufacturing Co.		9,053		9,053	38	.01
1966 Acquisitions:						
Le Febure, Inc.	164,967		358,778	358,778	619	.07
Globe Security Systems, Inc.	201,111		437,385	437,385	879	.11
Young Industries		2,525	2,525	2,525	—²	
Fenwal, Inc.; Fenwal Electronics; Fenwal Int'l. Ltd.	97,499	232,213	211,960	444,173	1,210	.18
Dura Corp.	469,109	1,020,239	1,020,239	1,020,239	2,530	.20
Interstate Security Services, Inc.	7,000	20,661	15,224	35,885	152	.02
1967 Acquisitions:						
Modern Refrigeration Services	396	422		422	12⁴	.01
Merit Protective Services, Inc. (N.J.)		858	862	1,720		
Sargent & Co.	113,780		247,453	247,453	741	.06
Lighting Corp. of America	255,968	556,788	556,691	1,113,479	3,612	.26
Wright Light Inc.; Sign Light Inc.		12,669	12,669	12,669	93	.01

396

Toledo Commutation Co. and Molded Elect. Co....

			52,766		.05
Grove Manufacturing Co.	50,237	348,767	109,258	458,025	1,550	.08
Houston Electronics Corp.		84,768		84,768	388	.04
Carpenter Manufacturing Co.		11,382		11,382	125[7]	.01
Dura Steel Products Co.		13,666		13,666	(276)	(.05)
Morrison Industries, Inc.		57,651		57,651	422	.05
Jade Corp.; Jade Tool		234,610		234,610	2,495[6]	.29
Garden State Tanning, Inc.; Pine Grove Tanning Co.; Chestnut Operating Co.; Tanning House, Inc.		75,931		75,931	562	.06
Crane Hoist Engineering Corp.		99,590		99,590	1,367	.16
1968 Acquisitions:						
H. Greenwald Mfg. Co., Inc., and rel. companies .... New Jersey Office Supply Co., Inc.; Armac Press, Inc.; Quick Snap Printing Corp.; New Jersey Office Machines, Inc.; Gerart Office Furniture	38,430	38,430		38,430	402	.05
Co., and Drecher Bros. of Bergen County	96,477	96,477		96,477	431	.02
Harrington & Richardson, Inc.	117,068	117,068		117,068	419	.01
American Crane and Hoist	37,269	37,269		37,269	271	.02
Georgian Court of America, Inc.	45,964	45,964		45,964	204[8]	.01
Halkey–Roberts Corp.	6,292	6,292		6,292	143[9]	.02
Work–O–Lite Co., Inc., and National Lighting Supply Co., Inc.	20,500	20,500		20,500	272	.03
Jersey Testing Labs, Inc.	16,088	16,088		16,088	113	.01
Tose Properties, Inc.	211,425	211,425		211,425	895	.03
Keystone Lamp Mfg. Corp. and subsids.	217,303	217,303		217,303	906	.03
First Theurer Corp.	63,974	63,974		63,974	424[10]	.03
	1,360,067	4,628,931	2,957,850	7,586,781	23,770	$3.13
Stock options exercised	22,384	169,678[11]	47,494[13]	217,172		
Conversion of subordinated notes		139,254[11]		139,254		
Conversion of preference into common	(925,648)	1,964,040[13]	(1,964,040)[13]			
Other[12]	(1,112)	76,296		76,296		
Walter Kidde & Co., Inc., 12/31/68	455,691	6,978,199	1,041,304	8,019,503	$24,687	$3.11

* See Notes, on p. 398.

Notes—Table 13-2

1. Adjusted for stock dividends of 4% in 1964; 3½% in 1965; 3% in 1966 and in 1967; 2½% in 1968; and assuming immediate conversion of 455,691 shares of Kidde $2.20 Cumulative Conversion "A" Preference stock.

2. Based on the latest year's net income figures reported for such companies in listing application or proxies filed at the time of acquisition; or other public sources.

3. Earnings contributed to consolidated earnings per share over and above earnings applicable to shares issued by Kidde to acquire such companies.

4. Net income reported for nine months only was $9,128; annualized it would be $12,170. Purchase price also included $20,000 in cash.

5. Net income of Toledo Commutation Company reported for five months only was $124,138; annualized it would be $297,931. Net income of Molded Electrical Company reported for nine months only was $31,105; annualized it would be $41,472.

6. Includes Jade Tool net income for nine months only of $874,275; annualized to $1,165,671.

7. Net income for six months only was $62,656; annualized it would be $125,312.

8. Net income for six months only of $102,231; annualized to $204,462.

9. Net income for six months only of $71,551; annualized to $143,102.

10. Net income of Gemini Inc. for seven and one-half months only was $8,309, and First Parkhurst Corporation for six months only was $13,229; annualized to $13,296 and $26,458, respectively, for these subsidiaries which are included in the total.

11. Assuming exercise or conversion occurred before stock dividend record date in each instance.

12. The table does not include S. W. Farber, Inc. (for which financial data could not be obtained), acquired in 1965 for approximately $10,000,000. However, the 1965 annual report indicated the purchase price exceeded related net assets by approximately $6,500,000. Also not included is Cardinal Electronics Company of Canada, Ltd. (for which financial data could not be obtained), acquired in 1967 for 60,575 adjusted common shares.

13. At current rate of 2.1218 as shown in 1968 annual report to shareholders.

In connection with an offering, in August 1969, of debentures and warrants of Kidde by selling security holders, the consolidated statement of income (loss) of United States Lines for 1968 included in the prospectus showed a loss of $8,877,737 before extraordinary items, and a loss of $24,692,017 after extraordinary items (net) resulting primarily from "the implementation of the new container services, the abandonment of break bulk trades and the cessation of passenger operations." In addition, United States Lines' financial statements showed a direct charge for 1968 of $5,622,750 to "Earnings retained in the business" for adjustments to accruals under an operating-differential subsidy agreement with the U. S. Goverment.

Income of Kidde for 1968 was restated at the close of 1969 to $26,380,384 to give retroactive effect to poolings of interest in the latter year. Shares outstanding and earnings per share on a fully diluted basis for 1968 were restated at 9,259,121 and $2.87 respectively. Reported income for 1969 was $33,604,040 equivalent to $3.30 per share applicable to the 10,462,043 shares outstanding at December 31, 1969, on a fully diluted basis.

With the substantial write-offs in 1968, prior to the inclusion of United States Lines' operations, this acquisition accounted for $0.27 per share of the $0.43 per share improvement in Kidde's consolidated results in 1969. A number of other acquisitions during 1969, accounted for as poolings of interests, further contributed to Kidde's improved results for that year.

Transactions in 1970

For the year 1970, Kidde reported a loss of $37,600,000 after a net extraordinary charge of $56,400,000. Such loss was equivalent to $3.82 per common share. Particulars of the net extraordinary charge follow:

1. A provision for loss of $42,000,000 resulting from an agreement dated November 9, 1970, with R. J. Reynolds Tobacco Company to sell United States Lines. Such loss was based on the excess of Kidde's cost and equity in earnings since acquisition of United States Lines over the $65,000,000 contractual sales price to Reynolds.

2. A provision for loss of $10,900,000 on the investment in Crum and Forster stock. During September 1970, Kidde sold 335,000 common shares of such stock at a substantial loss and the provision combines such loss plus the estimated loss on the remaining investment in Crum and Forster.
3. A charge of $9,200,000 related to the sale or discontinuance of several other operations.
4. A gain of $5,700,000, net of tax on the sale of 600,000 shares or 30% of its interest in Globe Security Systems, Inc.

CONCLUSION

Probably the competence of management of a conglomerate may be judged only when it stops acquiring for a period and demonstrates the ability to promote internal growth. Although it is too early to judge the performance, on this basis, of many conglomerates listed in Table 13–1, it is evident that some have relied solely on "deals" and leverage in types of securities issued to show improved earnings. Furthermore, the vaunted claim of furnishing overall management with resultant benefits and efficiencies has not been translated into improved operations in the case of others, and the ease with which they have been able to incur indebtedness to finance acquisitions has adversely affected the earnings and financial stability of several.

The real test of a successful conglomerate lies in its *long-term* ability to (a) provide and develop competent management, (b) develop component businesses to their optimum profit potential, and (c) obtain needed capital on a sound basis. Using these criteria, only a limited number of conglomerates could qualify as being presently successful. As in the case of other stocks, the quality of their earnings is of paramount importance.

PART IV

SPECIAL SITUATIONS

14

Valuations for
Dissenting Stockholders

Valuations pursuant to state laws for appraisal rights of stockholders and those subject to approval of the Securities and Exchange Commission, which has quasi-judicial powers, are discussed in this chapter.

In a statutory merger or consolidation, or the sale or other disposition of all or substantially all of the assets of a corporation, not in the ordinary course of business of the corporation, the states usually grant stockholders the right to dissent from such action and to appraisal of their shares and payment of the appraisal value in cash.

PROVISIONS OF STATE LAWS

A review of the *Corporation Manual*, 1969 Edition, published by United States Corporation Company, including revisions in state legislation during 1968, indicates a diversity of state laws in the area of stockholders' dissents and appraisal rights. The District of Columbia and all states with the exception of West Virginia have laws specifically providing the right of stockholders to dissent. A tabulation of pertinent rights and restrictions regarding dissenting stockholders, indicating states having unusual restrictions, is included as Appendix H.

A number of states have no apparent provisions restricting the right to dissent to plans of a merger or consolidation, while in a number of others the only apparent restriction is with respect to certain parent–subsidiary mergers. Some few states restrict the right to dissent in mergers and consolidations in specific circumstances, such as where shares held are registered or listed on national securities exchanges or held of record by not less than a certain number of shareholders, or no alteration of contract rights results.

Sale, Exchange, or Lease of Corporate Property

The majority of states specifically grant the right of shareholders to dissent to the sale, exchange, or lease of substantially all corporate property, except that no right is granted by a number of states in the case of a cash sale, prior to distribution in liquidation, or in sales pursuant to a court order.

Miscellaneous Rights and Obligations of Dissenting Stockholders

Other provisions regarding the right to dissent in statutory mergers or consolidations, or in the sale, exchange, or lease of substantially all corporate property follow:

> *Right to dissent to less than all shares held*—This right is either not mentioned or specifically denied in the majority of states, but is granted in some.
>
> *Filing of written objection to proposed corporate action*—This is required to be done prior to the meeting or prior to the corporate action in the majority of the states. In all cases the statutes provide that the dissenting stockholders may not have voted in favor of the proposal.
>
> *Right of dissenting stockholder to withdraw demand for payment of his stock*—This right may be withdrawn with corporate consent, or could effectually be withdrawn by the failure to take timely action in the majority of states. In a few states the language of the statutes appears to preclude withdrawal of demand.

Definition of Value Used in Various Statutes

The definitions used in the fifty jurisdictions having statutes relating to dissenting stockholders' rights of appraisal follow: in 33 states the term used is "fair value," in 7 "fair cash value," in 6 "value," and in 4 "fair market value." In 26 states such values are indicated to be exclusive of any element of value arising from the expectation or accomplishment of the proposed transaction.

Date at which value is to be determined—In 36 states such determination is indicated to be the date prior to the vote approving the action; in 9 it is as of the effective date of the corporate action; and in the remaining 5 states it is either not mentioned or indicated to be at other specified dates.

Persons determining value initially—In 22 states this is done by the corporation, in 23 by agreement between the parties, in 4 by dissenting stockholders, and in 1 by the court.

Persons determining value where no agreement is reached between corporation and dissenting stockholders—This is done by the court in 33 states, by court-appointed appraisers in 12 states, and by arbitration in 5 states. Where the court makes a determination of value the statutes of 15 states indicate that it may elect to appoint appraisers.

All dissenting stockholders made parties to court proceedings—This is required in 18 states, optional in 10, and not mentioned in 22.

Payment of interest to dissenting stockholders on cash value of shares in court actions—This is required in 37 states and is not mentioned in 13.

CASE RE STOCK OF DISSENTING STOCKHOLDERS

The cases where dissenting stockholders bring suit solely in a dispute over the valuation of their shares are very infrequent. Usually there are other issues involved, such as alleged bad faith on the part of corporate officers in negotiating a merger or consolidation or the sale of the assets of the corporation. Other issues included in such actions may be alleged violations of federal antitrust laws, the antifraud provisions of the securities laws, and fraud under state laws.

Great Western Sugar Company, et al.

A recent interesting action involving a suit by a common stockholder of The Great Western Sugar Company (Sugar), acting on behalf of herself and others to enjoin a proposed merger of that company and Colorado Milling and Elevator Company (Milling) into a subsidiary of Milling, The Great Western United Corporation (United), had all three companies named as defendants, in addition to the directors of Sugar and Milling. The judgment of the United States District Court in favor of the defendants was affirmed by the United States Court of Appeals and later upheld when the United States Supreme Court refused to review the lower court decision. The data below were summarized from the opinion of the Court of Appeals: [1]

Sugar was engaged in the production of sugar and its by-products from sugar beets and was the largest sugar beet producer in the country, accounting for about 25% of the beet sugar marketed in this country and having a net worth of approximately $93,000,000 as of February 28, 1967. Milling was principally engaged in the manufacture and sale of wheat, flour, and mixes, and animal feeds. It also bought and sold grains, beans, seeds and fertilizers, and stored grains for the public in company-owned elevators. Milling's net worth was approximately $24,000,000 as of May 31, 1967.

Acquisition of Voting Control. Milling, through a tender offer in 1966, acquired a sufficient number of preferred and common shares of Sugar to give it virtual voting control (47%) of the latter. The tender offer was aimed primarily at Sugar's preferred stock, since, by virtue of its unusual voting structure, each of the 150,000 preferred shares had one vote while each of the 1,800,000 shares of common had only $\frac{1}{12}$ of a vote, thereby giving the aggregate preferred holders 50% of the voting power.

Approval by Merging Companies. Standard Research Consultants, Inc. were engaged by Milling to recommend one or more plans for a merger of Sugar and Milling. Several different plans were drawn up, and other financial consultants were engaged by Sugar before a plan was approved by the latter's board of directors,

---

[1] Jane Levin, et al. v. The Great Western Sugar Co., et al., No. 17080 United States Court of Appeals, 3rd Cir., Decision, as amended, Feb. 20, 1969.

which at that point, except for one member, consisted of Milling designees. At a stockholders' meeting on September 15, 1967, 92% of the shares of Sugar were voted in favor of the merger, including approval by independent stockholders owning a substantial amount of all shares. It was also approved by Milling stockholders. Under the plan, which had been modified several times to improve the participation of Sugar stockholders, each share of Milling stock was to be exchanged for a share of United common, and each share of Sugar common would be exchanged for ⅓ share of United common and one share of United $1.88 non-convertible cumulative preferred. The merger was consummated on January 15, 1968.

Allegation of Fraud.   The plaintiff sought to enjoin the merger on the grounds of alleged fraud under Section 10(b) and Rule 10b–5 of the Securities Exchange Act of 1934, common-law fraud under New Jersey law, and lastly, but principally, that the terms of the merger were unfair to the Sugar common stockholders.

Kidder, Peabody & Company, financial consultants were engaged by Sugar to review the final merger plan submitted by the financial consultants of Milling, and concluded that the Sugar common stockholder:

1. Would find himself in a preferred equity position with respect to about 60% of market value of his new holdings;
2. Would receive securities with an indicated market value of $47.80 per share of equivalent (Sugar) common stock, or a value that is 21% higher than the present market for the common, and a value that also compares favorably with the price range of the common over the past ten years, with the exception of 1963;
3. Assuming that the dividend on [Milling] common is increased to $1.80, would receive a 20% increase in dividend income with 75% of such income in the form of a preferred and fixed payment; [The estimated total dividend package after merger for the Sugar common stockholders was $2.48, $1.88 on the preferred, and $.60 on the common. The pre-merger figure was $2.00.]
4. Would obtain an increase of ⅓ of a vote per share until such time as the cumulative preferred stock would be redeemed. Initially, the (Sugar) common shareholders would have about 53% of the votes of the surviving corporation;
5. Would also obtain an increase in book value from $24.95 to $34.70 per share;

6. On the other hand, would receive about a 10–15% dilution in per share earnings; and

7. Would be receiving "Section 306 Stock" and hence a favorable ruling from the IRS should be a condition for the exchange.

The plaintiff's principal objections were as to market values, dividends, and earnings per share, in respect of which she contended that Milling stockholders benefited disproportionately in the merger. The court agreed that the plaintiff and other Sugar common stockholders were entitled to a proportionate benefit in the merged corporation and turned to a close examination of the plaintiff's claims.

Findings of the Court. *Comparison of earnings.* A comparison of earnings of the two companies since 1962 showed a steady increase in Milling's earnings over the ensuing five years except for 1967, and a relatively static earnings pattern of Sugar, with a slight decline in earnings following a peak in 1964. The 1967 decline in Milling's earnings reflected expenditures and loans incurred with respect to stock purchases under the tender offer for Sugar stock. The court pointed out that the earnings comparison chart indicated that the prospectus for earnings growth of Milling was excellent, whereas the opposite seemed the case for Sugar. In view of the past performances of both companies, the court deemed it fair to accord greater weight to Milling's earnings potential and to reflect this in the disparate allocation to post-merger earnings (a 10 to 15% dilution to Sugar stockholders and approximately 100% increase to Milling stockholders). Furthermore, it was mentioned that Sugar common stockholders received a prior claim on earnings to the extent of their preferred holdings in United.

Post-Merger Dividends. As to post-merger dividends, the dividend increase to Milling stockholders was from $1.20 to an estimated $1.80, a 50% rise. The dividend increase for Sugar common stockholders was from $2.00 to an estimated $2.48, a 24% rise. The court held that $1.88 of the dividend to Sugar stockholders was on preferred stock, which fairly justified the percentage differential, particularly in view of the indicated policy of the new board of directors to retain earnings in the business for development and growth.

Market Values. As to market values, the pre-merger figures assigned to market values by Kidder, Peabody were $39.50 for Sugar and $49.00 for Milling. The post-merger figures traced into their equivalents in United stock were $47.80 for Sugar common and $57.00 for Milling. The plaintiff did not object to such increases as being disproportionate, but based her complaint on the after-market action. In the after-market, the Sugar common package in its equivalents fluctuated from a low of $50.00 to a high of $65.00; the Milling stock in United equivalents ranged from a low of $80.00 to a high of $116.00.

The court pointed out that "hindsight is a slippery base upon which to stand in passing judgment, particularly in matters of valuation. . . . Such later market action may be influenced by many factors having little or nothing to do with the fairness of a valuation judgment previously made." It expressed the belief that the estimates of market were properly arrived at on the basis of the then relevant information. The court held, on this point, that ". . . it was not only the Milling stock equivalent in United whose value rose above the predicted increase, but Sugar common stock's package as well, resulting in an even larger premium for plaintiff than projected."

Comment. This was a case where a company in a static industry that had little apparent prospect for improved earnings was taken over by a company with progressive growth-oriented management. The common stockholders of Sugar were better off from the standpoint of market values and dividends on their stock as a result of the merger. The main complaint of the plaintiff was to the effect that the Milling stockholders fared far better than those of Sugar, particularly with regard to post-merger earnings, i.e., an increase of 100% compared with a decrease of 10 to 15% for former Sugar stockholders. This earnings increase, of course, influenced the price of United stock in the after-market. As pointed out in Chapters 11 and 12, any company whose growth is achieved primarily through acquisitions and mergers endeavors to improve its earnings upon consummation of such deals. In this case it is a question of degree, as the fulfillment of Milling's earnings potential was immediately achieved by acquiring Sugar's earnings. Considering this, and also the fact that the Sugar board of directors who voted approval of the deal consisted of Milling designees with one exception, raises a question as to the so-called "proportionate benefits" obtained by stockholders of the respective interests in this deal.

CASES DECIDED BY THE SECURITIES AND EXCHANGE COMMISSION

The Securities and Exchange Commission may, upon application, become involved in a determination of the valuation of securities issued in an exchange under the Investment Company Act of 1940 and the Public Utility Holding Company Act of 1935, and in the valuation of utility assets or of any other interest in any business under the latter Act.

While the cases in which application is made to the SEC for such determinations have not been too numerous lately, it is interesting to note factors considered in making their determination in two recent cases. In one case the proposed exchange ratios of securities were revised by the Commission, and in the other, the ratio was approved as filed. In each case, the stockholders of the "absorbed" companies received a premium on the market prices of their stocks on the basis of comparison with those of the dominant companies in the business combinations.

Pennzoil and United Gas [2]

The purpose of valuation was determination of fairness and equity of a proposed exchange of shares under the consolidation plan filed under Section 11(e) of the Public Utility Holding Company Act of 1935 to the persons affected by such plan.

The exchange ratio of shares of United for Pennzoil United Inc. (Consolidated) under the proposed plan filed was one half share of $4 dividend preference common stock convertible into 0.588 share of Consolidated common.

---

[2] In the Matters of Pennzoil Co. and United Gas Corporation, SEC Release No. 15963, February 7, 1968.

As determined by the Commission, the exchange ratio was one half share of $4 dividend preference common stock convertible into 0.72 share of Consolidated common.

Description of Proceedings and Excerpts from Findings. Pennzoil and its subsidiaries were engaged in various non-utility businesses and owned and operated oil gathering and pipeline systems, refineries, canning and packaging plants, warehouses, and marketing facilities. United, which was registered as a holding company under the 1935 Act, and its subsidiaries, were engaged primarily in the production, purchasing, gathering, transportation, transmission, and sale of natural gas and petroleum products. They were also engaged in the mining and marketing of copper, molybdenum, potash, and crude sulphur.

During 1965, Pennzoil acquired 5,427,598 shares, approximately 42% of the 12,918,982 outstanding shares of common stock of United, at the time of the proceedings before the Securities and Exchange Commission. Of this amount 5,152,598 shares were acquired at a price of $41 per share pursuant to a tender offer, the remaining 275,000 shares having been purchased on the open market. After this acquisition Pennzoil registered as a holding company, as required under the 1935 Act. A plan was filed with the Commission which provided for the exchange of securities of the two companies for securities of Consolidated.

Under the plan, the public common stockholders of United were to receive one-half share of $4 dividend preference common stock of Consolidated for each share of United held (or alternatively ⅔ share of common stock of Consolidated). Each full share of the $4 dividend preference common was to be convertible (a) during the first six years following the effective date of the consolidation, into 1.176 shares of Consolidated common, equivalent to .588 shares per share of United; and (b) during the succeeding six years, into 1.053 shares of common, equivalent to .5265 shares per share of United.

Testimony of Witnesses. Testimony in support of the fairness of the plan was presented by two management representatives of Pennzoil and United and one non-management witness, who was retained after the plan was filed to testify as an expert that it was fair and equitable from a financial viewpoint. Although the witnesses introduced other evidence, their testimony appeared to be oriented around comparative market prices to judge the fairness of the exchange ratio.

Price–Earnings Ratios Developed. The expert witness prepared comparative earnings data both on companies and on a pro forma basis for Consolidated. He then developed price–earnings ratios for each company and for Consolidated. He considered the 1965 earnings of eight gas transmission companies and their related price–earnings ratios ranging from 13.5 to 18.7 and concluded that a multiple of 14 would be appropriate in capitalizing United's 1965 net income of $2.42 per share, resulting in a value of approximately $34 per share. Although he developed similar information for Pennzoil on a number of petroleum companies and from other indexes, he used these merely as a point of reference and not to indicate comparability. He also considered Pennzoil's 1965 net income of $3.01 per share and used a multiplier of 19.8 to arrive at a value of about $60 per share. This 19.8 multiple was obtained from a mathematical formula in a well known text on security analysis.[3]

Comparison of Market Values. The witness then referred to comparative market values on November 19, 1965, before the tender offer date, November 22, 1965. He found the prices of United and Pennzoil common stocks to be $35.75 and $56.75 respectively, a ratio of 0.63 to 1. Such prices and ratio were not inconsistent with his derived values, and he therefore chose to use them for purposes of his evaluation, stating further that experience of the companies since that time merely confirmed his conclusions as to relative values.

One management witness relied upon the prevailing market prices in December 1965, of $42 for United and $66 for Pennzoil, a ratio of 0.636 to 1. He also noted that on October 28, 1966, after announcement of the terms of the exchange, market prices were $48.375 for United and $73.25 for Pennzoil, a ratio of 0.66 to 1.

[3] GRAHAM, DODD, AND COTTLE, SECURITY ANALYSIS—PRINCIPLES AND TECHNIQUES (4th ed. 1962).

Market Action Before and After Tender Offer. The other management witness, although giving consideration to United's and Pennzoil's earnings history and potential, to book values, and to current and prospective earnings contributions, gave substantial weight to the market price history of the companies before and after the tender offer. He referred to the March 1966 market prices of United and Pennzoil common stocks which ranged respectively from $45 to $50 and from $70 to $75 (a ratio of approximately 0.655 to 1). He testified that ordinarily the price of a convertible security is set at a level which is 15 to 25% over the current market value or assumed equity value of the securities into which it is convertible. Accordingly, the right to convert one share of $4 dividend preference common stock into 1.176 shares of common stock of Consolidated (which is at the rate of one share of United for 0.588 of a share of Consolidated) reflects a discount of about 12% from his assumed parity of 0.667, based on market values.

Use of Mathematical Formula Rejected by Commission. The Commission rejected the use of the mathematical formula resulting in the 19.8 multiple of Pennzoil's 1965 earnings, stating that it was intended to indicate the theoretical or mathematical maximum which would apply to any company with an asserted future growth rate of 7.2% (which is assumed in the formula). According to the Commission's statement, ". . . neither the earnings forecast for Pennzoil for the years 1967 and 1968 nor any other part of the record justifies the use of the 19.8 multiplier."

Limited Weight Given Market Prices. In considering the testimony as to fairness presented by witnesses, the Commission concluded, among other things, that in determining the exchange ratios stipulated in the plan, too much weight had been given to market price considerations and the substantial effects of Pennzoil's acquisition of about 42% of United's stock had not been reflected.

In discussing the use of market prices in determining exchange value, the Commission noted: "Market price comparisons . . . are normally entitled to only limited weight . . . the market prices . . . prior to the tender offer . . . have little, if any, significance. . . . The market prices of United subsequent to the tender offer were affected by the tender offer itself . . . ; and the market prices of both United and Pennzoil were also substantially influenced by speculative and extraneous considerations. . . ."

Valuation Determinable When Stockholders Surrender Their Interest. After substantial borrowings to acquire United stock, the ratio of Pennzoil's debt to total capitalization at December 31, 1965, had increased to 78% from 21% at the end of the previous year. During 1966, the first full year of interest on the additional debt, Pennzoil's earnings covered interest charges 2.1 times, down from 16.3 times in 1964. The Commission noted that "under the 'fair and equitable' standards of Section 11(e), . . . valuation has primary relationship to values as of the time when stockholders surrender their interest for exchange under a plan, not as of an earlier date which does not take into proper account intervening developments, ..."

Projected Earnings Considered. The Commission, in its independent analysis, first calculated the proportion of pro forma earnings (based on adjusted figures for 1966 and 1967 and projected earnings for 1968, 1969, and 1970) of Consolidated for a five-year period to be contributed by United public stockholders and by Pennzoil. The resulting ratio of average income contributed was 55.58% for the United public stockholders and 44.42% for Pennzoil. Applying these ratios to the number of shares of Consolidated which would be outstanding, the Commission calculated that the 3,745,692 shares of Consolidated $4 dividend preference common issuable to United stockholders should be convertible into 5,766,227 shares of Consolidated common—equivalent to 0.77 share for each share of United.

Adjustment for Intangible Factors. This conversion rate was then adjusted in consideration of other relevant factors, including the following:

1. Pennzoil's dominant position in its field and strong marketing organization were factors favorable to continued earnings growth and indicated a lower conversion rate.
2. The preference nature of dividend rights which the United stockholders would receive warranted a reduction in the parity ratio.

3. Comparative coverage of fixed interest charges by earnings of United, Pennzoil, and Consolidated indicated a participation for United stockholders in earnings which were less secure and therefore justified a higher conversion rate. However, earnings coverage of fixed interest charges plus dividend payments of United compared with earnings coverage of fixed interest charges, plus preference stock dividends of Consolidated indicated an opposite trend.

4. Conversion at the parity rate would likely result in a decrease in dividends.

5. A suggestion that tax benefits contributed by Pennzoil be given weight in the calculation was rejected on the grounds that the contribution of earnings by United permitting utilization of the tax benefits was of equal weight.

Conclusions of Commission. After considering all relevant factors the Commission concluded that the conversion rate for the preference stock should be 1.44 shares of common for the initial six-year period—equivalent to 0.72 share of United. For the next succeeding six years the conversion rate should be equivalent to .648 share, a reduction of 10%, approximately the same percentage as proposed in the plan. Thus, assuming that all of the $4 preference common stock of Consolidated to be received by the United stockholders were converted at the initial rate of 0.72, they would receive 5,393,797 shares of Consolidated common constituting 53.9% of the total outstanding shares. In addition to the determination of the fairness and equity of the proposed exchange ratio of shares of Consolidated, the Commission dealt with other matters in this proceeding.

Comment. This case is of interest in that the Commission recognized the influence that a tender offer, and speculation over the outcome of a merger plan, had on market prices of the stocks of the constituent companies. The Commission evidently placed the greatest stress on the estimated earnings contribution of each of the merger constituents to the Consolidated company, allowing a slight mathematical edge to Pennzoil stockholders because of the preferred dividend rights accruing to United stockholders.

Electric Bond and Share and American & Foreign Power [4]

The purpose of valuation was determination that terms of proposed merger of two affiliated registered closed-end investment companies were reasonable and fair and did not involve overreaching on the part of any person concerned, as required under Section 17(b) of the Investment Company Act of 1940.

The exchange ratio of shares of Bond and Share for Foreign Power, under the proposed plan filed, was .6 to 1. As determined by the Commission, the exchange ratio was approved as filed.

Description of Proceedings and Excerpts from Findings. Bond and Share and its 56% owned subsidiary, Foreign Power, filed an application for an order exempting the proposed merger of the two companies from the provisions of the Investment Company Act of 1940. A stockholder of Bond and Share and a stockholder of Foreign Power opposed the application on the grounds that the exchange ratio of .6 share of Bond and Share for each share of Foreign Power was unfair to the stockholders of each of the respective companies.

Bond and Share's principal assets consisted of various operating subsidiaries including several service companies and a chemical company, securities of unaffiliated companies, and its holdings of Foreign Power stock. The Foreign Power stock amounted to 56.1% of Bond and Share's total stated net assets and had a market value of $72,110,000, or 32.7% of net asset value computed in accordance with the Act. The tax basis of the stock had been higher than market for several years, and in each year Bond and Share had sold a sufficient number of shares to realize tax losses which established Bond and Share's dividend as a return of capital to its shareholders. The tax losses had also been applied to offset realized capital gains, and a large capital loss carryover remained available for application against future capital gains. Bond and Share had followed the practice of replacing the Foreign Power shares sold.

---

[4] In the Matter of Electric Bond and Share Co. and American & Foreign Power Co., Inc., SEC Release No. 5215, December 28, 1967.

Foreign Power's principal assets consisted of utility operating companies in five Latin American countries, holdings of Latin American government dollar obligations, investments in several Latin American industrial ventures, and various short-term obligations. Expropriation of its Cuban properties in 1960 had produced a tax loss sufficient to offset its income since that date, plus an additional amount to be carried forward to future years.

The criteria considered in determining the fairness of the exchange ratio of shares were as follows.

Market Prices. For a fourteen-year period Foreign Power's year-end market prices had ranged from 31 to 57% of Bond and Share's. The proposed exchange ratio of .6 to 1 would provide Foreign Power shareholders with roughly a 20% premium over the market price ratio of .5 to 1 on the day negotiations began. Contrary to an assertion by one dissenting stockholder, the record showed that Bond and Share's sales and purchases of Foreign Power stock had no long-term effect upon the market.

Earnings and Capital Gains. According to the Commission's statement:

Bond and Share's earnings per share for the fiscal year ended December 31, 1966, on a corporate basis and a consolidated basis (including the consolidated net income of Bond and Share's domestic subsidiaries and Bond and Share's equity in the consolidated net income of Foreign Power) were $1.83 and $3.22, respectively. Bond and Share also realized $1.32 per share in capital gains, of which 21¢ was attributable to gains on transactions in Foreign Power stock. Foreign Power's earnings per share for the same period were $1.95 and $2.28, respectively. Thus, Foreign Power's corporate earnings were 66.3% of the total of Bond and Share's corporate earnings plus capital gains other than on transactions in Foreign Power stock, and Foreign Power's consolidated earnings were 52.7% of Bond and Share's consolidated earnings plus the same capital gains. . . . If gains realized by Bond and Share on its transactions in Foreign Power stock are included the percentages would be 61.9 and 50.2, respectively.

On a pro forma basis for 1966, giving effect to the merger, the earnings attributable to each share of Foreign Power stock would have decreased by 30¢ on a corporate basis and by 22¢ on a consolidated basis. If Bond and Share's realized capital gains (excluding gains on Foreign Power stock) are added to its corporate net income, then the amount attributable to a public shareholder of Foreign Power would have increased as a result of the merger (on the basis of the 1966 pro forma figures) by 19¢ to $2.14 per share, and if added to consolidated net income would have increased by 27¢ to $2.55 per share. Computed on the same pro forma basis, Bond and Share's net income, taken together with such capital gains, would have increased by 62¢ to $3.56 per share on a corporate basis and decreased 9¢ to $4.24 per share on a consolidated basis.

Depending upon the circumstances in which they are realized, gains from the sales of securities that are a recurring item are a factor to be taken into consideration in assessing the fairness of an allocation in a merger or reorganization. Here Bond and Share has had a substantial portfolio of marketable securities aside from its holdings of Foreign Power stock for twelve years. At September 30, 1967, such portfolio was valued at $54,400,000, and contained $18.4 million in unrealized appreciation. It expects to continue to maintain such a portfolio. In each of the years 1963 through 1966, Bond and Share's realized capital gains have equalled more than 60 percent of its corporate earnings and more than 34 percent of its consolidated earnings.

The Commission determined that the assumption by Bond and Share of Foreign Power's outstanding debt would not have a significant effect on the quality of Bond and Share's earnings. Similarly, two tax consequences of the merger were found to have limited significance.

Bond and Share's business was expected to continue and therefore its earnings could be projected and capitalized in estimating the value of its assets. However, Foreign Power's operations were changing and its past and present earnings could not be related to its future prospects. Therefore, the Commission found that only limited weight could be afforded to relative historical earnings as a measure of fairness.

Dividends. The proposed initial post-merger dividend represented a 16% increase for Bond and Share stockholders and a 3.4% increase for Foreign Power stockholders. In view of the uncertainties regarding Foreign Power's future earnings, the Commission did not attribute much significance to past dividend relationships. The merger would create a company whose financial resources would exceed those of either of the constituents. Foreign Power stockholders would benefit from the possibility of receiving a more liberal dividend in the future as well as the possibility of avoiding the severe fluctuations to which the Foreign Power dividend had been subject in the past.

Asset Values. The relative stated net asset values of the two companies indicated an exchange ratio of .67 to 1. However, Foreign Power's foreign government obligations and other investments in Latin America which at their face amount accounted for 89.5% of Foreign Power's consolidated net assets, were determined to be subject to an unspecified discount.

Bond and Share's operating subsidiaries included four service companies which provided engineering, construction, consulting and related services, and a chemical company. The Commission accepted as reasonable for purposes of testing the fairness of the proposed merger terms, the company's over-all valuation of its investment in these companies the stocks of which were not publicly traded. The method used to value the service companies consisted of a review for each company of the past and estimated earnings, significant past and anticipated developments, and the derivation of a representative net income for valuation purposes. A price–earnings multiplier for each company was selected by analyzing the earnings, dividends, and market performance of a group of comparable companies having publicly traded common stocks, using the results of their most recent 12 months as well as four previous years to evaluate trends.

In valuing the chemical company, income was adjusted to eliminate substantial losses sustained by an experimental plant and other items of a non-recurring nature and a value assigned to the experimental plant equivalent to a minimum recovery of a net tax saving in the event that the plant was abandoned. The method of valuation used was substantially similar to that used in valuing the service companies. Bond and Share's portfolio of marketable securities was deemed properly valued at market value.

Conclusions of Commission. The Commission's conclusions in this case read, in part, as follows:

> We have found that the market's evaluation of the stock of the two companies presents a guide to the value of the companies, and that on the basis of the market price relationship, both over the long term and as of the time negotiations commenced, the proposed exchange ratio would provide Foreign Power's shareholders with a premium over the market price ratio. On the other hand, the initial post-merger dividend will represent a far greater dividend increase for the shareholders of Bond and Share than for the Foreign Power shareholders. Relative net asset values at face amount point toward a higher exchange ratio than that proposed; however, as we have found, Foreign Power's assets cannot be accepted at their face amount.

We also note that on the basis of 1966 consolidated earnings, the exchange ratio would be favorable to Bond and Share's stockholders, but if consideration is given to realized capital gains the exchange ratio would be favorable to Foreign Power's shareholders. On a pro forma basis giving effect to the merger, Foreign Power stockholders would have suffered a decrease in their interest in consolidated earnings in 1966, while Bond and Share stockholders would have enjoyed an increase. If consideration is given to realized capital gains all stockholders would have benefitted.

The Commission then made the following observation:

We also consider it significant that the two financial advisers retained by the negotiating groups, both of which are expert in the evaluation of companies for merger purposes, on the basis of separate analyses recommended merger terms which were quite similar and not far removed from those finally agreed upon. . . . Under all the circumstances we conclude that the exchange ratio and other terms of the proposed merger are within a range that is reasonable and fair and do not involve overreaching on the part of any person concerned.

Comment. Although Foreign Power shareholders suffered a decrease in their interest in pro forma consolidated earnings and net assets, on the basis of the exchange ratio of .6 of a share for 1 share of Bond and Share, they did benefit from the standpoint of market value. Over the recent five-year period ended December 31, 1965, the relationship of market prices of Foreign Power stock to Bond and Share stock steadily increased from 31 to 50%. The evident prospect of a merger of the two companies was bound to influence the market price of Foreign Power stock during this period. Accordingly, a premium of 20% above the highest market price prevailing at the year-end, before formal merger negotiations, appears to have been a generous settlement for whatever Foreign Power stockholders gave up as a result of the merger.

15

Valuation in
Regulated Industries

Regulated industries are those subject to specific regulatory bodies, in addition to or in lieu of authorities such as the Securities and Exchange Commission, the stock exchanges, the Department of Justice, and the Federal Trade Commission, which exercise certain controls over such companies as well as industrial, commercial, and investment companies. The general reasoning behind the creation of these regulatory bodies is that the particular industries over which they have jurisdiction are considered to have a public interest from a customer or consumer standpoint.

Among the industries so regulated are airlines, banks, fire and casualty insurance companies, life insurance companies, intercity motor freight carriers, public utilities, railroads, and steamship companies. As in the valuation of industrial and commercial companies, earnings, potential earnings, and dividend policies play a large part in the market action of the common stocks of regulated industries.

Although there is a growing trend toward more uniformity, the accounting practices of some of these industries differ to such an extent that it is sometimes difficult for an investor to determine their earnings on a basis comparable with those of industrial and commercial companies. More importantly, their profit-making potential is restricted in varying degrees by rules, regulations, or actions of regulatory authorities.

Except for steamship companies, the significantly varying accounting practices of regulated industries will be discussed in the first section of this chapter, followed by comments on valuation data and characteristics, including the effects of regulatory restrictions on their profit potential. Steamship lines, with one or two notable exceptions, have shown substantial deficits in recent years, and several of them have been acquired by conglomerate-minded companies, so that the industry has lost its direct public investment interest.

ACCOUNTING PRACTICES

The Securities Acts amendments of 1964 extended the requirements of the 1933 and 1934 Securities Acts to certain companies whose shares are traded over the counter. Generally, all companies having total assets in excess of $1,000,000, and at least 500 shareholders of record of any class of securities on the last day of any fiscal year ending after July 1, 1966, must register with the Commission. Banks generally are required to comply with the law. State-chartered banks are regulated by the Federal Reserve Board and Federal Deposit Insurance Corporation, and national banks are subject to the Comptroller of the Currency.

Insurance companies received an exemption from the 1934 Act, provided they filed prescribed annual statements with the Commissioner of Insurance of their domiciliary state, and followed prescribed proxy regulations. This exemption is proposed to be deleted in 1971.

Some significant variations in accounting practices of regulated industries from generally accepted principles of accounting followed by industrial and commercial companies are summarized below.

Airlines

Airline accounting practices are prescribed by the Civil Aeronautics Board, and, with two exceptions, conform with generally accepted principles of accounting followed by industrial and commercial companies. Practices that are peculiar to airline accounting follow.

The costs of surveying new routes and preparing for the integration of new types of aircraft into an existing fleet are usually substantial. These costs are generally deferred and amortized over a period until the route or aircraft are in actual operation. This deferral treatment is permissive and not obligatory and, therefore, differences may exist among airlines in accounting for such costs and in the periods over which they are deferred.

Another difference exists with respect to foreign exchange rates for airlines having international operations. In translating foreign currency balances, the airlines are required to use rates in effect at the balance sheet date, and may not provide reserves for declines in rates between that date and the time the annual stockholders' report is ready for issuance. Where an airline has substantial foreign currency balances, this may be a factor for consideration.

Banks

As a result of the regulations and forms issued by the federal bank supervisory agencies, banks presented an "income" statement beginning in 1969. In earlier years, such items as securities gains and losses and provisions for loan losses, together with their income tax effects, were carried direct to undivided profits, or, alternatively, to a securities reserve, in the case of securities gains or losses. Thus, the reader of the financial statements was forced to use his own judgment regarding the financial results of the period's activities.

Generally, banks carry security investments at cost, less amortization when purchased at a premium, and, less often, at cost plus accretion when purchased at a discount. Some of the larger banks are dealers in government and municipal securities. Gains and losses on such trading transactions are included in operating income and amounts on hand at the year-end are valued at market, or in some cases at the lower of cost or market.

Banks came under a special provision of the Internal Revenue Code, through 1968, regarding gains and losses on portfolio securities. Capital gains were taxed at 27%, whereas capital losses were fully deductible against ordinary income at an approximate rate of 53%. These rates applied for the year 1968, including the surtax. Accordingly, banks endeavored to group their gains and realize them in one year and group their losses for realization in another year. Otherwise, capital losses would only be realized at the 27% rate, to the extent that capital gains had been realized. Inasmuch as portfolio securities are not revalued to market at the year-end, a bank could show realized capital gains for the year while, at the same time, it had substantial unrealized market depreciation in securities on hand. This special tax advantage was discontinued under the Tax Reform Act of 1969 and net gains from the sale or exchange of bonds or other securities are treated as ordinary income; net losses continue to be treated as ordinary losses.

Loan losses suffered by banks include those of the normal recurring type and those which occur at infrequent and unpredictable intervals. The latter generally result from economic depressions or international situations, such as an expropriation of properties. In recognition of this, the Internal Revenue Code prior to 1969 permitted banks to provide reserves, under a formula, up to 2.4% of the total loans outstanding.

Inasmuch as the amount of loss provision claimed for income tax purposes had to be booked, the provision for losses could be at the allowable limit or less than such amount. In any case, it usually had no relation to actual requirements. This special tax privilege was discontinued under the Tax Reform Act of 1969, and banks are now permitted to make reasonable additions to reserves only in amounts necessary to increase the reserve for bad debts to an amount equal to the net bad debt ratio of the particular taxpayer during the current and five preceding years applied to the loans outstanding at the end of the current taxable year. An alternative computation is permitted for those taxpayers whose reserves at the end of their base year (the last taxable year beginning on or before July 11, 1969) were in excess of the amount based on actual prior experience.

At a meeting on July 8, 1969, representatives of the Securities and Exchange Commission, The Federal Reserve Board, Comptroller of the Currency, and Federal Deposit Insurance Corporation, the American Bankers Association and the American Institute of Certified Public Accountants reached an understanding as to acceptable standards of financial reporting for commercial banks effective for the year 1969. The federal bank supervisory agencies pursuant to this understanding issued regulations covering the following revisions in the structure of bank statements to be included in stockholder reports.

1. Recognition of a loan loss factor in the operating expenses of banks. Any provision for loan losses not allocable against current operations shall be charged directly to the undivided profits account.

2. Inclusion of results of investment security transactions as realized in the report of income.

3. Designation of the last line in the statement of income as "net income."

Regulatory instruction for the allocation of loan losses to operating expense will include:

(a) *Minimum* charge equivalent to the five-year average ratio of losses computed on the basis of net charge-offs to total loans.

(b) An added amount based on management's judgment shall be permitted. Adequate disclosure of such discretionary action to be furnished in a referenced footnote.

(c) If the bank is on a charge-off basis of recognizing loan losses, the amount of actual charge-offs shall be reported against operating income.

Conforming to established bank accounting practice and in accordance with generally accepted accounting principles, gains and losses on investment securities shall be reported following the computation of operating income. Net security gains and losses shall be reflected in income in the period such results are realized and recorded in the accounts.

These revised reporting practices, and the elimination of the special federal income tax privileges regarding security transactions and loan losses bring bank reporting practices more in accord with those followed by industrial and commercial companies, except for the failure to revalue security investments at market.

Insurance Companies

Insurance companies are under the regulation of state agencies, and must report to each state in which they are qualified to do business. As in the case of banks, their financial reporting practices are concerned with the solvency and liquidity of the individual companies. One of the practices followed by insurance companies is not to recognize prepaid expenses or deferred charges. All costs such as commissions, premium taxes, medical examinations (for life insurance), and other items in connection with writing insurance and obtaining premiums are charged to income as incurred. Premiums, however, are taken into income over periods covered by the policies.

Accordingly, in a period of increasing premium volume, the results of statutory underwriting operations of a company are depressed to the extent of the expenses applicable to unearned premiums, which will be reflected in income of later years. Conversely, in a period of declining premiums, statutory underwriting results are benefited by premiums taken into income, whose related costs have been charged against income in prior periods.

Stocks are, in general, carried at market or appraised values, except that life insurance companies carry most preferred stocks at cost. However, no provision is made for tax on unrealized appreciation on such investments. While life insurance companies have a relatively small percentage of their assets invested in stocks, fire and casualty companies may have substantial amounts so invested.

Bonds, generally, are carried at amortized values. Because of sharply rising interest rates during recent years, such securities in portfolios of life insurance companies may be carried at aggregate amounts substantially in excess of current market values.

Life insurance companies reflect gains and losses on sales of investments, as well as changes in unrealized appreciation, or depreciation, in surplus. Fire and casualty companies, however, include realized gains and losses on investments in net income, but treat changes in unrealized appreciation, or depreciation, as surplus adjustments.

There are other accounting practices peculiar to the insurance industry such as the exclusion, as assets, of premiums in course of collection, or overdue premiums; the expensing of certain capital items such as equipment, furniture, and fixtures; and the maintenance of reserves for certain types of risks or reinsurance risks at amounts higher than estimated requirements.

Public Utilities

Accounting practices of electric, gas, water, telecommunication, and pipeline companies are influenced by regulatory authority concepts of property or investment upon which earnings are permitted, and the recording of related costs which are recoverable from revenues. Such authorities include the Federal Power Commission or the Federal Communications Commission as well as state regulatory commissions.

Generally speaking, there are two areas in which accounting practices prescribed for utilities may differ from those followed by industrial and commercial enterprises. First, in many states, the gross values of properties must be stated at the historical costs incurred when they were first placed in service. This is only important where a utility purchases property from another at a value substantially in excess of such original cost. Generally, it is not permissible, in these states, to recover any excess over such original cost through rates charged to customers. However, other states are more liberal, and permit recognition of the fair value of properties or replacement cost for rate-making purposes.

Second, depending upon the state regulatory authorities, utilities may claim depreciation for federal income tax purposes substantially in excess of amounts provided for book purposes, and not provide deferred taxes for such excess. These differences result from using, for tax purposes, accelerated methods and shorter depreciable lives, taking full allowance for the investment credit, and deducting interest, pensions, and taxes, which have been capitalized in construction for book purposes. This tends to increase substantially the current year's net income, but for rate-making purposes, the utility may be required to reduce its rates to consumers to the extent of the tax benefits gained. This practice is not universally followed; some states require utilities to provide deferred income tax for such depreciation differences, and to normalize investment credits over a period. In all cases, however, the accounting method followed with regard to such items must conform to that used for rate-making purposes.

However, effective January 1, 1970, the Federal Power Commission requires footnote disclosure to income statements of the difference between taxes payable under liberalized depreciation methods and those that would be payable under straight-line depreciation.

Railroads

Accounting practices of railroads are regulated by the Interstate Commerce Commission. In recent years, their accounting practices, in reporting to stockholders, have tended to conform closely with those followed by industrial and commercial companies, with two notable exceptions.

Federal income taxes are provided in the accounts generally on the basis of amounts payable, shown in returns filed for the current year, without any provision for deferred taxes attributable to depreciation claimed for tax purposes in excess of amounts provided for book purposes. This practice has the effect of substantially reducing tax provisions and increasing the current year's net income. A perusal of annual reports to stockholders of major railroads indicates the relatively low ratio of provision for federal income tax, to income before such provision.

The other exception exists with regard to certain depreciation practices. Prior to January 1, 1943, depreciation on road properties was not generally provided. Since that time, depreciation has been provided on such properties, other than track, grading, and tunnels, with the result that income is absorbing a reasonable charge therefor. Grading and tunnels generally are deemed to have an indefinite life and, therefore, are not subject to depreciation. Accounting for track costs is on a replacement basis, rather than through depreciation provisions. Costs are charged to property accounts when track is originally constructed, and replacements in kind are expensed. Additional amounts are added to the property account only when components of track are replaced with heavier or improved material. Over a period of years, charges to income may be reasonably comparable under either replacement accounting or depreciation accounting. However, income of a particular year may be affected by the extent to which track maintenance is carried out, under the replacement method.

Intercity Motor Freight Carriers

Although trucking companies use accelerated depreciation methods for federal income tax purposes, they are required, under Interstate Commerce Commission regulations, to write off equipment on a straight-line basis. However, in reporting to stockholders, their financial statements are prepared on the basis of generally accepted accounting principles. Thus, trucking companies, unlike railroads, provide for deferred income taxes so that their current earnings are not overstated.

SECURITIES MARKETS AND PERFORMANCE

The capital stocks of major airlines, public utilities, railroads, and intercity motor freight carriers are traded primarily on the principal stock exchanges. With rare exceptions, stocks of banks and insurance companies, having public stockholders, are traded in the over-the-counter market.

Comparative Tabulation

The tabulation on page 430 compares the stock market performance of Standard & Poor's industrial stocks with those of regulated industries under review for the 5½-year period ended June 30, 1970. January 1, 1965, has been used as the base period, in the tabulation, and given a value of 100 in all cases.

During the 5½-year period covered by the comparative study of market performance, the formation of holding companies by banks, insurance companies, and railroads, and public utilities to a lesser extent, with a view to diversifying their activities, coupled with acquisitions of some of these institutions by conglomerate-minded companies, has had an effect on their market action. However, the many mergers and acquisitions of industrial and commercial companies during this period has, no doubt, affected market action in a number of stocks included in the industrial price index. Standard & Poor's 425 industrial stocks were selling at an average price–earnings ratio of 17.26 at December 31, 1969.

	January 1, 1965, Index	Fluctuations During 5½-Year Period		June 30, 1970, Index
		Highest Index	Lowest Index	
Industrials	100.0	132.4	84.0	93.0
Airlines	100.0	244.4	67.3	67.3
Banks	100.0	126.9	86.3	97.0
Fire and casualty insurance	100.0	156.2	99.8	106.6
Life insurance	100.0	100.0	57.3	61.3
Public utilities	100.0	100.0	63.5	66.0
Railroads	100.0	124.3	54.6	63.2
Trucking companies	100.0	265.8	100.0	123.7

Indexes used:

Industrials—Standard & Poor's index of 425 industrials.

Airlines—Standard & Poor's index of six major U. S. airlines.

Banks—M. A. Schapiro & Co., Inc., index of 25 banks, 7 of which are in New York, 4 in California, and 14 in other centers.

Fire and casualty insurance—Best's Stock Index of 24 property-liability insurance companies.

Life insurance—Best's Stock Index of 30 life insurance companies.

Public utilities—Standard & Poor's index of 55 utilities.

Railroads—Standard & Poor's index of 20 railroads.

Trucking companies—Standard & Poor's index of 10 major truckers.

Comparable ratios, where pertinent, of the various regulated industries will be indicated under the specific sections following.

VALUATION DATA AND CHARACTERISTICS

Airlines, insurance companies, public utilities, railroads, and trucking companies must have approval from federal and/or state regulatory authorities for the rates they charge customers or consumers. Such rates are required by law to be established at levels which will attract sufficient capital to maintain adequate service and also provide a fair return to the investor. Generally, however, such regulated industries have to demonstrate hardship before rate increases are allowed.

It is not intended, nor is it practicable to cover here comprehensively the investment characteristics of the several regulated industries. For example, investment firms, such as M. A. Schapiro & Company, Inc., Blyth & Company, Inc., and the First Boston

Corporation produce considerable information on banks on a national scale. There are also dealers specializing in local stocks of a particular industry, such as John J. Ryan Company, Inc., who publish an annual review of New Jersey bank stocks, as well as interim reports.

Publications of the various national and local industry specialists include Moody's and Standard & Poor's, who publish manuals and reports on thousands of stocks and various industries, Best's (insurance), and many others who publish manuals and monthly magazines devoted to a particular industry. In addition to information produced by the industry specialists, many investment houses from time to time make current studies of various of the regulated industries with investment recommendations to their customers.

The discussions that follow will be devoted to highlights of data pertinent to the valuation of stocks of these industries and some of their investment characteristics. It should also be noted that the basic approaches outlined in the chapters on initial public offerings, valuations for estate, trust, and income tax purposes, and for acquisitions, mergers, and tender offers, apply to regulated industries in similar situations, subject to factors discussed herein affecting such industries.

AIRLINES

Reported profits for eleven domestic trunklines [1] aggregated $244.5 million in 1967, after six years of steady improvement, but fell sharply to $126.5 million in 1968, and further to $97.0 million in 1969.

Average passenger revenues per unit of traffic have been declining for a period of years, and with the large number of jets delivered in 1969 and 1970, integration costs continued to affect profits adversely. Also, inflationary wage settlements and airport traffic delays have added to the costs of airlines in recent years.

The six major airline stocks included in the index [2] reached

---

[1] American, Braniff, Continental, Delta, Eastern, National, Northwest, Pacific Southwest, Trans World, United, and Western.

[2] American, Delta, Eastern, Pan American, Trans World, and United.

their market peak in the first quarter of 1967 and steadily declined thereafter through June 30, 1970. Average price–earnings ratios of these stocks at December 31, 1969, would have no significance, as two of the six (Eastern and Pan American) operated at a loss for the year then ended.

Relief in the form of fare increases and expanded cargo services may be expected during the next several years, and future unit costs should decrease because of the greater capacity of the newer jets. However, capacity increases have continued to run ahead of traffic growth during the years so that the domestic load factor has dropped from 61.4% in 1959 to 50% in 1969. Accordingly, the market outlook in mid-1970 for airline stocks was somewhat uncertain.

BANKS

Although the rates of discount and interest charged by banks are generally not restricted, except by state laws on usury, their operations are circumscribed in other respects that affect earnings potentials. For example, there are governmental restrictions on the maximum rates of interest payable on savings, negotiable certificates of deposit, and other time deposits. This inhibits the growth of such deposits to the extent that competing types of investments may be more attractive to potential depositors.

Governmental Control of Credit

The Federal Reserve Board by raising the discount rate (i.e., interest rate at which banks borrow from the Federal Reserve) and increasing the cash reserve requirements on such borrowings, may compel banks to raise their interest rates to the point where potential borrowers will resort to other forms of financing. Due to the increase in the discount rate, the rate of interest paid on savings accounts, certificates of deposit, and other time deposits, as well as a general increase in expenses, banks increased their rate to prime business borrowers to an historic high of 8½% in June 1969. This compares with a prime rate that had been as low as 3½% during the preceding ten-year period. Also, banks are restricted, by the amount of their capital, to a maximum amount which may be loaned to a single customer, and, in total loans, by reserves to be maintained against depositors' balances. This subject is discussed in more detail in Chapter 1.

Territorial Restrictions

Deterrents to expansion exist in many states which restrict banks from establishing branches, such as outside the confines of county boundaries, etc. In fact, several states prohibit banks from having any branch offices at all.

Earnings and Market Action

The 25 bank or bank holding company stocks included in the Schapiro index had "net operating earnings" of $1,223.7 million for the year 1969, and "net income" of $1,121.5 million, after net realized security losses of $102.2 million. At the year-end, investments carried by the entire group aggregated $27,325.5 million, but only twelve of the banks, which accounted for $14,650.4 million disclosed the market value of such investments. Such market value was $13,065.3 million, or $1,585.1 million below carrying value.[3]

These bank stocks have shown a steady improvement in net operating income, net income (after net realized securities losses), and dividend payments throughout the five-year period ended in 1969. However, because of a somewhat predictable rate of improvement, and, to some extent, their unrealized investment portfolio losses, their market performance has not been spectacular. At the end of 1969 the 25 stocks were selling at a composite price multiple of 12.3 times net operating earnings.[4] This multiple would be slightly higher if net income (after security losses) were used as a factor instead of net operating earnings.

As in the case of other regulated industries, there is a growing trend on the part of banks to diversify their activities. This is accomplished through holding companies, a large number of which have been formed by banks during recent years. The holding company may own the capital stock of one or more banks (gener-

[3] Figures compiled from "Bank Stock Quarterly" June 1970, M. A. Schapiro & Co., Inc.

[4] Ibid.

ally one) together with the stock of non-banking subsidiaries. A liberalization of branch banking laws also could be forthcoming in a number of states. Such factors, and the continued expansion of the economy, should favorably affect bank "earnings."

INSURANCE COMPANIES

As mentioned earlier, insurance companies, by state laws, are required to exclude (in effect write off) certain types of assets which have definite and ascertainable value. Also, life insurance companies are generally restricted to investing only a small percentage of their assets in common stock. At the end of 1969, common stock investments constituted only slightly more than 5% of total life insurance companies' assets, compared with over 37% of the assets of fire and casualty insurance companies. Considering that fixed income securities have tended to decrease in value during recent years, such companies have been deprived of an opportunity to benefit from the inflationary rise in common stocks as have private pension and college endowment funds, and other institutional investors.

Fire and Casualty Stocks

Fire and casualty insurance stocks showed a sporadic and somewhat dull pattern during the three-year period ended December 31, 1967. However, they had a substantial market surge during 1968, and, although retreating through 1969 and the first six months of 1970, held up better than the stock market in general. Acquisition of several large insurance companies by merger-minded companies and attempted acquisition of others were in large part responsible for the market surge in 1968.

Total net premiums written in 1969 amounted to $29 billion for all lines of property and liability insurance, of which $12 billion was for automobile lines. These automobile lines continued to develop large underwriting losses. Also, "riot" losses and crime losses continued at a high level.[5]

---

[5] Insurance Information Institute, "Insurance Facts" (1970).

For purposes of determining earnings of fire and casualty insurance companies, investment analysts compute an equity in unearned premium reserve of a company at the beginning and end of the year, and adjust statutory income by the difference thereof. This procedure is a somewhat arbitrary method of reinstating expenses, which have been written off, applicable to premiums not yet taken into income. Also, if a company reflects realized gains and losses on investments in income, they adjust earnings for such amount, as unrealized gains and losses are reflected in surplus, on a statutory basis. A representative group of fire and casualty stocks averaged slightly under 16 times earnings on an adjusted basis at the close of 1969, and yielded nearly 4%.[6]

Life Stocks

Unlike fire and casualty insurance, where stock companies carry the bulk of insurance in force, stock life insurance companies had only 48% of insurance in force compared with 52% by mutual companies. At the close of 1969 a very substantial portion, approximately 40%, of net premiums on insurance in force was underwritten by five mutual insurance companies. Although stock companies account for more than nine tenths of the number of life companies in the United States, many of these are small. As a further indication of the relative stability of mutual life companies, they accounted for approximately 68% of the assets of all U. S. life companies at December 31, 1969.[7]

As in the case of fire and casualty insurance companies, investment analysts adjust reported earnings of stock life insurance companies. The principal adjustment is for changes during the year in estimated equities in the value of life insurance in force. This has been done generally by computing so much per $1,000 for the several types of life insurance in force at the beginning and end of the year. Also, other adjustments are made to reported net income, where information is available, for excess reserves required by statute.

[6] "Best's Review," February 1970 edition.
[7] Institute of Life Insurance, "Life Insurance Fact Book" (1970).

Life insurance stocks reached a peak prior to January 1, 1965, and beat a somewhat steady retreat during the 5½-year period ended June 30, 1970. A representative number of life stocks averaged about 17 times earnings on an adjusted basis at the close of 1969, and yielded slightly over 1½%.[8] This traditionally low dividend pay-out is one of the relative disadvantages of investing in life insurance stocks.

Acquisitions and Holding Companies

The acquisition of fire and casualty and life insurance companies by non-insurance companies, and the formation of holding companies for non-insurance business, has affected stock market prices of the industry. The liquidity and large surpluses of fire and casualty insurance companies have made them a prime target of acquisition-minded companies and also led to the formation of holding companies. Great American Insurance, which was acquired by National General Corporation, paid a dividend of $174 million to its parent in February 1969; Reliance Insurance paid a dividend of $38 million to its parent, Leasco, in August 1969; and Insurance Company of North America paid a dividend of $175 million to its holding company parent, INA Corporation, in September 1969.

PUBLIC UTILITIES

The earnings growth of public utilities has been inhibited by the high cost of borrowing in recent years. When a utility could issue a bond at an effective interest rate of 4%, it gained considerable leverage, for a period, in earnings on its common stock with, say, an allowable rate of return of 6 or 6½% on the investment of funds generated by the bond issue. However, when it rises to 8% or more, the cost of borrowing money may approximate the allowable rate of return on investment, in many cases.

Basic Utilities Industries

Utilities, in the Standard & Poor's index, include three basic industries: electric, natural gas, and telecommunications. As a

[8] "Best's Review," *op. cit.*

group, the utilities showed a relatively steady decline in market prices throughout the 5½-year period ended June 30, 1970.

Although public utilities were selling at a composite price–earnings ratio of 11.96 at December 31, 1969, stocks of telecommunications companies in the composite group, with the exception of American Telephone & Telegraph Company, were generally at higher levels. The return on investment of the telecommunications industry has been consistently higher than on electric and natural gas utility stocks, in recent years. Companies in both of the latter industries generally continued to show modest gains in earnings, but they have not been sufficiently improved during the several years ended December 31, 1969, to attract investment interest.

The long-term outlook for the telecommunications industry appears attractive at the beginning of the Seventies, with a continued increase in the number of telephones in service and the growth of data transmission and voice communication augmenting the computer service field. The electric and natural gas industries have been squeezed by rising costs, by state and local taxes, and by the high interest rates on new capital. Many companies apply periodically to regulatory authorities for rate increases but due to the time lag in granting such increases, they have failed to keep pace with increased income requirements.

As in the case of other regulated industries, some utilities are forming holding companies for the purpose of diversifying their operations. It remains to be seen what effect ventures into new fields will produce for them.

RAILROADS

Income of class I railroads (operating revenues of $5 million or more) was $461 million for 1969, down from $902 million in 1966. The return on investment of the class I railroads for 1969 was 2.38%, considerably less than half that of public utilities.[9] Because of this poor return, capital expenditures for equipment and the improvement of roadway facilities have been at a low

---

[9] Standard & Poor's Industry Survey, July 16, 1970.

level in recent years. It makes no sense to borrow money, at rates of 8% or more, when investments in capital items will yield a return of considerably less than that amount.

Railroads have been merging, and forming holding companies, to diversify into a wide range of non-transportation activities. In fact, non-rail activities accounted for a significant portion of net income for some of the larger roads in 1968 and 1969. However, expected savings on railroad operations, resulting from mergers, have not materialized in most cases, and the filing of a bankruptcy petition by Penn Central Transportation Co., in June 1970, came as a shock to the general public.

Railroad stocks, included in Standard & Poor's index, reached a market peak at the close of 1968, largely because of the optimism generated by the mergers during 1967 and 1968. As a result of steadily declining earnings, they started their downward path shortly thereafter and fell sharply during the six months ended June 30, 1970. At December 31, 1969, the 20 railroad stocks in Standard & Poor's index were selling at a composite price–earnings ratio of 10.83.

Some relief may be afforded through government and state subsidies for ailing passenger operations and for the purchase of new equipment. Also, significant freight increases could be forthcoming in the foreseeable future. Otherwise, the outlook for the railroad industry is rather bleak.

TRUCKING

The increase in revenues of class I and class II trucking companies (over $300,000 in operating revenues) from $6 billion in 1958 to almost $13 billion in 1969 has been impressive and largely at the expense of railroads. Trucking companies showed a substantial market surge during the 5½ years ended June 30, 1970, reaching a peak at December 31, 1968. Despite a revenue increase in 1969, rising costs cut estimated industry profits from $276 million in 1968 to $240 million in 1969. This, coupled with general conditions, accounted for the adverse market action of trucking stocks during 1969 and through mid-1970.

The average price–earnings ratio of stocks included in the Standard & Poor's trucking company index [10] at December 31, 1969, would have no significance, as some are closely held and others are unseasoned. While the outlook for continued growth in gross revenues remains good, control of costs is imperative for improved profits. During the next few years, this may be accomplished through mergers, and through better equipped terminals and materials handling facilities to offset high labor costs. The average annual wage paid in the trucking industry was some 40% higher than that paid by private industry in 1968.

[10] Associated Transport, Consolidated Freightways, Cooper Jarrett, McLean Trucking, Pacific Intermountain, Roadway Express, Spector Freight, T.I.M.E. D.C., Transcon Lines, and Yellow Transit.

APPENDIXES

A

Excerpts from Report to the Attorney General of the State of New York on New Issues of Securities

REPORT DATED OCTOBER 1969, TO THE HONORABLE LOUIS J. LEFKOWITZ

Survey of New Issues

In this recent new issue market, a pattern emerged whereby substantial sums of money went into new and highly speculative ventures. The securities of these companies generally rose, frequently beyond all rational value, and then returned somewhat to earth when the inevitable cooling-off period began.

At the time interest in the new issue market was particularly high, investments in these companies were rarely made on the basis of their merit. Rather, the atmosphere became one of pure gambling and in the process it was not too difficult to rig the game. The big winners were underwriters, insiders of these companies and those who had contacts with these groups. The losers were those investors who purchased at inflated prices and the economy itself. . . . As money poured into newly formed companies, these ventures had little choice but to seek quick investment of the funds received, thereby placing greater inflationary pressure on an already troubled economy.

In coming to these conclusions the study initially analyzed various aspects of some 103 companies all of which went public for the first time in the 1968–1969 period.

The first matter examined was the quality of the companies and the securities involved. A notable factor was the pattern in these new issues of *dilution* of the public equity. Corporate insiders acquired large blocks of stock at nominal prices. As a result, public investors purchasing at the offering price had the book value of their shares substantially reduced. The average dilution was 65% and one case reached the preposterous amount of 89%.

The dilution analysis prepared as part of the new issue survey utilized a sample of one hundred and three new issues whose initial offering ranged from $148,500 to $13,390,000. . . . The following schedule presents details as to the size of the new issue security offerings selected for use in this study:

Size of Offering	Number of New Issues
$ 300,000 or less	52
300,001 to 500,000	5
500,001 to 1,000,000	17
1,000,001 to 2,000,000	15
2,000,001 to 3,000,000	5
3,000,001 to 4,000,000	4
4,000,001 to 5,000,000	1
6,000,001 to 7,000,000	1
8,000,001 to 9,000,000	2
13,390,000	1
	103

These reductions in book value are of considerable significance as these ventures frequently had no other objective criteria of value for investors. Our findings showed that earnings per share, prior to the public offering, were non-existent for 16% of companies and where such figures were present they were of a negative variety in an additional 29%. The only other key factor left upon which a company could be judged is its potential for future development. Yet, there was little in the prospectuses of most of these new issues to indicate that the issuing companies had any great promise. Indeed as will be seen, faith in a company's long term prospects was not a significant factor in inducing purchases of their securities. . . .

Public participation and price movement were sometimes shocking. For example, the stock of one company with an appropriate space age name was issued at $2.00 and ran up to 7½ before severe swings downward. That particular company represented in its prospectus that 60% of the proceeds were to be used for such items as past due accounts, repayment of loans, back wages, back rents and similar items. The issuer was a constant loser in operations and had a working capital deficit. In effect we concluded that the public issue was the method used to delay bankruptcy. Yet the price of the stock more than tripled in a short period of trading.

The study reached the conclusion that many companies are merely manufactured by underwriters for stock profits rather than bona fide new enterprises seeking capital in the securities market. Because of this situation, the underwriter may be placed in an awkward position with respect to disclosure of adverse information about the company during the course of issuance or trading. . . . For example, in one case involving an underwriter which had made a $250,000 loan to create a new issue, later embarrassing information obtained about one of the new company's officers could not lead to relinquishment of the issue before actually going public. . . . Direct loans, guarantee of loans and similar common "manufacturing" aspects by underwriters remove much of the public protection which should be expected from a dealer in securities negotiating with the public. Moreover, in 67% of issues analyzed, underwriters obtained warrants generally at a price of $.01 (one cent) each which may be exercised at or within 10% of the original offering price during a three to five year period beginning one year after the offering. The blocks of stock involved ranged from 5 to 25% of the amount of stock in the original issue. . . .

Despite the obviously weak quality of most of the new issues analyzed, they were readily sold out and almost inevitably rose in price in the after-market. How this came to pass and the ramifications of it prove an interesting story.

To determine the motivations of purchasers of these issues, the study interviewed 122 persons who bought initial offerings. Certain patterns of behavior clearly emerged. In only a small minority of cases did investors state that the prospectus had any influence on their decision. In fact, the typical language in these documents indicating high risk was largely disregarded by readers, many of whom were less than certain of even the exact business the company was in.

What was occurring was a very different process than investors' selection of stock based upon judgment as to merit. Quite to the contrary, the most potent factor was a desire to obtain a new issue—preferably one regarding which they had received an "inside tip." In the great majority of instances, investors purchased at the original offering price with the intent of a quick resale at a premium above the offering price. Approximately 73% of this group who bought at the original issue price did in fact resell, usually quite soon after the time of purchase. . . .

Increased demand was brought about by such means as brokers frequently emphasizing to their customers the difficulty of obtaining these shares. These statements were of course often true, but by playing upon this fact still greater demand was created. Salesmen regularly predicted that the after market prices would be higher than the original or current prices. Cruder techniques include brokers informing customers that they must make additional purchases in the after market upon pain of being cut off from any further new issues. In addition, a steady flow of "tips" was fed into the market and purchasers often stated that it was this type of information which had stimulated their interest in a particular security. The question of the validity of this information is not even a logical one to ask—these companies were generally in such an early stage of development that any predictions as to their future were unwarranted. . . .

The study group uncovered instances where intra-office brokerage memoranda were inconsistent with offering literature. The former material no doubt provided the rudiments for customers men. In one case, a memo contained the following gem: "OTC initially, NYSE eventually." In another case where the prospectus contained a substantial risk section and a cover legend emphasizing such risks, the confidential underwriter memo contained a section called "Factors Limiting Risks: as an obvious offset." . . .

Some of the names chosen by companies were misleading on their face. Thus, a company with the word "aerosystems" in its title was mainly involved in manufacturing ball point pen parts. The latter stock was issued at $4.00, reached a high bid of $9\frac{1}{4}$ until the decline began.

Concurrently, various methods of reducing supply were utilized. In nearly all of these offerings substantial percentages of shares are reserved for sale to employees, principals and the like. Instances have been found indicating that this can run as high as 25% of the shares registered for sale. At times, the underwriter holds back some shares either for his own account or for those associated with or related to him.

At other times the underwriter makes an effort to limit supply once trading begins. Thus, a customer may be informed that if he sells his shares without permission he would receive no new shares from the underwriter. In other instances, underwriters recommended to customers that a stock had a good long term investment potential and should not be quickly resold. How an underwriter can determine this regarding a new untried company is impossible to answer.

The effect of all this of course was that the increased pressures of demand upon a shortened supply resulted in prices being bid sharply in the after market. A sampling was made of the price rise of some 40 companies from their various times of initial offering through January, 1969. The results were as follows:

Number of Companies	Percentage of Increase
7	Up to 50%
5	Between 51% and 100%
10	Between 101% and 200%
11	Between 201% and 300%
3	Between 301% and 700%
4	Over 1,000%
40	

Company insiders and investment bankers have taken full advantage of the opportunities presented to them by the generally heated situation—which was partially of their own creation. . . .

The most obvious method available to them is the acquisition of shares at a low price for resale when the time appeared right. Thus, at times, underwriters withhold part of the shares for their own account and then resell when they think the market has reached its peak. Company insiders of course would frequently do the same with stock they had received. An interesting factor is the heavy purchase of a new issue for discretionary accounts of the underwriter, giving him a large degree of effective trading control. Some such underwriters do not deal with the general public except for new issue distributions and trading. In one case involving such an underwriter, a new issue stock moved up in price ten times its issue price. After moving from $10 per share to approximately $100, it has recently been marketed at the $12 range. . . .

Resales by insiders occurred in approximately 23% of all cases analyzed. The figure which is based on questionnaires sent to 103 companies is undoubtedly low as further insider resales must have occurred since the various times the questionnaires were received. Further, in at least one instance insider resales appear to have been concealed.

Beyond this both underwriters and the issuers have fully utilized the opportunity to reward business associates, friends or favorite customers for either past transactions or anticipated future ones.

As new issues become progressively more difficult to obtain, the ability of issuers and their underwriters to allocate shares is a matter of some considerable import. That this was used to favor certain individuals is indicated by the fact that approximately ⅔ of the new issue purchasers interviewed had prior business or social contacts with either company insiders or the broker through whom the purchase was made. Several underwriters who were interviewed by the study stated that allocations were based upon the customer's prior business dealings with the firm and the likelihood of a continued relation with him. Interviews were held with several investment bankers who had been significantly involved in the new issue market.

The full value of the power to allocate is seen when it is realized that underwriters can usually predict which issues are most likely to be mercurial in price. An excellent barometer of this is the indications of interest received during the registration period. In extreme cases these indications have been as high as six times the shares available for public sale. The fact that such shares will sell at substantial premium in the after market would be realized by even the most simpleminded. In effect, in this situation, the power to allocate meant the ability to make a gift to the favorite few.

Obviously those investors truly in the favored group would receive neither threats nor suggestions that they hold the shares for any prolonged period. As noted earlier, most investors purchased for quick resale and of those original purchasers interviewed who did resell, only 2% took a loss on the transaction.

While this group was able to quickly turn over their shares at substantial profits, members of the public purchasing after the stock had risen in price were not so fortunate. A random sampling of 37 new issues has indicated that their price level in the majority of these companies has declined from the original issue price more than 40% from the end of January, 1969, through August 27, 1969. A fuller statement of the price behavior of these companies in this period is as follows:

Percent of Decrease from End of January, 1969 Through August 27, 1969

Number of companies that showed increase 2
Number of comapnies showing decrease up to 10% 4
Number of companies showing decrease 11%– 20% 2
Number of companies showing decrease 21%– 30% 2
Number of companies showing decrease 31%– 40% 7
Number of companies showing decrease 41%– 50% 5
Number of companies showing decrease 51%– 60% 9
Number of companies showing decrease 61%– 70% 3
Number of companies showing decrease 71%– 80% 1
Number of companies showing decrease 81%– 90% 1
Number of companies showing decrease 91%–100% 1
                                                                                    ——
                                                                                    37

The study also made random samplings of the use of proceeds by the issuing company, as against representations in the prospectus. We concluded that promoters interpreted the prospectus quite liberally in certain cases. In one $300,000 new issue that more than tripled in price after its issue, the prospectus enumerated the various purposes of the public issue. Not included were personal loans to officers. Yet $19,000 of the $247,000 net proceeds were applied to make loans to officers. In addition, the prospectus indicated that $130,000 of proceeds were to be used for asset acquisition. However, only $59,000 was used for such purpose. The company did adhere to its representation that $40,000 would be used for management salaries.

Even though the purpose of this inquiry was to report on the mechanics of new issues, we were forced to recommend immediate remedial action by one company with respect to the use of proceeds: In such situation a "prestige" offering that jumped 75 points inside of 4 weeks after being marketed to the public took 13.5 millions of dollars out of its proceeds and applied it to investments considered by this office inconsistent with the prospectus representations. On our insistence, the money was immediately redirected where it should have gone in the first place.

We have concluded that the last situation and similar ones are caused by the drive for company performance for the sake of maintaining an initial high market price.

Spin-offs

During the course of our initial inquiry into new issues it became apparent that the device of spin-offs was being employed in various ways that in effect resulted in new issues coming to market with special problems. . . . For this reason, it was felt that an analysis should be made of a particular situation that could provide information as to the problems involved and the possibility for solutions in the future. For that reason Assistant Attorneys General . . . and Principal Securities Accountant . . . were assigned to work on recording the history of spin-offs stemming from the activities of a publicly held corporation known as Herman & Appley, Inc. This is an attempt to record the conclusions of the study group based on the work and analysis by the aforesaid members. . . .

That spin-offs are fraught with evils is exemplified by our recent investigation of Herman & Appley, Inc. Herman & Appley, Inc. is a real estate company with over 700 stockholders, which was insolvent by the end of 1968. The corporation at that time was barely alive and in no position to go to the public for funds by any conventional registration process. However, by spinning off five asset-less subsidaries, the principals of Herman & Appley, Inc. not only succeeded in putting money into their own pockets, but bailed themselves out of certain bankruptcy, and placed, into the hands of the unwary public, hundreds of thousands of shares of spin-off companies whose actual merits, as compared with their traded market prices, was and is extremely dubious. . . .

To illustrate the last point, on the 20th day of May, 1969, a share of stock in Equity Group, Inc. (one of the spin-offs) was quoted on the over-the-counter market at $5 bid and $8 asked. Although this company had and has no assets whatsoever and is not operating in any fashion, its market price at its zenith would indicate the value of the company to be 5 to 8 million dollars, based on the outstanding stock of one million shares.

[A number of other manipulative deals involving Herman & Appley, Inc., its principals and several NYSE member firms are described in this section of the report to the Attorney General.]

B

Required Financial Statements
Under Schedule I, Regulation A
of the Securities Act of 1933

ITEM 11

11. Furnish appropriate financial statements of the issuer, or of the issuer and its predecessors, as required below. Such statements shall be prepared in accordance with generally accepted accounting principles and practices but need not be certified.

(a) If the issuer is a commercial, industrial or extractive company in the promotional exploratory or development stage, the following statements shall be furnished:

(1) Separate statements of (i) assets, (ii) liabilities, and (iii) capital shares, as of a date within 90 days prior to the filing of the notification, or such longer period of time, not exceeding six months, as the Commission may permit at the written request of the issuer upon a showing of good cause therefor.

(2) A statement of cash receipts and disbursements for each of at least two full fiscal years prior to the date of the statements furnished pursuant to paragraph (1) above, and for the period, if any, between the close of the last full fiscal year and the date of such statements, or for the period of the issuer's existence if less than the period specified above.

In such statements, dollar amounts shall be extended only for cash transactions and transactions involving amounts receivable or payable in cash. Amounts due to or from, or paid to or received from, underwriters, promoters, directors, officers, employees and principal stockholders, shall be stated separately for each such class of persons, if significant in amount. The statement of assets shall include as a separate item unrecovered promotional, exploratory and development costs. The statement of cash receipts and disbursements shall be itemized as appropriate to the nature of the enterprise.

(b) If paragraph (a) does not apply to the issuer, there shall be furnished a balance sheet of the issuer as of the date specified in subparagraph (a)(1) and profit and loss statements and analyses of surplus for the periods specified in subparagraph (a)(2). Even though paragraph (a) may apply to the issuer, a balance sheet in conventional form may nevertheless be furnished in lieu of the statements specified in subparagraph (a)(1) if the assets reflected therein which were acquired in exchange for capital stock are not carried at an amount in excess of identifiable cash cost to promoters, predecessor companies or other transferors.

C

Expediting Registration Statements
Filed Under the Securities Act of 1933

RELEASE NO. 4934 (NOVEMBER 21, 1968)

The Securities and Exchange Commission today invited the cooperation of the industry, the bar, underwriters, accountants and other experts in a program which will assist the Commission's staff in its processing of the increased volume of registration statements filed under the Securities Act of 1933.

The work load of the Commission's Division of Corporation Finance has greatly increased recently due in part to the substantial increase in the number of filings of registration statements under the Securities Act of 1933. 2,473 registration statements were filed in the fiscal year ending June 30, 1968 as compared to 1,543 in 1967. For the first quarter of fiscal 1969, 840 registration statements were filed as compared to 507 for the like period in 1968. There has also been a substantial increase in the number of registration statements filed by issuers which never before have been subjected to the registration process. For example, of the 840 registration statement filings in the first quarter of fiscal 1969, 414 were filed by such issuers as compared to 149 for the first quarter of 1968. These filings most often require time-consuming review by the staff. The substantial increase in the volume of filings, and the high percentage of new filings, have resulted in a lengthening of the period between the filing and effective dates of registration statements. Further, as a result of the Securities Acts Amendments of 1964 approximately 3,200 additional companies became subject to the Commission's proxy rules. The number of definitive proxy statements filed with the Commission has increased from 2,661 in fiscal 1964 to 5,244 in fiscal 1968. The review of these filings has fallen almost entirely on the Division of Corporation Finance.

The backlog of registration statements to be processed by the staff of that Division has now reached an unprecedented high (852 as of October 31, 1968 as compared to 410 at October 31, 1967) because of the enormous increase in the number of filings and accompanied at the same time by a reduction of personnel in the Division due to budgetary cuts. While proposals for meeting this problem have been under constant study by the Commission and its staff and certain steps have been taken from time to time to that end, further measures now must be taken to reduce the backlog. Of course, the statutory standards of disclosure remain unchanged. Under the circumstances the Commission has directed the staff of the Division of Corporation Finance to adopt the following procedures until such time as normal procedures may be resumed.

A Division officer will make a cursory review of every registration statement and will make one of the following three decisions:

1. That the registration statement is so poorly prepared or otherwise presents problems so serious that no further review will be made. Oral or written comments will not be issued for to do so would delay the review of other registration statements which do not appear to contain comparable disclosure problems. Counsel will be notified;

2. That counsel shall be advised that the staff has made only a cursory review of the registration statement; no written or oral comments will be provided; and review by the staff whether extensive as is customary or cursory as in this case, may not be relied upon in any degree to indicate that the registration is true, complete or accurate. Particularly, with respect to companies which have never before been subject to the registration process, counsel will be requested to furnish as supplemental information letters from the chief executive officer of the issuer, the auditors, and the managing underwriter on behalf of all underwriters. These letters shall include representations that the respective persons are aware that the staff has made only a cursory and not a customary review of the registration statement, which may not be relied upon in any degree to indicate that the registration statement is true, complete or accurate, and are also aware of their statutory responsibilities under the Securities Act. Counsel will be advised that upon receipt of such supplemental information in satisfactory form, the staff will recommend clearance of the registration statement upon request, not earlier than 20 days after the date of original filing; or

3. That the filing will be subject to the regular review process.

With respect to (1), the company's counsel will be advised that acceleration of the effective date of the registration statement will not be recommended and should it become effective in such form, the Division would then decide what action, if any, to recommend to the Commission. Such action could include recommendations for examination or private investigation under Section 8(e) or 20(a) of the Securities Act of 1933, stop-order public hearing under Section 8(d) of the Act, and an injunctive proceeding or criminal reference under Section 20(b) of the Act.

With respect to both (1) and (2), counsel for the companies will be advised that the statutory burden of full disclosure is on the issuer, its affiliates, the underwriter and experts, that as a matter of law this burden cannot be shifted to the staff, and that the current work load is such that the staff cannot undertake additional review and comment. Attention is directed to the case of *Escott* v. *BarChris Construction Corporation, et al.*, 283 F. Supp. 643 (DC, S.D.N.Y., 1968).

Need for Full Cooperation of the Bar and Financial Community

This program and the efforts of the staff of our Division of Corporation Finance to reduce the record backlog of registration statements and the length of the pre-effective period in a manner consistent with the tradition of high standards of disclosure can only be accomplished with the full cooperation of issuers, counsel, underwriters, accountants and others. Such persons are therefore urged to proceed as follows:

1. Do not file a registration statement with the Commission unless it fully meets the statutory standards. Filing a piece of paper to "get in line" or in expectation that the staff's comments will enable you to meet these standards will not be productive.

2. By reason of the period elapsing between the filing date and the effective date, it is frequently necessary to request that financial statements be updated. Registrants should anticipate such requests and be prepared to furnish financial data to the latest practicable date.

3. Cooperate with the staff in pinpointing to them in your letter of transmittal possible trouble spots and in explaining to them the desired time schedule. Such time schedule should of course be realistic. The registration process of the S.E.C. is not and was not designed to be an adversary proceeding. We are trying to assist bona fide efforts to comply with the disclosure requirements of the statute so that prospective investors can exercise sound and informed judgments as to the merits of securities.

4. Exercise great restraint in considering whether to communicate with members of the staff, in person or by telephone.

D

Valuation of Stocks and Bonds Under Revenue Ruling 59-60

In valuing the stock of closely held corporations, or the stock of corporations where market quotations are not available, all other available financial data, as well as all relevant factors affecting the fair market value must be considered for estate tax and gift tax purposes. No general formula may be given that is applicable to the many different valuation situations arising in the valuation of such stock. However, the general approach, methods, and factors which must be considered in valuing such securities are outlined.

Revenue Ruling 54-77, C.B. 1954-1, 187, superseded.

Sec. 1. Purpose.

The purpose of this Revenue Ruling is to outline and review in general the approach, methods and factors to be considered in valuing shares of the capital stock of closely held corporations for estate tax and gift tax purposes. The methods discussed herein will apply likewise to the valuation of corporate stocks on which market quotations are either unavailable or are of such scarcity that they do not reflect the fair market value.

Sec. 2. Background and Definitions.

.01 All valuations must be made in accordance with the applicable provisions of the Internal Revenue Code of 1954 and the Federal Estate Tax and Gift Tax Regulations. Sections 2031(a), 2032 and 2512(a) of the 1954 Code (sections 811 and 1005 of the 1939 Code) require that the property to be included in the gross estate, or made the subject of a gift, shall be taxed on the basis of the value of the property at the time of death of the decedent, the alternate date if so elected, or the date of gift.

.02   Section 20.2031–1(b) of the Estate Tax Regulations (section 81.10 of the Estate Tax Regulations 105) and section 25.2512–1 of the Gift Tax Regulations (section 86.19 of Gift Tax Regulations 108) define fair market value, in effect, as the price at which the property would change hands between a willing buyer and a willing seller when the former is not under any compulsion to buy and the latter is not under any compulsion to sell, both parties having reasonable knowledge of relevant facts. Court decisions frequently state in addition that the hypothetical buyer and seller are assumed to be able, as well as willing, to trade and to be well informed about the property and concerning the market for such property.

.03   Closely held corporations are those corporations the shares of which are owned by a relatively limited number of stockholders. Often the entire stock issue is held by one family. The result of this situation is that little, if any, trading in the shares takes place. There is, therefore, no established market for the stock and such sales as occur at irregular intervals seldom reflect all of the elements of a representative transaction as defined by the term "fair market value."

Sec. 3.   Approach to Valuation.

.01   A determination of fair market value, being a question of fact, will depend upon the circumstances in each case. No formula can be devised that will be generally applicable to the multitude of different valuation issues arising in estate and gift tax cases. Often, an appraiser will find wide differences of opinion as to the fair market value of a particular stock. In resolving such differences, he should maintain a reasonable attitude in recognition of the fact that valuation is not an exact science. A sound valuation will be based upon all the relevant facts, but the elements of common sense, informed judgment and reasonableness must enter into the process of weighing those facts and determining their aggregate significance.

.02   The fair market value of specific shares of stock will vary as general economic conditions change from "normal" to "boom" or "depression," that is, according to the degree of optimism or pessimism with which the investing public regards the future at the required date of appraisal. Uncertainty as to the stability or continuity of the future income from a property decreases its value by increasing the risk of loss of earnings and value in the future. The value of shares of stock of a company with very uncertain future prospects is highly speculative. The appraiser must exercise his judgment as to the degree of risk attaching to the business of the corporation which issued the stock, but that judgment must be related to all of the other factors affecting value.

.03   Valuation of securities is, in essence, a prophesy as to the future and must be based on facts available at the required date of appraisal. As a generalization, the prices of stocks which are traded in volume in a free and active market by informed persons best reflect the consensus of the investing public as to what the future holds for the corporations and industries represented. When a stock is closely held, is traded infrequently, or is traded in an erratic market, some other measure of value must be used. In many instances, the next best measure may be found in the prices at which the stocks of companies engaged in the same or a similar line of business are selling in a free and open market.

Sec. 4.   Factors To Consider.

.01   It is advisable to emphasize that in the valuation of the stock of closely held corporations or the stock of corporations where market quotations are either lacking or too scarce to be recognized, all available financial data, as well as all relevant factors affecting the fair market value, should be considered. The following factors, although not all-inclusive are fundamental and require careful analysis in each case:

(a) The nature of the business and the history of the enterprise from its inception.

(b) The economic outlook in general and the condition and outlook of the specific industry in particular.

(c) The book value of the stock and the financial condition of the business.

(d) The earning capacity of the company.

(e) The dividend-paying capacity.

(f) Whether or not the enterprise has goodwill or other intangible value.

(g) Sales of the stock and the size of the block of stock to be valued.

(h) The market price of stocks of corporations engaged in the same or a similar line of business having their stocks actively traded in a free and open market, either on an exchange or over-the-counter.

.02 The following is a brief discussion of each of the foregoing factors:

(a) The history of a corporate enterprise will show its past stability or instability, its growth or lack of growth, the diversity or lack of diversity of its operations, and other facts needed to form an opinion of the degree of risk involved in the business. For an enterprise which changed its form of organization but carried on the same or closely similar operations of its predecessor, the history of the former enterprise should be considered. The detail to be considered should increase with approach to the required date of appraisal, since recent events are of greatest help in predicting the future; but a study of gross and net income, and of dividends covering a long prior period, is highly desirable. The history to be studied should include, but need not be limited to, the nature of the business, its products or services, its operating and investment assets, capital structure, plant facilities, sales records and management, all of which should be considered as of the date of the appraisal, with due regard for recent significant changes. Events of the past that are unlikely to recur in the future should be discounted, since value has a close relation to future expectancy.

(b) A sound appraisal of a closely held stock must consider current and prospective economic conditions as of the date of appraisal, both in the national economy and in the industry or industries with which the corporation is allied. It is important to know that the company is more or less successful than its competitors in the same industry, or that it is maintaining a stable position with respect to competitors. Equal or even greater significance may attach to the ability of the industry with which the company is allied to compete with other industries. Prospective competition which has not been a factor in prior years should be given careful attention. For example, high profits due to the novelty of its product and the lack of competition often lead to increasing competition. The public's appraisal of the future prospects of competitive industries or of competitors within an industry may be indicated by price trends in the markets for commodities and for securities. The loss of the manager of a so-called "one-man" business may have a depressing effect upon the value of the stock of such business, particularly if there is a lack of trained personnel capable of succeeding to the management of the enterprise. In valuing the stock of this type of business, therefore, the effect of the loss of the manager on the future expectancy of the business, and the absence of management-succession potentialities are pertinent factors to be taken into consideration. On the other hand, there may be factors which offset, in whole or in part, the loss of the manager's services. For instance, the nature of the business and of its assets may be such that they will not be impaired by the loss of the manager. Furthermore, the loss may be adequately covered by life insurance, or competent management might be employed on the basis of the consideration paid for the former manager's services. These, or other offsetting factors, if found to exist, should be carefully weighed against the loss of the manager's services in valuing the stock of the enterprise.

(c) Balance sheets should be obtained, preferably in the form of comparative annual statements for two or more years immediately preceding the date of appraisal, together with a balance sheet at the end of the month preceding that date, if corporate accounting will permit. Any balance sheet descriptions that are not self-explanatory, and balance sheet items comprehending diverse assets or liabilities, should be clarified in essential detail by supporting supplemental schedules. These statements usually will disclose to the appraiser (1) liquid position (ratio of current assets to current liabilities); (2) gross and net book value of principal classes of fixed assets; (3) working capital; (4) long-term indebtedness; (5) capital structure; and (6) net worth. Consideration also should be given to any assets not essential to the operation of the business, such as investments in securities, real estate, etc. In general, such nonoperating assets will command a lower rate of return than do the operating assets, although in exceptional cases the reverse may be true. In computing the book value per share of stock, assets of the investment type should be revalued on the basis of their market price and the book value adjusted accordingly. Comparison of the company's balance sheets over several years may reveal, among other facts, such developments as the acquisition of additional production facilities or subsidiary companies, improvement in financial position, and details as to recapitalizations and other changes in the capital structure of the corporation. If the corporation has more than one class of stock outstanding, the charter or certificate of incorporation should be examined to ascertain the explicit rights and privileges of the various stock issues including: (1) voting powers, (2) preference as to dividends, and (3) preference as to assets in the event of liquidation.

(d) Detailed profit-and-loss statements should be obtained and considered for a representative period immediately prior to the required date of appraisal, preferably five or more years. Such statements should show (1) gross income by principal items; (2) principal deductions from gross income including major prior items of operating expenses, interest and other expense on each item of long-term debt, depreciation and depletion if such deductions are made, officers' salaries, in total if they appear to be reasonable or in detail if they seem to be excessive, contributions (whether or not deductible for tax purposes) that the nature of its business and its community position require the corporation to make, and taxes by principal items, including income and excess profits taxes; (3) net income available for dividends; (4) rates and amounts of dividends paid on each class of stock; (5) remaining amount carried to surplus; and (6) adjustments to, and reconciliation with, surplus as stated on the balance sheet. With profit and loss statements of this character available, the appraiser should be able to separate recurrent from nonrecurrent items of income and expense, to distinguish between operating income and investment income, and to ascertain whether or not any line of business in which the company is engaged is operated consistently at a loss and might be abandoned with benefit to the company. The percentage of earnings retained for business expansion should be noted when dividend-paying capacity is considered. Potential future income is a major factor in many valuations of closely-held stocks, and all information concerning past income which will be helpful in predicting the future should be secured. Prior earnings records usually are the most reliable guide as to the future expectancy, but resort to arbitrary five-or-ten-year averages without regard to current trends or future prospects will not produce a realistic valuation. If, for instance, a record of progressively increasing or decreasing net income is found, then greater weight may be accorded the most recent years' profits in estimating earnings power. It will be helpful, in judging risk and the extent to which a business is a marginal operator, to consider deductions from income and net income in terms of percentage of sales. Major categories of cost and expense to be so analyzed include the consumption of raw materials and supplies in the case of manufacturers, processors and fabricators; the cost of purchased merchandise in the case of merchants; utility services; insurance; taxes; depletion or depreciation; and interest.

(e) Primary consideration should be given to the dividend-paying capacity of the company rather than to dividends actually paid in the past. Recognition must be given to the necessity of retaining a reasonable portion of profits in a company to meet competition. Dividend-paying capacity is a factor that must be considered in an appraisal, but dividends actually paid in the past may not have any relation to dividend-paying capacity. Specifically, the dividends paid by a closely held family company may be measured by the income needs of the stockholders or by their desire to avoid taxes on dividend receipts, instead of by the ability of the company to pay dividends. Where an actual or effective controlling interest in a corporation is to be valued, the dividend factor is not a material element, since the payment of such dividends is discretionary with the controlling stockholders. The individual or group in control can substitute salaries and bonuses for dividends, thus reducing net income and understating the dividend-paying capacity of the company. It follows, therefore, that dividends are less reliable criteria of fair market value than other applicable factors.

(f) In the final analysis, goodwill is based upon earning capacity. The presence of goodwill and its value, therefore, rests upon the excess of net earnings over and above a fair return on the net tangible assets. While the element of goodwill may be based primarily on earnings, such factors as the prestige and renown of the business, the ownership of a trade or brand name, and a record of successful operation over a prolonged period in a particular locality, also may furnish support for the inclusion of intangible value. . . .

(g) Sales of stock of a closely held corporation should be carefully investigated to determine whether they represent transactions at arm's length. Forced or distress sales do not ordinarily reflect fair market value nor do isolated sales in small amounts necessarily control as the measure of value. This is especially true in the valuation of a controlling interest in a corporation. Since, in the case of closely held stocks, no prevailing market prices are available, there is no basis for making an adjustment for blockage. It follows, therefore, that such stocks should be valued upon a consideration of all the evidence affecting the fair market value. The size of the block of stock itself is a relevant factor to be considered. Although it is true that a minority interest in an unlisted corporation's stock is more difficult to sell than a similar block of listed stock, it is equally true that control of a corporation, either actual or in effect, representing as it does an added element of value, may justify a higher value for a specific block of stock.

(h) Section 2031(b) of the Code states, in effect, that in valuing unlisted securities the value of stock or securities of corporations engaged in the same or a similar line of business which are listed on an exchange should be taken into consideration along with all other factors. An important consideration is that the corporations to be used for comparisons have capital stocks which are actively traded by the public. In accordance with section 2031(b) of the Code, stocks listed on an exchange are to be considered first. However, if sufficient comparable companies whose stocks are listed on an exchange cannot be found, other comparable companies which have stocks actively traded in on the over-the-counter market also may be used. The essential factor is that whether the stocks are sold on an exchange or over-the-counter there is evidence of an active, free public market for the stock as of the valuation date. In selecting corporations for comparative purposes, care should be taken to use only comparable companies. Although the only restrictive requirement as to comparable corporations specified in the statute is that their lines of business be the same or similar, yet it is obvious that consideration must be given to other relevant factors in order that the most valid comparison possible will be obtained. For illustration, a corporation having one or more issues of preferred stock, bonds or debentures in addition to its common stock should not be considered to be directly comparable to one having only common stock outstanding. In like manner, a company with a declining business and decreasing markets is not comparable to one with a record of current progress and market expansion.

Sec. 5. Weight To Be Accorded Various Factors.

The valuation of closely held corporate stock entails the consideration of all relevant factors as stated in section 4. Depending upon the circumstances in each case, certain factors may carry more weight than others because of the nature of the company's business. To illustrate:

(a) Earnings may be the most important criterion of value in some cases whereas asset value will receive primary consideration in others. In general, the appraiser will accord primary consideration to earnings when valuing stocks of companies which sell products or services to the public; conversely, in the investment or holding type of company, the appraiser may accord the greatest weight to the assets underlying the security to be valued.

(b) The value of the stock of a closely held investment or real estate holding company, whether or not family owned, is closely related to the value of the assets underlying the stock. For companies of this type the appraiser should determine the fair market values of the assets of the company. Operating expenses of such a company and the cost of liquidating it, if any, merit consideration when appraising the relative values of the stock and the underlying assets. The market values of the underlying assets give due weight to potential earnings and dividends of the particular items of property underlying the stock, capitalized at rates deemed proper by the investing public at the date of appraisal. A current appraisal by the investing public should be superior to the retrospective opinion of an individual. For these reasons, adjusted net worth should be accorded greater weight in valuing the stock of a closely held investment or real estate holding company, whether or not family owned, than any of the other customary yardsticks of appraisal, such as earnings and dividend paying capacity.

Sec. 6. Capitalization Rates.

In the application of certain fundamental valuation factors, such as earnings and dividends, it is necessary to capitalize the average or current results at some appropriate rate. A determination of the proper capitalization rate presents one of the most difficult problems in valuation. That there is no ready or simple solution will become apparent by a cursory check of the rates of return and dividend yields in terms of the selling prices of corporate shares listed on the major exchanges of the country. Wide variations will be found even for companies in the same industry. Moreover, the ratio will fluctuate from year to year depending upon economic conditions. Thus, no standard tables of capitalization rates applicable to closely held corporations can be formulated. Among the more important factors to be taken into consideration in deciding upon a capitalization rate in a particular case are: (1) the nature of the business; (2) the risk involved; and (3) the stability or irregularity of earnings.

Sec. 7. Average of Factors.

Because valuations cannot be made on the basis of a prescribed formula, there is no means whereby the various applicable factors in a particular case can be assigned mathematical weights in deriving the fair market value. For this reason, no useful purpose is served by taking an average of several factors (for example, book value, capitalized earnings and capitalized dividends) and basing the valuation on the result. Such a process excludes active consideration of other pertinent factors, and the end result cannot be supported by a realistic application of the significant facts in the case except by mere chance.

Sec. 8. Restrictive Agreements.

Frequently, in the valuation of closely held stock for estate and gift tax purposes, it will be found that the stock is subject to an agreement restricting its sale or transfer. Where shares of stock were acquired by a decedent subject to an option reserved by the issuing corporation to repurchase at a certain price, the option price is usually accepted as the fair market value for estate tax purposes. See Rev. Rul. 54–76, C.B. 1954–1, 194. However, in such case the option price is not determinative of fair market value for gift tax purposes. Where the option, or buy and sell agreement, is the result of voluntary action by the stockholders and is binding during the life as well as at the death of the stockholders, such agreement may or may not, depending upon the circumstances of each case, fix the value for estate tax purposes. However, such agreement is a factor to be considered, with other relevant factors, in determining fair market value. Where the stockholder is free to dispose of his shares during life and the option is to become effective only upon his death, the fair market value is not limited to the option price. It is always necessary to consider the relationship of the parties, the relative number of shares held by the decedent, and other material facts, to determine whether the agreement represents a bonafide business arrangement or is a device to pass the decedent's shares to the natural objects of his bounty for less than an adequate and full consideration in money or money's worth. In this connection see Rev. Rul. 157 C.B. 1953–2, 255, and Rev. Rul. 189, C.B. 1953–2, 294.

Sec. 9.   Effect on Other Documents.

Revenue Ruling 54–77, C.B. 1954–1, 187, is hereby superseded.

E

Requirements for Certified Financial Statements of Companies Acquired or To Be Acquired—Securities Act of 1933, Release No. 4950

RELEASE NO. 4950 (FEBRUARY 20, 1969)

The increasing number of business acquisitions has led to numerous requests for relief from the requirements for certification of financial statements of the acquired businesses on the representation that it is impossible to obtain certification. When an acquiring company plans to register securities under the Securities Act the necessity for furnishing financial statements for the new business must be considered by it. Item 27 of Schedule A of the Securities Act of 1933 and Instructions 11 and 12 to Form S–1 for registration under the Act require certified financial statements for a company acquired or to be acquired. Instruction 13 of Form S–1 permits the Commission to grant relief from this requirement of certification where such relief is consistent with the protection of investors. Generally, relief has been requested because no independent certified public accountant has observed the taking of inventory of the acquired company necessary for certification of financial statements for three years and alternative methods of verification were not available.

When a representation is made that certification of financial statements of acquired companies for a full three year period cannot be obtained and compelling and satisfactory evidence in support of such representation is furnished, the Commission considers the relationship of the following items of the acquired companies to those of the registrant (on a consolidated basis without inclusion of such companies) in determining whether relief from the three-year certification requirement should be granted:

1. gross sales and operating revenues;
2. net income;
3. total assets;
4. total stockholder equity; and
5. total purchase price compared to total assets of registrant.

The above items will be evaluated as follows:

A. If none of the items exceed 10 percent, certified statements will not be required;

B. If any of the items exceed 10 percent but none exceed 25 percent, certification of the balance sheet and the income statement for not less than six months will be required;

C. If any of the items exceed 25 percent but none exceed 45 percent, certification of the balance sheet and the income statement for at least twelve months will be required.

D. If any of the items exceed 45 percent, certification of the balance sheet and the income statement for three years will be required, consistent with similar requirements as to the registrant.

In connection with any request for relief from the three-year certification requirement the items of information mentioned above should be furnished in tabular form, comparing the five items set forth therein of the acquired companies (individually and in the aggregate) with the registrant on a consolidated basis (without the acquired companies), with dates of acquisition and other pertinent data. To the extent any of the data is not based on audit reports, the basis or lack of basis for reliance on the data should be fully stated (including the nature and method of checking the accuracy of the underlying figures).

Income statements for periods not certified shall not be combined with the certified statements if to do so would result in a qualification by the auditors on grounds of materiality.

Note: This release does not apply to the financial statements of a company to be acquired where the securities to be registered are to be offered to the security holders of that company in exchange for their securities. In such a case certified financial statements of that company shall be furnished in accordance with the requirements of the applicable registration form.

F

Valuation of Intangibles
Under Revenue Ruling 68-609

Gain or loss: Amount: Valuation of intangibles: "Formula" approach restated.—The "formula" approach may be used in determining the fair market value of intangible assets of a business only if there is no better basis available for making the determination.

A. R. M. 34, C. B. 2, 31; A. R. M. 68, C. B. 3, 43; O. D. 937, C. B. 4, 43; and Rev. Rul. 65–192, C B. 1965–2, 259, superseded. Back references: ¶ 3970.06, 4430.1973, 4430.215, 4430.221, 4430.276, 4430.28, 4430.302, 4430.3021, 4430.3022, 4430.3067, 4430.319, 4430.3285, 4430.3295, 4430.3335, 4430.343 and 4430.344.

The purpose of this Revenue Ruling is to update and restate, under the current statute and regulations, the currently outstanding portions of A. R. M. 34, C. B. 2, 31 (1920), A. R. M. 68, C. B. 3, 43 (1920), and O. D. 937, C. B. 4, 43 (1921).

The question presented is whether the "formula" approach, the capitalization of earnings in excess of a fair rate of return on net tangible assets, may be used to determine the fair market value of the intangible assets of a business.

The "formula" approach may be stated as follows:

A percentage return on the average annual value of the tangible assets used in a business is determined, using a period of years (preferably not less than five) immediately prior to the valuation date. The amount of the percentage return on tangible assets, thus determined, is deducted from the average earnings of the business for such period and the remainder, if any, is considered to be the amount of the average annual earnings from the intangible assets of the business for the period. This amount (considered as the average annual earnings from intangibles), capitalized at a percentage of say, 15 to 20 percent, is the value of the intangible assets of the business determined under the "formula" approach.

The percentage of return on the average annual value of the tangible assets used should be the percentage prevailing in the industry involved at the date of valuation, or (when the industry percentage is not available) a percentage of 8 to 10 percent may be used.

The 8 percent rate of return and the 15 percent rate of capitalization are applied to tangibles and intangibles, respectively, of businesses with a small risk factor and stable and regular earnings; the 10 percent rate of return and 20 percent rate of capitalization are applied to businesses in which the hazards of business are relatively high.

The above rates are used as examples and are not appropriate in all cases. In applying the "formula" approach, the average earnings period and the capitalization rates are dependent upon the facts pertinent thereto in each case.

The past earnings to which the formula is applied should fairly reflect the probable future earnings. Ordinarily, the period should not be less than five years, and abnormal years, whether above or below the average, should be eliminated. If the business is a sole proprietorship or partnership there should be deducted from the earnings of the business a reasonable amount for services performed by the owner or partners engaged in the business. See *Lloyd B. Sanderson Estate v. Commissioner,* 42 F. 2d .160 (1930). Further, only the tangible assets entering into net worth, including accounts and bills receivable in excess of accounts and bills payable, are used for determining earnings on the tangible assets. Factors that influence the capitalization rate include (1) the nature of the business, (2) the risk involved, and (3) the stability or irregularity of earnings.

The "formula" approach should not be used if there is better evidence available from which the value of intangibles can be determined. If the assets of a going business are sold upon the basis of a rate of capitalization that can be substantiated as being realistic, though it is not within the range of figures indicated here as the ones ordinarily to be adopted, the same rate of capitalization should be used in determining the value of intangibles.

Accordingly, the "formula" approach may be used for determining the fair market value of intangible assets of a business only if there is no better basis therefor available.

See also Revenue Ruling 59–60, C. B. 1959–1, 237, as modified by Revenue Ruling 65–193, C. B. 1965–2, 370, which sets forth the proper approach to use in the valuation of closely held corporate stocks for estate and gift tax purposes. The general approach, methods, and factors, outlined in Revenue Ruling 59–60, as modified, are equally applicable to valuations of corporate stocks for income and other tax purposes as well as for estate and gift tax purposes. They apply also to problems involving the determination of the fair market value of business interests of any type, including partnerships and proprietorships, and of intangible assets for all tax purposes.

A. R. M. 34, A. R. M. 68, and O.D. 937 are superseded, since the positions set for therein are restated to the extent applicable under current law in this Revenue Ruling. Revenue Ruling 65–192, C. B. 1965–2, 259, which contained restatements of A. R. M. 34 and A. R. M. 68, is also superseded.

G

Digest of Department of Justice
Merger Guidelines

On May 30, 1968, the Department of Justice released guidelines outlining its standards for determining whether to oppose corporate acquisitions or mergers under Section 7 of the Clayton Act. The announced purpose of the guidelines is to insure that the business community, the legal profession, and other interested persons are informed of the Department's policy of enforcing Section 7 of the Clayton Act.

"The Department anticipates that it will amend the guidelines from time to time, to reflect changes in enforcement policy that might result from subsequent court decisions, comments of interested parties, or Department reevaluations.

"Because changes in enforcement policy will be made as the occasion demands and will usually precede the issuance of amended guidelines, the Department said that the existence of unamended guidelines should not be regarded as barring it from taking any action it deems necessary to achieve the purposes of Section 7."

Summarized below are some of the pertinent data contained in the guideline release, which covers 21 topical items in some 26 pages of text:

General Enforcement Policy

The primary role of Section 7 enforcement is to preserve and promote market structures conducive to competition, and the enforcement activity is directed toward the identification and prevention of mergers which alter market structure or permit noncompetitive conduct.

Market Definition

A market is any grouping of sales in which each of the firms whose sales are included enjoys some advantage in competing with those firms whose sales are not included. It is defined both in terms of its product dimension (line of commerce) and its geographic dimension (section of the country).

Horizontal Mergers

With respect to mergers between direct competitors, the Department's enforcement activity has the following interrelated purposes:

1. Preventing elimination as an independent business entity of any company likely to have been a substantial competitive influence in a market.
2. Preventing any company or small group of companies from obtaining a position of dominance in a market.
3. Preventing significant increases in concentration in a market.
4. Preserving significant possibilities for eventual deconcentration in a concentrated market.

Primary significance is placed on the comparative size of the acquiring and acquired firms. The Department has applied the following standards relating to the size of the merger participants in determining whether to challenge a merger:

1. In a highly concentrated market in which the four largest firms account for 75% or more of the market, the Department will ordinarily challenge mergers between firms accounting for, approximately, the following percentages of the market:

Percentages of the Market

Acquiring Firm	Acquired Firm
4%	4% or more
10%	2% or more
15% or more	1% or more

2. Less highly concentrated market:

Percentages of the Market

Acquiring Firm	Acquired Firm
5%	5% or more
10%	4% or more
15%	3% or more
20%	2% or more
25% or more	1% or more

A stricter standard is applied in markets in which there is a significant trend toward increased concentration. Such a trend is considered present if any grouping of companies from the two largest to the eight largest has increased their share of the market by 7% or more over the past 5–10 years.

The Department may also challenge mergers for other reasons such as (a) acquisition of a competitor which is a particularly "disturbing," "disruptive," or otherwise unusually competitive factor in the market; and (b) a merger involving a substantial firm and a firm which, despite an insubstantial market share, possesses an unusual competitive advantage (for example, the acquisition by a leading firm of a newcomer having a patent on a significantly improved product or production process).

Failing Company

A merger which the Department would otherwise challenge will ordinarily not be challenged if (a) the resources of one of the merging firms are so depleted and its prospects for rehabilitation so remote that the firm faces the clear probability of a business failure, and (b) good faith efforts by the failing firm have failed to elicit a reasonable offer of acquisition more consistent with the purposes of Section 7 by a firm which intends to keep the failing firm in the market. The standards will only be applied where a company is failing "in the clearest of circumstances."

Economies

Unless there are exceptional circumstances, the Department will not accept as a justification for an acquisition normally subject to challenge under its horizontal merger standards the claim that the merger will produce economies.

Vertical Mergers

The Department's enforcement with respect to vertical mergers (i.e., acquisitions "backward" into a supplying market or forward into a purchasing market) is intended to prevent changes in market structure that are likely to lead, over the course of time, to significant anticompetitive consequences. Such consequences occur when mergers raise barriers by (a) foreclosing equal access to potential customers, (b) foreclosing equal access to potential suppliers, or (c) facilitating promotional product differentiation, when the merger involves a manufacturing firm's acquisition of firms at the retail level.

The Department will look at both the supplying firm's market and the purchasing firm's market and will ordinarily challenge a merger in which the supplying firm accounts for 10% or more of the sales in its market, and the purchasing firm accounts for 6% or more of the total purchases in that market. Even where the respective market shares are less, mergers may be challenged "on the ground that they raise entry barriers in the purchasing firm's market, or disadvantage the purchasing firm's competitors. . . ." If a product is a significant feature or ingredient of a manufactured end product, the merger will be challenged if the supplying firm accounts for 20% or more of the sales in its market and the purchaser firm accounts for 10% or more of the sales in the market in which it sells the manufactured products.

Comments regarding failing companies and the fact that expected economies do not justify a merger, similar to those under "horizontal mergers," are also included in this category of mergers.

Conglomerate Mergers

Conglomerate mergers are mergers that are neither horizontal or vertical. The Department's enforcement activity in this area is to prevent changes in market structure that appear to cause a substantial lessening of competition that would otherwise exist. A market extension merger, i.e., one involving two firms selling the same product, but in different geographic areas, is classified as a conglomerate merger. The three categories of conglomerate mergers that will be challenged are (a) mergers involving potential entrants, (b) mergers creating a danger of reciprocal buying, and (c) mergers which threaten to entrench or enhance the market power of the acquired firm.

The Department will challenge mergers between one of the most likely entrants into a market and:

1. A firm with 25% or more of the market
2. One of the two largest firms in a market in which the two largest firms account for 50% or more
3. One of the four largest firms in a market in which the shares of the eight largest firms amount to approximately 75%, providing the merging firm's share of the market amounts to 10% or more
4. One of the eight largest firms in a market in which the shares of these firms amount to approximately 75% or more provided either (1) the merging firms' share of the market is not insubstantial and there are no more than one or two likely entrants into the market, or (2) the merging firm is a rapidly growing firm

The Department will challenge a merger which creates a danger of reciprocal buying if 15% or more of the total purchases in a market in which one of the merging firm's (the selling firm) sales are accounted for by firms which also make substantial sales in markets where the other merging firm (the buying firm) is both a substantial buyer and a more substantial buyer than all or most of the competitors of the selling firm.

The Department will investigate mergers that may serve to entrench or enhance the market power of a firm such as (a) a merger which produces a very large disparity between the merged firm and the largest remaining firms in the relevant markets, (b) a merger of firms producing related products which may induce purchasers to buy products of the merged firm rather than those of a competitor, and (c) a merger which may enhance the ability of the merged firm to increase product differentiation in the relevant markets.

The standards set forth under "Horizontal Mergers" for failing companies are normally applied in determining whether to challenge a conglomerate merger, except for certain exceptions in marginal cases.

H

Provisions of State Laws Regarding
Rights of Dissenting Stockholders

States having laws specifically providing right to dissent: 49 and District of Columbia

States without such provision: West Virginia

1. Extent of right to dissent to plans of merger or consolidation:

No apparent provisions restricting right to dissent:

Alabama	Maine	New Hampshire
Arizona	Massachusetts	Oklahoma
District of Columbia	Michigan	Rhode Island
Florida	Minnesota	South Dakota
Georgia	Missouri	Vermont
Kansas	Nevada	

No apparent restrictions except that right of dissent is not available to stockholders of the surviving corporation in certain parent–subsidiary mergers (law specifies percentage of ownership of which the lowest is 90%):

Alaska	Montana	Texas
Arkansas	Nebraska	Utah
Colorado	New Mexico	Virginia
Illinois	North Carolina	Washington
Indiana	North Dakota	Wisconsin
Iowa	Oregon	Wyoming
Mississippi	South Carolina	

Note: The laws of the following states include the above restriction in addition to the other restrictions noted below:

Delaware	New York	Pennsylvania *
New Jersey	Ohio	

No apparent restrictions except that right of dissent is not available to holders of classes of shares whose terms and provisions specifically set forth the amount to be paid (or the method of determining the amount to be paid) in the event of consolidation or merger:

California

Hawaii

Note: Also Kentucky, in addition to another restriction.

No apparent restriction provided corporation has sufficient net assets to make payment:

Idaho
Tennessee

No right of dissent available to shareholders of surviving corporation unless the merger alters the contract rights of the shares held:

Connecticut
Maryland
New York

No right of dissent available to holders of shares which are:

Listed on a national securities exchange or quoted in an over-the-counter market (New Jersey)

Registered on a national securities exchange or held by not less than 2,000 stockholders (Delaware, Louisiana)

Listed on the New York Stock Exchange or the American Stock Exchange or held of record by not less than 2,500 stockholders (Pennsylvania)

and

The shareholders are required to accept only shares or shares and cash in lieu of fractional shares of the surviving corporation:

Delaware
Louisiana **

* Restriction also applies to stockholders of subsidiary.
** Further restricted; see below.

New Jersey

Pennsylvania *

No right of dissent available if action approved by at least 80% of the total voting power (Louisiana)

No right to dissent available "if only shares or other securities of the surviving corporation, other than shares of common stock of the surviving corporation, are to be issued or exchanged for shares of any other constituent corporation" (Kentucky)

Right to dissent restricted to mergers where the shareholders of the other constituent corporation or corporations would, when the merger becomes effective, own shares of the surviving corporation entitling them to exercise one-sixth or more of the voting power in the election of directors of the surviving corporation

or

contract rights of the shares are altered (Ohio)

2. Extent of right to dissent to sale, exchange or lease of substantially all corporate property:

Right to dissent substantially unrestricted. (Included in this category are those statutes where no right to dissent is granted in the case of a cash sale prior to distribution in liquidation or in sales pursuant to a court order)—36 states

No provision located covering right to dissent to this type of transaction—10 states

Various restrictions, as follows—4 states

Connecticut—Right to dissent "if a corporation sells all or substantially all its assets primarily in consideration for securities of another corporation, domestic or foreign, and such transaction is part of a general plan of liquidation and distribution substantially equivalent to a merger."

Louisiana—No right to dissent if action approved by 80% of total voting power.

New Jersey—No right to dissent (1) where shares are listed on a national securities exchange or are regularly quoted in an over-the-counter market (2) to a transaction pursuant to a plan of dissolution where the transaction is wholly for (a) cash, (b) securities listed on a national securities exchange or regularly quoted in an over-the-counter market, or (c) cash and such securities.

---

* Restriction not applicable if contract rights of shares are altered.

Pennsylvania—No right to dissent applies "to a sale, lease, or exchange of substantially all of the property and assets of a business corporation which directly or indirectly owns all of the outstanding shares of another corporation, to such corporation: provided" (no change in contract rights).

3. Right to dissent to less than all shares held:

Right granted in statute—11 states
Right denied in statute—3 states (New Jersey, New York, Oregon)
Right granted to nominee of corporate fiduciary only—2 states (Alabama, Pennsylvania)
No mention—34 states

4. Statute provides that dissenting stockholder must file a written objection to the proposed corporate action prior to the meeting or prior to the vote on the action—36 states. In all cases the statutes provide that the dissenting stockholder may not have voted in favor of the proposal.

5. Right of dissenting stockholder to withdraw demand for payment for his stock:

Statute states that demand may be withdrawn with corporate consent. However, it appears that in some cases demand could effectively be withdrawn by failure to take timely action—21 states
No provision other than requirement to take timely action—14 states
Demand may be withdrawn up to some specified point in time, e.g., prior to determination of fair value—6 states
Language of statute appears to preclude withdrawal of demand—4 states (Florida, Georgia, Indiana, Nevada)
No mention—5 states (Idaho, Maine, New Hampshire, Tennessee, Vermont)

6. Definition of value used in the various statutes:

Fair value—12 states
Fair value, exclusive of any element of value arising from the expectation or accomplishment of the corporate transaction (or similar language)—19 states
Fair cash value—4 states
Value—4 states
Value, exclusive of any element of value arising from the expectation or accomplishment of the corporate transaction—2 states

Fair market value—2 states

Fair cash value, exclusive of any element of value arising from the expectation or accomplishment of the corporate transaction—2 states

Fair value, based on its pro rata share of the fair value of the net assets of the corporation as of the date of the consolidation meeting—Arizona

Fair market value, excluding any appreciation or depreciation in consequence of the proposed transaction—California

Fair cash value defined as "the amount which a willing seller, under no compulsion to sell, would be willing to accept and a willing buyer, under no compulsion to purchase, would be willing to pay . . . , provided that in no event shall the amount thereof exceed that specified in the demand of the particular shareholder. There shall be excluded from such value any appreciation or depreciation resulting from the proposal voted upon at such meeting" (Ohio)

Fair value defined as "market value thereof as of the day before the vote was taken authorizing such corporate action, excluding any appreciation or depreciation in consequence of such proposed action. If such shares be listed upon a recognized stock exchange and any of such shares shall have been sold upon such exchange upon the day aforesaid, the fair value thereof shall be presumed to be the highest price at which such shares were thus sold upon such day in the absence of any evidence of fraud or collusion" (Oklahoma)

Full and fair value shall "be deemed to be the amount which the owners of such shares would have been entitled to recover at an action at law with respect thereto in case of a conversion thereof" (Rhode Island)

7. Date of valuation:

Day prior to vote approving action—36 states

Date of authorization meeting—5 states

Effective date of corporate action—4 states

Day prior to the date on which notice of the proposed corporate transaction was mailed—1 state

Date agreement was recorded—1 state

No mention—3 states

8. Persons determining value initially:

No specification other than agreement between the parties—23 states
Corporation—22 states
Price specified by dissenting stockholder to which corporation may make counter offer (Ohio, Oklahoma, Rhode Island, Texas)—4 states
Court (Maine)—1 state

9. Persons determining value where no agreement is reached between corporation and dissenting shareholder:

Court—17 states
Court, which may elect to appoint appraisers—15 states
Court-appointed appraisers—12 states
Arbitration (Georgia, Idaho, Minnesota, New Hampshire, Vermont)—5 states
Court determines initially (Maine)—1 state

10. In case of court action, all dissenting stockholders with whom no agreement has been reached are made parties to the proceeding:

Required—18 states
Optional—10 states
No mention—22 states

11. Certificates of dissenting stockholder are required to be presented for endorsement:

Required—20 states
Option of corporation—1 state (Ohio)
Option of court—3 states (Delaware, Maryland, Massachusetts)
Required to be deposited with court—2 states (Kansas, Maine)
Required to be deposited with a bank—1 state (Louisiana)
No mention—23 states

12. In case of court action, statute provides that interest shall be paid to stockholder:

Required—37 states
No mention—13 states

Note: The foregoing data have been summarized from the *Corporation Manual*, 1969 Edition, published by United States Corporation Company.

I

Interest on Indebtedness Incurred by Corporation To Acquire Stock or Assets of Another Corporation — Internal Revenue Code Section 279

[Sec. 279(a)]

(a) GENERAL RULE.—No deduction shall be allowed for any interest paid or incurred by a corporation during the taxable year with respect to its corporate acquisition indebtedness to the extent that such interest exceeds—

(1) $5,000,000, reduced by

(2) the amount of interest paid or incurred by such corporation during such year on obligations (A) issued after December 31, 1967, to provide consideration for an acquisition described in paragraph (1) of subsection (b), but (B) which are not corporate acquisition indebtedness.

[Sec. 279(b)]

(b) CORPORATE ACQUISITION INDEBTEDNESS.—For purposes of this section, the term "corporate acquisition indebtedness" means any obligation evidenced by a bond, debenture, note, or certificate or other evidence of indebtedness issued after October 9, 1969, by a corporation (hereinafter in this section referred to as "issuing corporation") if—

(1) such obligation is issued to provide consideration for the acquisition of

(A) stock in another corporation (hereinafter in this section referred to as "acquired corporation"), or

(B) assets of another corporation (hereinafter in this section referred to as "acquired corporation") pursuant to a plan under which at least two-thirds (in value) of all the assets (excluding money) used in trades and businesses carried on by such corporation are acquired,

(2) such obligation is either—

(A) subordinated to the claims of trade creditors of the issuing corporation generally, or

(B) expressly subordinated in right of payment to the payment of any substantial amount of unsecured indebtedness, whether outstanding or subsequently issued, of the issuing corporation,

(3) the bond or other evidence of indebtedness is either—

(A) convertible directly or indirectly into stock of the issuing corporation, or

(B) part of an investment unit or other arrangement which includes, in addition to such bond or other evidence of indebtedness, an option to acquire, directly or indirectly, stock in the issuing corporation, and

(4) as of a day determined under subsection (c)(1), either—

(A) the ratio of debt to equity (as defined in subsection (c)(2)) of the issuing corporation exceeds 2 to 1, or

(B) the projected earnings (as defined in subsection (c)(3)) do not exceed 3 times the annual interest to be paid or incurred (determined under subsection (c)(4)).

[Sec. 279(c)]

(c) RULES FOR APPLICATION OF SUBSECTION (b)(4).—For purposes of subsection (b)(4)—

(1) TIME OF DETERMINATION.—Determinations are to be made as of the last day of any taxable year of the issuing corporation in which it issues any obligation to provide consideration for an acquisition described in subsection (b)(1) of stock in, or assets of, the acquired corporation.

(2) RATIO OF DEBT TO EQUITY.—The term "ratio of debt to equity" means the ratio which the total indebtedness of the issuing corporation bears to the sum of its money and all its other assets

(in an amount equal to their adjusted basis for determining gain) less such total indebtedness.

(3) PROJECTED EARNINGS.—

(A) The term "projected earnings" means the "average annual earnings" (as defined in subparagraph (B)) of—

(i) the issuing corporation only, if clause (ii) does not apply, or

(ii) both the issuing corporation and the acquired corporation, in any case where the issuing corporation has acquired control (as defined in section 368(c)), or has acquired substantially all of the properties, of the acquired corporation.

(B) The average annual earnings referred to in subparagraph (A) is, for any corporation, the amount of its earnings and profits for any 3-year period ending with the last day of a taxable year of the issuing corporation described in paragraph (1), computed without reduction for—

(i) interest paid or incurred,

(ii) depreciation or amortization allowed under this chapter,

(iii) liability for tax under this chapter, and

(iv) distributions to which section 301(c)(1) applies (other than such distributions from the acquired to the issuing corporation),

and reduced to an annual average for such 3-year period pursuant to regulations prescribed by the Secretary or his delegate. Such regulations shall include rules for cases where any corporation was not in existence for all of such 3-year period or such period includes only a portion of a taxable year of any corporation.

(4) ANNUAL INTEREST TO BE PAID OR INCURRED.—The term "annual interest to be paid or incurred" means—

(A) if subparagraph (B) does not apply, the annual interest to be paid or incurred by the issuing corporation only, determined by reference to its total indebtedness outstanding, or,

(B) if projected earnings are determined under clause (ii) of paragraph (3)(A), the annual interest to be paid or incurred by both the issuing corporation and the acquired corporation, determined by reference to their combined total indebtedness outstanding.

(5) SPECIAL RULES FOR BANKS AND LENDING OR FINANCE COMPANIES.—With respect to any corporation which is a bank (as defined in section 581) or is primarily engaged in a lending or finance business—

> (A) in determining under paragraph (2) the ratio of debt to equity of such corporation (or of the affiliated group of which such corporation is a member), the total indebtedness of such corporation (and the assets of such corporation) shall be reduced by an amount equal to the total indebtedness owed to such corporation which arises out of the banking business of such corporation, or out of the lending or finance business of such corporation, as the case may be;
>
> (B) in determining under paragraph (4) the annual interest to be paid or incurred by such corporation (or by the issuing and acquired corporations referred to in paragraph (4)(B) or by the affiliated group of which such corporation is a member) the amount of such interest (determined without regard to this paragraph) shall be reduced by an amount which bears the same ratio to the amount of such interest as the amount of the reduction for the taxable year under subparagraph (A) bears to the total indebtedness of such corporation; and
>
> (C) in determining under paragraph (3)(B) the average annual earnings, the amount of the earnings and profits for the 3-year period shall be reduced by the sum of the reductions under subparagraph (B) for such period.

For purposes of this paragraph, the term "lending or finance business" means a business of making loans or purchasing or discounting accounts receivable, notes, or installment obligations.

[Sec. 279(d)]

(d) TAXABLE YEARS TO WHICH APPLICABLE.—In applying this section—

(1) FIRST YEAR OF DISALLOWANCE.—The deduction of interest on any obligation shall not be disallowed under subsection (a) before the first taxable year of the issuing corporation as of the last day of which the application of either subparagraph (A) or subparagraph (B) of subsection (b)(4) results in such obligation being corporate acquisition indebtedness.

(2) GENERAL RULE FOR SUCCEEDING YEARS.—Except as provided in paragraph (3), (4), and (5), if an obligation is determined to be

corporate acquisition indebtedness as of the last day of any taxable year of the issuing corporation, it shall be corporate acquisition indebtedness for such taxable year and all subsequent taxable years.

(3) REDETERMINATION WHERE CONTROL, ETC., IS ACQUIRED.—If an obligation is determined to be corporate acquisition indebtedness as of the close of a taxable year of the issuing corporation in which clause (i) of subsection (c)(3)(A) applied, but would not be corporate acquisition indebtedness if the determination were made as of the close of the first taxable year of such corporation thereafter in which clause (ii) of subsection (c)(3)(A) could apply, such obligation shall be considered not to be corporate acquisition indebtedness for such later taxable year and all taxable years thereafter.

(4) SPECIAL 3-YEAR RULE.—If an obligation which has been determined to be corporate acquisition indebtedness for any taxable year would not be such indebtedness for each of any 3 consecutive taxable years thereafter if subsection (b)(4) were applied as of the close of each of such 3 years, then such obligation shall not be corporate acquisition indebtedness for all taxable years after such 3 consecutive taxable years.

(5) 5 PERCENT STOCK RULE.—In the case of obligations issued to provide consideration for the acquisition of stock in another corporation, such obligations shall be corporate acquisition indebtedness for a taxable year only if at some time after October 9, 1969, and before the close of such year the issuing corporation owns 5 percent or more of the total combined voting power of all classes of stock entitled to vote of such other corporation.

[Sec. 279(e)]

(e) CERTAIN NONTAXABLE TRANSACTIONS.—An acquisition of stock of a corporation of which the issuing corporation is in control (as defined in section 368(c)) in a transaction in which gain or loss is not recognized shall be deemed an acquisition described in paragraph (1) of subsection (b) only if immediately before such transaction (1) the acquired corporation was in existence, and (2) the issuing corporation was not in control (as defined in section 368(c)) of such corporation.

[Sec. 279(f)]

(f) EXEMPTION FOR CERTAIN ACQUISITIONS OF FOREIGN CORPORATIONS.—For purposes of this section, the term "corporate acquisition indebtedness" does not include any indebtedness issued to any person to provide consideration for the acquisition of stock in, or assets of, any foreign corporation substantially all of the income of which, for the

3-year period ending with the date of such acquisition or for such part of such period as the foreign corporation was in existence, is from sources without the United States.

[Sec. 279(g)]

(g) AFFILIATED GROUPS.—In any case in which the issuing corporation is a member of an affiliated group, the application of this section shall be determined, pursuant to regulations prescribed by the Secretary or his delegate, by treating all of the members of the affiliated group in the aggregate as the issuing corporation, except that the ratio of debt to equity of, projected earnings of, and annual interest to be paid or incurred by any corporation (other than the issuing corporation determinded without regard to this subsection) shall be included in the determinations required under subparagraphs (A) and (B) of subsection (b)(4) as of any day only if such corporation is a member of the affiliated group on such day, and, in determining projected earnings of such corporation under subsection (c)(3), there shall be taken into account only the earnings and profits of such corporation for the period during which it was a member of the affiliated group. For purposes of the preceding sentence, the term "affiliated group" has the meaning assigned to such term by section 1504 (a), except that all corporations other than the acquired corporation shall be treated as includible corporations (without any exclusion under 1504(b)) and the acquired corporation shall not be treated as an includible corporation.

[Sec. 279(h)]

(h) CHANGES IN OBLIGATION.—For purposes of this section—

(1) Any extension, renewal, or refinancing of an obligation evidencing preexisting indebtedness shall not be deemed to be the issuance of a new obligation.

(2) Any obligation which is corporate acquisition indebtedness of the issuing corporation is also corporate acquisition indebtedness of any corporation which becomes liable for such obligation as guarantor, endorser, or indemnitor or which assumes liability for such obligation in any transaction.

[Sec. 279(i)]

(i) CERTAIN OBLIGATIONS ISSUED AFTER OCTOBER 9, 1969.—For purposes of this section, an obligation shall not be corporate acquisition indebtedness if issued after October 9, 1969, to provide consideration for the acquisition of—

(1) stock or assets pursuant to a binding written contract which was in effect on October 9, 1969, and at all times thereafter before such acquisition, or

(2) stock in any corporation where the issuing corporation, on October 9, 1969, and at all times thereafter before such acquisition, owned at least 50 percent of the total combined voting power of all classes of stock entitled to vote of the acquired corporation.

Paragraph (2) shall cease to apply when (at any time on or after October 9, 1969) the issuing corporation has acquired control (as defined in section 368(c)) of the acquired corporation.

[Sec. 279(j)]

(j) EFFECT ON OTHER PROVISIONS.—No inference shall be drawn from any provision in this section that any instrument designated as a bond, debenture, note, or certificate or other evidence of indebtedness by its issuer represents an obligation or indebtedness of such issuer in applying any other provision of this title.

J

Excerpts from Tender Offer
Disclosure Act

SECTIONS 13(d) AND (e), AND 14(d), (e), AND (f)
OF THE SECURITIES EXCHANGE ACT

Information To Be Filed by Five Per Cent Beneficial Owners

Sec. 13(d)(1) Any person who, after acquiring directly or indirectly the beneficial ownership of any equity security of a class which is registered pursuant to section 12 of this title, or any equity security of an insurance company which would have been required to be so registered except for the exemption contained in section 12(g)(2)(Ġ) of this title, or any equity security issued by a closed-end investment company registered under the Investment Company Act of 1940, is directly or indirectly the beneficial owner of more than 5 per centum of such class shall, within ten days after such acquisition, send to the issuer of the security at its principal executive office, by registered or certified mail, send to each exchange where the security is traded, and file with the Commission, a statement containing such of the following information, and such additional information, as the Commission may by rules and regulations prescribe as necessary or appropriate in the public interest or for the protection of investors—

(A) the background and identity of all persons by whom or on whose behalf the purchases have been or are to be effected;

(B) the source and amount of the funds or other considerations used or to be used in making the purchases, and if any part of the purchase price or proposed purchase price is represented or is to be represented by funds or other consideration borrowed or otherwise obtained for the purpose of acquiring, holding, or trading such security, a description of the transaction and the names of the parties thereto, except that where a source of funds is a loan made in the ordinary course of business by a bank, as defined in section 3(a)(6) of this title, if the person filing such statement so requests, the name of the bank shall not be made available to the public;

(C) if the purpose of the purchases or prospective purchases is to acquire control of the business of the issuer of the securities, any plans or proposals which such persons may have to liquidate such issuer, to sell its assets to or merge it with any other persons, or to make any other major change in its business or corporate structure;

(D) the number of shares of such security which are beneficially owned, and the number of shares concerning which there is a right to acquire, directly or indirectly, by (i) such person, and (ii) by each associate of such person, giving the name and address of each such associate; and

(E) information as to any contracts, arrangements, or understandings with any person with respect to any securities of the issuer, including but not limited to transfer of any of the securities, joint ventures, loan or option arrangements, puts or calls, guaranties of loans, guaranties against loss or guaranties of profits, division of losses or profits, or the giving or withholding of proxies, naming the persons with whom such contracts, arrangements, or understandings have been entered into, and giving the details thereof.

Sec. 13(d)(2) If any material change occurs in the facts set forth in the statements to the issuer and the exchange, and in the statement filed with the Commission, an amendment shall be transmitted to the issuer and the exchange and shall be filed with the Commission, in accordance with such rules and regulations as the Commission may prescribe as necessary or appropriate in the public interest or for the protection of investors.

Syndicate, Group as "Person"

Sec. 13(d)(3) When two or more persons act as a partnership, limited partnership, syndicate, or other group for the purpose of acquiring, holding, or disposing of securities of an issuer, such syndicate or group shall be deemed a "person" for the purposes of this subsection.

Percentage of Class of Security Computations

Sec. 13(d)(4) In determining, for purposes of this subsection, any percentage of a class of any security, such class shall be deemed to consist of the amount of the outstanding securities of such class, exclusive of any securities of such class held by or for the account of this issuer or a subsidiary of the issuer.

Simplified Statement Authority

Sec. 13(d)(5) The Commission, by rule or regulation or by order, may permit any person to file in lieu of the statement required by paragraph (1) of this subsection or the rules and regulations thereunder, a notice stating the name of such person, the number of shares of any equity securities subject to paragraph (1) which are owned by him, the date of their acquisition and such other information as the Commission may specify, if it appears to the Commission that such securities were acquired by such person in the ordinary course of his business and were not acquired for the purpose of and do not have the effect of changing or influencing the control of the issuer nor in connection with or as a participant in any transaction having such purpose or effect.

Exemptions

Sec. 13(d)(6) The provisions of this subsection shall not apply to

(A) any acquisition or offer to acquire securities made or proposed to be made by means of a registration statement under the Securities Act of 1933;

(B) any acquisition of the beneficial ownership of a security which, together with all other acquisitions by the same person of securities of the same class during the preceding twelve months, does not exceed 2 per centum of that class;

(C) any acquisition of an equity security by the issuer of such security;

(D) any acquisition or proposed acquisition of a security which the Commission, by rules or regulations or by order, shall exempt from the provisions of this subsection as not entered into for the purpose of, and not having the effect of, changing or influencing the control of the issuer or otherwise as not comprehended within the purposes of this subsection.

Contravention of Rules and Regulations

Sec. 13(e)(1) It shall be unlawful for an issuer which has a class of equity securities registered pursuant to section 12 of this title, or which is a closed-end investment company registered under the Investment Company Act of 1940, to purchase any equity security issued by it if such purchase is in contravention of such rules and regulations as the Commission, in the public interest or for the protection of investors, may adopt (A) to define acts and practices which are fraudulent, deceptive, or manipulative, and (B) to prescribe means reasonably designed to prevent such acts and practices. Such rules and regulations may require such issuer to provide holders of equity securities of such class with such information relating to the reasons for such purchase, the source of funds, the number of shares to be purchased, the price to be paid for such securities, the method of purchase, and such additional information, as the Commission deems necessary or appropriate in the public interest or for the protection of investors, or which the Commission deems to be material to a determination whether such security should be sold.

Purchase by Issuer

Sec. 13(e)(2) For the purpose of this subsection, a purchase by or for the issuer, or any person controlling, controlled by, or under the common control with the issuer, or a purchase subject to control of the issuer or any such person, shall be deemed to be a purchaser by the issuer. The Commission shall have power to make rules and regulations implementing this paragraph in the public interest and for the protection of investors, including exemptive rules and regulations covering situations in which the Commission deems it unnecessary or inappropriate that a purchase of the type described in this paragraph shall be deemed to be a purchase by the issuer for purposes of some or all of the provisions of paragraph (1) of this subsection.

Filing of Information for Tender Offers

Sec. 14(d)(1) It shall be unlawful for any person, directly or indirectly, by use of the mails or by any means or instrumentality of interstate commerce or of any facility of a national securities exchange or otherwise, to make a tender offer for, or a request or invitation for tenders of, any class of any equity security which is registered pursuant to section 12 of this title, or any equity security of an insurance company which would have been required to be so registered except for the exemption contained in section 12(g)(2)(G) of this title, or any equity, security issued by a closed-end investment company registered under the Investment Company Act of 1940, if, after consummation thereof, such person would, directly or indirectly, be the beneficial owner of more than 5 per centum of such class, unless at the time copies of the offer or request or invitation are first published or sent or given to security holders such person has filed with the Commission a statement containing such of the information specified in section 13(d) of this title, and such additional information as the Commission may by rules and regulations prescribe as necessary or appropriate in the public interest or for the protection of investors. All requests or invitations for tenders or advertisements making a tender offer or requesting or inviting tenders of such a security shall be filed as a part of such statement and shall contain such of the information contained in such statement as the Commission may by rules and regulations prescribe. Copies of any additional material soliciting or requesting such tender offers subsequent to the initial solicitation or request shall contain such information as the Commission may by rules and regulations prescribe as necessary or appropriate in the public interest or for the protection of investors, and shall be filed with the Commission not later than the time copies of such material are first published or sent or given to security holders. Copies of all statements, in the form in which such material is furnished to security holders and the Commission, shall be sent to the issuer not later than the date such material is first published or sent or given to any security holders.

Syndicate, Group as "Person"

Sec. 14(d)(2) When two or more persons act as a partnership, limited partnership, syndicate, or other group for the purpose of acquiring, holding, or disposing of securities of an issuer, such syndicate or group shall be deemed a "person" for purposes of this subsection.

Computation of Percentage of Class of Security

Sec. 14(d)(3) In determining, for purposes of this subsection, any percentage of a class of any security, such class shall be deemed to consist of the amount of the outstanding securities of such class, exclusive of any securities of such class held by or for the account of the issuer or a subsidiary of the issuer.

Recommendations Regarding Acceptance or Rejection of Tender Offer

Sec. 14(d)(4) Any solicitation or recommendation to the holders of such a security to accept or reject a tender offer or request or invitation for tenders shall be made in accordance with such rules and regulations as the Commission may prescribe as necessary or appropriate in the public interest or for the protection of investors.

Withdrawal of Securities Deposited Under Tender Offer

Sec. 14(d)(5) Securities deposited pursuant to a tender offer or request or invitation for tenders may be withdrawn by or on behalf of the depositor at any time until the expiration of seven days after the time definitive copies of the offer or request or invitation are first published or sent or given to security holders, and at any time after sixty days from the date of the original tender offer or request or invitation, except as the Commission may otherwise prescribe by rules or regulations, or order as necessary or appropriate in the public interest or for the protection of investors.

Pro Rata Acceptance

Sec. 14(d)(6) Where any person makes a tender offer, or request or invitation for tenders, for less than all the outstanding equity securities of a class, and where a greater number of securities is deposited pursuant thereto within ten days after copies of the offer or request or invitation are first published or sent or given to security holders than such person is bound or willing to take up and pay for, the securities taken up shall be taken up as nearly as may be pro rata, disregarding fractions, according to the number of securities deposited by each depositor. The provisions of this subsection shall also apply to securities deposited within ten days after notice of an increase in the consideration offered to security holders, as described in paragraph (7), is first published or sent or given to security holders.

Changed Terms of Offer

Sec. 14(d)(7) Where any person varies the terms of a tender offer or request or invitation for tenders before the expiration thereof by increasing the consideration offered to holders of such securities, such person shall pay the increased consideration to each security holder whose securities are taken up and paid for pursuant to the tender or request or invitation for tenders whether or not such securities have been taken up by such person before the variation of the tender offer or request or invitation.

Exemptions

Sec. 14(d)(8) The provisions of this subsection shall not apply to any offer for, or request or invitation for tenders of, any security—

(A) if the acquisition of such security, together with all other acquisitions by the same person of securities of the same class during the preceding twelve months, would not exceed 2 per centum of that class;

(B) by the issuer of such security; or

(C) which the Commission, by rules or regulations or by order, shall exempt from the provisions of this subsection as not entered into for the purpose of, and not having the effect of, changing or influencing the control of the issuer or otherwise as not comprehended within the purposes of this subsection.

Fraudulent, Deceptive, or Manipulative Practices

Sec. 14(e) It shall be unlawful for any person to make any untrue statement of a material fact or omit to state any material fact necessary in order to make the statements made, in the light of the circumstances under which they are made, not misleading, or to engage in any fraudulent, deceptive, or manipulative acts or practices, in connection with any tender offer or request or invitation for tenders, or any solicitation of security holders in opposition to or in favor of any such offer, request, or invitation. The Commission shall, for the purpose of this subsection, by rules and regulations define, and prescribe means reasonably to prevent such acts and practices as are fraudulent, deceptive or manipulative.

Directors Without a Meeting

Sec. 14(f) If, pursuant to any arrangement or understanding with the person or persons acquiring securities in a transaction subject to subsection (d) of this section or subsection (d) of section 13 of this title, any persons are to be elected or designated as directors of the issuer, otherwise than at a meeting of security holders, and the persons so elected or designated will constitute a majority of the directors of the issuer, then, prior to the time any such person takes office as a director, and in accordance with rules and regulations prescribed by the Commission, the issuer shall file with the Commission, and transmit to all holders of record of securities of the issuer who would be entitled to vote at a meeting for election of directors, information substantially equivalent to the information which would be required by subsection (a) or (c) of this section to be transmitted if such person or persons were nominees for election as directors at a meeting of such security holders.

Index of Companies Undertaking Initial Public Offerings

(See Tables 4–2 and 4–3.)

Index of Companies Involved in Business Combinations

(See Tables 11–1, 12–1, 12–2, 12–3, 13–1, and 13–2.)

General Index

507

"*Valuing a Company* is an interesting collection of matters dealing with securities offerings, business combinations, and evaluations for tax purposes. It contains the kind of general information helpful to the younger accountant, lawyer, or business executive. The many case digests and extensive tables are useful to the more seasoned practitioner."—*The CPA Journal*

McCarthy and Healy bring together, in a single professional reference, detailed guidelines for valuing a corporation or non-corporate business. This guide covers all aspects of the subject — pointing out what to do, what to avoid — and supplies exhaustive data on actual valuations for companies of every size in all major industries and provides extensive tables to aid in valuation calculations.

It fully explains the steps to follow in handling valuation for:

- **Public Offerings** — reviews every valuation factor affecting the offering from overall economic conditions and securities to problems of assessing a firm's current assets and future prospects. Each stage of planning and implementing is covered, and supported by relevant information on SEC and stock exchange rules and regulations, accounting procedures, underwriter practices, and tax considerations.

- **Estate and Gift Taxes** — outlines the approaches followed by the IRS in establishing a "fair market value" for a company. Numerous illustrative examples and extensive reviews of twenty-one pivotal court cases point out specific opportunities for lessening the impact of estate and gift taxes.

- **Acquisitions and Mergers** — after pointing out how to handle each element in the valuation study, this section offers specific advice on meeting the objectives of buyers and sellers and arriving at a satisfactory approach for transferring ownership. Explores the pros and cons of outright purchase, installment sales, and tax-free exchanges, and devotes major attention to the subject of tender offers.

- **Special Situations** — gives procedures for dealing with the problems posed by dissenting stockholders, and shows how to deal with the special valuation problems of regulated industries.